Advanced Macroeconomics

Advanced Macroeconomics

Edited by Charlie Taylor

MURPHY & MOORE
www.murphy-moorepublishing.com

Murphy & Moore Publishing,
1 Rockefeller Plaza,
New York City, NY 10020, USA

ISBN: 978-1-63987-011-0

Cataloging-in-Publication Data

Advanced macroeconomics / edited by Charlie Taylor.
p. cm.
Includes bibliographical references and index.
ISBN 978-1-63987-011-0
1. Macroeconomics. 2. Economics. I. Taylor, Charlie.
HB172.5 .A38 2022
339--dc23

For information on all Murphy & Moore Publications
visit our website at www.murphy-moorepublishing.com

MURPHY & MOORE

Contents

Preface

Macroeconomics is a branch of economics that investigates the performance, structure, behavior, and economic issues of a nation or the world altogether. It takes interest rates, taxes, and government spending into consideration to regulate an economy's growth and stability. Advanced macroeconomics covers some complex topics such as multiple equilibria, global games, international trade and finance, etc. It addresses the issues of national output, unemployment, and inflation through its monetary and fiscal policies. It analyzes the aggregate indicators and microeconomic factors that impact the economy. This book is a compilation of chapters that discuss the most vital concepts and emerging trends in this field. The topics covered herein deal with the core subjects of advanced macroeconomics. Researchers and students in this field will be assisted by this book.

The researches compiled throughout the book are authentic and of high quality, combining several disciplines and from very diverse regions from around the world. Drawing on the contributions of many researchers from diverse countries, the book's objective is to provide the readers with the latest achievements in the area of research. This book will surely be a source of knowledge to all interested and researching the field.

In the end, I would like to express my deep sense of gratitude to all the authors for meeting the set deadlines in completing and submitting their research chapters. I would also like to thank the publisher for the support offered to us throughout the course of the book. Finally, I extend my sincere thanks to my family for being a constant source of inspiration and encouragement.

Editor

1

A New Approach of Investment for the Future Economic Policies

Alin OPREANA*

Lucian Blaga University of Sibiu

The investment takes the form of sums of money spent for the acquisition of capital goods, changes in business inventories, and the purchases of new residential housing that are not currently consumed, but will be used in the future for the growth of the wealth. The work covered by this study aims to identify the model that presents, in the best possible way, the method of investment's calculation and to determine the factors of influence. In the first part, the investment is analyzed as a linear function dependent on the interest rate; and the second part implies a new model for determining long-term investments.

***Keywords**: investment, interest rate, taxes, regression equation*

1. Introduction

According to Keynesian theory, the investment depends on what he called "marginal efficiency of capital" - that is, the expected rate of return for the acquisition cost of the capital goods. This is compared with the market interest rate. If the marginal efficiency of the capital is higher than the interest rate, the investment will increase, and if it is lower, the investment will decrease. Keynes (1936) stated that "the investment rate will increase to the point where the marginal efficiency of capital in general is equal to the market interest rate". Thus, given the "propensity to consume" and "incentive to invest" (determined jointly by the marginal efficiency of capital and the market interest rate), the employment rate is uniquely determined.

This paper aims to identify factors that influence investments in a large economy, like the case of the U.S. economy. In macroeconomic models, the equilibrium condition is given by the equality between savings and investment. Also, in these equilibrium models (IS-LM and Mundell-Fleming), an important relationship is that planned investment depends on the interest rate indirectly.

2. Literature Review

Keynes (1936, p.199) defined the marginal efficiency of capital as "equal to the discount rate that would determine that the present value of a series of annuities given by the expected benefits brought by the capital asset over its lifetime to be equal to its price offer".

Starting from this point, Keynes (1936, p.199) defined the function of investment demand as a function meant to link the rate of aggregate investment with the marginal efficiency of the capital determined that the level of the aggregate investment rate.

* Correspondence:
Alin Opreana, Lucian Blaga University of Sibiu, E-mail address: alin.opreana@ulbsibiu.ro

The size of the investment depends on the relationship between the interest rate and the correlation between the marginal efficiency of capital and the various dimensions of current investments , while the marginal efficiency of capital depends on the relationship between the offer price of a capital good and the future benefits it will bring (Keynes, 1936, p.211) If the marginal efficiency of capital is higher than the interest rate, investment will grow, if it is lower, the investment will decrease. Keynes argued that "the investment rate will increase to the point at which the marginal efficiency of capital is approximately equal, in general lines, to interest rate" (Keynes,1936 p. 314). Given the "propensity to consume" and "incentive to invest" (determined jointly by the marginal efficiency of capital and the market interest rate), the employment rate is uniquely determined.

Classical economists assumed that aggregate demand - production cost in monetary units - adjust quickly and flexibly to changes in expectations of sales profitability, keeping the economy at full employment rate. Keynes's denial that this must happen , is the crux of his denial of Say's Law - that supply always creates its own demand. Assuming that an employer's expected sales arise from N workers hiring, employment falls below the cost of employing that number; in Keynes's model, employers reduce their production costs through layoffs of workers. This reduces total demand in the economy. It is not wage cuts, but the decrease in employment rate that removes excess supply of output. This would be equivalent to the statement that the excess of savings over investment is eliminated by the fall in income (Skidelsky, 2010, pp.154-155).

The amount of work that entrepreneurs decide to employ depends on effective demand, i.e. the sum regarding what the company expects to spend on consumption and what the company expects to be devoted to new investments (Keynes, 2009, p.88). From the definitions of income and consumption provided by Keynes (1936, pp.123), it follows that savings are equal to $A_1 - U$, while net savings are expressed as a surplus of income over consumption equal to $A_1 - U - V$.

Starting from the definition of income, the current investment can defined as "current addition to the value of the technical capital resulting from the productive activity of the period under consideration ... this addition is equal to what we have just defined as savings, because it is that part of the income that has not passed into consumption"(Keynes, 1936, pp.123-124).

In other line of ideas, the excess income, expressed as $A - U$, over the part of income already in consumption, with the value of $A - A_1$, namely $A_1 - U$, is the addition to the technical capital as a result of the productive activity in the timeframe and represents the investment of that period.

Regarding the net investment, this equals $A_1 - U - V$, representing the net addition to technical capital after the normal depreciation of its normal value.

The study of the relationship between investment and interest rate has also been achieved in 2010 and the current research subject of this study is a continuation of that research (Opreana, 2010, pp.227-237). Thus, the research from 2010 has been disproved hypothesis that "investments are expressed by a function dependent on interest rates" and proposed a different function to identify factors that influence investments. These limits of that particular research consisted of the invalidation of the hypothses of homoskedasticity, normality and independence of values.

In this framework, the current research aims precisely to eliminate these limitations and to identify new investment functions to highlight the factors influencing investment in the U.S. economy.

3. Research Methodology

The next step implies the testing of the research assumptions in relation to this study's objectives to verify the validity of Keynes's model equations. In this research I will use a multiple linear regression model to test and determine the impact that different independent variables have on the dependent variables.

The general form of the multiple linear regression equation is:

$$Y_t = \beta_t^{X_1} X_{i1} + \beta_t^{X_2} X_{i2} + \cdots + \beta_t^{X_n} X_{in} + \beta_0 + \varepsilon$$

For simple linear models, regression coefficients measure the marginal contribution of the independent variable to the dependent variable, holding all the other variables fixed. If there is a constant (β), it represents the basic level of the prediction when all the other independent variables are zero. The other coefficients are interpreted as the slope of the relationship between the independent variable and the corresponding dependent variable, assuming all other variables do not change (Quantitative Micro Software, 2007, p.12).

Regression estimated by the method of least squares are determined by the following formula (Quantitative Micro Software, 2007, p.11):

$$\beta = (X'X)^{-1} X'y \tag{2.47}$$

For the inference based on the results of the multiple linear regression to be valid, I will use the following set of tests:

(i) The *F-Test* for testing the validity of the model. This test measures how well the independent variables explain the evolution of the dependent variable. Under the null hypothesis of normally distributed errors, this test has an *F* distribution with *k-1* degrees of freedom for the numerator and *T-k* degrees of freedom for the denominator. If the *p* value is less than the relevant level that is considered for the research, then at least one of the coefficients of the regression is statistically significant. But if the p-value is higher than the relevant level of the research, then all the regression coefficients are considered statistically insignificant (equal to zero) (Quantitative Micro Software, 2007, p.15).

(ii) The *coefficient of determination* R^2 and *adjusted coefficient of determination* $\bar{R}^2$ are used to determine the intensity link between values and measure the quality of the adjustment

(iii) *t-statistic* is used for testing the validity of the coefficients - t-statistic, calculated as the ratio between the estimated coefficient and its standard error, is used to test the hypothesis that a coefficient is equal to zero (Quantitative Micro Software, 2007, p.12).

(iv) *White test* for testing the hypothesis of homoskedasticity of the residual variable. The White test is a statistical test that determines whether the residual variance of a variable in a regression model is constant (homoskedasticity assumption).

(v) *Jarque-Bera test* for normality testing of the random variable distribution. Jarque-Bera tests whether a distribution is normally distributed. The test measures the difference between the asymmetry coefficient (skewness) and vaulting coefficient (kurtosis) of the analyzed distribution with that of a normal distribution. The test has the following null hypothesis: the series is normally distributed. If the probability associated with the test is higher than the relevancy level chosen, the test indicates the acceptance of the normality assumption and the fact that the series is normally distributed; otherwise, it indicates the rejection of the hypothesis of normality.

(vi) *Durbin-Watson test* and *Breusch-Godfrey test* for testing the hypothesis of independence of the residual variable values. The Durbin Watson test (DW) is a statistical test that examines the serial correlation of errors. If errors are not correlated, then the value of DW is about 2, in the same way, if the DW is less than 2, there is evidence of a positive correlation series. If there is a negative correlation, statistical test will show a value between 2 and 4 (Quantitative Micro Software, 2007, p.14). The existence of serial correlation, shown by correlogram errors, is confirmed by the Serial Correlation LM test. To obtain certain results, the *F-Statistic*, R^2 and their associated probabilities are analyzed. If the probability associated with the two tests is below the level of relevance chosen for the analysis, then there is a serial correlation of the residuals; otherwise there is no serial correlation (Codîrlaşiu, 2007, p.47).

This methodology will be applied using Eviews 6 software on empirical data, in order to attain the research objectives. In the process of the research, the methodology will be applied on time series of the U.S. economy, obtained from the Federal Reserve of St. Louis in the timeframe of 1959-2011.

4. Analysis and Results

The Identification of the Linear Regression Theoretical Model and the Verification of the Model's Validity

In the following section the investment equation is presented, based on the equation offered by the model:

$$LI = I_0 + i * LR$$

where *I*– Investment, I_0 – Autonomous Investment, i – Investment Sensitivity to Interest Rate Change, r – Interest Rate, *LI* – Logarithm of Investment and *LR* – Logarithm of Interest Rate

After applying the linear regression model of the historical data, the following investment equation is obtained:

$$LI = 7.069075 - 0.366704 * \text{LR}$$

Table 1. *The Investment Regression Equation*

Dependent Variable: LI
Method: Least Squares
Date: 10/15/12 Time: 22:16
Sample (adjusted): 1962 2011
Included observations: 50 after adjustments

Variable	Coefficient	Std. Error	t-Statistic	Prob.
LR	-0.366704	0.380933	-0.962648	0.3405
C	7.069075	0.714306	9.896421	0.0000

R-squared	0.018940	Mean dependent var	6.395430
Adjusted R-squared	-0.001498	S.D. dependent var	1.012555
S.E. of regression	1.013313	Akaike info criterion	2.903505
Sum squared resid	49.28656	Schwarz criterion	2.979986
Log likelihood	-70.58764	Hannan-Quinn criter.	2.932630
F-statistic	0.926692	Durbin-Watson stat	0.017955
Prob(F-statistic)	0.340549		

After analyzing the equation obtained, the following g conclusions arise:

(i) Prob (F-statistic) = 0.3405 > 0.05, indicates that the model is not statistically significant.

(ii) R-squared = 0.0189 and Adjusted R-squared = -0.0015 show a reduced intensity of the connection between interest rate (LR) and investment (LI).

(iii) t-Statistic for the LR parameter has Prob = 0.3405>0.05, illustrating the fact that the parameter is not significant.

Table 2. *White test for homoskedasticiy*

Heteroskedasticity Test: White

F-statistic	11.60237	Prob. F(2,47)	0.0001
Obs*R-squared	16.52648	Prob. Chi-Square(2)	0.0003
Scaled explained SS	8.816072	Prob. Chi-Square(2)	0.0122

Test Equation:
Dependent Variable: RESID^2
Method: Least Squares
Date: 12/29/13 Time: 19:42
Sample: 1962 2011
Included observations: 50

Variable	Coefficient	Std. Error	t-Statistic	Prob.
C	1.658087	2.501907	0.662729	0.5107
LR	0.952836	2.758052	0.345474	0.7313
LR^2	-0.689024	0.741635	-0.929062	0.3576

R-squared	0.330530	Mean dependent var	0.985731
Adjusted R-squared	0.302041	S.D. dependent var	1.071363
S.E. of regression	0.895059	Akaike info criterion	2.674269
Sum squared resid	37.65310	Schwarz criterion	2.788991
Log likelihood	-63.85673	Hannan-Quinn criter.	2.717956
F-statistic	11.60237	Durbin-Watson stat	0.149490
Prob(F-statistic)	0.000080		

(iv) Prob. F(2,47) = 0.001 < 0.05 indicates that after applying the White test, the hypothesis of homoskedasticity is verified in the regression function.

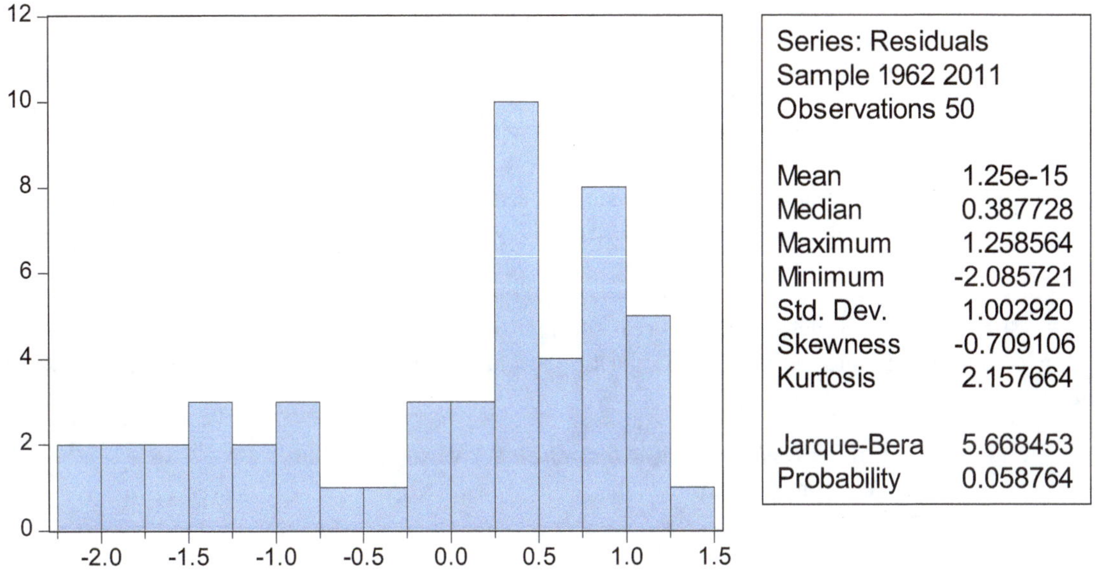

Figure 1. *Jarque Berra test for normality testing*

(v) Prob(Jarque-Berra Test) = 0.0588 > 0.05 indicates that the assumption of normality, checked through the the Jarque-Berra test, is accepted.

Table 3. *Breusch-Godfrey Serial Correlation LM Test*

F-statistic	212.7050	Prob. F(2,46)	0.0000
Obs*R-squared	45.12102	Prob. Chi-Square(2)	0.0000

Test Equation:
Dependent Variable: RESID
Method: Least Squares
Date: 12/29/13 Time: 19:43
Sample: 1962 2011
Included observations: 50
Presample missing value lagged residuals set to zero.

Variable	Coefficient	Std. Error	t-Statistic	Prob.
LR	0.213376	0.127841	1.669080	0.1019
C	-0.375669	0.238433	-1.575572	0.1220
RESID(-1)	0.941917	0.148031	6.362954	0.0000
RESID(-2)	0.019544	0.150952	0.129469	0.8976

R-squared	0.902420	Mean dependent var	1.25E-15
Adjusted R-squared	0.896056	S.D. dependent var	1.002920
S.E. of regression	0.323344	Akaike info criterion	0.656419
Sum squared resid	4.809363	Schwarz criterion	0.809381
Log likelihood	-12.41047	Hannan-Quinn criter.	0.714667
F-statistic	141.8033	Durbin-Watson stat	1.070316
Prob(F-statistic)	0.000000		

(vi) The results of the Durbin-Watson test (0.14) and Prob. F (Breusch-Godfrey) = 0.00 <0.05 show that the assumption of independence of the residual variable values is rejected, meaning that the errors of the models have positive autocorrelation, and are not independent.

Thus, after verifying the validity of the model, it can be stated that it is not valid, and that the investment is not a linear function of the interest rate.

Next, in this paper, the investments' function will be achieved, and also factors determining the investments will be identified.

Following the re-estimation model, it results in a new form of the equation according to the type of economy and the influence of external factors. The results yielded the following equation:

$$LI = LI(-1) + \Delta(LD) + LT(-1) + I_0$$

where LI – Logarithm of Investment, $LI(-1)$ – Logarithm of investment in the previous period, LD – Logarithm of Discount Rate, $LT(-1)$ – Logarithm of taxes of the previous period, I_0 – Autonomous Investment

Table 4. *The New Investment Regression Equation*

Dependent Variable: LI
Method: Least Squares
Date: 10/26/12 Time: 21:46
Sample (adjusted): 1960 2011
Included observations: 52 after adjustments

Variable	Coefficient	Std. Error	t-Statistic	Prob.
LI(-1)	0.693979	0.115135	6.027511	0.0000
Δ(LD)	0.150015	0.021536	6.965871	0.0000
LT(-1)	0.287056	0.110573	2.596072	0.0125
C	0.330209	0.099269	3.326397	0.0017

R-squared	0.996112	Mean dependent var	6.317287
Adjusted R-squared	0.995869	S.D. dependent var	1.068041
S.E. of regression	0.068645	Akaike info criterion	-2.445939
Sum squared resid	0.226181	Schwarz criterion	-2.295843
Log likelihood	67.59441	Hannan-Quinn criter.	-2.388396
F-statistic	4099.371	Durbin-Watson stat	1.639700
Prob(F-statistic)	0.000000		

The Verification of the Proposed Model's Validity

After testing the validity, through the F test, the following two conclusions arise:

(i) Prob (F-statistic) = 0.0000 < 0.05, indicates that the model is statistically significant (valid).

(ii) Giving the R-squared of 0.6413 and the Adjusted R-squared of 0.6384, leads to the conclusion that there is a strong intensity of the relationship between the endogenous variables and the exogenous variable.

(iii) t-Statistic for the parameters of the analysis show that these are statistically significant.

Table 5. *White test for homoskedasticiy*

Heteroskedasticity Test: White

F-statistic	1.739522	Prob. F(9,42)	0.1100
Obs*R-squared	14.11996	Prob. Chi-Square(9)	0.1181
Scaled explained SS	12.56367	Prob. Chi-Square(9)	0.1834

Test Equation:
Dependent Variable: RESID^2
Method: Least Squares
Date: 12/29/13 Time: 19:37
Sample: 1960 2011
Included observations: 52

Variable	Coefficient	Std. Error	t-Statistic	Prob.
C	-0.088833	0.083703	-1.061294	0.2946
LI(-1)	0.138502	0.189585	0.730555	0.4691
LI(-1)^2	-0.137750	0.119273	-1.154918	0.2547
LI(-1)*(D(LD))	0.039933	0.033204	1.202678	0.2358
LI(-1)*LT(-1)	0.274421	0.228206	1.202516	0.2359
D(LD)	-0.031842	0.026327	-1.209476	0.2332
(D(LD))^2	-0.002228	0.002250	-0.990497	0.3276
(D(LD))*LT(-1)	-0.038411	0.032379	-1.186286	0.2422
LT(-1)	-0.113906	0.179483	-0.634635	0.5291
LT(-1)^2	-0.138967	0.109365	-1.270674	0.2108

R-squared	0.271538	Mean dependent var	0.004350
Adjusted R-squared	0.115439	S.D. dependent var	0.006347
S.E. of regression	0.005970	Akaike info criterion	-7.233199
Sum squared resid	0.001497	Schwarz criterion	-6.857960
Log likelihood	198.0632	Hannan-Quinn criter.	-7.089341
F-statistic	1.739522	Durbin-Watson stat	2.130446
Prob(F-statistic)	0.109961		

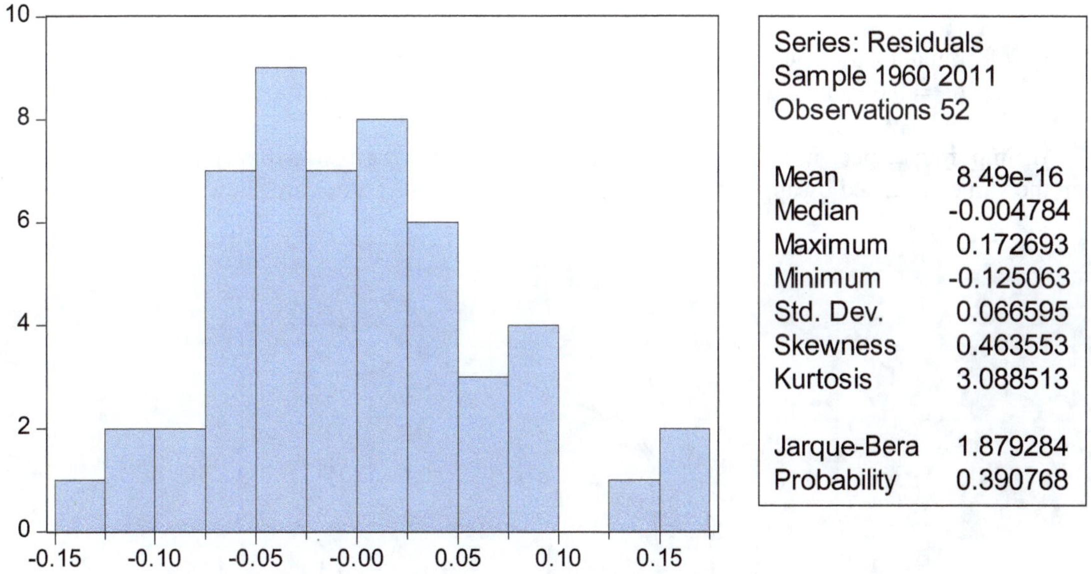

Figure 2. *Jarque Berra test for normality testing*

(iv) Prob(Jarque-Berra Test) = 0.3908 > 0.05 indicates that the assumption of normality, verified through the Jarque-Berra test, is accepted.

Table 6. *Breusch-Godfrey Serial Correlation LM Test*

F-statistic	1.736657	Prob. F(2,46)	0.1875
Obs*R-squared	3.650702	Prob. Chi-Square(2)	0.1612

Test Equation:
Dependent Variable: RESID
Method: Least Squares
Date: 12/29/13 Time: 19:41
Sample: 1960 2011
Included observations: 52
Presample missing value lagged residuals set to zero.

Variable	Coefficient	Std. Error	t-Statistic	Prob.
LI(-1)	-0.030592	0.148090	-0.206579	0.8373
D(LD)	0.000995	0.021832	0.045574	0.9638
LT(-1)	0.029510	0.141223	0.208963	0.8354
C	0.021349	0.124748	0.171137	0.8649
RESID(-1)	0.219687	0.182384	1.204533	0.2345
RESID(-2)	-0.199533	0.166376	-1.199291	0.2366

R-squared	0.070206	Mean dependent var	8.49E-16
Adjusted R-squared	-0.030859	S.D. dependent var	0.066595
S.E. of regression	0.067615	Akaike info criterion	-2.441808
Sum squared resid	0.210302	Schwarz criterion	-2.216664
Log likelihood	69.48701	Hannan-Quinn criter.	-2.355493
F-statistic	0.694663	Durbin-Watson stat	2.019578
Prob(F-statistic)	0.630114		

(iv) The results of the Durbin-Watson test (1.64) and Prob. F (Breusch-Godfrey) = 0.1875> 0.05 show that the assumption of independence of the residual variable values are accepted, meaning that the errors of the models are not positively auto-correlated, as the patterns are independent.

By reformulating the equation, we get the following situation:

$$LI = 0.6940 * LI_{n-1} + 0.15 * LD - 0.15 * LD_{n-1} + 0.2871 * LT_{n-1} + I_0$$

An important aspect in the analysis process is to analyze the residual variable, i.e. the differences between the values obtained by applying the model and the observed values are shown in Figure 3.

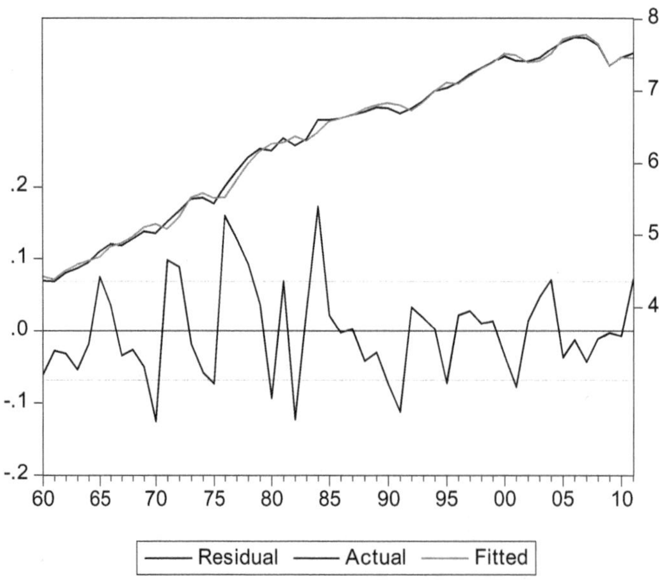

***Figure 3.** Residual variables in the investment functions*

5. Conclusion

The short-term model proposed by Mundell and Fleming, in terms of investment as a linear function dependent on the interest rate, is not a valid model in the long term. Long-term investments are expressed with the following equation:

$$LI = 0.6940 * LI_{n-1} + 0.15 * LD - 0.15 * LD_{n-1} + 0.2871 * LT_{n-1} + I_0$$

Thus, we see that the economic developments of the past 50 years have led to major changes in terms of the structure and influencing factors underlying investments. Regarding the U.S. economy, investments are positively influenced by the volume of investments in the previous period, the interest rate (discount rate) of the monetary policy of the current timeframe, and the amount of taxes in the current period, and are negatively influenced by the interest rate of the monetary policy of the previous year.

This change of the investment structure also determined a change in terms of the equilibrium models that rely on the classical investment function. Thus, this new approach to investments directly influences the IS-LM model, and the Mundell-Fleming model.

References

Codîrlaşiu, A., 2007. *Econometrie aplicată utilizând Eviews 5.1- note de curs*, ASE Bucureşti

Keynes, J. M., 1936. *The General Theory of Employment, Interest, and Money.* London: MacMillan

Skidelsky, R., 2010. *Keynes: The Return of the Master.* London: PublicAffairs

Opreana, A., 2010. The Long-Run Determinants Of Investment: A Dynamic Approach For The Future Economic Policies. *Studies in Business and Economics*, 5(3), pp.227–237. Available at: http://eccsf.ulbsibiu.ro/RePEc/blg/contents/contents_vol5.3.pdf.

Quantitative Micro Software, 2007. *EViews 6 User's Guide.* Irvine CA: Quantitative Micro Software, LLC

2

Pretension Strategy in the Surviving Game

Andrejs JAUNZEMS*

Ventspils Augstskola, Latvia

Presently, we cannot find the scientific analysis that clearly explains the deepest roots of global economical and moral crisis. Because of that many famous politicians, economists, sociologists denote the understanding of current situation as the most valuable attainment. Under traditional influence of the doctrine of spontaneous harmony of egoistic individual behavior many economists believe that competition and private property rights through the markets' price mechanism leads in the long run to the Pareto efficiency equilibrium. At the same time the social and economic reality categorically asks to ascertain the market failure and to revision the classical statements of microeconomics. The perfect competition market has lost its attributes due to dialectics of interactions of agents. The investigation of the interactions strategies of the individuals are based on the game theory, what also helps to understand the role of asymmetric information as a specific market failure factor. In the present paper the Martin Shubik classical surviving game is analyzed and some statements of Herbert Gintis concerning this game are critically appraised. The solution of Martin Shubik game in the original geometrical form is offered. The problem of Martin Shubik "does the fittest necessary survive?" is transformed according the case of asymmetric information in problem "does the pretender survive?", for which the answer "if the agent is not the weakest, but he pretends to be the weakest, than this agent survives with high probability" is offered. The results of the present paper appear to be innovative, not discussed in literature available to the author of the present paper.

***Keywords**: game, probability of surviving, interactions of the agent's strategies, Nash equilibrium, asymmetric information, pretension*

1. Introduction

The view about wide diversity of game theory applications offers, for instance, the content of the Gintis's (2009, p.390) book: "*Game Theory Evolving: A Problem Centered Introduction to Modelling Strategic Interaction.*"

The applications of game theory as tool for decision support is given in the books of Baye (1997, p. 578), Байе (1999, p. 743), Binmore (2007, p. 184), Jaunzems (2008, p. 555; 2009a, p.311; 2009b, p. 360). In paper of Jaunzems (2009c) the analysis of some social economical processes in Latvia with help of game theory is presented. There is no lack of literature and sources, nevertheless in the practice of social and economic analysis in Latvia the game theory introduces too slowly.

---

* Corresponding Author:
Andrejs Jaunzems, Ventspils Augstskola, Inženieru iela 101, Ventspils, LV-3600

In Gintis's book (2009, p. 23) under the title "*When Weakness Is Strength*" the model "The surviving game of three agents" offered by game theorist *Martin Shubik* (1954, 43-46) is considered. With help of this model the surviving example which contradicts to the fundamental thesis of Charles Darvin "*survival of the fittest*" is constructed. In this example the highest probability to survive has the weakest player. However this example is too simplified. The deepest investigation of the problem discovers that probability of surviving depends on mutual proportion of agents' strength and from behavior of agents as well. Unfortunately the author of present paper was not able to get original paper of Martin Shubik (Shubik, 1954, pp. 43-46). Therefore the aim of present paper is dispute with Herbert Gintis (2009) and more wide interpretation of Charles Darvin thesis. The limitation of some statements of Herbert Gintis (2009) empirically is proved. In this paper exact definition of surviving game is given, the mathematical model of surviving game under definite comparatively universal assumptions is constructed and with help of model multi-shaped numerical experiments are performed. Besides that the Nash equilibrium of surviving game is identified, the classical surviving game is modified according asymmetric information and instead the theme "*When Weakness Is Strength*" the theme "*When Pretension Is Strength*" is discussed. The authors have never met the mentioned results in literature, therefore comments are welcomed and, if is not proved the opposite, results of the present paper have to be evaluated as innovative.

2. The Definition of the Surviving Game

The definition of the surviving game comes next, with comments.

Three individuals – Ansis, Basis, Casis take part in the surviving game.

At first the sequence of shooting during lottery is determined. As result one from six possible sequences (ABC), (ACB), (BAC), (BCA), (CAB), (CBA) is fixed. The probability of each sequence is 1:6.

The game is extensive – in the each step or act of the game one of players has rights to shot.

Explanation. Let us consider, for instance, the sequence (ABC). The sequence (ABC) means, that Ansis shot the first. Ansis has three strategies: Ansis may shot Basis, Ansis may shot Casis and Ansis may shot in the air.

(1) Let us assume that Ansis shot Basis; we will denote that as A→B. If Ansis hits Basis than Basis exits the game (we will say Basis is shot down or Basis is eliminated) and farther sequence of shooting is (CA). If Ansis miss Basis then the farther sequence of shooting is (BCA).

(2) Let us assume that Ansis shot Casis; we will denote that as A→C. If Ansis hits Casis than Casis exits the game, he is eliminated and farther sequence of shooting is (BA). If Ansis miss Casis then the farther sequence of shooting is (BCA).

(3) Let us assume that Ansis shot in the air; we will denote that as A→O. The farther sequence of shooting is (BCA).

The five another sequences are interpreted analogically.

The definition of surviving game continued. Let us assume that the following probabilities are given.

The probability that Ansis hits is p_A. The probability that Ansis miss we denote as q_A: $p_A + q_A = 1$.

The probability that Basis hits is p_B. The probability that Basis miss we denote as q_B: $p_B + q_B = 1$.

The probability that Casis hits is p_C. The probability that Casis miss we denote as q_C: $p_C + q_C = 1$.

The each of agents is interested to stay alive. The game is finished when only one of the players has left alive. Let us observe that the surviving game may have infinite acts because of possibility that players miss and miss and all three agents or at least two of them have infinite chances of shooting. In the each act the agent, who has the move, chooses the strategy from set of three strategies, if three players are still alive, or only one strategy if two players are remain.

Our main goal is the determination of the Nash equilibrium of this game.

Let us illustrate the Nash equilibrium in the simple, but nevertheless a very pithy case.

Suppose $p_A = 1$, $p_B = 1$, $p_C = 1$ and the sequence (ABC) during lottery is determined. It is easy to see that the triple of strategies (A→O, B→O, C→O) determines a situation that is very stable Nash equilibrium. Indeed, if Ansis shot Basis, Basis is eliminated and the next moves Casis who shots down Ansis and wins. So, Ansis would be unwise if he shots Basis or Casis. The best strategy for Ansis is shot in the air. When the right of move has Basis he judges similarly and makes decision that shot in the air is the best strategy for him. The same decision makes Casis. So the eternal peace exists between these three antagonistic and strong warriours.

The given surviving game associates with popular but wrong thesis about bipolar world as peace guarantee. If only two players Ansis and Basis take part in surviving game and $p_A = 1$, $p_B = 1$, than shooter who has rights to shot first unswerving eliminates the enemy. We recognize here the first move advantage often discussed by military experts.

Conclusion. The antagonistic bipolar world is unstable. The antagonistic tripolar world is very stable.

Important remark. Everywhere further, if especially is not formulated another assumption, we will examine comparatively universal case, namely, we will suppose that $0 < p_C < p_B < p_A \leq 1$. We will say that Ansis is the strongest but Casis is the weakest shooter.

What is the payoff of the player? The payoff of the player could be the surviving probability. However, if we are going to investigate this game analytically with help of mathematical methods we need correct agents' surviving probability definition, what unfortunately we do not meet in Gintis's book (2009) published by Princeton University Press.

Let us illustrate with help of simplest stochastic experiment – dice throw the theoretical difficulties what arise when we are going to definite agents' surviving probability. Try to understand the meaning of following question: "Is the probability that first will come in sight even number bigger than the probability that first will come in sight number one?"

It is possible to calculate, for instance, probability of event "five times throwing the dice the even number will come in sight earlier than number one". In the same time the cardinality of the set of all outcomes when the first comes in sight even number is continuum. Also the cardinality of the set of all outcomes when the first comes number one is continuum.

In order to depict the extensive process of the surviving game graphically as decision-state tree we have to use infinite graph with infinite volume of infinite sub-branches.

2.1. Two Agents' Surviving Game

Before investigation of three agents' surviving game is purposeful to start with two agents' surviving game analysis, what is sufficiently simpler because of each player has only one strategy – to shot enemy.

For instance, let us examine the case when Casis is eliminated and further sequence is (AB). Such a game is possible to depict geometrically as decision-state tree with infinite volume of finite sub-branches and one infinite subbranche.

We are going to define the probability that Ansis survives as sum of infinite geometric series. Let us denote probability that Ansis has eliminated Basis after 2k+1 shoots or earlier with $P_A\{(AB) \mid 2k+1\}$. Let the sign "+" means "hits", the sign "–" means "miss".

Then, for instance, in the case 2k+1 = 5 the event we are interested in consists from the following results of shooting: (A+), (A–, B–, A+), (A–, B–, A–, B–, A+).

We calculate $P_A\{(AB) \mid 5\}$ as follows:

$$P_A\{(AB) \mid 5\} = p_A + q_A q_B p_A + (q_A q_B)^2 p_A = p_A [1 + q_A q_B + (q_A q_B)^2].$$

It is easy to see by analogy that $P_A\{(AB) \mid 2k+1\} = p_A [1 + q_A q_B + \ldots + (q_A q_B)^k]$.

We calculate the limit of partial sum of the geometric series:

$$P_A(AB) := \lim_{k\to\infty} P_A\{(AB) \mid 2k+1\} = \frac{p_A}{1 - q_A q_B}.$$

Number $P_A(AB)$ will be interpreted as probability that Ansis survives.

The probability $P_B(AB)$ is defined analogically: $P_B(AB) := \lim_{k\to\infty} P_B\{(AB) \mid 2k\} = \frac{q_A p_B}{1 - q_A q_B}$.

As a check on our formulas, note that $P_A(AB) + P_B(AB) = 1$.

Remark. In book published in Princeton University (Gintis, 2009) the probability $P_A(AB)$ has calculated from the recursion equation: $P_A(AB) = p_A + q_A P_A(BA) = p_A + q_A q_B P_A(AB)$.

Solving, we get $P_A(AB) = \frac{p_A}{1 - q_A q_B}$.

Let us mark that this method is heuristic but mathematically incorrect.

In the analysis of three agents' surviving game we will make use of the following theorem about two agents' game what confirms the intuitive suspected connection: the weakest enemy of Ansis, the higher is for Ansis probability to survive.

Theorem. $P_A(AB) < P_A(AC)$ if and only if $p_B > p_C$.

The proof follows from equalities $P_A(AB) = \dfrac{p_A}{1-q_Aq_B}$; $P_A(AC) = \dfrac{p_A}{1-q_Aq_C}$.

Consequence. $P_A(BA) < P_A(CA)$ if and only if $p_B > p_C$.

2.2. The Nash Equilibrium of the Sub-Game of the Surviving Game and Nash Equilibrium of the Martin Shubik Game

As it was showed before in general case of surviving game the cardinality of agents' strategies set is continuum. We are going to make important assumption about agents' behavior in three shooters game, which will relieve us the analysis of game and will allow us to get important and pithy interpreted conclusions.

Let us suppose that each of agents chooses his strategy in the very beginning of the game and after that each time when agent has right to move, he acts according this strategy. It means, that Ansis in the very beginning of the game chooses one of three strategies A→B, A→C, A→O, and then utilizes this strategy each time when he has rights to move (naturally, till there are three players in the game). Analogically, Basis chooses one of strategies B→A, B→C, B→O and Casis chooses one of strategies C→A, C→B, C→O.

Taking in account this assumption all together $3\times3\times3 = 27$ triples of strategies exist.

Concrete triple of strategies, for instance, (A→B; B→A; C→O) allows us to follow the extensive process of game so say in the probabilities tongue and analogically as it was did in the case of two players to define agents' surviving probabilities as sum of geometric series.

Given sequence of acts (ABC) and given triple of strategies (A→B; B→A; C→O) determine three surviving probabilities: $P_A(ABC)$, $P_B(ABC)$ $P_C(ABC)$.

The game what corresponds to the concrete sequence determined during lottery we will call as sub-game of the surviving game. We have six sub-games all together, each of that corresponds to one of six possible shooting sequences (ABC), (ACB), ... , (CBA).

The Martin Shubik game is completely defined, if we construct the (27×3)-table represented strategy-surviving probabilities for all sub-games. Thus, in order to investigate Martin Shubik game we calculate $6\times27\times3 = 486$ probabilities. After that, taking in account that initial sequences are stochastic, we calculate the (27×3)-table of mathematical expectations of strategy-surviving probabilities. These table allows us to determine Nash equilibrium of Martin Shubik game and to make different another conclusions.

Let us utilize heiristic method of surviving probabilities determination from the recursion equations offered by Herbert Gintis. (The same results can be get as limits of geometric series.) Than, for instance, we will get the following expressions for Ansis, Basis and Casis surviving probabilities in the sub-game (ABC) concerning strategies triple N := (A→B; B→A; C→O):

$$P_A^N(ABC) = p_A\, P_A(CA) + q_A\, P_A^N(BCA) = p_A\, P_A(CA) + q_A\, q_B\, P_A^N(CAB) =$$
$$= p_A\, P_A(CA) + q_A\, q_B\, P_A^N(ABC). \text{ Solving, we get } P_A^N(ABC) = \frac{p_A P_A(CA)}{1-q_Aq_B}.$$

$$P_B^N(ABC) = q_A\, P_B^N(BCA) = q_A\, [p_B\, P_B(CB) + q_B\, P_B^N(CAB)] =$$
$$= q_A\, p_B\, P_B(CB) + q_A\, q_B\, P_B^N(ABC)]. \text{ Solving, we get } P_B^N(ABC) = \frac{q_A p_B P_B(CB)}{1-q_Aq_B}.$$

$$P_C^N(ABC) = p_A\, P_C(CA) + q_A\, P_C^N(BCA) = p_A\, P_C(CA) + q_A\, [p_B\, P_C(CB) + q_B\, P_C^N(CAB)] =$$
$$= p_A\, P_C(CA) + q_A\, p_B\, P_C(CB) + q_A\, q_B\, P_C^N(ABC).$$

Solving, we get $P_C^N(ABC) = \dfrac{p_A P_C(CA) + q_A p_B P_C(CB)}{1-q_Aq_B}$.

As a check on our formulas, note that $P_A^N(ABC) + P_B^N(ABC) + P_C^N(ABC) =$

$$= \frac{p_A P_A(CA)}{1-q_Aq_B} + \frac{q_A p_B P_B(CB)}{1-q_Aq_B} + \frac{p_A P_C(CA) + q_A p_B P_C(CB)}{1-q_Aq_B} = 1$$

Remark. The symbols $P_A^N(ABC)$, $P_B^N(ABC)$, $P_C^N(ABC)$ reflect the sub-game (ABC) and strategies triple N = (A→B; B→A; C→O) choosen as well.

What strategy does Ansis choose? Our intuition predict us that Ansis will try to eliminate the most dangerous enemy, namely, the enemy with higher hit probability. That is Basis. In Basis turn purposeful is eliminate Ansis. For the weakest shooter Casis purposeful is shot in the air in order the strongest enemies shot each other.

Let us stress that just told mathematically is incorrect. That is typically for game theory: correct are solely statements inside the frame of mathematical concepts, any other debate as usually is defective and leads to the wrong conclusions. By my opinion directly that creates objective difficulties for the wide applications of the game theory in the research of social-economical processes.

The next lemma has universal character.

Lemma. Conditional Nash equilibrium of the sub-game.

Let us assume, that $0 < p_C < p_B < p_A \leq 1$; suppose that we have freely chosen some sub-game. Let us assume that Casis as strategy leader decides shot in the air. Than situation associated with strategy triple N := (A→B; B→A; C→O) is conditional Nash equilibrium.

Let us mark the idea of proof.

Let us suppose that sub-game is determined by sequence (ABC) and Casis chooses strategy C→O. We will prove that situation N = (A→B; B→A; C→O) is the conditional Nash equilibrium of the sub-game with corresponding payoffs $P_A^N(ABC)$, $P_B^N(ABC)$, $P_C^N(ABC)$.

The proof for each sub-game consists from two steps.

First, we make certain that in the situations S := (A→C; B→A; C→O), T := (A→O; B→A; C→O) probability for Ansis to survive decreases to compare with probability $P_A^N(ABC)$.

Let us calculate:

$$P_A^S(ABC) = p_A P_A(BA) + q_A P_A^S(BCA) = p_A P_A(BA) + q_A q_B P_A^S(CAB) =$$

$$= p_A P_A(BA) + q_A q_B P_A^S(ABC), \text{ Solving, we get } P_A^S(ABC) = \frac{p_A P_A(BA)}{1 - q_A q_B}.$$

Comparing probability $P_A^S(ABC)$ with probability $P_A^N(ABC)$ getting before, and taking in acount that $P_A(BA) < P_A(CA)$, we get $P_A^S(ABC) < P_A^N(ABC)$.

Comparing probability $P_A^T(ABC)$ with probability $P_A^N(ABC)$ is easier:

from $P_A^T(ABC) = P_A^T(BCA) = q_B P_A^T(CAB) = q_B P_A^T(ABC)$ follows that $P_A^T(ABC) = 0$.

In the second step we make certain that in the situations U := (A→B; B→C; C→O), V := (A→B; B→O; C→O) probability for Basis to survive decreases to compare with probability $P_B^N(ABC)$.

Let us calculate:

$$P_B^U(ABC) = q_A P_B^U(BCA) = q_A p_B P_B(AB) + q_A q_B P_B^U(CAB) =$$

$$= q_A p_B P_B(AB) + q_A q_B P_B^U(ABC). \text{ Solving, we get } P_B^U(ABC) = \frac{q_A p_B P_B(AB)}{1 - q_A q_B}.$$

Comparing probability $P_B^U(ABC)$ with probability $P_B^N(ABC)$ getting before, and taking in acount that $P_B(AB) < P_B(CB)$, we get $P_B^U(ABC) < P_B^N(ABC)$.

We have also $P_B^V(ABC) = q_A P_B^V(BCA) = q_A P_B^V(ABC)$, from what follow $P_B^V(ABC) = 0$.

It may be prooved analogically, that situation associated with strategy triple N = (A→B; B→A; C→O) is conditional Nash equilibrium in other five sub-games.

Consequence. The conditional Nash equilibrium in Martin Shubik game. Let us asume that $0 < p_C < p_B < p_A \leq 1$. Let Casis is strategy leader and chooses strategy C→O. Then situation associated with strategy triple N = (A→B; B→A; C→O) is conditional Nash equilibrium in Martin Shubik game.

Although it is not assert in explicit form the content of theme 1.32 "*When Weakness Is Strength*" in Gintis (2009) creates impression, that triple of strategies N = (A→B; B→A; C→O) determines Nash equilibrium in the each sub-game and in the Martin Shubik game. In the example examined in details this statement is true. Multishaped numerical experiments also signalized that this statement could be true. However the aspirations to prove this statement mathematically leads to the conclusion that for some triple of probabilities p_A, p_B, p_C situation associated with triple of strategies N = (A→B; B→A; C→O) is not the Nash equilibrium.

Let us examine, for instance, the sub-game (ABC). Taking in account the proof of lemma it would be proved that strategy triple N = (A→B; B→A; C→O) determines the Nash equilibrium in the sub-game (ABC), if we were be able to prove that in the situations W := (A→B; B→A; C→A), Y := (A→B; B→A; C→B) the payoff of Casis decreases to compare with P_C^N (ABC).

It is possible to get the following expression:

$$P_C^W(ABC) = p_A P_C(CA) + q_A P_C^W(BCA) = p_A P_C(CA) + q_A [p_B P_C(CB) + q_B P_C^W(CAB)] =$$
$$= p_A P_C(CA) + q_A p_B P_C(CB) + q_A q_B [p_C P_C(BC) + q_C P_C^W(ABC)].$$

Solving, we get $P_C^W(ABC) = \dfrac{p_A P_C(CA) + q_A p_B P_C(CB) + q_A q_B p_C P_C(BC)}{1 - q_A q_B q_C}$.

Before we have got the expression $P_C^N(ABC) = \dfrac{p_A P_C(CA) + q_A p_B P_C(CB)}{1 - q_A q_B}$.

We are interested in investigation of the the set $\{(p_A, p_B, p_C)\}$ of inequality $P_C^W(ABC) < P_C^N(ABC)$ solutions and in the set $\{(p_A, p_B, p_C)\}$ of inequality $P_C^Y(ABC) < P_C^N(ABC)$ solutions. The problem arises: how to haracterize the sets of solution of inequalities $P_C^W(ABC) < P_C^N(ABC)$, $P_C^Y(ABC) < P_C^N(ABC)$.
We are interested also in investigation of the the sets of analogical inequality solutions for the other five sub-games in order to discover conditions what guarantee that strategy triple N = (A→B; B→A; C→O) determines the Nash equilibrium.

I could not receive explicit algebraic description for these solution sets. However I have received empirical descriptions of the inequality $P_C^W(ABC) < P_C^N(ABC)$, $P_C^Y(ABC) < P_C^N(ABC)$ solution sets, displayed in the table 1 and in the figure 1. In the table 1 information about minimal value of probability p_C (depending of values p_A, p_B) is given; with this probability or bigger probability in the situation, determined by strategy triple N = (A→B; B→A; C→O), Casis does not refuse the strategy C→O. If, in addition $p_C < min\{p_A, p_B\}$, then strategy triple N = (A→B; B→A; C→O) determines the Nash equilibrium of the Martin Shubik game.

In the figure 1 dates of the table 1 are depicted graphically. For each value of probability p_A, namely, $p_A = 0{,}1$; $p_A = 0{,}2$; $p_A = 0{,}3$; $p_A = 0{,}4$; $p_A = 0{,}5$; $p_A = 0{,}6$; $p_A = 0{,}7$; $p_A = 0{,}8$; $p_A = 0{,}9$, $p_A = 1$ corresponds curve, what show connection between probabilities p_B, p_C, holding value of p_A constant. Higher the probability p_A, higher is dislocated corresponding curve.
The figure 1 could be considered as empirical solution of the Martin Shubik game.

Table 1. *Information about Nash equilibrium conditions in Martin Shubik game.*

p_A	p_B	*min* p_C	p_A	p_B	*min* p_C
0,1	0,02	0,7754	0,6	0,5	0,0431

0,1	0,04	0,5041	0,6	0,6	0,0409
0,1	0,06	0,2501	0,7	0,05	0,9242
0,1	0,08	0,0561	0,7	0,1	0,8310
0,1	0,085	0,0326	0,7	0,2	0,5894
0,1	0,09	0,0227	0,7	0,3	0,2653
0,2	0,02	0,8954	0,7	0,4	0,0721
0,2	0,05	0,6973	0,7	0,5	0,0512
0,2	0,10	0,3309	0,7	0,6	0,0462
0,2	0,12	0,1925	0,7	0,7	0,0448
0,2	0,15	0,0483	0,8	0,05	0,9345
0,2	0,18	0,0257	0,8	0,1	0,8549
0,2	0,19	0,0237	0,8	0,2	0,6506
0,3	0,02	0,9325	0,8	0,3	0,3698
0,3	0,05	0,8073	0,8	0,4	0,1059
0,3	0,10	0,5596	0,8	0,5	0,0617
0,3	0,15	0,2874	0,8	0,6	0,0524
0,3	0,20	0,0673	0,8	0,7	0,0493
0,3	0,23	0,0385	0,8	0,8	0,0485
0,3	0,25	0,0328	0,9	0,05	0,9424
0,3	0,28	0,0289	0,9	0,1	0,8732
0,4	0,02	0,9503	0,9	0,2	0,6977
0,4	0,05	0,8600	0,9	0,3	0,4560
0,4	0,10	0,6804	0,9	0,4	0,1666
0,4	0,15	0,4695	0,9	0,5	0,0762
0,4	0,20	0,2407	0,9	0,6	0,0602
0,4	0,25	0,0714	0,9	0,7	0,0546
0,4	0,30	0,0413	0,9	0,8	0,0525
0,4	0,35	0,0347	0,9	0,9	0,0519
0,5	0,02	0,9608	1	0,05	0,9488
0,5	0,05	0,8905	1	0,1	0,8876
0,5	0,1	0,7520	1	0,2	0,7350
0,5	0,2	0,3959	1	0,3	0,5265
0,5	0,3	0,0714	1	0,4	0,2516
0,5	0,4	0,0408	1	0,5	0,0973
0,6	0,05	0,9103	1	0,6	0,0699
0,6	0,1	0,7985	1	0,7	0,0610
0,6	0,2	0,5078	1	0,8	0,0570
0,6	0,3	0,1501	1	0,9	0,0553
0,6	0,4	0,0530	1	1	0,0548

The explanation of the table 1 and figure 1.

For instance, we can read in table 1 and observe visually in figure 1: if $p_A = 0{,}8$; $p_B = 0{,}4$, then for each probability p_C bigger then 0,1059 Casis shots in the air. Let us remember, that in Martin Shubik game Ansis shots Basis and Basis shots Ansis because of $p_C < p_B$, $p_C < p_A$, namely, Casis is the weakest. Therefore, if probability p_C satisfates inequality $0{,}1059 < p_C < min\{p_A, p_B\} = 0{,}4$, then the strategy triple N = (A→B; B→A; C→O) determines the Martin Shubik games' Nash equilibrium. If $p_C < 0{,}1059$, then strategy triple N = (A→B; B→A; C→O) does not determine the Nash equilibrium because of Casis shots Ansis.

If $p_C > 0{,}4$, then Casis shots in the air if conditions A→B; B→A fulfil. But Casis is now stronger than Basis. What reason in this case is for Ansis to shot Basis?

*Another exam*ple. We can read in table 1 and observe visually in figure 1: if $p_A = 0{,}5$; $p_B = 0{,}2$, then for each probability p_C bigger then 0,3959 Casis shots in the air. However with such probability the conditions of Martin Shubik game does not fulfil. If probabilities follow in order $p_B < p_C < p_A$, then in Martin Shubik game Ansis shots Casis not Basis, because of Basis is weakest. But just $p_C < 0{,}2$ immediately Casis shots

Ansis. Obviously, in the case $p_A = 0{,}5$; $p_B = 0{,}2$ such probability $p_C < min\{p_A, p_B\}$ that strategy triple (A→B; B→A; C→O) determines Martin Shubik games' Nash equilibrium does not exist.

In figure 1 especially is depicted the point $(p_B, p_C) = (0{,}8; 0{,}5)$ in order to illustrate the very special case $(p_A, p_B, p_C) = (1; 0{,}8; 0{,}5)$ examined by Herbert Gintis (2009). Let us mark, that this very special case does not expose the complication of surviving game. Our calculations and figure 1 shows: still the probability p_C satisfies inequalities $0{,}0570 < p_C < 0{,}8$ strategy triple (A→B; B→A; C→O) determines Nash equilibrium, namely, Casis shots in the air. In the same time if, for instance, $(p_A, p_B, p_C) = (1; 0{,}8; 0{,}05)$ then Casis shots Ansis not in the air.

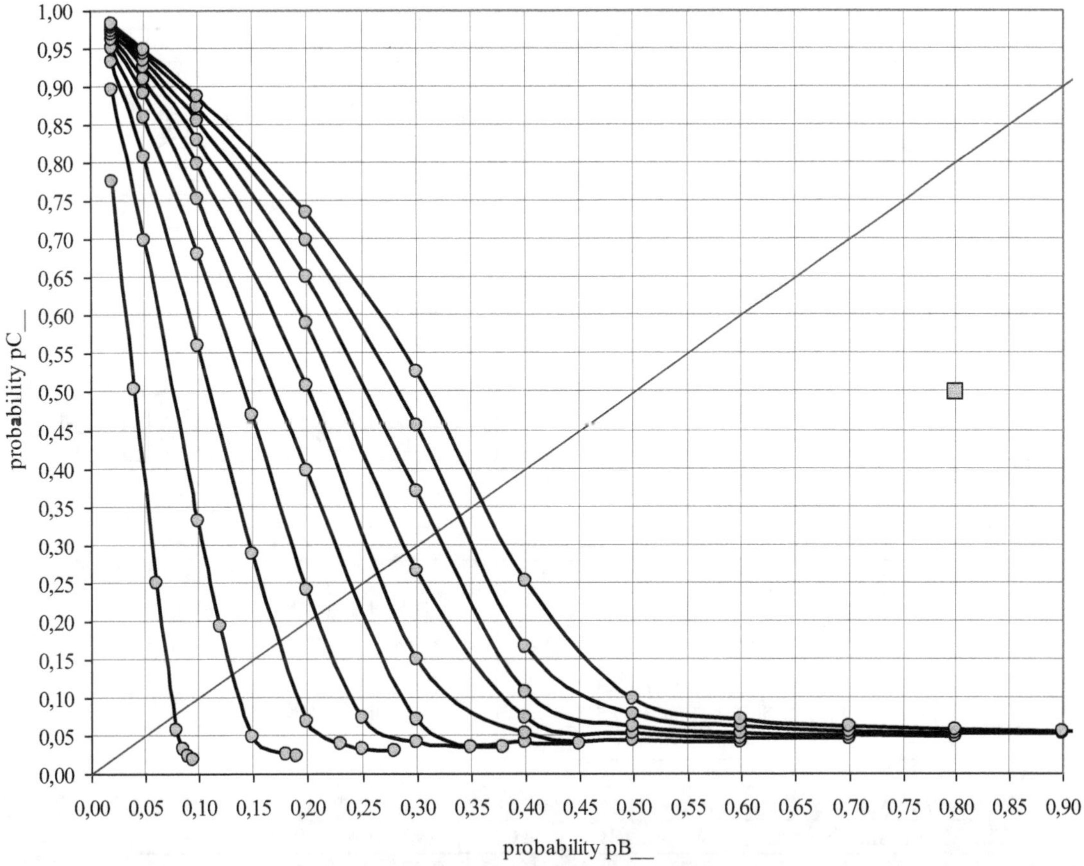

Figure 1. *Graphical solution of the Martin Shubik game.*

3. Some Conclusions Empirically Proven

3.1. Example "When Weakness Is Strength".

Let us theoretical examination of matter done before illustrate now with numerical example. Let us assume, that $p_A = 0{,}9$; $p_B = 0{,}6$; $p_C = 0{,}4$. Note, that probabilities satisfies requirements of table 1: $p_C = 0{,}4 > 0{,}0602$.

The surviving probabilities of two agents fighting game are showed in table 2. In table 3 the Nash situations of the sub-games and situations beside to the Nash equilibrium are exposed. In the table 4 the Nash equilibrium of Martin Shubik game is exposed.

Table 2. *Surviving probabilities in the two agents game if $p_A = 0{,}9$; $p_B = 0{,}6$; $p_C = 0{,}4$.*

$P_A(AB)$	0,93750	$P_A(AC)$	0,95745
$P_A(BA)$	0,37500	$P_A(CA)$	0,57447
$P_B(AB)$	0,06250	$P_B(BC)$	0,78947
$P_B(BA)$	0,62500	$P_B(CB)$	0,47368

$P_C(AC)$	0,04255	$P_C(BC)$	0,21053
$P_C(CA)$	0,42553	$P_C(CB)$	0,52632

Table 3. *The Nash equilibriums of the sub-games if $p_A = 0,9$; $p_B = 0,6$; $p_C = 0,4$.*

Sub-game (ABC)	**A**	**B**	**C**	**P_A(ABC)**	**P_B(ABC)**	**P_C(ABC)**
The Nash equilibrium	shot B	shot A	shot air	0,53856	0,02961	0,43183
	shot C	shot A	shot air	0,35156		
	shot B	shot C	shot air		0,00391	
	shot B	shot A	shot A			0,42820
Sub-game (ACB)	A	B	C	P_A(ACB)	P_B(ACB)	P_C(ACB)
The Nash equilibrium	shot B	shot A	shot air	0,53856	0,02961	0,43183
	shot C	shot A	shot air	0,351563		
	shot B	shot C	shot air		0,00391	
	shot B	shot A	shot A			0,42044
Sub-game (BAC)	A	B	C	P_A(BAC)	P_B(BAC)	P_C(BAC)
The Nash equilibrium	shot B	shot A	shot air	0,21543	0,29605	0,48852
	shot C	shot A	shot air	0,14063		
	shot B	shot C	shot air		0,03906	
	shot B	shot A	shot A			0,48396
Sub-game (BCA)	A	B	C	P_A(BCA)	P_B(BCA)	P_C(BCA)
The Nash equilibrium	shot B	shot A	shot air	0,21543	0,29605	0,48852
	shot C	shot A	shot air	0,14063		
	shot B	shot C	shot air		0,03906	
	shot B	shot A	shot A			0,45224
Sub-game (CAB)	A	B	C	P_A(CAB)	P_B(CAB)	P_C(CAB)
The Nash equilibrium	shot B	shot A	shot air	0,53856	0,02961	0,43183
	shot C	shot A	shot air	0,35156		
	shot B	shot C	shot air		0,00391	
	shot B	shot A	shot A			0,34113
Sub-game (CBA)	A	B	C	P_A(CBA)	P_B(CBA)	P_C(CBA)
The Nash equilibrium	shot B	shot A	shot air	0,21543	0,29605	0,48852
	shot C	shot A	shot air	0,14063		
	shot B	shot C	shot air		0,03906	
	shot B	shot A	shot A			0,37459

Table 4. *The Nash equilibrium of the Martin Shubik game if $p_A = 0,9$; $p_B = 0,6$; $p_C = 0,4$.*

The Martin Shubik game	A	B	C	P_A	P_B	P_C
The Nash equilibrium	shot B	shot A	shot air	0,37699	0,16283	0,46018
	shot C	shot A	shot air	0,24609		
	shot B	shot C	shot air		0,02148	
	shot B	shot A	shot A			0,41676

The examined example allows us to formulate following conclusions.

1. Strategy triple (A→B, B→A, C→O) in all six sub-games and, of course, also in Martin Shubik game leads to the Nash equilibrium.

2. In the Martin Shubik game in the Nash equilibrium situation the strategy "shot in the air" insures to Casis the highest surviving probability comparing other two agents. The weakest shooter has the biggest probability to survive! Exactly this result as universal conclusion Gintis (2009) sprightly discuss under the title "When Weakness Is Strength". By opinion of Herbert Gintis this result contradicts to the fundamental thesis of Charles Darvin "*survival of the fittest*".

Below in the example 2.2 "When Weakness Is Not Strength" the case when conclusion of Herbert Gintis does not hold is exposed.

3. Let us observe, that in some sub-games, for instance, in sub-game (ACB) the surviving probability of Casis is lower then surviving probability of Ansis. However if Ansis shots Basis and Basis shots Ansis, then in the each sub-game Casis shots in the air.

3.2. Example "When Weakness Is Not Strength".

Suppose $p_A = 0{,}9$; $p_B = 0{,}7$; $p_C = 0{,}2$.

Note, that probabilities satisfies requirements of table 1: $p_C = 0{,}2 > 0{,}0546$.

The surviving probabilities of two agents fighting game are showed in table 5. In table 6 the Nash situations of the sub-games and situations beside to the Nash equilibrium are exposed. In the table 7 the Nash equilibrium of Martin Shubik game is exposed.

Table 5. *Surviving probabilities in the two agents game if $p_A = 0{,}9$; $p_B = 0{,}7$; $p_C = 0{,}2$.*

$P_A(AB)$	0,92784	$P_A(AC)$	0,97826
$P_A(BA)$	0,27835	$P_A(CA)$	0,78261
$P_B(AB)$	0,07216	$P_B(BC)$	0,92105
$P_B(BA)$	0,72165	$P_B(CB)$	0,73684
$P_C(AC)$	0,02174	$P_C(BC)$	0,07895
$P_C(CA)$	0,21739	$P_C(CB)$	0,26316

Table 6. *The Nash equilibriums of the sub-games if $p_A = 0{,}9$; $p_B = 0{,}7$; $p_C = 0{,}2$.*

Sub-game (ABC)	A	B	C	$P_A(ABC)$	$P_B(ABC)$	$P_C(ABC)$
The Nash equilibrium	shot B	shot A	shot air	0,72613	0,05317	0,22069
	shot C	shot A	shot air	0,25826		
	shot B	shot C	shot air		0,00521	
	shot B	shot A	shot A			0,21982
Sub-game (ACB)	A	B	C	$P_A(ACB)$	$P_B(ACB)$	$P_C(ACB)$
The Nash equilibrium	shot B	shot A	shot air	0,72613	0,05317	0,22069
	shot C	shot A	shot air	0,258263		
	shot B	shot C	shot air		0,00521	
	shot B	shot A	shot A			0,21718
Sub-game (BAC)	A	B	C	$P_A(BAC)$	$P_B(BAC)$	$P_C(BAC)$
The Nash equilibrium	shot B	shot A	shot air	0,21784	0,53174	0,25042
	shot C	shot A	shot air	0,07748		
	shot B	shot C	shot air		0,05208	
	shot B	shot A	shot A			0,24936
Sub-game (BCA)	A	B	C	$P_A(BCA)$	$P_B(BCA)$	$P_C(BCA)$
The Nash equilibrium	shot B	shot A	shot air	0,21784	0,53174	0,25042
	shot C	shot A	shot air	0,07748		
	shot B	shot C	shot air		0,05208	
	shot B	shot A	shot A			0,24170
Sub-game (CAB)	A	B	C	$P_A(CAB)$	$P_B(CAB)$	$P_C(CAB)$
The Nash equilibrium	shot B	shot A	shot air	0,72613	0,05317	0,22069
	shot C	shot A	shot air	0,25826		
	shot B	shot C	shot air		0,00521	
	shot B	shot A	shot A			0,19165
Sub-game (CBA)	A	B	C	$P_A(CBA)$	$P_B(CBA)$	$P_C(CBA)$
The Nash equilibrium	shot B	shot A	shot air	0,21784	0,53174	0,25042
	shot C	shot A	shot air	0,07748		
	shot B	shot C	shot air		0,05208	
	shot B	shot A	shot A			0,21528

Table 7. *The Nash equilibrium of the Martin Shubik game if $p_A = 0{,}9$; $p_B = 0{,}7$; $p_C = 0{,}2$.*

The Martin Shubik game	A	B	C	P_A	P_B	P_C
The Nash equilibrium	shot B	shot A	shot air	0,47199	0,29246	0,23556
	shot C	shot A	shot air	0,16787		
	shot B	shot C	shot air		0,02864	
	shot B	shot A	shot A			0,22250

The examined example allows us to formulate following conclusions.

1. Strategy triple (A→B, B→A, C→O) in all six sub-games and, of course, also in Martin Shubik game leads to the Nash equilibrium.

2. In the Nash equilibrium situation of the Martin Shubik game surviving probability for Casis is the lowest to compare with two others agents. The weakest shooter has the lowest probability to survive! This result contradicts to the conclusion of Herbert Gintis (2009, p. 23).

3.3. The example for approving the Nash equilibrium condition.

Let us suppose, that $p_A = 0{,}7$; $p_B = 0{,}2$; $p_C = 0{,}1$.

The probabilities satisfies requirements of table 1: $p_C = 0{,}1 < 0{,}5894$.

The surviving probabilities of two agents fighting game are showed in table 8. Tables 9 and 10 show, that strategy triple (A→B, B→A, C→O) does not lead to the Nash equilibrium.

***Table 8.** Surviving probabilities in the two agents game if $p_A = 0{,}7$; $p_B = 0{,}2$; $p_C = 0{,}1$.*

$P_A(AB)$	0,92105	$P_A(AC)$	0,95890
$P_A(BA)$	0,73684	$P_A(CA)$	0,86301
$P_B(AB)$	0,07895	$P_B(BC)$	0,71429
$P_B(BA)$	0,26316	$P_B(CB)$	0,64286
$P_C(AC)$	0,04110	$P_C(BC)$	0,28571
$P_C(CA)$	0,13699	$P_C(CB)$	0,35714

***Table 9.** The situations of sub-games.*

Sub-game (ABC)	**A**	**B**	**C**	**$P_A(ABC)$**	**$P_B(ABC)$**	**$P_C(ABC)$**
It is no Nash equilibrium	shot B	shot A	shot air	0,79488	0,05075	0,15437
	shot C	shot A	shot air	0,67867		
	shot B	shot C	shot air		0,00623	
	shot B	shot A	shot A			0,15839
Sub-game (ACB)	A	B	C	$P_A(ACB)$	$P_B(ACB)$	$P_C(ACB)$
It is no Nash equilibrium	shot B	shot A	shot air	0,79488	0,05075	0,15437
	shot C	shot A	shot air	0,67867		
	shot B	shot C	shot air		0,00623	
	shot B	shot A	shot A			0,15784
Sub-game (BAC)	A	B	C	$P_A(BAC)$	$P_B(BAC)$	$P_C(BAC)$
It is no Nash equilibrium	shot B	shot A	shot air	0,63590	0,16917	0,19492
	shot C	shot A	shot air	0,54294		
	shot B	shot C	shot air		0,02078	
	shot B	shot A	shot A			0,19770
Sub-game (BCA)	A	B	C	$P_A(BCA)$	$P_B(BCA)$	$P_C(BCA)$
It is no Nash equilibrium	shot B	shot A	shot air	0,63590	0,16917	0,19492
	shot C	shot A	shot air	0,54294		
	shot B	shot C	shot air		0,02078	
	shot B	shot A	shot A			0,20833
Sub-game (CAB)	A	B	C	$P_A(CAB)$	$P_B(CAB)$	$P_C(CAB)$
It is no Nash equilibrium	shot B	shot A	shot air	0,79488	0,05075	0,15437
	shot C	shot A	shot air	0,67867		
	shot B	shot C	shot air		0,00623	
	shot B	shot A	shot A			0,17112
Sub-game (CBA)	A	B	C	$P_A(CBA)$	$P_B(CBA)$	$P_C(CBA)$
It is no Nash equilibrium	shot B	shot A	shot air	0,63590	0,16917	0,19492
	shot C	shot A	shot air	0,54294		
	shot B	shot C	shot air		0,02078	
	shot B	shot A	shot A			0,20650

***Table 10.** The situations of the Martin Shubik game.*

The Martin Shubik game	A	B	C	P_A	P_B	P_C
It is no Nash equilibrium	shot B	shot A	shot air	0,71539	0,10996	0,17464

	shot C	shot A	shot air	0,61080		
	shot B	shot C	shot air		0,01350	
	shot B	shot A	shot A			0,18331

The examined example confirms characterization of the Nash equilibrium given into table 1 and in the figure 1 and allows to appraise critically the exposition of the theme "When Weakness Is Strength" in Gintis (2009).

4. Survives agent who is not the weakest but pretends to be weakest

As before we suppose that inequality $0 < p_C < p_B < p_A \leq 1$ holds.
Let us examine surviving game in circumstance when special kind of asymmetric information present.

4.1. Ansis is the strongest but pretends to be weakest.

Let us start with case when Ansis pretends to be weakest. Ansis assures Basis and Casis that probabilities satisfy the inequality $p_A < p_C < p_B$ and he – Ansis will shot in the air. In the reality Ansis is going to shot Basis.

If Basis and Casis believe that $p_A < p_C < p_B$ and A→O, then, as it was showed before, the strategies of Basis and Casis are B→C, C→B, which leads to the illusory conditional Nash equilibrium in the Basis and Casis imaginations. In the reality strategy triple (A→B, B→C, C→B) is realized, and that strategy triple guaranteed to Ansis the highest surviving probability.

Let us illustrate the case when Ansis is the strongest but pretends to be weakest with help of some examples.

Example 1. *"When pretence is strenght".*

Let us asume that in reality $p_A = 0{,}9$; $p_B = 0{,}6$; $p_C = 0{,}4$, but Ansis pretends to be weakest and Basis and Casis believe that $p_A < p_C < p_B$, namely, they believe that Ansis is the weakest and will shot in the air. The situations what arise in the six sub-games as result of strategy triple (A→B, B→C, C→B) are exposed in the table 11. Situation what arise in the Martin Shubik game is exposed in the table 12.

Table 11. *The situations of the sub-games if Ansis pretends to be the weakest.*

Sub-game (ABC)	B	C	A	$P_B(ABC)$	$P_C(ABC)$	$P_A(ABC)$
	shot C	shot B	shot B	0,03842	0,10115	0,86043
Sub-game (ACB)	B	C	A	$P_B(ACB)$	$P_C(ACB)$	$P_A(ACB)$
	shot C	shot B	shot B	0,03842	0,15766	0,80392
Sub-game (BAC)	B	C	A	$P_B(BAC)$	$P_C(BAC)$	$P_A(BAC)$
	shot C	shot B	shot B	0,02305	0,11161	0,86533
Sub-game (BCA)	B	C	A	$P_B(BCA)$	$P_C(BCA)$	$P_A(BCA)$
	shot C	shot B	shot B	0,00231	0,25288	0,74482
Sub-game (CAB)	B	C	A	$P_B(CAB)$	$P_C(CAB)$	$P_A(CAB)$
	shot C	shot B	shot B	0,00384	0,39309	0,60306
Sub-game (CBA)	B	C	A	$P_B(CBA)$	$P_C(CBA)$	$P_A(CBA)$
	shot C	shot B	shot B	0,00231	0,39414	0,60355

Table 12. *The situations of the Martin Shubik game if Ansis pretends to be the weakest.*

Martin Shubik game	B	C	A	P_B	P_C	P_A
	shot C	shot B	shot B	0,01806	0,23509	0,74685

Let us compare this example with example "When Weakness Is Strength" in the section 2.1.
We have $p_A = 0{,}9$; $p_B = 0{,}6$; $p_C = 0{,}4$ in both examples. In the tables 2 and 3 are exposed surviving probabilities of all agents in case when all players now real proportion. In the tables 11 and 12 are exposed surviving probabilities of all agents in case when the strongest player pretends to be weakest, but two other agents do not know true. In the first case in the Martin Shubik game $P_A = 0{,}38$, in the second case $P_A = 0{,}75$. It is advantageous do not expose ones power! Let us note, that in the second case very low surviving probability has Basis because of not only Ansis shots to him, but also Casis shots Basis.

Example 2. *"When pretence is strenght".*

Let us asume that in reality the predominance of Ansis is smaller: $p_A = 0{,}7$; $p_B = 0{,}6$; $p_C = 0{,}5$. Ansis pretends to be weakest and Basis and Casis believe that Ansis is the weakest and will shot in the air. The situations what arise in the Martin Shubik game as result of strategy triple (A→B, B→C, C→B) are exposed in the table 13. Obviously, the pretence of Ansis helps him to survive.

Table 13. *The situation of the Martin Shubik game if Ansis pretends to be the weakest.*

Martin Shubik game	B	C	A	P_B	P_C	P_A
	shot C	shot B	shot B	0,06746	0,28692	0,64562

4.2. The second strongest player Basis pretends to be weakest.

Now we are going to demonstrate that pretence strategy provides the highest surviving probability also for the second strongest player – Basis.

For instance, let us examine the case, whe in the reality $p_A = 0{,}7$; $p_B = 0{,}6$; $p_C = 0{,}5$. Basis pretends to be weakest and Ansis and Casis believe that $p_A < p_C < p_B$, namely, they believe that Basis is the weakest and will shot in the air. The situations what arise as result of strategy triple (A→C, B→A, C→A) in the six sub-games are exposed in the table 14. The situation what arises in the Martin Shubik game is exposed in the table 15.

Table 14. *The situations of the sub-games if Basis pretends to be the weakest.*

Sub-game (ABC)	A	C	B	P_A(ABC)	P_C(ABC)	P_B(ABC)
	shot C	shot A	shot A	0,23694	0,09973	0,66332
Sub-game (ACB)	A	C	B	P_A(ACB)	P_C(ACB)	P_B(ACB)
	shot C	shot A	shot A	0,23694	0,13564	0,62742
Sub-game (BAC)	A	C	B	P_A(BAC)	P_C(BAC)	P_B(BAC)
	shot C	shot A	shot A	0,11847	0,19282	0,68871
Sub-game (BCA)	A	C	B	P_A(BCA)	P_C(BCA)	P_B(BCA)
	shot C	shot A	shot A	0,04739	0,33245	0,62016
Sub-game (CAB)	A	C	B	P_A(CAB)	P_C(CAB)	P_B(CAB)
	shot C	shot A	shot A	0,09478	0,41489	0,49033
Sub-game (CBA)	A	C	B	P_A(CBA)	P_C(CBA)	P_B(CBA)
	shot C	shot A	shot A	0,04739	0,45213	0,50048

Table 15. *The situations of the Martin Shubik game if Basis pretends to be the weakest.*

Martin Shubik game	A	C	B	P_A	P_C	P_B
	shot C	shot A	shot A	0,13032	0,27128	0,59840

Numerical experiments performed show us that the surviving probability which Basis gets do to pretending is the largest to compare with another two surviving probabilities. In some sub-games surviving probability of pretenders is even larger then pretenders probability to hit.

5. Conclusions

The author is convinced of cardinal role of game theory in the investigation of individuals' strategy interaction what is fundament for understanding absolutely all social and economic processes. In the circumstance of global confidence crisis the investigation of asymmetric information role in individuals' interactions seems for us especially actual. In present paper the surviving game of three agents, what essence is the competition fight, is investigated. It is established that the shape of Nash equilibrium in a specific way depends of surviving probabilities of the agents. In the paper the limitation of some statements of Herbert Gintis empirically is proved. By opinion of author, the most valuable result of this research is the solution of Martin Shubik surviving game exposed in geometrical form. It is recognized that statement of Martin Shubik "survives the weakest" in circumstances of asymmetric information transforms in statement "survives agent who is not the weakest but pretends to be weakest". My recommendation is to include the surviving game as topic in the game theory course taught in academic program of economics.

References

Binmore, K., 2007. *Game Theory. A Very Short Introduction.* Oxford: Oxford University Press

Gintis H., 2009. *Game Theory Evolving: A Problem Centered Introduction to Modelling Strategic Interaction – 2nd Edition.* Princeton, NJ: Princeton University Press

Jaunzems, A., 2008. *Mikroekonomika. Vidēja teorētiskā līmeņa kurss - 1. daļa.*, Ventspils Augstskola, "LiePA"

Jaunzems, A., 2009a. *Mikroekonomika. Vidēja teorētiskā līmeņa kurss - 2. daļa.*, Drukātava

Jaunzems, A., 2009b. *Risku analīze un vadīšana*. Drukātava

Jaunzems, A., 2009c. Trimatricu spēles: interpretācijas un pielietojumi sociālekonomisko situāciju stabilitātes analīzē, in Medveckis A. (editor), *Sabiedrība un kultūra*. Rakstu krājums, XI / Sastād, Liepāja: LiePA, pp. 521-534

Майкл, Р.Б., 1999. *Управленческая экономика и стратегия бизнеса*. Москва: Юнити, 743 стр.

Shubik, M., 1954. *Readings in Game Theory and Political Behavior*, New York: Doubleday

Байе, М.Р., 1999. *Управленческая экономика и стратегия бизнеса.* Москва: Юнити,

3

Investment under Financial Liberalization: Post 1980 Turkey Case

Onur TUTULMAZ*, Burcu DOĞAN

Hitit University, Turkey

In the history of the modern state of Turkey many policies have been developed and applied in order to transform ineffective economy to a dynamic and steady one. The liberal policies have been effectively applied except for war periods. The main activity of liberal policies in Turkey's economy was conducted on January 24, 1980 with some important structural adjustment decisions. These decisions aimed to integrate the economy with the global system by applying global economic order that widely adopted all over the world. The decisions aimed also to activate a financial liberalization in the country. Financial liberalization generally includes the principles related to removing the pressure on the interest rate, currency control and investment mobility. More liberalization steps came in 1989 aiming to increase the investment and growth. Foreign Direct Investment (FDI) was seen important for those purposes. However, short term capital flows, having been more effective in real investments than FDI, have led to several negative effects in this period. In this study some of the drawbacks of that process of financial liberalization have been discussed. The relation between FDI and Gross Domestic Product in the financial liberalization process has been tested with econometric implementation. Econometric estimation has been applied for this purpose to test this relationship for post 1980 era for Turkey as a developing country.

Keywords: *financial liberalization, foreign direct investment, FDI, economic growth*

1. Introduction

Although a lot of economic policies have been applied in Turkey's history since 1923, the interventionist policies had been always more dominant until 1980. Especially the war or crisis periods have been the times that were detached from the liberal policies.

State interventionism was started to be left gradually in the post 1980 period. By the effect of liberalization era in the world, economic liberalization transformation reforms were declared on January 24th, 1980. These decisions were primarily used to establish the stability in its domestic and international markets. Because the stability is the primary feature that foreign direct investment (FDI) looks for when entering a country. Therefore, the stimulus programs prepared in order to promote to domestic production are facilitated

* Corresponding Author:
Onur Tutulmaz, Hitit University, Department of Economics, Turkey

for also FDI. FDI was expected to bring technology, knowledge and know-how so that it was expected to help in growing economy. In this aspect FDI was given an important place in the macroeconomic policy of the country.

The reforms planed in 1980`s financial liberalization decisions were brought into the reality in a large extent in a decade. By the means of that policy the controls over the interest rates and currency exchange were removed and the capital flows were liberalized. However, this financial liberalization had not brought the expected positive effect on the growth or decrease in the dependence on foreign capital. This experience brings the questions on the effectiveness of liberalization policies in developing countries since the success of the liberalization in developed world has not been generally seen in the developing countries. The liberalized interest rates led an increase in incoming short term foreign capital instead of an increase in domestic savings. Liquidity of short term foreign capital leads to fast capital outflows in the crisis times. This liquidity, consequently, increases the economic instability of the system in the crisis. Accordingly, there have seen an increase in the number of crisis in the country; in contrast, the portion of FDI in developed economies has been higher before and after economic liberalization.

In this paper, first the concepts of liberalization and financial liberalization are investigated in the second section. In the third section, the process of the liberalization and financial liberalization in Turkey is taken into account. In the third section, an empirical model is applied for the relationship of FDI with economic growth.

2. Liberalization

Liberalization, literally means making free; applied in economics, it means to make the economy (in a large extent) free from the state and to let the market run the economy as much as possible.

As one of the important concepts that affected modern economies in the world, liberalization can be defined in general terms as 'removal of uncompetitive factors and of the obstacles against the free circulation of goods, services, labors and capital' (GEU, 2009).

Going through the definitions, we can see that liberalization aims to abolish the economic borders among the countries whether they are developed or developing countries; in this aspect of the meaning of the word, it closes to the 'globalization'.

2.1. Financial Liberalization

In a narrow definition, financial liberalization means to remove the controls on bank account and credit interests; in a wider definition, it means to abolish the classifications of the activity of institutions, to decrease and abolish the controls on exchange, to remove the obstacles on the foreign accesses to domestic financial system, and the obstacles on the national access to international financial system (Williamson and Mahar, 1998:2).

In a different definition financial liberalization is defined as a result of the deregulation activities by which the controls and restrictions on the financial and banking system are abolished; therefore, it is defined as a process of opening to international capital flows.

The justification of the financial liberalization lies beneath the criticizing of the government intervention and control on the economy. According to that analysis, an intervention to economy means the external determination of interest rates to the market and the restriction of the capital flows. In this concept, a maximum level of interest rates would distort the consumption plans towards today, meaning inter-periodic changes. This kind of inter-periodic changes decrease today`s savings and therefore negatively affect the investments. Moreover, a maximum level of interest rate causes a negative real interest rates in inflation times, leading to a valuation of national money and damage in export sector. With this analysis, financial liberalization criticizes the government intervention and defends the efficiency of the liberal policies.

Another important issue with the financial liberalization is its different efficiency levels according to the development levels of countries. Developed financial infrastructure and financial tools of developed countries prepare an available base for liberalization policies. However, the liberalization situation in developing countries is not only related with the financial markets but it is related with the radical economic transformations coming up in their development path (Tuncel, 2010: 100).

There are different applications of financial liberalization in domestic and international markets. However, they should both be applied in order to be efficient. Domestic financial liberalization means the removal of controls and restrictions which causes financial shrinking and to obtain that the nominal interest rates should be determined by banks instead of the government and the interest rates should be determined in the market according to demand and supply. The foreign financial market liberalization, on the other hand, is defined as the removal of the controls on exchange rates in order to unification with the foreign financial markets and to maintain of that the exchange rates are determined in the market by exchange demand and supply. Moreover, the unlimited capital circulation of capital and the equalization of factor prices in long term consists the other expected results from the liberalization process (Williamson and Maher, 1998: 8-11).

At first the developing countries followed a negative attitude against the financial liberalization. After 1980, the maximum interest rates, obligatory reciprocal rates and the restrictions on the international capital flows were abolished. (Demirgulec and Detragiache, 1998: 2). Therefore, the domestic and international financial liberalization movements can be evaluated as that they brought a wider scale economic liberalization and preceded the financial globalization.

3. Post 1980 Turkish Economy

3.1. 1980-1989 Period

In this period of 1980-1989, Turkey had done important changes in economic policy and applied domestic financial liberalization. There were political openings aiming the real sector and trade liberalization in the first step; but the policies for financial liberalization were also added to them.

In 1980, the first step in liberalization of economy was taken by the January 24th decisions. The January 24th decisions are an important milestone showing that Turkey connects world markets. There are 2 opinions on this process. First opinion defends that this process is a revolutionary integration process by which the country opened itself to the world; second opinion proposes that the policies of detachment from national industry, national trade and promoting agriculture are actually the continuation of the harmonization policies used to open the country to the international capital (Öztürk, Nas and Içöz, 2008: 16). These two opinions show that there are positive and negative evaluations on the January 24th decisions. The main points of January 24th decisions are listed as below:

1. The macro level decisions instead of micro level decisions should be preferred in order to maintain integrity, consistency and compatibility in economy.
2. The potential and dynamism of the private sector should be maximally facilitated in production and export sectors.
3. The control of inflation should be maintained primarily. A healthy growth should be aimed after controlling inflation.
4. In order to control inflation the monetary and credit policies should be under control and the government financial deficit should be eliminated gradually; the central bank loans to the Treasury should be followed tightly.
5. The unutilized capacity should be first facilitate before initiating new investments
6. To increase the export rapidly, a realist and elastic exchange policy should be followed parallel to the other precautions.
7. A realistic interest policy should be followed in order to increase savings and channeling them by fiscal institutions.
8. The foreign private capital should be promoted in order to eliminate the domestic and foreign financial deficit and in order to increase the investments so as to increase employment (Parasız, 2003: 283-284).

After the January 24th decisions listed above, the main changes performed in this period can be given as below:

1. Lira (TL) was devaluated from 1 US Dolar = 1.47 TL to the exchange rate of 1 US Dolar = 70 TL.
2. Export Promotion Fund (EPF) was founded by the Central Bank and a certain amount from the Support and Price Stability Fund and from the export guarantee deposits were transferred to the EPF.
3. Efforts to eliminate the KİT deficits and governmental sector deficits were conducted (Cura, 1998: 134).

The economic program of 24 January 1980 deemed the foreign capital as a must for economic growth, therefore, the private foreign capital has been regarded a privileged place in the program. First, a bylaw, called 'Foreign Capital Frame Bylaw' (Yabancı Sermaye Çerçeve Kararnamesi), was legislated in order to remove the bureaucratic obstacles in front of foreign capital inflow. With this bylaw, a condition that a part of production depends on foreign investment must be exported was legislated (Savrul, Ozekicioğlu and Ozel, 2013: 230). The purpose of this regulation was to decrease the government role in economy and stimulate the export.

3.2. 1989-2001 Period

The liberalization movement that started after 1980 first became effective in the trade and production areas. Between 1980 and 1989 all necessary financial regulations were made and the integration to market economy was completed.

By the decisions of 24 January 1980 various policies were applied to increase the investments and to establish the stability and eventually an improvement was observed. This improvement went into another phase with the introduction of Decree No. 32 in 1989 to continue the liberalization reforms by financial liberalization steps, which can be seen as advance level of liberalization (Unsal, 2003: 191). By Decree No.32, first, all exchange controls were established and consequently the international capital flows started to be effective in the domestic markets (Kar and Tatlısoz, 2008: 4).

In 1984, a regulation, Decree No.30 related to the law numbered 1567, launched a quasi-control regime for currency exchange and this regime lasted until 1989. By the Decree No.32 this transformation had been completed in 1989 and all hurdles against the liberalization of capital circulation in domestic markets were removed. Some of the important articles of the Bylaw are given below:

On the foreign capital to come to the country:

Article 12- (1) Foreign investments aiming Turkey will be evaluated according to the Law no. 4875, the Law on Foreign Direct Investments.

(2) The profit, sales revenue, license, compensation, interest and other expenses which are outcomes of the foreign investor`s activities in Turkey can be freely transferred to abroad.

(3) According to Petroleum Law no 6326 the activities in Turkey and transfer demands subject to this law.

On the domestic capital to leave the country:

Article 13- (1) Individual placed in Turkey can freely transfer capital abroad via banks to invest or to conduct trade activity, to establish incorporation, under the custom rules.

(2) Individual placed in Turkey can freely transfer the establishment or running expenses of their abroad brands, representatives or bureaus.

(3) Banks and custom authorities inform the Ministry Undersecretriat about the exporting capital to abroad in 30 days.

(4) Ministry is authorized on requesting the information and the documents from individuals related with applications of this law (TCMB, 1989).

Beginning from 1989, the governmental authorities launched a new economic policy that aims to keep the devaluation of Turkish Lira (TL) against Dolar and Mark under the inflation. TL started to evaluate against foreign exchanges especially in 1989 and 1990; and after 1991 the high interest policy to attract the foreign capital helped to expand the exchange supply (Uysal, Mucuk and Alptekin, 2008: 53).

The Decree No. 32 came into effect in 1989 was effective to change the country`s economic direction. However, it had been observed that the liberal policies could not be effective to increase the real investments, rather it helped that the short term capital had a major role in operating of the country`s economy.

3.3. Post 2001 Period

After the Decree No. 32 came into effect in 1989, Turkish economy experienced a several economic crises in 1994, 1997-1998, 2001 and consequently went under IMF stability programs.

A program to deal with the 2001 crisis was announced on 14 April and 15 May 2001 in two steps. The program was called as national program first, and afterwards as ‘Program for Transition to a Strong Economy’ (Ay and Karaçor, 2006: 71).

The Program for Transition to a Strong Economy (PTSE) was put into effect in three steps. It was announced that it had been planned to get financial sector under control in first step, the foreign deficit and inflation would be dealt in second step and the growth rate would be increased by the applications aiming the structural changes in the last step (Karacor and Kol, 2012: 387). The program generally focused on the opportunity to facilitate from the strong international economic resources; however, it didn’t take the negative parts of the short term foreign capital in account. Actually, the program can be seen as a continuum of the rule of the Decree No. 32 on the manner of capital mobilization. The program did not either consider on that an exchange expand could lead to an import surge and its consequences as capital outflow. With this arguments, the program has been criticized as the possible outcomes might be reverse of what was aimed; and it could have possibly leaded to a total dependence to international capital instead of facilitating from the foreign economic resources (for example see, BSB, 2001). Parallel to these critiques, after PTSE launched in 2001 the dependence on short term foreign capital and foreign currency financing deficit has increased.

4. Foreign Direct Investment (FDI) and Growth in Financial Liberalization Process: An Application

4.1. The Literature Survey on the Relationship between FDI and Growth

There are quite a lot studies investigating the relation of financial liberalization with economic variables. These studies show different results according to the countries they were applied. A brief scan of literature is given below.

Mario Carcovic and Ross Levine (2002) tested the relationship between FDI and growth by using a data set including 72 countries. The application uses countries' data for the period 1960-1995 and. Ordinary least square (OLS) method is used in the first step of the application, a dynamic panel data is structured by using the 5 year averages in the second step. A negative relationship between FDI and growth is detected in the paper.

The relationship between FDI and economic growth has been tested by the paper of Fatma Turan Koyuncu (2011). The paper used the causality test for analyzing the relationship. 3 month data set for the period of 1990-2010 taken from Central Bank`s data base is used in the paper. The analysis resulted that the variables are stable and FDI affects the economic growth in positively.

De Mello (1997) used a data set consists of 32 non-OECD countries. The paper detected a positive relationship between FDI and economic growth.

Onur Sara (2005) tested the relationship between a set of variables consist of openness, financial development and financial liberalization with the economic growth by using Granger causality test. The paper detected a single direction relationship in 1 % significant level between openness and financial liberalization, growth and financial liberalization, growth and financial development. The paper detected a double direction relationship in 1 % significant level between growth and openness. It is also detected a single direction relationship in 5 % significant level between financial development and financial liberalization, financial liberalization and openness, financial liberalization and growth, financial development and growth.

Ayberk Nuri Berkman (2011) tested the relationship between FDI and economic growth using a data set consists of quarter data between the periods 1987: 01 and 2011: 02. Causality test detected a causality relationship from financial liberalization to growth.

Ağayev, Seymur (2010) tested the relationship between FDI and economic growth for 25 transition economies by panel data, panel cointegration and panel causality tests. The paper detected a positive effect of FDI on economic growth.

Okuyan and Erbaykal (2008) conducted an empirical research by using causality test on 9 developing countries. These 9 developing countries consists of Brazil, Mexico, Malaysia, South Korea, Thailand, Turkey, Singapore, Indonesia and India. For the period of 1970-2006; and tested the causality relationship of FDI with economic growth. Authors concluded that the economic growth cause an increase in FDI for the 6 of these countries including Brazil, Mexico, Malaysia, South Korea, Thailand and Turkey. Moreover, a reciprocal causality is detected for the data of Singapore and Indonesia, and a causality relationship from FDI to economic growth is determined for India.

Babajide Fowowe (2008) used Generalized Moments Method (GMM) to test the relationship of financial liberalization with economic growth for the data set of Sub-Sahara Africa for the 1978-2000 period. The research concluded a positive relationship between financial liberalization and economic growth.

Ben McLean and Sona Shrestha (2002) conducted a panel data analysis consists of 40 countries for the period of 1976-1995. The econometric model analyzed the effects of various capital flows to the economic growth and concluded that the FDI and portfolio investments affected growth positively; on the other hand, bank credits affected growth negatively.

Imran Sharif Chaudhry (2007) determined a positive relationship between financial liberalization and economic growth for Pakistan for the period of 1972-2006. Chaudhry concludes that the financial liberalization process pulled the growth rates upward.

David T. Tswamuno, Scott Pardee and Phanindra V. Wunnava (2007) tested the relationship between the financial liberalization and economic growth for South Africa for the time period of 1973:3 – 2005:1. Estimations showed that financial liberalization affected growth positively in the first years, yet the volatility experienced recent terms has not positively affected to South African economy.

As it can be seen here the biggest part of the financial liberalization literature consists of researches investigating the effects of FDI on economic growth. The role of economic crisis and the other macroeconomic variables in this relationship is also tested in literature.

4.2. Data and Method

The empirical model applied in this paper was first applied for Uganda by M.B. Obwana (2001) and then for Turkey by Onur Demirel (2006). Both papers used simultaneous models. Our paper, taking the model for a Turkey application, also estimates as single equations by using the Ordinary Least Square (OLS) method and compare the results with the ones from the estimations of simultaneous equations. Our paper tries to test the relationship of FDI with economic growth in Turkey after the financial liberalization takes start off in 1980 until 2013. On the other hand, because of encountered data problems for some of variables, the data set was restructured as 1984-2010.

During constructing the data set for the econometric model we facilitated the online data from the official websites of Turkish Statistical Institute (TurkStat), Ministry of Development, Treasury Undersecretariat, Central Bank of the Republic of Turkey (CBRT/TCMB), Ministry of Economy and Ministry of Finance. Most of these data are in current terms. Real data series of the variables GDP, FDI and S (domestic savings) have been obtained from global data networks of IMF, WB, OECD and UNCTAD in real terms. IMF: International Money Fund (www.imf.org); WB: World Bank (www.worldbank.org); OECD: Organizations of economic Cooperation and Development (www.oecd.org); UNCTAD: United Nations Conference on Trade and Development (www.unctad.org). Explanations of the variables are given under the Eq. (2) and (3) of the model.

4.3. Econometric Application and the Results

The estimated econometric model aims to determine the direction of the relationship between GDP and FDI in post 1980 Turkey. The aim of our paper is to determine the effect of the liberalization on the country`s economy, therefore especially the after 1980 data are used for this purpose.

$$Y_i = \beta_1 + \beta_1 X_i + e_i \tag{1}$$

First, the single equations as represented in Eq. (1) are estimated separately by OLS method. In these estimations it is aimed to determine that the effect of FDI and other variables on economic growth (GDPG) in the first equation; similarly, the effect of economic growth and other variables on FDI in the second equation.

The open forms of the estimated equations are given in Eq. (2) and (3) below:

$$GDPG_t = \beta_0 + \beta_1 FDI + \beta_2 S + \beta_3 XG + \beta_4 FA + e_{1t} \tag{2}$$

β_0: Constant term
GDPG: GDP growth rate (%)
FDI: Foreign Direct Investment (Milyon $)
S: Domestic savings rate (%)
XG: Export growth rate (%)
FA: Foreign aid income
e_{1t}: Error term

$$FDI_t = \beta_0 + \beta_1 GDPG + \beta_2 GDP + \beta_3 INF + \beta_4 S + \beta_5 PI + \beta_6 Dummy + e_{1t} \tag{3}$$

β_0: Constant term
GDPG: GDP growth rate (%)
GDP: Gross Domestic Product (Milyon $)
INF: Inflation (TUFE) (%)
S: Domestic savings rate (%)
PI: Public investment as percentage of GDP (%)
DUMMY: Dummy for GDP
e_{1t}: Error term

Table 1. *Estimations of OLS Model*

Growth Equation		
Variable	**Coefficient**	**t-stat**
C	-4.60	-0.76
FDI	-6.89	-0.26
FA	-4.05	-1.01
S	8.02	1.24
XG	0.16	2.04**
$R^2 = 0.27$		

*10%, **5%, ***1% significance levels

FDI Equation		
Variable	**Coefficient**	**t-stat**
C	-2.63	-0.81
GDP	0.14	4.47***
GDPG	-84332831	-0.55
INF	-56113526	-1.96**
S	5.33	2.58***
DUMMY	1.5	0.82
PI	-3.27	-2.66***
$R^2 = 0.78$		

Table 1 shows the estimations results of econometric application. The coefficient of determination (R^2) shows to what extent dependent variable can be explained by the independent variables. In growth equation, R-square is determined 0.27. This explanation level of dependent variable by independent variables can be thought as a low value. R^2 is 0.78 in FDI equation, higher than the one in the growth equation, it can be deemed as good level for estimations.

In the estimations of growth equation, XG and S are determined positive; FA and FDI are determined negative. XG was estimated in 5% significance level. It is normal that increases in export increase the economic growth; however FDI was not estimated significant by the data of investigated period. The significant role of FDI in economic growth of developed countries could not be determined for Turkey. More importantly F statistics cannot confirm overall significance for first equation. This result puts the statistical inability of the model for Turkey data more clearly signaling insignificant role of FDI in recent growth experience of Turkey.

This study aiming to re-test the explaining power of the previously applied simultaneous equation by referencing Obwana (2009) finds an inability in this aspect. The estimations of the simultaneous model doesn't give meaningful results, and this is consistent with the growth equation insignificant estimation above and the Hausman test for simultaneity as well.

The empirical simultaneous equations estimated in this paper are given in Eq. (4). The same variables as used in Eq (2) and (3) are used here, therefore they are not explained again here.

$$GDPG_t = \beta_{20} + \beta_{21} FDI + \beta_{22} S + \beta_{23} XG + \beta_{24} FA + e_{1t}$$

$$FDI_t = \beta_{10} + \beta_{11} GDPG + \beta_{12} GDP + \beta_{13} INF + \beta_{14} S + \beta_{15} PI + \beta_{16} DUMMY + e_{1t} \quad (4)$$

In this sense our results contradict with the results of another Turkey application of the Obwana model (see, Demirel, 2006). This difference should be caused by the different data structure and source because the data sources and the lengths are different. However, this apparent differentiation also puts a question in terms of the reliability of the simultaneous model.

Despite the fails of the simultaneous model application of (4), single equation estimation of FDI equation gives reliable results. In FDI equation, GDP, DUMMY and S are determined as positive; INF, GDPG and PI are determined negative. In the estimations, PI, S and GDP are determined statistically significant at 1% level; INF is determined significant at 5% level. GDP level has been found significantly related with FDI. PI can be related with the consumption behavior; therefore it is included in the model. PI can be deemed as a way to affect the consumption behavior in a society; in this aspect, the increasing consumption behavior has affected GDP level in this period (despite the overall insignificance of the first equation). S and INF are also found significant for describing FDI. S and stable INF can be effective in determination of FDI via affecting the GDP levels.

5. Conclusion

Starting from 1980 the liberal policies brought a real unlimited freedom to Turkish economy. In this period of transformation the country has introduced many new regulations.

However, these regulations could not bring the intended success. Financial liberalization has worked for the profit realizing foreign capital at the high interest periods instead of intended stability and growth. The failure in achieving the stability and growth in the country also affected back in attracting FDI, in a vicious circle. The result of the econometric application in this paper showed signs in this way. Having been significant in FDI numbers, growth in GDP could not be stable enough to make FDI numbers effective and significant in describing the GDP itself.

As a result, the outcomes for Turkey remind us the differentiation of the successes of FDI in developing and developed countries. Not having stability in their economy, developing countries could not be successful in FDI applications. On the contrary, the liberal policies have led insatiability to escalate inside the countries. In this context, the escalated instability can be seen related with the high number of economic crises of modern economies in recent decades.

References

Ay, A. and Karaçor, Z., 2006. 2001 Sonrası Dönemde Türkiye Ekonomisinde Krizden Büyümeye Geçiş Üzerine bir Tartışma. *S.Ü. Sosyal Bilimler Enstitüsü Dergisi*, 16, pp.67-86.

BSB-Bağımsız Sosyal Bilimciler, 2001. Güçlü Ekonomiye Geçiş Programı Üzerine Değerlendirmeler. (http://www.bagimsizsosyalbilimciler.org/bsbmetin.html. (Accessed August 20, 2014).

Berkman, A.N., 2011. Finansal Liberalizasyonun Gelişmekte olanÜlkeler ve Türkiye Üzerindeki Etkileri, Adana: Çukurova Üniversitesi Sosyal Bilimler Enstitüsü, *Doktora Tezi*.

Carkovic, M. and Levine, R., 2002. Does Foreign Direct Investment Accelerate Economic Growth? University of Minnesota, Department of Finance, *Working Paper*, June, pp.195-220. Available online at: http:// papers.ssrn.com/sol3/papers.cfm?abstract_id=314924 Paper Download. (Accessed May 10, 2014).

Chaudhry, I.S., 2007. Financial Liberalization and Macroeconomic Performance: Empirical Evidence from Pakistan. Available online at: http:// www.gredeg.cnrs.fr/ Colloques/NFI/ Papers/ PapierOnLine/ Chaudry.pdf. (Accessed August 27, 2014).

Cura, K., 1998. Türkiye'de 1980 Sonrası İzlenen Para politikası, *Selçuk Üniversitesi Sosyal Bilimler Meslek Yüksek Okulu Dergisi*, 1, pp.129-145.

De Mello. Jr. By Luiz Re., 1997). Foreign Investment in Developing Countries and Growth: A Selective Survey. *The Journal of Development Studies*, 34 (1), pp.133-151

Demirel, O., 2006. *Doğrudan yabancı yatırımlar, ekonomik büyümeye etkileri ve Türkiye uygulaması*. Master thesis, Suleyman Demirel University

Demirgüleç, A. and Detragiache Kunt E., 1998. Financial Liberalization and Financial Fragility. *Policy Research Working Paper 1917*, Available at http://wwwwds.worldbank.org/ servlet/WDSContentServer/ WDSP/ IB/1998/05/01/ 000009265_3980630181025/ Rendered/PDF/multi_page.pdf. (Accessed May 22, 2015).

Fowowe, B., 2008. Financial Liberalization Policies and Economic Growth: Panel Data Evidence from Sub-Saharan Africa. *African Development Review*, 20(3), pp.549-574.

GEU, 2009. *Glossary for the European Union*. Economic Development Foundation. Available at http: // www.ikv.org.tr/sozluk.asp?bas_harf=L&anahtar=&sayfa=&id=1193#kancasosluk1193. Accessed May 2, 2014.

Kar, M. and Tatlısöz, F., 2008. Türkiye'de Doğrudan Yabancı Sermaye Hareketlerini Belirleyen Faktörlerin Ekonometrik Analizi. *KMU İİBF Dergisi,* 14(10), pp.1-23.

Kol, E. N. and Karaçor, Z., 2012), "2001 Güçlü Ekonomiye Geçiş Programı ve İstihdam Üzerine Etkileri", *Maliye Dergisi*, 162, pp.379-395.

Obwona, M.B., 2001. Determinants of FDI and their Impact on Economic Growth in Uganda. *African Development Bank*, 13(1), pp.46-81.

Okuyan, A. and Erbaykal E., 2008. Gelişmekte Olan Ülkelerde Doğrudan Yabancı Yatırımlar ve Büyüme İlişkisi. *Ekonomik Yaklaşım Dergisi*, 19(67), pp.47-58.

Öztürk, Ş., Nas F. and İçöz, E., 2008. 24th January Decisions Neo-Liberal Policies and Agriculture of Turkey. *PAU J Soc Sci Ins*, 1 (2), pp.15-32.

Parasız, I., 2003. *Türkiye Ekonomisi*, Bursa: Ezgi Kitabevi Yayınları.

Sara, O., 2005. Finansal Liberalizasyon ve GSMH arasındaki İlişki. *ZKÜ Sosyal Bilimler Dergisi*, 1(1), pp.127-151.

Savrul Kılıc, B., Özal, H.A. and Kılıç, C., 2013. Osmanlı'nın Son Döneminden Günümüze Türkiye'de Dış Ticaretin Gelişimi. *Girişimcilik ve Kalkınma Dergisi,* 1(8), pp.55-78.

Seyidoğlu, H., 2002. *Ekonomik Terimler Ansiklopedik Sözlük*, İstanbul: Güzem Can Yayınları.

TCMB, 1989). Türk Parası Kıymetini Koruma Hakkında 32 Sayılı Karar, Available at http://www.tcmb.gov.tr/ yeni/mevzuat/ DISILISKILER/32sayilikarar.htm. Accessed May 13, 2014.

Tswamuno, D. T., Pardee, S., and Wunnava, P.V., 2007. Financial Liberalization and Economic Growth: Lessons from the South African Experience. *International Journal of Applied Economics*, 4(2), pp.75-

89.
Tuncel, C.O., 2010. Finansal Liberalizasyon ve Küresel Krizin Yapısal Nedenleri: Gelişmekte Olan Ülkeler İçin Dersler. *Finans Politik & Ekonomik Yorumlar Dergisi*, 47 (545), pp.93-105.
Unsal, H., 2003. Türkiye'de Finansal Serbestleşme Sürecinde İç Borçlanma ve Sermaye Piyasası Üzerindeki Etkileri. *G.Ü. İ.İ.B.F. Dergisi*, 3, pp.191-205.
Uysal, D., Mucuk, M., Volkan, A., 2008. Finansal Serbestleşme Sürecinde Türkiye Ekonomisinde Faiz Kur İlişkisi. *KMU IIBF Dergisi*, 15(10), pp.48-64.
Williamson, J. and Mahar, M., 1998. *A Survey of Financial Liberalization, Issue 211*. Princeton University, New Jersey

4

Identification of Key Productive Sectors in the Mexican Economy

David REVILLA[1], Adelaido GARCÍA-ÁNDRES[2] and Isaac SÁNCHEZ-JUÁREZ[3]*

[1]Instituto Nacional de Estadística y Geografía, Oaxaca, México
[2]Universidad Autónoma de Nuevo León, Monterrey, México
[3]Universidad Autónoma de Ciudad Juárez, Chihuahua, México

This article focuses on identifying what are the key sectors with high potential for drag induced investment in the Mexican economy, also characterizes the sectors according to their hierarchy, impact and degree of articulation. To achieve this the input-output matrix national 2003 was used (disaggregated into 20 sectors and 79 sub-sectors), provided by the official government agency responsible for generating statistical information, which applied the traditional method of calculation of multipliers which takes into account both relations hierarchical such as circular between the productive sectors of Rasmussen (1956). The originality of the work lies in the application of the social networks theory to determine (García, Morillas and Ramos 2005, 2008): a) total effects, b) immediate effects, and c) mediative effects of sectors and thus have a full diagnosis of key sectors of the economy under study. In general, the findings indicate that for the promotion of growth and productive development, efforts should focus on manufacturing industries, which means to apply an active industrial policy.

Keywords: *input-output analysis, social network theory, inter-sectorial relations, key sectors, Mexico, development, economic growth.*

1. Introduction

Mexico is a developing country facing a myriad of problems, one of the most important, in economic terms, is the low rate of growth of its economy, which has had severe consequences on the ability to generate jobs and therefore income that help to improve the welfare of the population. On annual average, between 1982 and 2014 the economy, in per capita terms, barely grew 0.5%, a truly insignificant figure. Given this situation, it becomes relevant, studies that contribute to clarify the way in which the authorities could act to solve the problem.

* Corresponding Author:
Isaac Sánchez-Juárez, Universidad Autónoma de Ciudad Juárez, Chihuahua, México

This paper seeks to contribute in this regard, using information contained in the matrix of national input-output for 2003 with the aim of identifying those sectors that are the most important, through their productive linkages, both forward and backward, sectors with a high potential for drag. This is vital, since before resources that normally are scarce, its use in this way should be prioritized, and thus the paper by identifying sectors of greatest relevance contributes with information for decision-makers that are focused on the promotion of economic growth.

It should be stressed that the analysis of the productive structure of an economy based on so-called inter-sectorial linkages allows to characterize the degree of interaction and dependence between productive sectors, this type of analysis provides the following advantages: a) allows you to identify what are the key sectors with high potential for investment induced drag, b) characterizes the sectors according to their hierarchy (impact and degree of articulation, and c) provides information of practical use for planning the growth and productive development.

In the paper the task of identifying key sectors from the input-output matrix is performed using as a reference the traditional works of Leontief (1936) and Rasmussen (1956), but particularly García, Morillas and Ramos (2005 and 2008). The identification is carried out with 20 sectors (1: Agriculture, forestry, and fishing; 2: Mining; 3: Electricity, water and gas; 4: Construction; 5: Manufacturing industries; 6: Commerce; 7: Transportation; 8: Post office and storage; 9: Information in mass media; 10: Financial and insurance services; 11: Real estate and rental services; 12: Professional, scientific and technological services; 13: Corporate management and business; 14): Business support services; 15: Educational services; 16: Health and social care services; 17: Recreational services; 18: Hotels, food and beverages; 19: Other services; 20: Government activities) and 79 subsectors (by extension are specified in table 3).

The paper innovates in the Mexican case making use of the Social Networks Theory (SNT), which unlike the traditional analysis, focused the study on a set of observed relationships between the actors in a network or group –for example, the structure of supply and demand of an economy– and not on the individual characteristics of the same –e.g. volume of production in a sector, final demand, value-added, etc. –. In particular, the study of the productive structure allows us to respond to the following questions: What are the key productive sectors, driving, strategic and independent in the economy derived from their production chains? What is the relative influence that has, by its position, a sector particularly on the overall economy? What is the capacity and speed of diffusion of the relative influence between elements –sectors and subsectors of activity– and particular substructures of the economic framework?

The work was structured in three parts. The first summarizes the existing literature in this regard, according to a scan performed in the electronic databases Repec, Scielo, Dialnet and Jstor. The second presents a synthesis of the methodology used, as well as the source of the data. The third part presents the results of identification of key sectors with a breakdown of 20 and 79 subsectors. Finally the findings are summarized and brief suggestions of economic policy are made for the promotion of economic growth in Mexico.

2. Literature Review

Efforts to identify key sectors of an economy based on the information provided by the input-output matrix are numerous internationally, a first work encountered was that of Meller and Marfan (1981), who studied the relevance of the small and large industry in relation to the problem of job creation in a developing country. His work examines the forward and backward linkages and identifies key sectors for the generation of employment within the Chilean industrial sector. One of his most important findings is that the sectors associated with the manufacturing of large scale are those who have a greater positive effect on employment generation, particularly: large industry-food, beverages, textiles, wood, paper, leather, and basic metals; small industry-wood, machinery except electrical, and diverse manufacturing.

On the other hand, with information from the input-output matrix of the Andalusian economy for 1980, Cuadrado and Aurioles (1984), analyzed the intersectorial relationships with a simple and conventional methodology proposed by Chenery and Watanabe (1958), from which found that there are two separate structural imbalances in this economy, and prevailing high participation of the primary activities and a reduced share of industrial activities. The identified key sectors are agribusiness, certain branches linked to the export of natural resources and construction. His work also able to determine industrial sites that rely heavily on imported components that sell most of their production abroad.

Using the SNT and the input-product matrix of the Andalusian economy, García, Morillas and Ramos (2005) calculated the total, immediate and mediative effects, finding that the productive relations are not structured around branches of high technology that is an obstacle to the spread and development of it, their work is the first encountered in the implementation of this new approach and hence its reply to the Mexican case in this paper. These authors recognize that although manufacturing industries continue to be key in the development, increasingly charges a greater boost the role of the services associated with the knowledge economy. García, Morillas and Ramos (2008) updated its previous research with information from the Spanish economy for 71 industries and the European Union for the year 1995 with 25 branches. Unlike the previous work, now added an index of sectorial influence, so that their results suggest that Spain shows a similar performance to the European Union, with the construction sector pushing the economy and an essential industry for the whole activity. The manufacturing sector reveals the basic differences between the two territories. Spain still shows a traditional structure with an important presence of the metallurgic sector due to its history, while Europe has a better relative position in the high technological segment. On other hand, the tertiary sector presents a similar position in both economies.

In the case of the Chilean economy, Soza-Amigo (2011), identifies the products and activities that are key to the Chilean regions, forming clusters and structural similarity that exists between them. For this, used a combination of so-called Important Coefficients and Fields of Influence. Their study lets you know the productive structure of each of the regions of that country from which makes a number of recommendations for economic growth.

Hernandez (2012), using data from the Colombian economy for 2007, to which applies the method of chains and multipliers of the input-output matrix, which allows you to determine that there are strong links between sectors and sectors of petroleum, chemical, plastics, electricity and gas, transport and communications have a great influence on the demand and the supply of others. Finally, it concludes that the sectors of civil works, other services and chemicals and plastics are the greatest generators of employment in the economy.

Finally, regarding the international review, in a recent study of the Spanish economy, Cansino *et al* (2013) present the social accounting matrix corresponding to 2007 at basic prices. From this, key sectors of the economy are identified through three different methodologies: the methodology proposed by Rasmussen, hypothetical extraction method and finally the method of product matrix multiplier. The analysis of key sectors with the use of these methodologies leads to conclusions which, in some cases, are very different and contradictory.

For the Mexican case highlights the work of Fuentes and Sastré (2001) and Fuentes (2009) who performed the identification of key sectors for two subnational economies; while Sobarzo (2011), from an applied general equilibrium model reproduces an input-output model, which serves as a basis for estimating Leontief's multipliers, allowing you to perform some exercises of impact of economic policy in a context of crisis. Finally, Albornoz, Canto and Becerril (2012), carried out the estimation of the input-output matrix for a sub-national economy in southeastern Mexico from which identified key sectors and propose how to best allocate resources to those sectors with greater linkages and therefore a notorious multiplier effect resulting in increased growth. The review shows that the exercise proposed in this article fills a gap existing in the literature by applying a new methodology for the identification of key sectors of the Mexican economy.

3. Research Methodology

The information contained in the matrix of the input-output from 2003, published by the National Institute of Statistics and Geography (INEGI in spanish), was used in the estimation of key sectors of the Mexican economy in two versions: one made up of 20 sectors and the other disaggregated 79 subsectors of economic activity. The input-output matrix of Mexico that was used was constructed using the rules of the North America Industry Classification System (NAICS).

For the construction of the matrix is required to put in place a set of activities, as the concentrating, analyzing and processing of basic information from multiple sources: economic censuses, agricultural, population censuses, household income and expenditure surveys, administrative records and fundamentally national accounts.

The information that concentrates the input-output matrix has its origin in the balance of supply and aggregate demand, that consists of comparing product-by-product supply and use of goods and services available in the economy, both domestic production and imports of products and services. Figure 1 details the sources of information used by the INEGI for building national matrix.

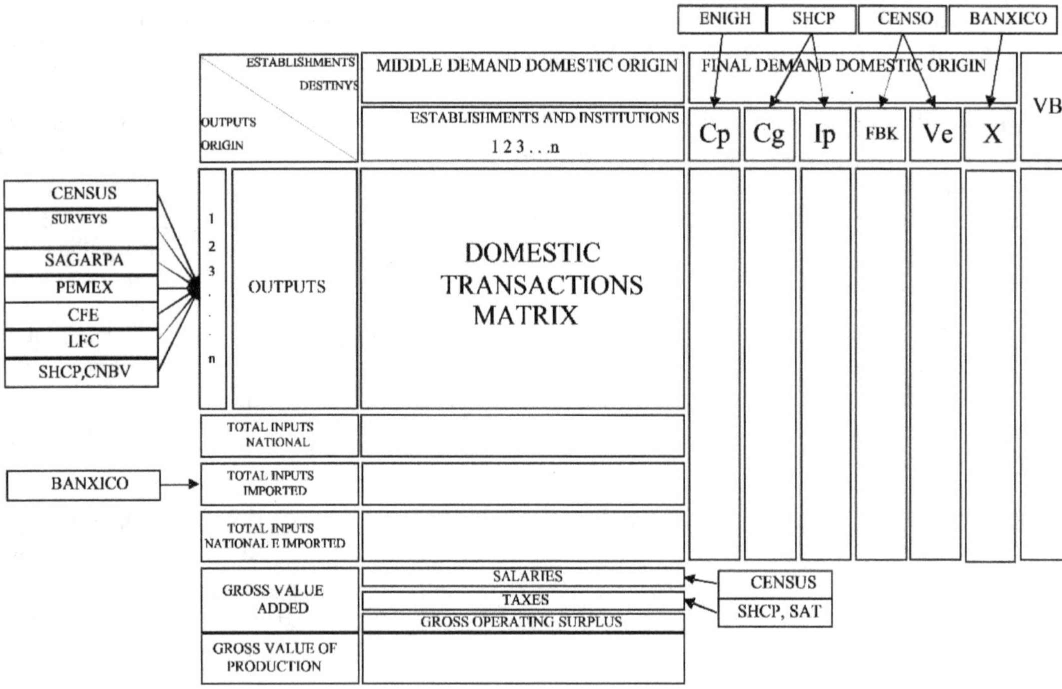

Cp: Private consumption
Ip: Public investment
Ve: Variation of stock
VBP: Gross value of production
Cg: Public consumption
FBK: Gross fixed capital formation
X: Exports

***Figure 1**. Sources of information to construct the input-output matrix in Mexico*
Source: Own elaboration

From the matrix, two procedures were used for estimation of key sectors, on the one hand chains of Rasmussen (R) method and the Social Networks Theory (SNT). Rasmussen (1956) posed a quantification of linkages from the inverse matrix of the input-output table. Thus, adding the columns of the inverse scattering power of a sector or the expansion of its effects on the production network is obtained. Adding rows of the same matrix gets the sensitivity of dispersion of a sector or the extent in which the sector is dragged by the expansion of the economic framework. Thus, suggests two measures based on Leontief inverse matrix to quantify the direct and indirect effects backward (BL^R) and forward (FL^R) that a may experience a sector. The normalized measurements are obtained from the following expressions:

$$BL^R = \frac{ni'(I-A)^{-1}}{i'(I-A)^{-1}i}$$

$$FL^R = \frac{n(I-A)^{-1}i}{i'(I-A)^{-1}i}$$

Thus we have (BL^R) which is known as scattering power and (FL^R) as sensitivity of dispersion. From this indicator, the activities are grouped into four types: 1) sectors with weak backward and forward linkages (independent); 2) sectors with high forward linkages and low backward linkages (driving sectors); 3) sectors with low forward linkages and high backward linkages (base sectors); and 4) sectors with strong forward and backward linkages (key sectors). Due to which these measures are sensitive to extreme values, instead of using the arithmetic means the coefficient of variation (standard deviation from the average in their classification) was used for each indicator. With respect to the limitations of this technique, see Fuentes and Sastré (2001).

***Table 1**. Rasmussen's (R) production chains*

	BL^R < Average	**BL^R > Average**
FL^R > Average	II. Driving sectors	IV. Key sectors
FL^R < Average	I. Independent sectors	III. Base or strategic sectors

Source: Own elaboration

The SNT has erupted into economic science as a new tool for structural analysis based on the work developed by Bavelas (1948), Granovetter (1973), Friedkin (1991), Rauch and Castella (2001), Garcia, Morillas and Ramos (2005 and 2008), among others. This approach focuses the analysis on the set of observed relationships between actors in a network or group –for example, the structure of supply and demand in an economy– and not on the individual characteristics of the same –e.g., volume of production of a sector final demand, value added, and so on–. Similarly, the SNT allows to evaluate what are the effects generated by the central actors on the whole of the network, the speed with which an actor is related to the others and its transmission capacity of such effects.

The above is collected within the generic concept called centrality, to analyze the structural properties and the location of agents in the network. The concept determines the position of an agent in the network, either by its importance, influence, relevance or prominence. Similarly, this notion of centrality led input-output model helps to determine the relevance of a sector in the economic framework.

Following the methodology of Friedkin (1991) and Garcia, Morillas and Ramos (2008), the following indicators of centrality were used: a) total effects, b) immediate effects and c) mediative effects. These measures allow identifying the position, impact and degree of articulation presenting each of the productive sectors through the determination of the total effects exerted a sector on the whole economy, the speed with which relate to other sectors and importance as a transmitter element within the network of exchanges.

The indicator of total effects of centrality, as its name implies measuring the total effects of a sector and their relative influence on the other sectors in the economic framework, in the context of the input-output analysis global cross-sectorial effects are essentially determined by the number and length of the existing roads between sectors through specified productive relationships, this effect is captured from the following expression:

$$V=(I-\alpha A)^{-1}(1-\alpha)=(I+\alpha A+\alpha^2 A^2+\alpha^3 A^3+...)(1-\alpha) \qquad 0<\alpha<1$$

In this case, V is an associated matrix from development of inversion matrix known as the method of expansion of powers, this technique captures the direct and indirect transactions, and may assert that the sector j influences globally relative to sector i, for $v_{ij}\neq 0$, being the v_{ij} the i,j-th coefficient of the matrix V; and at the same time the parameter (α) is a weighting which allows to quantify the capacity of influence between sectors. The matrix of full cross-sectorial effects (V) meets several conditions among which we can point to that it is a stochastic matrix by rows:

$$0\le v_{ij}\le 1$$

and

$$\Sigma_j^n v_{ij}=1$$

Of the foregoing, the more central is the position of a sector to interact with the rest –less number of steps through which two sectors are interrelated– the greater impact of their transactions; while equal distances between sectors caused effect depends on the intensity of the relationship in (αa_{ij}).

Assuming the existence of a network of influence regular; i.e., without sectorial extreme polarization and the hypothesis that the cross-sectorial influences weighting coefficient tends to the unit ($\alpha \to 1$) the matrix V could converge to a V_u matrix defined as:

$$V_u=\begin{bmatrix} c_1 & \dots & c_n \\ \dots & \dots & \dots \\ c_1 & \dots & c_n \end{bmatrix}$$

With the characteristic that the total cross-sectorial effects j are constant, i.e., $v_{ij}=c_i$, where $(0\leq c_i\leq 1)$ convergence of the matrix of total effects of centrality is guaranteed if and only if (for a formal demonstration see Friedkin and Johnsen, 1990):

$$V = \lim_{\alpha\to 1} -(I-\alpha A)^{-1}(I-\alpha) = A^{\infty} = V_u$$

Such that A^{∞} coincide with the matrix V_u which in turn reflects the steady state of the process $(c_1,\ldots,c_n)$. Hence the total effect of centrality of a particular sector j in the network are listed in column j of the matrix $V=V_u$, such that the total effect of centrality $(T_{TEC(j)})$ is defined as:

$$T_{TEC(j)} = \mathbf{V'\Phi}$$

Where T is a vector (nx1) order; $\Phi = \{1/n\}$ is a vector (nx1) order and V' is the transposed matrix V. The matrix expression is simply the average of the elements in the columns of the matrix V, in such a way that the higher this value, greater force shall in the sector totals on the overall economy.

The second measure of centrality of a sector refers to the speed of transmission of the sectorial total effects in the network, in other words, sectors whose effects are transmitted through long paths of economic relations have one smaller economic impact than those others with a high number of direct transactions. In this way, not only are seen smaller multiplier effects (Morillas, 1983), also there is a minor effect in the transmission of processes of innovation (García, Morillas and Ramos, 2008).

To formalize this measure requires two assumptions: first, the sequence of cross-cutting influence of sector j to a sector i in which the first sector appears only once, and second, take again the hypothesis that $(\alpha\to 1)$ in the context of a network of regular influence, once obtained such effects is defined influence relative of a sector j, as the average length of their economic transactions weighted sequences each of them by the force of established sectorial relations (Kemeny & Snell, 1960, p. 79, quoted in Friedkin, 1991, p. 1486).

$$M = (I - Z + EZ_{dg})D$$

Where D is a diagonal matrix with elements $d_{ii}= \{1/c_i\}$, c_i is an element of the matrix V_u; Z the fundamental matrix defined as $Z=(I-\alpha A + A^{\infty})^{-1}$; E is a unitary matrix of order (nxn); and Z_{dg} is Z setting to zero the elements outside the main diagonal.

How quickly a sector relates to which economically with others is expressed in the respective columns of the matrix M. The immediate effects $(T_{IEC(j)})$ indicator is calculated as the inverse of the average lengths of intersectorial relations (roads) a sector j-th.

$$T_{IEC(j)} = \left(\frac{\sum_{i=1}^{n} m_{ij}}{n}\right)^{-1}$$

In matrix is expressed as:

$$\mathbf{r} = \mathbf{n\varphi}$$

Where

$$\varphi=\{\varphi_j\}=\left\{1\Big/\sum_{i=1}^{n} m_{ij}\right\}$$

is a vector (nx1) order and m_{ij} is an element of M. From the above we have that, the greater the value of the index's immediate effects $(T_{IEC(j)})$, the greater the rapidity with which to propagate the total effects of the sector considered. It is important to note that the immediate effects of centrality or the speed of dissemination of the full effects are not considered by the traditional approach, so it is a contribution of the SNT to the structural analysis (García, Morrillas and Ramos, 2008).

The third measure of centrality indicates the degree of importance that a particular sector has as the overall effects transmitter; in other words, it indicates those sectors that provide the performance and economic interconnection. These economic sectors operate in the system as connectors and are relevant to the joint development of the economy.

The estimation of the mediative effects is obtained from the matrix M by decomposition in the number of steps from one sector j to another sector i, through several intermediate steps:

$$m_{ij} = \sum_{k=1}^{n} t_{(j)ik} \qquad i \neq j \neq k$$

Where $t_{(k)ik}$ is the i_k generic element of the matrix T, which is defined as:

$$T_{(j)} = (I - \tilde{A}_{(j)})^{-1}$$

So $\tilde{A}_{(j)}$ is the resulting matrix of eliminating the j-th row and column of the matrix A (Kemeny and Snell, 1960 cited in García, Morillas, and Ramos, 2008). The mediative effects ($T_{MEC(j)}$) indicates the relevance of a j-th block as a transmitter for connecting the economic framework.

$$T_{MEC(j)} = \left(\frac{\sum_{k=1}^{n} \bar{t}_{(k)j}}{n} \right) \qquad j \neq k$$

Where:

$$\bar{t}_{(k)j} = \left(\frac{\sum_{k=1}^{n} t_{(k)ij}}{(n-1)\iota_{(k)ij}} \right) \qquad i \neq j$$

The effects of intermediation, indicative of the importance of a particular sector as a transmitter or as a crossroads for the economic network connection can be expressed from the definition of the matrix

$$\bar{T} = \{\bar{t}_{(k)j}\}$$

$$\mathbf{c} = \bar{\mathbf{T}}\boldsymbol{\varphi}$$

Where

$\boldsymbol{\varphi}$ is a column vector (nx1) whose elements are (1/n).

It should be added that the indicator of mediative effects to quantify the importance of intersectoral linkages effects, have similar coefficients Streit (1969) interpretation. However, the mediatives effects not only collect direct relations between the different sectors but also the indirect. Therefore it is a global indicator of the intensity of the total transactions; additionally, this indicator can clarify questions relating to the speed of diffusion of the considered total effects measuring the average length of the sequences of economic exchanges. The program Excel (hypothetical matrix), Matlab (calculation of the inverse matrix) and Netminer (social network analysis) was used for the calculations.

4. Analysis and Results

In what follows are presented the results of the application of the methods exposed to the information contained in the input-output matrix to determine the key sectors of the Mexican economy. The exercise was conducted with 20 sectors and 79 subsectors. In order to compare the results of the approach of SNT with traditional methods (Rasmussen, 1956), in the first order the sectorial management is presented from the economic weight of the relations of causality or productive backward and forward linkages.

The reason for exposing these indices is due to the advantages with regard to measures made by Chenery and Watanabe (1958), since they incorporate in estimating the effects of global chain that occur between both the supply side and the demand side, also include the effect of sectorial dispersion and weightings in the sectorial chains according to their relative importance in the final demand (Hazari, 1970). The results are presented in Graph 1.

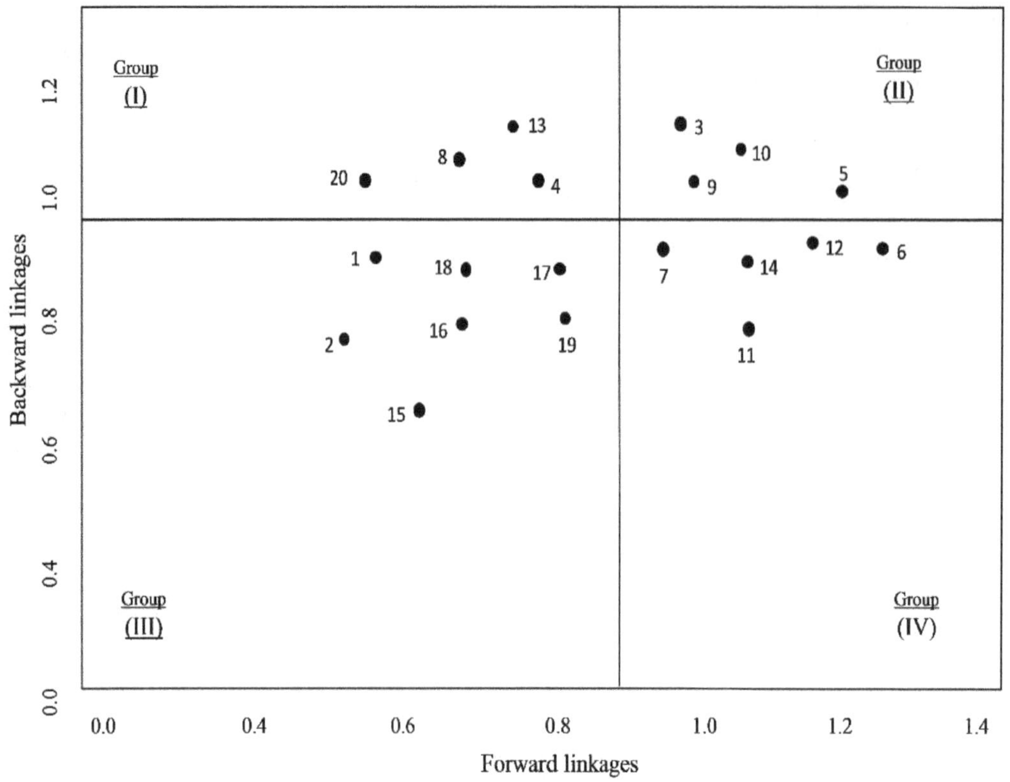

Graph 1. *Rasmussen's productive chains (R)*
* Every number correspond to one sector, see the Table 2
Source: Own elaboration with information from input-output matrix at 20 sectors

From the obtained classification, group sectors base or strategic –most demanded in an economy sectors, but which in turn are plaintiffs, which are important for the cross-sectorial sales– make up sectors of commerce (6), transportation (7), real estate and rental services (11), professional, scientific and technological services (12) and business support services (14).

The group of key sectors –characterized for being strong intersectorial applicants suppliers of intermediate inputs and products, which are forced to step sectorial flows in an economy consists of the activities of electricity, water and gas (3), manufacturing industries (5) information in mass media (9) and financial and insurance services (10).

The group of drive sectors –that have few linkages forward, but which are, in general, sectors that have wide possibilities of drag and induce economic growth– includes construction (4), postal office and storage (8), corporate management and business (13) and government activities (20).

Within the group of independent or little linked with other sectors and to produce without great requirements or by other sectors –basically demanding supplies primary– have the sectors of agriculture, forestry and fishing (1), mining (2), educational services (15), health and social care services (16), recreational services (17), and other services, except government activities (19).

The above sectorial classification relating to sectorial global linkages based on the criteria of Rasmussen (1956) shows that five of them are classified as base or strategic activities, seven activities are independent, four activities are classified as drivers, and finally only four activities make up the group called key sectors.

The previous analysis is illustrative of the structural characteristics of the economic activities in terms of their chains or links with other sectors of the economy, but at the same time is incomplete, because that takes economic activities separate and depending only of the economic weight of each sector.

In an effort to complement the analysis, presents the results obtained when you enter the capacity for intersectoral influence; in other words, when we focus on the existence and intensity of cross connections from a global point of view, perspective posed by network theory. In the first order, the sectorial management based on the ability to pick intersectorial influence through rates overall effects of centrality as network theory is presented (see Graph 2). The results were classified into four groups according to their centrality: I) semi-peripheral position, II) center position, III) peripheral position and IV) semi-central position.

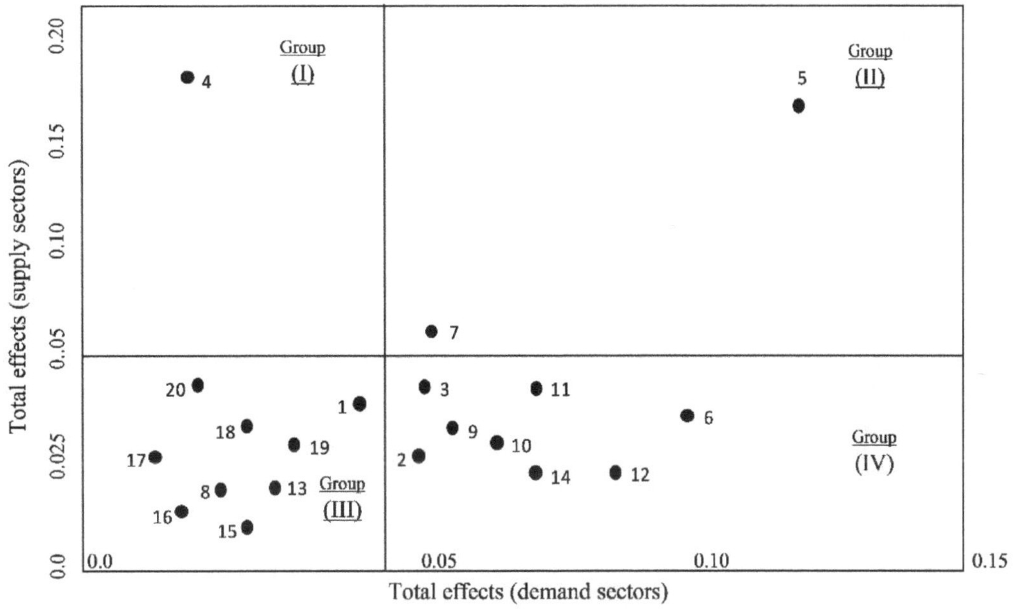

Graph 2. *Total effects of centrality ($T_{TEC(j)}$)*
* Every number correspond to one sector, see the Table 2
Source: Own elaboration with information from input-output matrix at 20 sectors

A first difference from traditional analysis approach relates to the classification of the 20 economic activities in Mexico; only two activities have a central location; nine of them have a peripheral location; eight form the classification of semi-central location; and, finally, just one sector presented semi-peripheral localization.

Introducing weighting relative to the capacity of cross-cutting influence on the coefficients input-output, clearly presents a disturbing element that allows you to pick up the sensitivity of the sectors to its structural location within the network, an aspect not considered in the classical approach.

As it can be seen from Graph 2 the group of core sectors –which have a position of centrality in the economic network and play a key role in the intermediation of intersectorial linkages in the rest of the production set– is composed only by manufacturing industries (5) and transportation (7).

The peripheral sectors – that have a less central position and therefore, under the possible effects on the set economic network– consist of agriculture, forestry and fishing (1), corporate management and business (13), business support services (14), educational services (15), health and social care assistance (16), recreational services (17), hotels, food and beverage (18), other services except the government (19) and activities of the government (20).

The group of semi-central sectors –which are in a better position within the structure to influence– exclusively includes construction (4). Within the group of semi-peripheral sectors –which are best placed within the structure to be influenced– stand mining (2), electricity, water and gas (3), commerce (6), information in mass media (9), financial and insurance services (10), real estate and rental services (11), professional, scientific and technological services (12) and business support services (14).

As it was expected, the grouping of sectors depending on the centrality substantially change considering the capacity of intersectorial influence, appear only in this case, the manufacturing industries (5) and transportation (7) as key sectors. Moreover, by having a position of important centrality in the economic network, construction (4), manufacturing industries (5), commerce (6) and transportation (7), can transmit the total effects on the whole of the economy relatively quickly, playing an important role in the intermediation of intersectorial linkages with the rest of the productive sectors.

Continuing with the analysis, management sector now comes from the intensity of interconnections between sectors measured from the immediate effects of centrality. The sector with the greatest immediate effects of centrality is manufacturing (5) located in group I and construction (4) in group II. Followed with a wide gap sectors located in group IV which include primary activities such as agriculture, forestry and fishing

(1), mining (2), electricity, water and gas (3) secondary activities or commerce (6) and tertiary activities such as information in mass media (9), financial and insurance services (10), professional, scientific and technological services (12), educational services (15) and government activities (20), among others. In this indicator, the highlights were manufacturing industries (5) and construction (4) sectors, productive activities with greater impact and effects send all the activities of the national economy (see Graph 3).

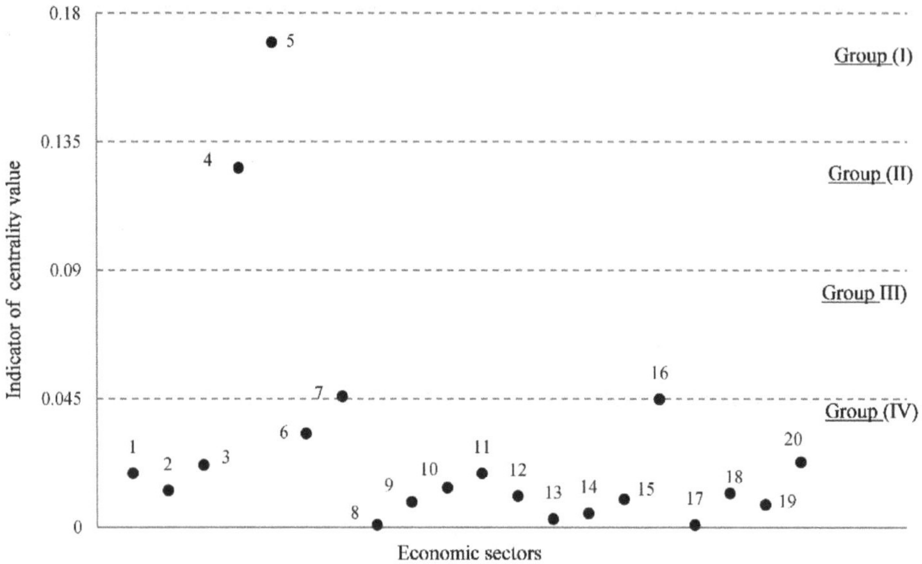

Graph 3. *Immediate effects of centrality ($T_{IEC(j)}$)*
* Every number correspond to one sector, see the Table 2
Source: Own elaboration with information from input-output matrix at 20 sectors

Mediative effects of centrality indicator results are presented in Graph 4. Like previous results, the analysis confirms the relevance of manufacturing industries (5) as the sector with the highest overall effect of interconnection. In the following order –above the average level– are construction (4), commerce (6), transportation (7) and government activities (20). The former sectors are characterized by their direct and indirect effects that can be transmitted to other activities are very significant.

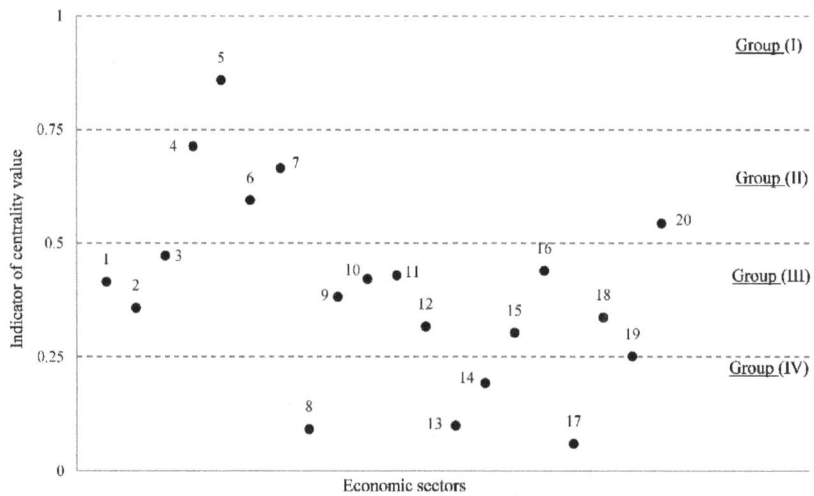

Graph 4. *Mediative effects of centrality ($T_{MEC(j)}$)*
* Every number correspond to one sector, see the Table 2
Source: Own elaboration with information from input-output matrix at 20 sectors

Among the sectors with lower transmission effects are post office and storage (8), corporate management and business (13), business support services (14) and recreational services (17). Similarly, highlights the low involvement of sectors related to human resources training, professional, scientific and technological services (12) and educational services (15).

In general terms, the structural analysis at this level of disaggregation indicates that there are strongly related sectors whose production dynamics is relevant within the economic structure. However, a better approach to structural analysis requires studying the national productive structure at a higher level of disaggregation, hence interest analysis to level for the 79 subsectors of activity.

As the first element of the input-output 79 subsectors of activity analysis, shows the sectorial management based on the productive chains according to the method proposed by Rassmusen (1956) (see Graph 5).

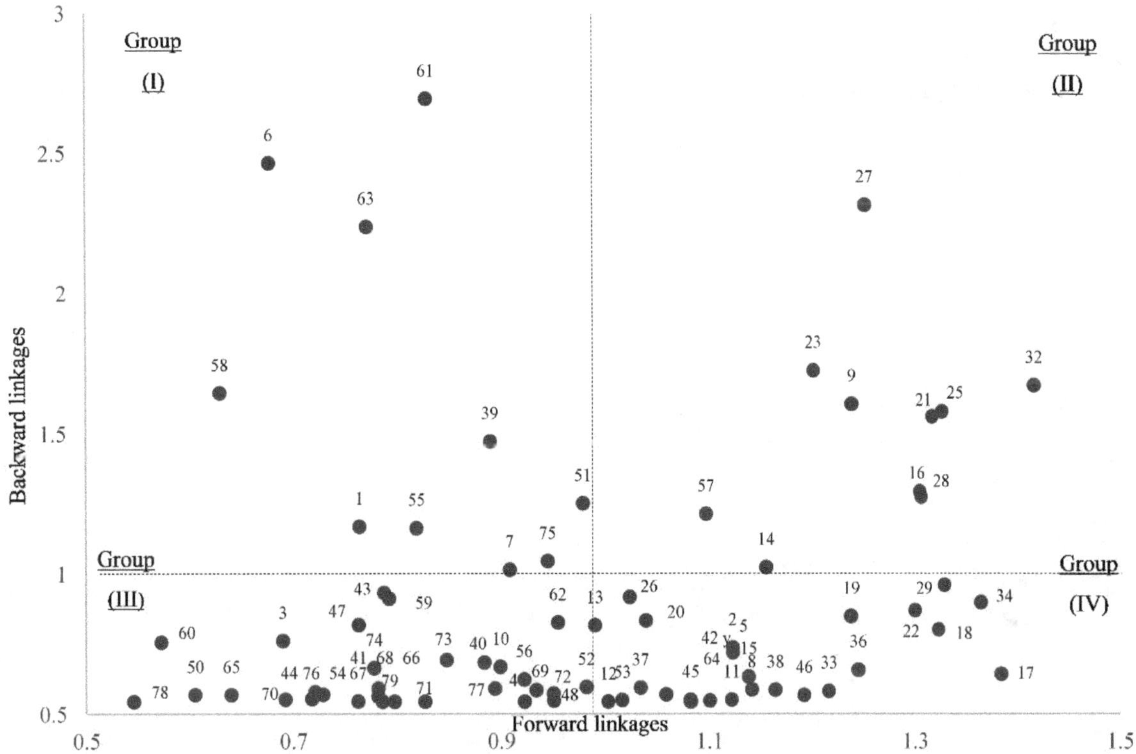

Graph 5. *Rasmussen's productive chains (R)*
* Every number correspond to one subsector, see the Table 3
Source: Own elaboration with information from input-output matrix at 79 subsectors

Based on this classification, the group of sub-sectors classified as strategic or base –which are the sectors most demanded in an economy, but which in turn are plaintiffs, which are important for the cross-sectorial sales– is made up of 27 sub-sectors (34%) where industry-related activities are observed: beverage and tobacco industry (15), manufacture of textile products, except apparel (17), manufacture of garments (18) wood industry (20), paper industry (21), plastics industry and rubber (25), manufacture of machinery and equipment (29), transport by rail (37), tourist transport (42), courier and parcel services (45), among others.

The group of key sectors –characterized for being strong intersectorial applicants suppliers of intermediate inputs and products, which are forced to step sectoral flows in an economy– is made up of 10 sub-sectors (13% of total). Again as expected, chiefly for industry related activities: generation, transmission and supply of electricity (9), food industry (14), manufacture of textile inputs (16), paper industry (21), petroleum and coal products manufacturing (23), plastic and rubber industry (25), basic metal industries (27), manufacture of metal products (28), manufacture of transport equipment (32), bonding, insurance and pensions (57).

The group of driving sectors –which have few linkages forward, but they are, in general, sectors that have significant potential to drag and economic growth-inducing– include 10 sub-sectors (13% of total) of the economy; in this group are primary activities: agriculture (1), oil and gas extraction (6), mining of metal ores, except oil and gas (7), and related human resource training high activities level as telecommunications (51), professional, scientific and technical services (61), business support services (63), repair and maintenance services (75).

Finally, within the group of independent sectors or loosely bound to the rest and produce no major requirements from other sectors are 32 subsectors (40% of total) of the economy, this block concentrated activities mainly related to the services sector: passengers, except railway transport (40), pipeline transportation (41), postal services (44), editing publications and software, except for internet (47), creation and dissemination of content via Internet (50), central banking (54), foreign exchange trading activities and financial investment (56), business support services (63), educational services (65), consultation external an related medical services (66), residences of welfare and health care (68), artistic, sports and other related services (70), museums, historical sites, botanical and similar gardens (71), personal services (76), among others .

In this way, analysis of productive linkages to 79 sub-sectors reveals in greater detail the workings of the economy as a whole, at this level of disaggregation is possible to determine in terms of their productive connections, what are the key activities, base or strategic, independent and driving. However, it is incomplete because it takes economic activities separate and depending only of the economic weight of each subsector.

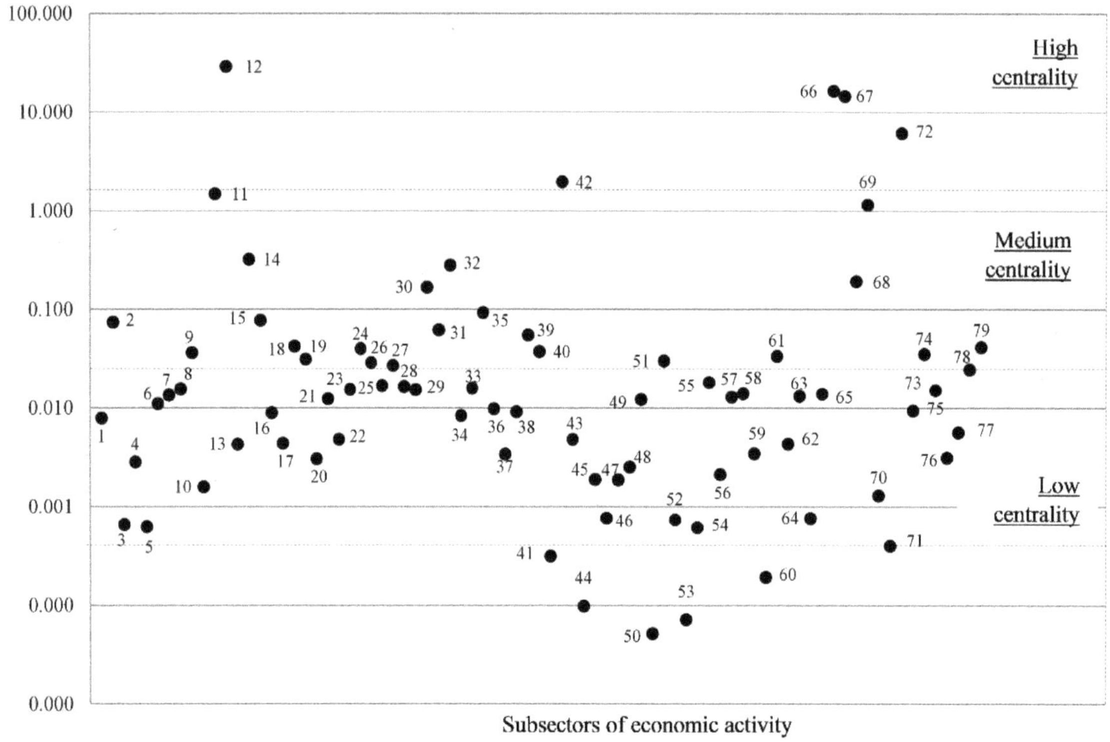

Graph 6. *Total effects of centrality ($T_{TEC(j)}$)*
* Every number correspond to one subsector, see the Table 3.
The centrality indicator values are presented on a logarithmic scale
Source: Own elaboration with information from input-output matrix at 79 subsectors

In order to perform a better representation of the structure and functioning of the economy, measures of centrality based on social network theory (SNT) were calculated. As the first element of the SNT total effects (see Graph 6) centrality indices are presented. After entering the relative ability of intersectorial influence on input-output coefficients, it is possible to observe the sensitivity of the subsectors of their structural location within the network, an aspect not considered in the traditional approach of input-output analysis.

As is clear from the analysis, the group of sectors "high centrality" – that have a position of centrality in the economic network and play a key role in the intermediation of intersectorial linkages in the rest of the production set– brings together seven subsectors (9% of total) which include: building (11), construction of civil engineering works or heavy work (12), food industry (14), tourist transport (42), hospitals (67), and other welfare services (69).

In the group of "medium centrality" activities or semi-central sub-sectors –who are in a better position within the structure– are 37 subsectors (47% of the total), some of these sectors are: livestock (2), generation, transmission and supply of electricity (9), beverages and tobacco industry (15), manufacture of transport equipment (32), government activities (79), among others.

Finally, in the activities of the "low centrality" or peripherals group – which have a less central position and therefore least potential effects on economically network– they are 37 subsectors (44% of the total) and are as follows: forest harvesting (3), services related to agricultural and forestry activities (5), transportation by pipelines (41), postal services (44), creation of and dissemination of content via the internet (50), central banking (54), rental of trademarks, patents and franchises (60), and others.

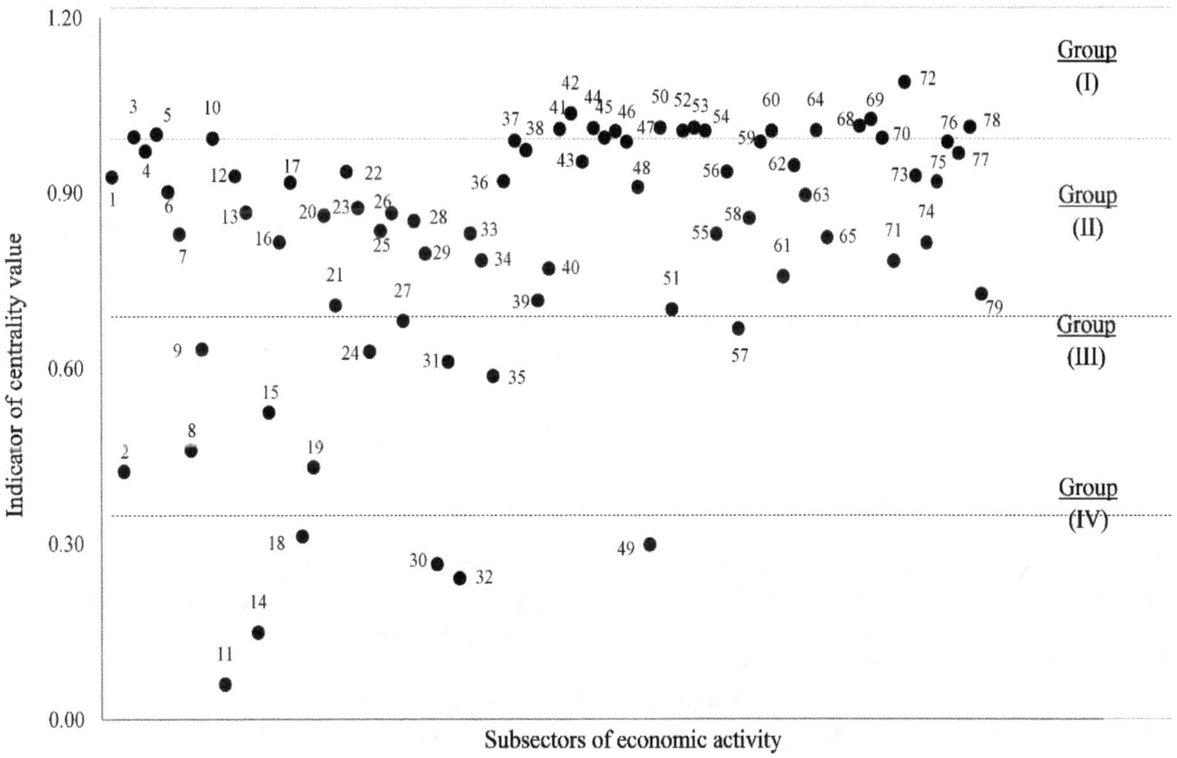

Graph 7. *Immediate effects of centrality ($T_{IEC(j)}$)*
* Every number correspond to one subsector, see the Table 3
Source: Own elaboration with information from input-output matrix at 79 subsectors

Continuing with the analysis, sector classification is presented in terms of the intensity of interconnections as the immediate effects of centrality (see Graph 7). Highest to lowest impact on the speed of transmission in the economic fabric shows that Group I agglomerates 25 subsectors (32% of total), the group II 29 subsectors (49% of total); Group III to nine subsectors (11% of total); and finally, the group IV to six subsectors (8% of total).

Among the sectors most direct interconnection are transport services in general: rail (37), water transport (38), pipeline transportation (41), tourist transport (42); postal services (44), courier and parcel services (45), storage services (46), providers of internet access, search services in the network and information processing (52), other information services (53); movable property rental services (59), rental of trademarks, patents and franchises (60); residences of welfare and health care (68), other welfare services (69). These subsectors are characterized by their high capacity to transmit direct effects on the total economic framework.

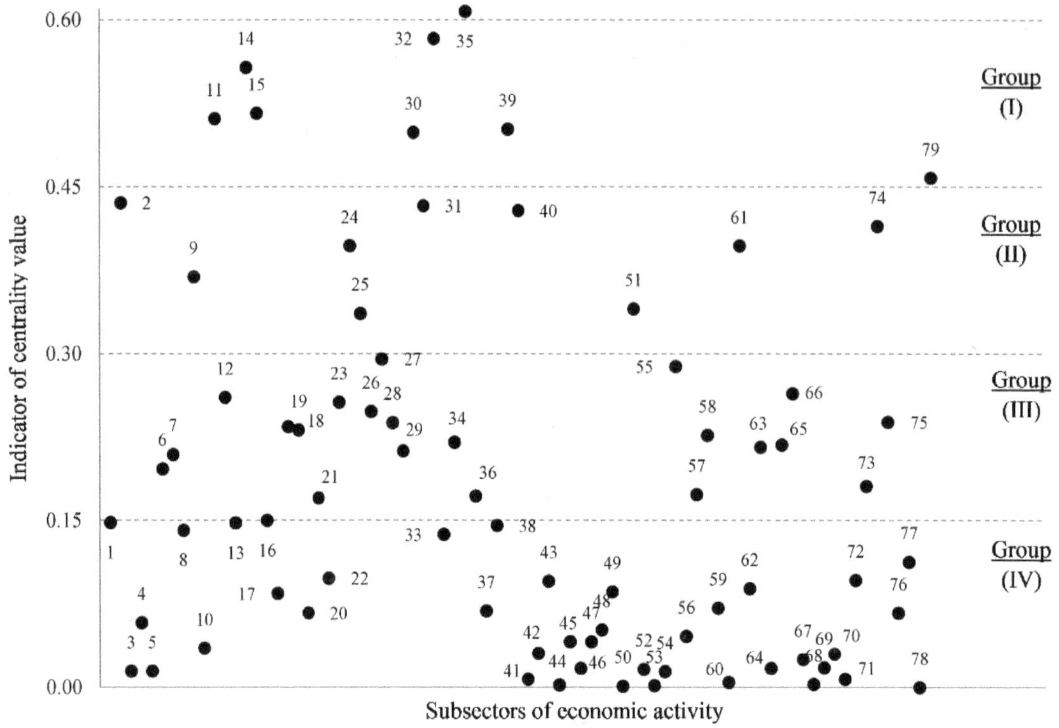

Graph 8. *Mediative effects of centrality* ($T_{MEC(j)}$)
* Every number correspond to one subsector, see the Table 3
Source: Own elaboration with information from input-output matrix at 79 subsectors

Finally, to identify the intensity of global interconnections are used to gauge mediative effects of centrality (see Graph 8). From this measure of centrality, the sub-sectors of importance for its transmitters or nodal effects for economic networking results in the following classification. The first group focuses eight subsectors (10% of total), the second group to nine subsectors (11% of total), and the third group of 21 subsectors (27% of total); finally, the fourth group 41 subsectors (52% of total). Among the sub-sectors with higher overall effects of interconnection with the rest of the economy are: building (11), food industry (14) beverages and tobacco industry (15), commerce (35), and government activities (79), among others.

An important result derived from this indicator is lower interconnection capacity of just over half of economic activities; mainly related subsectors primary industries: agriculture (1), forest harvesting (3), fishing, hunting and capture (4), services related to agricultural and forestry activities (5), mining-related services (8); service activities: tourist transport (42), transport-related services (43), postal services (44), courier and parcel services (45), radio and television, except vita the internet (49), and so on. The latter group also includes activities of the financial sector: central banking (54), no brokerage credit and financial institutions (55), foreign exchange trading activities and financial investment (56).

5. Discussion and Conclusion

Applying Rasmussen indexes at 20 sectors highlights the group of key sectors, manufacturing, electricity, water and gas supply pipelines to the final consumer, mass media information, and financial services and insurance. When the analysis is completed and arises from the point of view of the SNT, stand out, the total effects of centrality indices, those who have a central position, such as the manufacturing industry and transportation. In terms of the immediate effects of centrality, excels the manufacturing industry (again) and construction. The mediative effects of centrality emphasizes and confirms the importance of the manufacturing sector, followed by construction, commerce and transport.

The results of analysis of productive chains based on Rasmussen for the 79 sub-sectors, show that in the group of key subsectors, ten subsectors that comprise it, nine belong to the sector of manufacturing, which once again ranks as one of the most important in the economic network. By analyzing through the SNT, with indices of total effects of centrality, highlights the Group's "high centrality" subsectors, which are key in the intermediation of intersectorial linkages, they are seven, among which is the construction, the food industry and hospitals. The immediate effects of centrality show that the sub-sectors with higher direct interconnection have related to transport by rail, by water, services and tourism; storage and postal services. Finally, the mediative effects of centrality highlights eight subsectors, including construction, food industry, beverage industry and tobacco, commerce and government activities.

From the techniques used to identify key sectors of the Mexican economy was reached results that are consistent with other studies (Sánchez, 2011, 2013, 2013a; Palacios, 2013 and Olmedo, 2014), which underline the importance of manufacturing as the engine of economic growth. The evidence presented serves as an input for the establishment of an active industrial policy that will allow to overcome the current stage of economic stagnation. In the hands of a State that intervenes creatively in key sectors, supported axis of budgetary transparency and efficient management of resources, the economy of Mexico can become one of the most dynamic of the American continent, which would translate into job creation and greater well-being for its inhabitants.

To finish, indicate that as part of the research agenda is making new estimates with the array of input-output matrix of 2008 which was published in 2013, which will help to compare our present results and know if they continue to be consistent, especially towards the implementation of an active industrial policy as a strategy for promoting economic growth.

References

Albornoz, L., Canto, R. and Becerril, J. 2012. La estructura de las interrelaciones productivas de la economía del estado de Yucatán. Un enfoque de insumo-producto. *Región y Sociedad*, vol. 24, num. 54, pp. 135-174.

Bavelas, A. 1948. A mathematical model for group structures. *Applied Anthropology*, vol 7, num 3, pp. 16-30.

Cansino, J., Cardenete, M., Ordoñez, M. and Román, R. 2013. Análisis de sectores clave de la economía española a partir de la matriz de contabilidad social de España 2007. *Estudios de Economía Aplicada*, vol. 31, num. 2, pp. 621-654.

Chenery, H. and Watanabe, T. 1958. International comparisons of the structure of productions. *Econometrica*, vol. 26, num. 4, pp. 487-521.

Cuadrado, J. and Aurioles. J. 1984. Relaciones intersectoriales y sectores clave en la economía andaluza actual. *Estudios Regionales*, num. 14, pp. 61-101.

Friedkin, N. 1991. Theoretical foundations for centrality measures. *American Journal of Sociology*, vol. 96, num 6, pp. 1478-1504.

Friedkin, N. y Johnsen, E. 1990. Social influence and opinions. *Journal of Mathematical Sociology*, vol. 15, num 3-4, pp. 193-205.

Fuentes, N. and Sastré, M. 2001. Identificación empírica de sectores clave de la economía sudbajacaliforniana. *Frontera Norte*, vol. 13, num. 26, pp. 51-76.

Fuentes, N. 2009. Encadenamientos intersectoriales de la industria maquiladora de exportación en Baja California. *Región y Sociedad*, vol. 21, num. 44, pp. 171-194.

García, A., Morillas, A. and Ramos C. 2005. Relaciones interindustriales y difusión de la innovación: una aproximación desde la teoría de redes. *Estadística Española*, vol. 47, num. 160, pp. 475-499.

García, A., Morillas, A. and Ramos C. 2008. Key sectors: A new proposal from network theory. *Regional Studies*, vol. 42, num. 7, pp. 1013-1030.

Granovetter, M. 1973. The strength of weak ties. *American Journal of Sociology*, vol. 78, num. 6, pp. 1360-1380.

Hazari, B. 1970. Empirical identification of key sector in the Indian economy. *Review of Economics and Statistics*, vol. 52, num 3, pp. 301-305.

Hernández, G. 2012. Matrices de insumo-producto y análisis de multiplicadores: una aplicación para Colombia. *Revista de Economía Institucional*, vol. 14, num. 26, pp. 203-221.

Leontief, W. 1936. Quantitative input and output relations in the economic system of the United States. *The Review of Economic Statistics*, vol. 18, num. 3, pp. 105-125.

Meller, P. and Marfán, M. 1981. Small and large industry: employment generation, linkages, and key sectors. *Economic Development and Cultural Change*, vol. 29, num. 2, pp. 263-274.

Morillas, A. 1983. *La teoría de grafos en el análisis input-output. La estructura productiva Andaluza*. Malaga: Editorial Universidad de Malaga.

Olmedo, B. 2014. Desafíos de una política industrial y tecnológica en tiempos de reindustrialización mundial: reflexiones para México. In Girón, A. (coord.). *Democracia, financiarización y neoextraccionismo ante los desafíos de la industrialización y el mercado de trabajo*. México: Universidad Nacional Autónoma de México and Instituto de Investigaciones Económicas, pp. 167-182.

Palacios J. 2013. Más allá del discurso económico liberal: Por una política industrial para el siglo XXI en México. *Espiral, Estudios sobre Estado y Sociedad*, vol. 20, num. 56, pp. 69-105.

Rasmussen, P. 1956. *Studies in intersectoral relation*. Amsterdam: North Holland.

Rauch, J. and Castella, A. 2001. *Networks and markets*. New York: Russel Sage Foundation.

Sánchez, I. 2011. *Insuficiencia dinámica manufacturera y estancamiento económico en México, 1982-2010: Análisis y recomendaciones de política*. Ciudad Juárez: Editorial UACJ.

Sánchez, I. 2013. (Re) industrializar para superar la desaceleración en México. *Revista Equilibrio Económico*, vol. 9, num. 36, pp. 225-252.

Sánchez, I. 2013a. Política industrial activa como estrategia para el crecimiento de la economía mexicana. Estudios regionales en economía, población y desarrollo. Cuadernos de trabajo de la UACJ, vol. 3, num 15, pp. 1-40.

Sobarzo, H. 2011. Modelo de insumo-producto en formato de matriz de contabilidad social. Estimación de multiplicadores e impactos para México, 2003. *Economía Mexicana*, vol. 20, num. 2, pp. 237-280.

Soza-Amigo, S. 2011. Encadenamientos y similitudes estructurales para las regiones de Chile. *Revista de Análisis Económico*, vol. 26, num. 2, pp. 81-110.

Streit, M. 1969. Spatial associations and economic linkages between industries. *Journal of Regional Science*, vol. 9, num 2, pp. 177-188.

Appendices

Table 2. *Total effects ($T_{TEC(j)}$), immediate effects ($T_{IEC(j)}$),mediative effects ($T_{MEC(j)}$), 20 sectors*

Number	Sectors	Total effects		Immediate effects	Mediative effects
		TTEC(i)	TTEC(j)	TIEC(j)	TMEC(j)
1	Agriculture, forestry, and fishing	0.023	0.036	0.019	0.416
2	Mining	0.014	0.044	0.013	0.359
3	Electricity, water and gas	0.028	0.045	0.022	0.473
4	Construction	0.266	0.008	0.126	0.714
5	Manufacturing industries	0.247	0.245	0.170	0.859
6	Commerce	0.036	0.117	0.033	0.595
7	Transportation	0.051	0.054	0.046	0.666
8	Post office and storage	0.001	0.004	0.001	0.092
9	Information in mass media	0.011	0.062	0.009	0.383
10	Financial and insurance services	0.017	0.067	0.014	0.422
11	Real estate and rental services	0.019	0.084	0.019	0.430
12	Professional, scientific and technological services	0.011	0.104	0.011	0.318
13	Corporate management and business	0.003	0.017	0.003	0.100
14	Business support services	0.006	0.079	0.005	0.193
15	Educational services	0.010	0.001	0.010	0.304
16	Health and social care services	0.030	0.032	0.005	0.145
17	Recreational services	0.001	0.001	0.001	0.060
18	Hotels, food and beverage	0.012	0.0140	0.012	0.338
19	Other services	0.008	0.0232	0.008	0.252
20	Government activities	0.025	0.0027	0.023	0.544

Source: Own elaboration with information from input-output matrix at 20 sectors.

Table 3. Total effects ($T_{TEC(j)}$), immediate effects ($T_{IEC(j)}$),mediative effects ($T_{MEC(j)}$), 79 subsectors

No.	Subsectors of economic activity	Total effects		Immediate effects	Mediative effects
		TTEC(i)	TTEC(j)	TIEC(j)	TMEC(j)
1	Agriculture	0.000	0.026	0.928	0.148
2	Livestock	0.001	0.039	0.424	0.436
3	Forest harvesting	0.000	0.052	0.996	0.014
4	Fishing, hunting, and capture	0.000	0.064	0.972	0.058
5	Services related to agricultural and forestry activities	0.000	0.077	1.001	0.014
6	Oil and gas extraction	0.000	0.090	0.902	0.197
7	Mining of metal ores, except oil and gas	0.000	0.103	0.830	0.210
8	Mining-related services	0.000	0.116	0.460	0.141
9	Generation, transmission and supply of electricity	0.000	0.129	0.633	0.369
10	Water and supply of gas by pipeline to the final consumer	0.000	0.141	0.994	0.035
11	Building	0.019	0.154	0.060	0.511
12	Construction of civil engineering works or heavy work	0.373	0.155	0.929	0.261
13	Specialized construction works	0.000	0.180	0.867	0.148
14	Food industry	0.004	0.193	0.149	0.557
15	Beverages and tobacco industry	0.001	0.205	0.525	0.516
16	Manufacture of textile inputs	0.000	0.218	0.816	0.150
17	Manufacture of textile products, except apparel	0.000	0.231	0.919	0.085
18	Manufacture of garments	0.001	0.244	0.313	0.234
19	Manufacture of products of leather, leather except apparel	0.000	0.257	0.431	0.231
20	Wood industry	0.000	0.270	0.862	0.067
21	Paper industry	0.000	0.282	0.708	0.171
22	Printing and allied industries	0.000	0.295	0.937	0.098
23	Petroleum and coal products manufacturing	0.000	0.308	0.875	0.256
24	Chemical industry	0.001	0.321	0.629	0.397
25	Plastic and rubber industry	0.000	0.334	0.836	0.336
26	Manufacture of non-metallic mineral products	0.000	0.346	0.866	0.248
27	Basic metal industries	0.000	0.359	0.681	0.295
28	Manufacture of metal products	0.000	0.372	0.853	0.238
29	Manufacture of machinery and equipment	0.000	0.385	0.797	0.213
30	Manufacturing equipment of computing, common, measurement and other equipment, components and electronic accessories	0.002	0.398	0.266	0.499
31	Manufacture of equipment of power generation, equipment and electrical accessories	0.001	0.411	0.612	0.433
32	Manufacture of transport equipment	0.004	0.423	0.241	0.583
33	Manufacture of furniture and related products	0.000	0.436	0.831	0.137
34	Other manufacturing industries	0.000	0.449	0.785	0.220
35	Commerce	0.001	0.462	0.587	0.608
36	Air transport	0.000	0.475	0.920	0.172
37	Transport by rail	0.000	0.487	0.990	0.069
38	Water transport	0.000	0.500	0.974	0.145
39	Freight trucking	0.001	0.513	0.716	0.502
40	Passengers, except railway transport	0.000	0.526	0.771	0.429
41	Pipeline	0.000	0.539	1.010	0.007
42	Tourist transport	0.025	0.539	1.037	0.031
43	Transport-related services	0.000	0.564	0.954	0.095
44	Postal services	0.000	0.577	1.012	0.002
45	Courier and parcel services	0.000	0.590	0.995	0.041
46	Storage services	0.000	0.603	1.007	0.017
47	Editing publications and software, except for Internet	0.000	0.616	0.988	0.041
48	Industry film and video, and sound industry	0.000	0.629	0.910	0.052
49	Radio and television, except via the Internet	0.000	0.641	0.299	0.086
50	Creation and dissemination of content via the Internet	0.000	0.654	1.012	0.001
51	Telecommunications	0.000	0.667	0.701	0.340
52	Providers of Internet access, search services in the network and information processing	0.000	0.680	1.007	0.016
53	Other information services	0.000	0.693	1.012	0.002
54	Central banking	0.000	0.705	1.007	0.014

No.	Subsectors of economic activity	Total effects		Immediate effects	Mediative effects
		TTEC(i)	TTEC(j)	TIEC(j)	TMEC(j)
55	No brokerage credit and financial institutions	0.000	0.718	0.830	0.289
56	Foreign exchange trading activities and financial investment	0.000	0.731	0.936	0.046
57	Bonding, insurance and pensions	0.000	0.744	0.668	0.174
58	Real estate services	0.000	0.757	0.857	0.227
59	Movable property rental services	0.000	0.770	0.988	0.071
60	Rental of trademarks, patents and franchises	0.000	0.782	1.007	0.005
61	Professional, scientific and technical services	0.000	0.795	0.758	0.397
62	Corporate management and business	0.000	0.808	0.947	0.089
63	Business support services	0.000	0.821	0.897	0.216
64	Management of wastes and remediation services	0.000	0.834	1.007	0.017
65	Educational services	0.000	0.846	0.824	0.218
66	Consultation external and related medical services	0.212	0.846	1.257	0.264
67	Hospitals	0.187	0.859	1.210	0.025
68	Residences of welfare and health care	0.002	0.872	1.015	0.003
69	Other welfare services	0.015	0.885	1.027	0.018
70	Artistic, sports and other related services	0.000	0.911	0.995	0.030
71	Museums, historical sites, botanical and similar gardens	0.000	0.923	0.784	0.007
72	Entertainment recreational institutions and other services	0.078	0.923	1.090	0.096
73	Temporary accommodation services	0.000	0.949	0.929	0.181
74	Food and beverage preparation services	0.000	0.962	0.816	0.415
75	Repair and maintenance services	0.000	0.975	0.920	0.239
76	Personal services	0.000	0.987	0.988	0.067
77	Associations and organizations	0.000	1.000	0.969	0.113
78	Households with household employees	0.000	1.000	1.013	0.000
79	Government activities	0.001	1.026	0.727	0.458

Own elaboration with information from input-output matrix at 79 subsectors.

5

A New Perspective of Investment Modelling at the European Union Level

Alin OPREANA*

Lucian Blaga University of Sibiu

The study that represents the subject of this paper follows the analysis of the investment function and the influencing factors at the European Union level. The research has, as a starting point, the hypothesis that there is a negative relationship between the European Union investments and tax rates. For verifying this hypothesis, the structural equation modeling is used (SEM), and the same technique is applied in the second part of the research, which will track the development of the investments' model at the European Union level. The results will highlight the relationships that are established between specific variables that characterize the volume of investments.

Keywords: *investment, interest rate, taxes, gross domestic product, European Union*

1. Introduction

This work is a continuation of previous research regarding the modeling the investment function in in relation to specific factors. Previous research had as their starting point the elimination of the limitation according to which the investment function is a function dependent on interest rate and I introduced in the analysis the aspect related to fiscal pressure. Following these previous studies, I obtained the following results:

- a new model for determining long-term investments, but also an identification of the measures that would lead to increased investments (Opreana, 2010, pp.227-237, and Opreana, 2013, pp.4-12);
- obtaining a model in terms of investment analysis that will also allow us to identify a set of tools and measures to boost investments that can be used by countries with economies that are experiencing difficult periods in the current economic context (Opreana, 2014).

Maintaining the same direction research, in this current study which represents the object of this continued work on investment analysis and identifying the relationships that are established between investments and specific factors at the level of EU.

2. Literature Review

The analysis of investment represents the research objective of many researchers who approach, on the one hand, investments at a macroeconomic level and their relationships with consumption, and on the other hand,

* Corresponding Author:
Alin Opreana, Lucian Blaga University of Sibiu, Faculty of Economic Sciences, Romania

investments on financial markets. Therefore, the analysis presented in this article falls into the following research framework.

In a post-Keynesian/Kaleckian model of growth and distribution, Commendatore, Pinto, Sushko (2014: 12-28) suggested a constraint on firms' investment induced by increasing adjustment costs and/or limited financial resources.

Eslamloueyan & Jafari (2014: 209-220) used the correlated effects mean group (CCEMG) technique to a set of balanced panel error correction model and they studied the repercussions of the 1997's Asian financial crisis and of 2008's global financial crisis on the savings and investing behavior in East Asian countries. Eslamloueyan & Jafari (2014: 209-220) found that the rates of both savings and investments are highly dependent across countries of East Asia.

García-Belenguer & Santos (2013: 150-169) explored a simple version of the neoclassical growth model and studied empirically the main determinants of aggregate investment across countries. In their work, the neoclassical growth model predicts that aggregate investment may be influenced by income growth, capital income share, relative price of capital, taxes, and other market distortions (García-Belenguer & Santos, 2013: 150-169).

Using a fully general specification for the instantaneous utility function, Furlanetto & Seneca (2014: 111-126) presented that the size of the wealth effect on labor supply is largely inconsequential for macroeconomic dynamics.

Casalin & Dia (2014: 60-79) developed a simple theoretical model of investment by assuming that financial frictions generate certain adjustment costs that are different from those of industrial origin which are usually discussed in the literature.

Lim (2014: 160-177) analyzed 129 developed and developing economies in terms of their institutional and structural factors related to their investment activity. The author introduced these institutional and structural factors to a standard neoclassical investment function for open economies and found that financial development and institutional quality tend to be determinants of cross-country capital formation. Nonetheless, institutional quality seemed to show o higher level of stability in its sign and significance of its coefficient.

Rieger (2012: 239-240) developed and proved a formula for the computation of optimal financial investments in an expected utility framework with arbitrary (not necessarily concave) utility functions.

In their paper, Pirvu & Zhang (2014:142:150) approached the problem of consumption and investment in a financial market within a continuous time stochastic economy. Their results show that a change in the discount rate leads to time inconsistencies of the investor's decisions.

In another paper about optimal investment, Zeng, Wu, Lai (2013: 462-470) explored the multi-period optimal strategies for an investment-only problem and an investment–consumption problem.

Moreover, Di Corato, Moretto, Vergalli (2014: 80-89) introduced an analytical approximation of the short-run investment rule and presented how such an approximation can be used in order to derive the corresponding i) steady-state distribution of the optimal stock of capital and ii) the long-run average rate of capital accumulation.

Zhao, Shen and Wei (2014: 824-835) considered the consumption–investment problem with a general discount function and a logarithmic utility function in a non-Markovian framework. Their model's coefficients follow the assumption of adapted stochastic processes, including the coefficients of the interest rate, appreciation rate, and volatility of the stock. The work of Zhao, Shen and Wei (2014: 824-835) demonstrate that a time-consistent equilibrium consumption–investment strategy of the original problem consists of a deterministic function and the ratio of the market price of risk to the volatility. Nonetheless, the corresponding equilibrium value function can be described by the unique solution of a family of BSDEs parameterized by a time variable.

3. Research Methodology

To achieve the purpose of the research, the structural equation model (SEM) technique will be used to verify the hypotheses of the proposed model.

A structural equation model is a set of assumptions about how the variables in an analysis are generated and related to each other (Hu and Bentler, 1999).

This methodology will be applied by using the SPSS AMOS software on empirical data to achieve the main objective of the research and examine the hypotheses. Thus, for hypotheses testing, I used quarterly macroeconomic data, from Eurostat, related European Union, during the 2001Q1-2014Q4 timeframe.

For the empirical analysis of the investment function I will use independent variables such as interest rate and the level of fiscal pressure expressed by tax volume or tax rate.

4. Analysis and Results

4.1. Verification of the model in terms of the existence of a relationship between investment (EU28_I) and tax rate (EU28_T/Y) at the European Union level

Current research is a continuation of previous research (Opreana, 2014), in which it was observed that at EU level, there is a negative relationship is established between investments (EU28_I) and tax rate (EU28_T/Y). The main objective of this step is to verify the relationship between investment and tax rate. The hypotheses of this model are the following:

H1: There is a relationship between investment (EU28_I) and tax rate (EU28_T/Y)

Structural equation modeling was used to test the hypotheses proposed for the model examined in this paper. The structural model was tested in accordance with the criteria established by Hu and Bentler (1999).

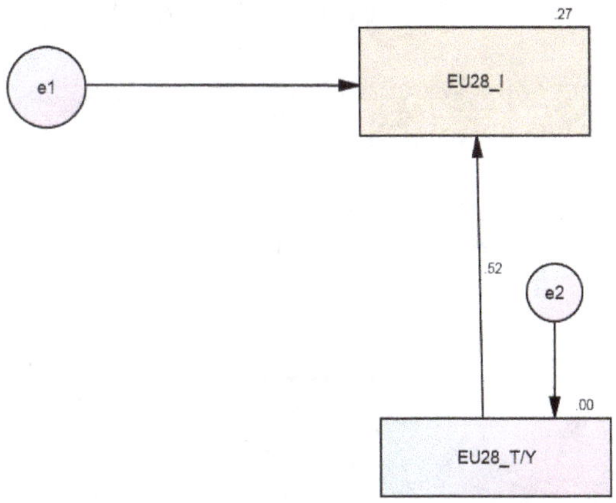

Figure 1. *Standardized results of the model*

Note: EU28_I = Investment at European Union level, EU28_T/Y = tax rate at European Union level

After applying the criteria set by Hu and Bentler (1999), the proposed model did not concur to the validation criteria in this form and needs a improvement by including more relationships between endogenous and exogenous variables.

Regarding the analysis of the hypotheses considered were obtained the following results presented in the following tables:

Table 1.1. *Regression Weights*

	Estimate	S.E.	C.R.	P
EU28_I <--- EU28_TY	16542514.109	3644604.846	4.539	***

Table 1.2. *Standardized Regression Weights*

	Estimate
EU28_I <--- EU28_TY	.522

Table 1.3. *Intercepts*

	Estimate	S.E.	C.R.	P	Label
EU28_TY	0.104	0.000	371.286	***	par_3
EU28_I	-1072116.344	377769.672	-2.838	.005	par_2

Table 1.4. *Variances*

	Estimate	S.E.	C.R.	P	Label
e2	.000	.000	5.244	***	par_4
el	3130322122.303	596929007.181	5.244	***	par_5

Table 1.5. Standardized Direct Effects

	EU28_TY
EU28_I	.522

Table 1.6. Standardized Indirect Effects

	EU28_TY
EU28_I	.000

From the obtained results, it can be observed that there is a relationship between tax rate and investment at an EU level, but the model is not statistically valid. Thus, there is a need for developing a new conceptual model.

Also, table 1.1. shows that Hypothesis 1 is confirmed, and there is a relationship between these 2 variables.

From table 1.3 it can be observed that the result of the residual value is statistically invalid. Therefore, this shows the need for a new working model, which includes other related relationships.

4.2. Proposing a new model regarding investments at the European Union level

Next, in this upcoming paper and research, the investments' function will be achieved, and also factors determining the investments will be identified. Following the re-estimation model, it results in a new form of the model according to the type of European Economy and the influence of other factors.

The hypotheses considered in terms of obtaining this model are:

H_2: Taxes affect investments in the European Union

H_3: GDP influences the amount of taxes in the European Union

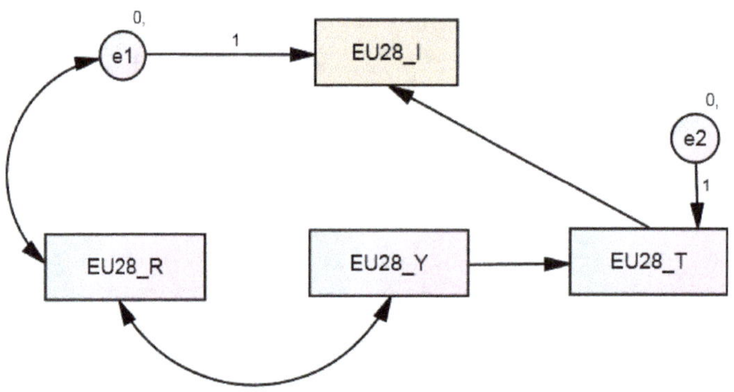

Figure 2. *The New Investment Model*

Note: EU28_R = Interest Rate at the EU level, EU28_Y = EU Gross Domestic Product, EU28_T = Taxes at the EU level, EU28_I = Investment at the EU level

Again, structural equation modeling was used to test the hypotheses proposed for the model examined in this section. The structural model was tested in accordance with the criteria established by Hu and Bentler (1999) and developed in Table 2.

Table 2.1. *Model accuracy*

Measurement	*Measurement model result*	*Recommended values*
χ^2	8.373 (p=0.015, 2df)	$p \leq 0.05$
χ^2/df	4.187	≤ 5
NFI	0.975	≥ 0.90
RFI	0.925	≥ 0.90
CFI	0.981	≥ 0.90
RMSEA	0.241	≤ 0.10

Note: χ^2 =Chi-square, χ^2/df = ratio of Chi-square and degrees of freedom, GFI = Goodness of fit index, NFI = Normed fit index, RFI = Relative fit index, CFI = Comparative fit index, RMSEA = Root mean square error of approximation.

To analyze the new investment model using the structural equation modeling technique, I analyzed the path coefficients of the hypothetical relationships between variables.

The following tables reflect information regarding the unstandardized and standardized coefficients estimates, statistical significance, and standard error of each relationship.

Table 2.2. *Regression Weights*

	Estimate	S.E.	C.R.	P	Label
EU28_T <--- EU28_Y	.111	.003	44.340	***	par_2
EU28_I <--- EU28_T	1.553	.144	10.769	***	par_1

Table 2.3. *Standardized Regression Weights*

	Estimate
EU28_T <--- EU28_Y	.986
EU28_I <--- EU28_T	.820

Table 2.4. *Intercepts*

	Estimate	S.E.	C.R.	P
EU28_T	-23299.594	7683.829	-3.032	.002
EU28_I	152005.080	45816.036	3.318	***

Table 2.5. *Covariances*

	Estimate	S.E.	C.R.	P
e1 <--> EU28_R	16079.333	3695.867	4.351	***
EU28_R <--> EU28_Y	-142194.580	36248.761	-3.923	***

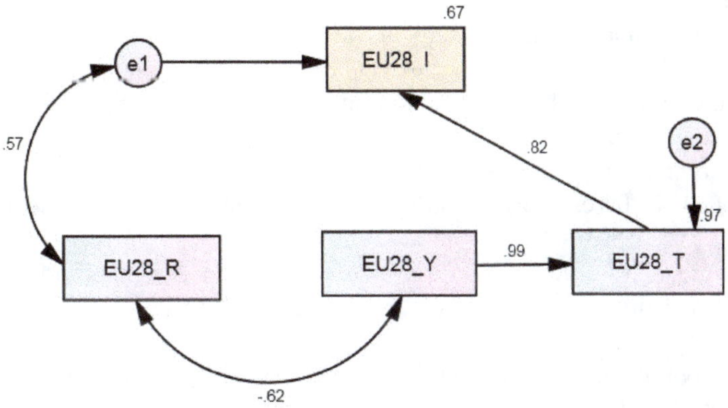

Figure 3. *Standardized results of the new investment model*

Table 3. *Estimates of hypotheses testing*

Hypotheses	*Significance*	*Hypothesis Result*
H_2. EU28_T→EU28_I	***	Confirmed
H_3. EU28_Y →EU28_T	***	Confirmed

***** *Significant at a 0.001 level (Two-tailed)*
*** *Significant at a 0.005 level (Two-tailed)*
** Significant at a 0.010 level (Two-tailed)*

5. Conclusions

Following this present research, a new model regarding the investment function was identified. The results obtained confirm the three proposed hypotheses, namely:

H1: There is a relationship between investment and tax rates.
H2: Taxes affect investment in the European Union
H3: GDP influences the amount of taxes in the European Union

Regarding the limits of this research it should be mentioned that the RMSEA value in Table 2.1. shows that the new model of investments needs a development and it is necessary to identify specific variables that influence the behavior of variables at the level of the European Union's economies.

However, the results from this research will enable us to achieve and identify a new set of specific measures for each country, which will lead to boosted investments in the current economic context.

6. References

Casalin, F. & Dia, E. (2014). Adjustment costs, financial frictions and aggregate investment. *Journal of Economics and Business* 75: 60-79.

Commendatore, P., Pinto, A., Sushko, I. (2014). A post-Keynesian model of growth and distribution with a constraint on investment. *Structural Change and Economic Dynamics* 28: 12-24.

Di Corato, L., Moretto, M. & Vergalli, S. (2014). Long-run investment under uncertain demand. *Economic Modelling* 41: 80-89.

Eslamloueyan, K. & Jafari, M. (2014). Financial crisis and saving–investment dynamics in the presence of cross-sectional dependence: The case of East Asia. *China Economic Review* 30: 209-220.

Furlanetto, F. & Seneca, M. (2014). Investment shocks and consumption. *European Economic Review* 66: 111-126.

García-Belenguer, F. & Santos, M.S. (2013). Investment rates and the aggregate production function. *European Economic Review* 63: 150-169.

Hu, L., Bentler, P. (1999), Cutoff criteria for fit indexes in covariance structure analysis: Conventional criteria versus new alternatives. *Structural Equation Modeling: A Multidisciplinary Journal*, 6(1): 1-55

Keynes, J. M. (1936). *The General Theory of Employment, Interest, and Money.* London: MacMillan

Lim, J.J. (2014). Institutional and structural determinants of investment worldwide. *Journal of Macroeconomics* 41:160-177.

Opreana, A. (2010). The Long-Run Determinants Of Investment: A Dynamic Approach For The Future Economic Policies. *Studies in Business and Economics* 5(3): 227–237.

Opreana, A. (2013). A New Approach of Investment for the Future Economic Policies. *Expert Journal of Economics* 1(1): 4-12

Opreana, A. (2014). Modelling Investment Function in Relationship to Specific Factors from European Economies. Paper presented at *Joint International Conference of Doctoral and Post-Doctoral Researchers, Craiova, 12-13 September 2014*

Pirvu, T.A. & Zhang, H. (2014). Investment–consumption with regime-switching discount rates. *Mathematical Social Sciences* 71: 142-150.

Quantitative Micro Software, (2007). *EViews 6 User's Guide.* Irvine CA: Quantitative Micro Software, LLC

Rieger, M.O. (2012). Optimal financial investments for non-concave utility functions. *Economic Letters* 114: 239-240.

Vinerean, S. (2013). Applying Online Behavioral Models in Internet Retailing. LAP Lambert Academic Publishing, Saarbrucken, Germany

Zeng, Y., Wu, H. & Lai, Y. (2013). Optimal investment and consumption strategies with state-dependent utility functions and uncertain time-horizon. *Economic Modelling* 33: 462-470.

Zhao, Q., Shen, Y., Wei, J. (2014). Consumption–investment strategies with non-exponential discounting and logarithmic utility. *European Journal of Operational Research* 238: 824-835.

Acknowledgement

This work was supported by the strategic grant POSDRU/159/1.5/S/133255, Project ID 133255 (2014), co-financed by the European Social Fund within the Sectorial Operational Program Human Resources Development 2007-2013.

6

Accessibility to Nodes of Interest: Demographic Weighting the Logistic Model

Gioacchino DE CANDIA*

Studio de Candia, Italy

This research fits into the genre of spatial analysis, aimed at better understanding of population dynamics in relation to the presence and distribution of infrastructure and related services. Specifically, the analysis uses a model of the gravitational type, based on the assumption of the impedance (attractiveness) territorial, based on a curve of type logistics to determine the accessibility of the same, to which to add a system of weights. In this sense, the model was weighted according to the population, to determine the level of "population served" in terms of infrastructure and related services included in the model.

Keywords: *accessibility, regional development, impedance curves, territorial statistics, infrastructures, logistic form, weighted indices.*

1. Introduction

Over the past few decades, from the end of the 50s of XX century, the attention to a greater knowledge of the territories, the relative accessibility, attractiveness and consequent control of the same has affected more and more governmental authorities of the countries.

It has gone from a simple "personalist conception" of the territorial governance to approaches more and more technical - scientific, based on the possibility of obtaining information as capillaries in the area, as well as the application of real equations can explain the distribution of resources in the same territory, in order to better government.

A pioneer in this kind of approaches was Hansen (1959), who first applied a mathematical model called "gravity" to the territory.

The excellent results obtained by this author have prompted other researchers, subsequently, to continue on the path taken, as well as to test new approaches (Andy and Niemeier, 1997).

That is how the measures defined as "cumulative opportunities" and "the utilitarian choice", due to the collaboration of multiple authors.

However, the approach of "gravity", to date, has provided the highest and best contribution to the knowledge of the territory, also because it is the most objective among those produced so far.

The writer has had occasion to apply the gravity model, suitably elaborated, three Italian regions: Tuscany, Trentino - Alto - Adige and Friuli - Venezia – Giulia (de Candia and Chiocchini, 2014).

---

* Corresponding Author:
Gioacchino de Candia, Studio de Candia, via Salgari, 6 – 70038 Terlizzi (BA), Italy

For Tuscany was produced a real benchmarking, whereas three distinct functions of impedance (exponential, logistic and linear) summarizing the results both by arithmetic average, either by MPI (Mazziotta and Pareto, 2007).

For Trentino - Alto - Adige and Friuli - Venezia - Giulia was produced map accessibility and consequent attractiveness at the municipal level, whereas function of impedance is the logistic curve and synthesis by arithmetic mean, which has been shown to be the best approach to territorial representation.

This paper aims to provide a further contribution to the field, building a system of weights based on the resident population, in order to pinpoint what is the degree of distribution of the services offered to the population, in terms of infrastructure in the area.

2. Materials and Methods

The research focuses on the areas of Tuscany, which are analyzed for the presence of the following infrastructure: hospitals with emergency room, upper secondary grade schools, railway stations and airports.

Following the approach of gravity, we arrive at the following synthetic formulation:

$$A_i = \sum_{j \in D} W_j^{\beta} \; f(c_{i,j}, \alpha)$$

Where A_i is the accessibility of a resident of the area i with respect to the node j in the region D, W_j^{β} is a measure of the activities or services (mass of opportunity) located in zone j, β is a calibration parameter (used to account for the effects agglomeration) and $f(c_{i,j})$ is a function of impedance generally decreasing with the cost (or with the distance or travel time).

Using the impedance in the form of logistics, we arrive at the following equation:

$$f(c_{i,j}) = \left(\frac{1}{1 + \exp - k(c_{i,j} - c_0)}\right)$$

with

$$c_0 = \frac{1}{2}(c_{min} + c_{max})$$

where

c_{min} is the minimum cost

c_{max} the maximum cost observed and

$k = 2\ln(\frac{1}{\gamma} - 1)/(c_{max} - c_{min})$

$\gamma > 0$

To get good results, γ must be greater than zero, but not too big. Following previous approaches, which have proved more encouraging that, there is γ equal to 0.05.

The summary of the results is achieved by weighted arithmetic mean, using the resident population as calculated from the XV Census of the Italian population and housing.

Were produced two different approaches, one called "weighted average", the other "index weighted average" according to the following formulations:

$$\mu_i = \Sigma_{ij}(x_{ij}/p_i) * 100 \qquad \mu = \Sigma_{ij}\, \mu_i/n \qquad \text{(Weighted average)}$$

$$\mu_i = \Sigma_{ij}(x_{ij} p_i)/p_i \qquad \mu = \Sigma_{ij}\, \mu_i/n \qquad \text{(Index weighted average)}$$

where

x_{ij} is the impedance function developed for the common i and for infrastructure j,

p_i is the population of the municipality,

μ_i is the weighted arithmetic mean for each municipality i.

3. GIS Analysis to Calculate Impedance Distances

The impedance distance (travel time) were calculated through the GIS software ArcGIS Network Analyst module. For the calculation is used the road graph Multinet of Tom Tom where the data on road conditions are updated at the end of 2013. The starting points used as source data are the centroids of the municipalities of Tuscany (ISTAT 2012) and centroid of the sub-municipal areas (ISTAT 2010) only for the city of Florence. The destination points used are all the considered infrastructures (hospitals, railway stations, secondary schools and airports). The infrastructure used are derived from georeferencing public administrative archives and these are integrated with the Point of Interest that are included in the graph road datasets. The facilities used, are:

- Railway stations (platinum, gold e silver) year 2012 RFI (Railway Italian Infrastructures) source;
- Airport year 2010 ENAC (Italian Civil Aviation Authority) source;
- Public and private hospital with first aid year 2007 Health and Care Ministry source;
- Secondary school year 2011 Ministry of Education source.

The output OD cost matrix, that is the result of GIS processes, consists of all drivetime and kilometric distances from origins to destinations. The calculations are performed in ideal conditions and in the absence of traffic and using a traveling speed that is set on the road graph. The traveling speed used, is referred to the highway code speed and to road signs contained in the updated road graph. The tool used is ArcGIS "find closest facilities" contained in the Network Analyst package; this tool allows you to calculate all the driving distance starting from closest to farthest.

4. Results and Discussion

The Tuscan territory is divided administratively into ten provinces: Arezzo, Florence, Grosseto, Livorno, Lucca, Massa - Carrara, Pisa, Pistoia, Prato, and Siena. There are in total 287 municipalities and 3,672,202 inhabitants, according to the latest Census of Population and Housing (ISTAT, 2011).

In developing the model, as explained above, we proceeded to isolate the metropolitan area of Florence, for which data on districts were available.

Also, have been eliminated island communities (as "isolated" by definition) resulting in a matrix of impedance functions for the remaining 276 municipalities.

The results of the weighted models are summarized in the pie charts below:

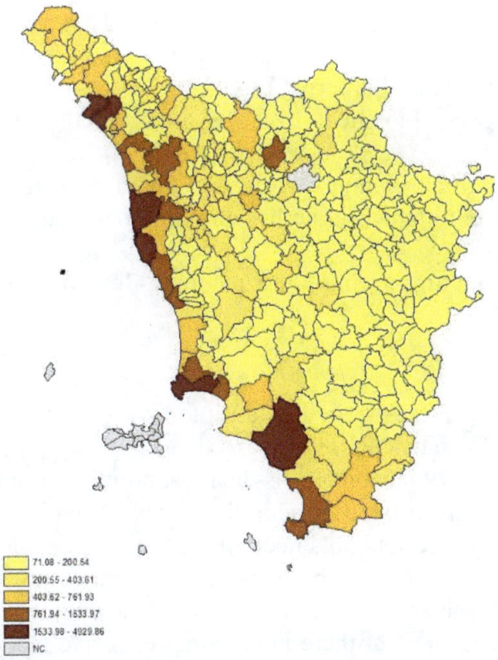

***Figure 1.** Synthesis of the model by index weighted average*

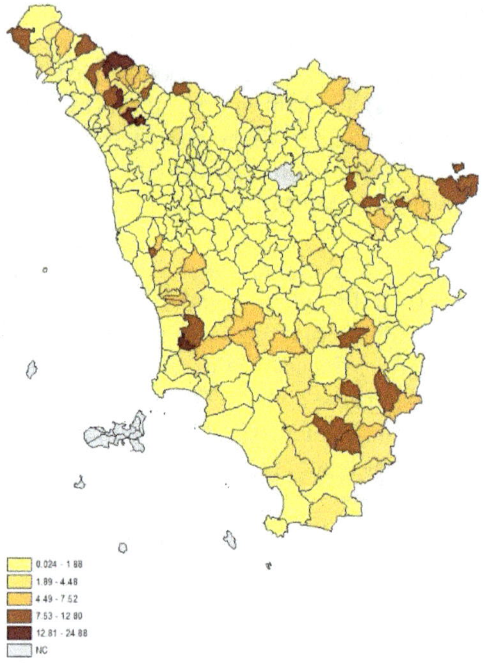

Figure 2. *Synthesis of the model by average weighted*

The pie charts show the results are quite dissimilar between the two models. In particular, the weighting obtained with "weighted average index" shows a situation "in leopard spots", where the municipalities are served less than riparian, with the area between Florence - Pisa - Livorno, which records accessibility of medium - low, depending on the population served by infrastructure.

Conversely, municipalities pertaining to the part of the Apennine region are those that are best served.

This weighting system shows its limits, as the common Apennines are among the least accessible (and therefore attractive) in terms of infrastructure in the area. The work already published by the authors (de Candia and Chiocchini, 2014), therefore, lead to reject this weighting system.

With regard to the synthesis achieved by "weighted average", the results presented in Figure 2 show a more homogeneous. In general, the Tuscan towns showed a good accessibility on the population served. The common "least served" are those of the Apennines bordering Umbria and partly those bordering Lazio. A similar situation for ordinary Apennines bordering Liguria.

In addition, the area between Florence - Pisa - Livorno with the best infrastructure, the best is the one with the population served.

In fact, the system "weighted average" works like this: low accessibility and low population pays a low rate for the population served; high accessibility and high population corresponds to a high rate for the population served.

In between, common from time to time show medium - low to medium - high rates for the population served.

4.1. Florence

The metropolitan area of Florence is divided into five districts: Centro storico, Campo di Marte, Gavinana - Galluzzo, Isolotto - Legnaia e Rifredi.

With a population of 358,079 inhabitants, is the most populous region.

For the city of Florence was made to develop the model of synthesis only according to the "weighted average" (not very useful given the results obtained with the synthetic "index weighted average" using only hospitals equipped with first aid (distributed by area) in analyzed as other infrastructure (airports, railway stations) are present in only "exemplary" (respectively "Leonardo da Vinci" and "Santa Maria Novella"). As for the upper secondary school level, data there is no comprehensive mapping and ultimately for the same constituency.

***Table 1**. Summary by "weighted average" for districts*

Districts	Population 2011	Weighted average
Isolotto - Legnaia	66,430	0.00063
Centro Storico	62,516	0.00068
Rifredi	102,834	0.00042
Gavinana - Galluzzo	39,663	0.00109
Campo di Marte	86,636	0.00052

Table 1 summarizes the data on population for districts of the city of Florence (ISTAT, 2011) and summarizes the impedance function in the form of logistics according to the "weighted average".

The results show a great addition plexus hospital for each district, as well as a strong homogeneity between the districts themselves.

If you want to try the classic "nit-picking" the district Galluzzo - Certosa shows the index lower, further proof that good accessibility but low population corresponds to a lower index of population served. It is, however, of infinitesimal.

5. Conclusions

Research has further helped to define and improve the map of the accessibility in relation to the territorial breakdown at local authority in which the authors have been discussing extensively in the past.

The addition of a weighting system that takes into account the "population served" not only contributes to the improvement of the primitive model, but adds a new connotation and new information available to policy makers and governance of the territory.

In addition, the report also has carried a real benchmarking between the approach called "index weighted average" and the approach "weighted average", preferring the latter.

Further progress in the application of such a model of accessibility weighted territory can be applied and extented in other regions (as in the authors'), but also in new infrastructures, economic data and environmental data, according to the availability of data and the degree of capillarity of information of local authority.

6. Acknowledgements

Thanks to Raffaella Chiocchini for processing the figures.

References

Ballin, M, Falorsi, P.D. and Russo, A., 2000. Condizioni di Coerenza e Metodi di Stima per le Indagini Campionarie sulle Imprese, *Rivista di Statistica Ufficiale*, n. 2, pp. 31-52.

Barnett, G.A, 2010, A measure of centrality for dense networks with valued ties, *Connections*, n. 30, pp. 11-20.

Dong, X., Ben-Akiva, M.E., Bowman, J.L. and Walker, J., 2006, Moving from Trip-Based to Activity-Based Measures of Accessibility, *Transportation Research Part A: Policy and Practice*, Volume 40, Issue 2, pp. 163-180.

Black, W.R., 1992. Network Autocorrelation in Transport Network and Flow Systems, Geographical Analysis, *Ohio State University Press*, Vol. 24, No. 3, pp. 207-222.

de Candia, G. and Chiocchini, R., 2014. Accessibility to nodes of interest: a practical application of the various forms of the impedance curves of two border regions, *Journal of the Geographical Institute "Jovan Cvijić" SASA,* 64(2), pp. 215-232.

de Candia, G. and Chiocchini, R., 2014. Accessibility to nodes of interest: a practical application of the various forms of the impedance curves, *Romanian Review of Regional Studies*, Volume X, Number 1, pp. 47-56.

Delvecchio, F., 1995. *Scale di misura e indicatori sociali*, Bari:Cacucci editore.

Deville, J.C., 1999. Simultaneous Calibration of Several Surveys. Proceedings of statistic Canada Symposium 99. *Combining Data from Different Sources*, Ottawa: Statistics Canada, May 1999, pp. 207-212.

Dronen, N. and Lv, Q., 2011. Return probability and k-step measures, [online] Available at: http://arxiv.org/pdf/1105.4479.pdf [Accessed on May 13, 2015]

Handy, S.L. and Niemeier, D.A., 1997. Measuring accessibility: an exploration of issues and alternatives, *Environment and Planning A*, volume 29, number 7, pp. 1175-1194.

Hansen, W.G., 1959. How accessibility shapes land-use, Journal of the American Institute of Planners, n. 25, pp. 73-76.

ISTAT, 2011. *Censimento generale della popolazione e delle abitazioni,* XV. [online] Available at: http://www.istat.it/it/censimento-popolazione/censimento-popolazione-2011 [Accessed on May 13, 2015]

Mazziotta, M. and Pareto, A., 2007. Un indicatore sintetico di dotazione infrastrutturale: il metodo delle penalità per coefficiente di variazione, in: Lo sviluppo regionale nell'Unione Europea – Obiettivi, strategie, politiche. *Atti della XXVIII Conferenza Italiana di Scienze Regionali*, AISRe, Bolzano.

Neal, Z.P., 2013. Does world city network research need eigenvectors?, *Urban Studies*, n. 50, pp. 1648-1659.

Piccolo, D., 2000. *Statistica*, Bologna: Il Mulino.

Weir, M., Rongerude, J. and Ansell, C.K., 2009. Collaboration is not enough: virtuous cycles of reform in transportation policy, *Urban Affairs Review*, n. 44, pp. 455-489.

7

Inequality Fragility Hypothesis

Sebastian-Ilie DRAGOE*

Lucian Blaga University of Sibiu, Romania

The last four decades have been marked by growing inequality. The inequality of income and wealth is one of the most important macroeconomic issues of our time. Inequality contributed to Global Savings Glut and Global Financial Crisis through riskiness channel and a greater propensity to borrow for poor people. This paper presents evidence that besides structural factors, monetary policy, high leverage and the development of new money substitutes are critical in explaining the inequality trend in advanced countries. Increasing economic inequality acts as financial instability enhancer and if left untreated it poses a significant threat to economic sustainability.

Keywords: *inequality, wage share, wealth distribution, debt, financial instability*

1. Introduction

Although Piketty's Capital in the 21st Century in which he stated that capitalism is prone to inequality, became a commercial success, inequality is still a poor treated subject in literature and a challenge for policymakers. Several books, papers and articles have pointed out the relevance of income and wealth distribution in macroeconomics. Stiglitz (2013) provides a variety of issues caused by inequality. The price of inequality is slower GDP growth, a weakened democracy and a diminished sense of fairness. Rajan (2010) explains how inequality entailed political pressure to ease consumption through credit growth. Kumhof and Ranciere (2010) investigate how changes in income distribution can lead to high leverage and crises. Confronted with declining or stagnant incomes, workers will limit their drop in consumption with credit expansion. Large debt-to-income ratios generate financial fragility. They also find a mechanism to explain global current account imbalances by considering the counterpart of a capital account surplus to be an increase in current account deficit. Berg and Ostry (2011) explore the relationship between income inequality and sustained economic growth. Their research concludes that inequality is the most important factor associated with longer growth spells.

The paper differs from most studies on this topic in that it analyzes inequality from a monetary perspective and its main purpose is to raise awareness regarding distributional effects of monetary policy. This paper claims that rising inequality wasn't just the consequence of structural factors, it also had a monetary cause.

The rest of this paper is structured as follows: In section II I present the role of inequality in disequilibrium economics and a holistic approach of distributional effects, in the third section I present the

* Corresponding Author:
Sebastian-Ilie Dragoe, Lucian Blaga University of Sibiu, Faculty of Economics, Romania

main reasons why distribution is an important for economic stability and the resemblance between the Keynesian and a self proposed Kaleckian multiplier. In Section IV I investigate the the link between inflation, wages and unemployment. The following section focuses on recommendations and an analysis of distributional consequences of monetary policy.

The data which was used for Granger causality test to show the substitution between human capital and financialisation was retrieved from Philippon (2014) Supporting Data. For detecting fat tails in loan impulse and testing that an increase in credit precedes an asset price boom I used Federal Board Reserve database and updated Stock market data from Shiller's book "Irrational Exuberance".

2. Inequality and Disequilibrium

In this paper I propose a new theory called "Inequality Fragility Hypothesis" as a new framework for crises involving four attributes:

1) As wealth inequality is higher, the gap between aggregate supply and demand is growing.
There are two types of transactions: GDP and non-GDP, money doesn't only serve as a mean of exchange, but is also used for wealth accumulation, resulting in an unproductive circuit (non-GDP transactions). Speculations lead to growing inequalities, which means more wealth and more opportunities to speculation for the wealthy. Even in an exchange economy, Say's Law cannot be valid, in case of high unequal wealth distribution, demand would collapse. Say's law is not restored on long-term because is possible to accumulate wealth in excess of the limits of practicable consumption. "Business men habitually aspire to accumulate wealth in excess of the limits of practicable consumption, and the wealth so accumulated is not intended to be converted by a final transaction of purchase into consumable goods or sensations of consumption" (Veblen, 1909). This event is evident because not only the number of billionaires has multiplied since 1987 (see figure 1), but also in 2014 the richest 80 people had amassed as much wealth as the bottom half of the world's population, down from 388 in 2010 (Oxfam, January 2015).

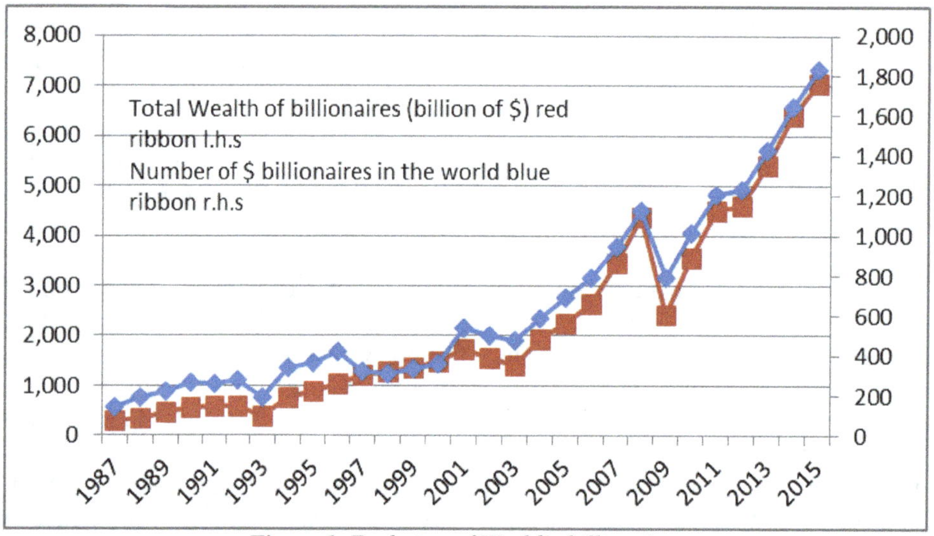

Figure 1. *Evolution of World's billionaires*
Source: http://piketty.pse.ens.fr/en/capital21c2 and Forbes

When inequality grows the wealth-income ratio increases and so the top decile/percentile is flooded with excess capital over time. Less and less of all that money will be allocated to productive investment, instead it will be devoted to speculations or lent to speculative and Ponzi units, thus keeping the system away from equilibrium. In U.S. speculations contributed to wealth concentration, which in turn gave rich people more resources to make unproductive gains.

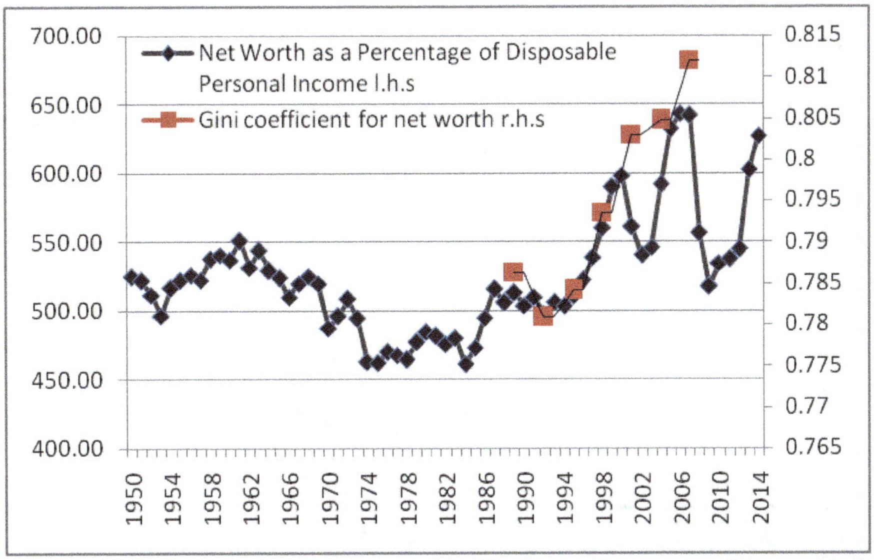

Figure 2. *U.S. Households and Nonprofit Organizations Net Worth as a Percentage of Disposable Personal Income and Gini Coefficient for net worth*

Sources: Net Worth as a Percentage of Disposable Personal Income from Board of Governors of the Federal Reserve System, Z.1 Financial Accounts of the United States, Series ID HNONWPDPI, Not Seasonally Adjusted, Frequency Annual, Aggregation Method Average, Units Percent, Gini Coefficient for net worth: Kennickell (2009)

This spiral has continued until crises took place (see figure 2). So money is employed in real production (GDP) and in capital gains (do not count in GDP). Fisher's equation of exchange proved to be false.

$M * V = P * Q$

M – money supply, V – velocity of money, P – prices, Q – quantity.

Aggregate supply is equal to aggregate demand, if money is used only for consumption purposes (money is used just for exchange, not for wealth accumulation).

Other disturbances, in dynamic equilibrium this time, appear to arise from changes in aggregate demand which produce disruptions in income (future expenditure plans count for determining aggregate demand). "If income is to grow, financial markets, where the various plans to invest and save are reconciled must generate an aggregate demand that, aside from brief intervals, is ever rising. For real aggregate demand to be increasing, given that commodity and factor prices do not fall readily in the absence of substantial excess supply, it is necessary that current spending plans be greater than current received income and that some market technique exist by which aggregate spending in excess of aggregate anticipated income can be financed. It follows that over a period during which economic growth takes place, at least some sectors finance a part of their spending by emitting debt or selling assets. For such planned deficits to succeed in raising income… it is necessary for some of the spending to be financed either by portfolio changes which draw money from idle balances into active circulation (that is, by an increase in velocity) or by creation of new money" (Minsky, p. 6, 1982). Equation (1) is the equation of growth if we ignore the leakages from and injections into the circular flow of income and idle balances (Palley, 2014).

Ex-post definition AD = Y + Net Bank Credit Creation ex-ante definition

where, AD - aggregate demand (goods and services), Y – nominal income, Net Bank Credit Creation – change in bank credit stock or new bank credit creation minus repayment of debt as only credit from commercial banks creates purchasing power, while in case of bonds, existing purchasing power is transferred between parties.

Therefore, temporarily, income is not equal to aggregate demand with a single exception (point X). X is the point where the change in credit creation is 0 and $Y = Y_{(-n)}$, before that point the flow of credit is negative implying $Y < Y_{(-n)}$, beyond point X, $Y > Y_{(-n)}$. Volatility in credit expansion takes place with a design to fuel speculative booms that aggravate wealth and income distribution, subject treated in section 6.

But, disequilibrium is at its best observed at the microeconomic level, where there can be overproduction or overconsumption.

Production – Consumption = Change in Stocks (2)

$Supply_{t1}(Production_{t1} + Stocks_{t0}) – Demand_{t1}(\text{or } Consumption_{t1}) = Stocks_{t1}$ (3)

From equation (3) supply seems to be always greater than demand, however there may be also shortages (crops, oil, energy) meaning that demand is greater than its supply. This supply-demand gap can be covered with fiscal deficits for a short time because on long-term it can lead to indebtedness. The other approach consists in inequality reduction. Relative income hypothesis developed by James Duesenberry states that the propensity to consume of an individual is a decreasing function of his percentile position in the income distribution. As a result, decreasing income inequality can stimulate demand and will avoid misalignments in production structure, as the poor can't afford the same lifestyle after a credit crunch.

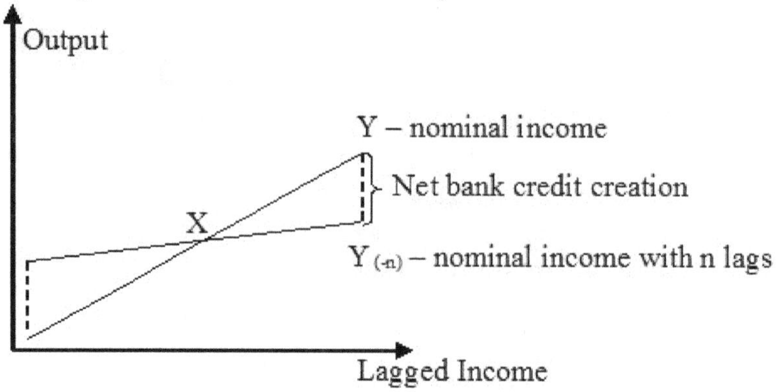

Figure 3. *Aggregate demand and credit*

From equation (3) supply seems to be always greater than demand, however there may be also shortages (crops, oil, energy) meaning that demand is greater than its supply. This supply-demand gap can be covered with fiscal deficits for a short time because on long-term it can lead to indebtedness. The other approach consists in inequality reduction. Relative income hypothesis developed by James Duesenberry states that the propensity to consume of an individual is a decreasing function of his percentile position in the income distribution. As a result, decreasing income inequality can stimulate demand and will avoid misalignments in production structure, as the poor can't afford the same lifestyle after a credit crunch.

2) Income and wealth inequality amplify financial instability.

Inside deregulated markets, low income households borrow in order to adhere to the same living standards with wealthy individuals. Marginal tax rate cuts on high incomes, a relatively stagnant minimum wage and development of monopsonies have contributed to higher inequality. Public policies have enhanced rent extraction and rent opportunities, especially at the expense of others (Stiglitz, 2013). The most gifted in doing so are the top 0.01% if we take a look at a Taleb's analysis:

"The one percent of the one percent of the population is vastly more sensitive to inequality than total GDP growth (which explains why the superrich are doing well now, and should do better under globalization, and why it is a segment that doesn't correlate well with the economy). For the super-rich, one point of GINI causes an increase equivalent to 6-10% increase in total income (say, GDP). More generally, the partial expectation in the tail is vastly more sensitive to changes in scale of the distribution than in its centering." (Taleb 2013, p. 153)

In addition to financial sector deregulation, U.S government encouraged banks to help meet the credit needs of the communities in which they operate, mainly low income neighborhoods (NINJA loans, NINJA – No Income, No Job or Assets) through credit promotion policies (Community Reinvestment Act):

"The political response to rising inequality – whether carefully planned or an unpremeditated reaction to constituent demands – was to expand lending to households, especially low-income ones. The benefits – growing consumption and more jobs – were immediate, whereas paying the inevitable bill could be postponed into the future. Cynical as it may seem, easy credit has been used as a palliative throughout history by governments that are unable to address the deeper anxieties of the middle class directly. [...] In the United States, the expansion of home ownership – a key element of the American dream – to low and middle-income households was the defensible linchpin for the broader aims of expanding credit and consumption. But when easy money pushed by a deep-pocketed government comes into contact with the profit motive of a sophisticated, competitive, and amoral financial sector, a deep fault line develops." (Rajan 2010, p. 9) As expressed by Austrians (Huerta de Soto 2009, p. 409), the money creation process ensures a redistribution of income and wealth in favor of those who get the new injections of money over the rest of society who will pay higher prices. This did not work in U.S and other developed countries because of low inflation which didn't give them an advantage and as well because of the massive wave of speculations. This inequality and indebtedness trends weren't present just in U.S (see annex 6), it has been to the fore in most developed countries (see annexes 1 and 2).

3) *Inequality worsened current account imbalances. Increasing savings of foreign and domestic investors, due to income and wealth inequality produced current account disequilibrium.*

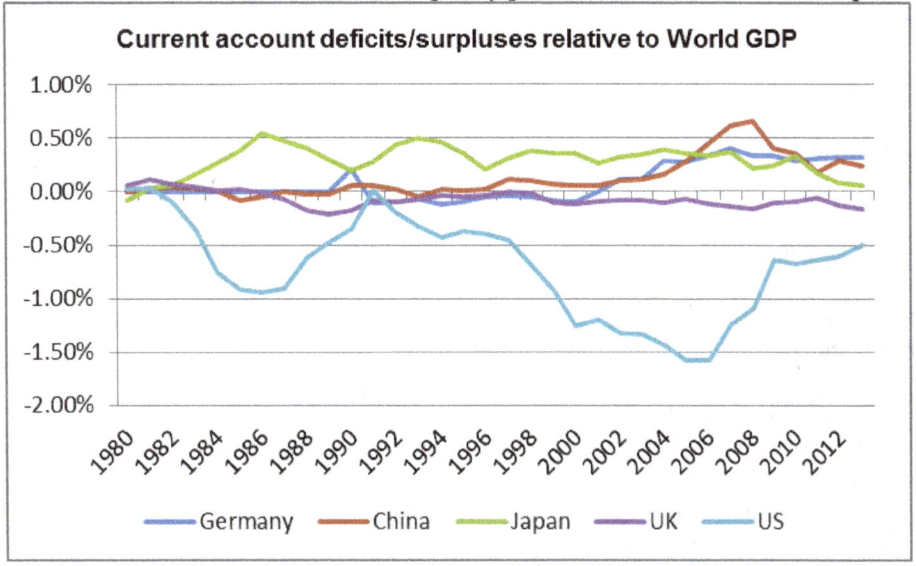

Figure 4. *Current account disequilibrium*
Source: data from UNCTADstat, author's calculations

US has become the "deficit of last resort" (Stiglitz, 2012). The reason, behind this phenomenon is the use of dollar as a global reserve currency, thereby, creating a counter-sense force that makes dollars leave United States and leads to a current account deficit (see figure 4). The current account disequilibrium was amplified by wealth and income concentration at the top end across the world. While some papers (Milanovic and Lakner, 2013) claim that global income inequality has fallen by using Global Gini Coefficients, in fact the Top 1 %/Average annual incomes per capita ratio has been climbing over the years (see table 1) and the global wage share followed a downward trend (see annex 3).

Table 1. *Income inequality evolution*

Average annual incomes per capita (in 2005 PPP-adjusted USD) Top 1%						**1988-2008 change**	**1993-2008 change**
Year	1988	1993	1998	2003	2008		
	38964	39601	46583	51641	64213	64.8%	62.1%
Average annual incomes per capita (in 2005 PPP-adjusted USD)							
	3295	3287	3471	3631	4097	24.3%	24.6%
Top 1 %/Average	11.82519	12.0477639	13.42063	14.22225	15.67317549	32.54%	16.78%

Source: (Milanovic and Lakner, 2013), author's calculations

Regarding global wealth inequality, there is another story (see annex 4). It may seem that global inequality decreased between 2001 and 2009, yet it could be only a distraction. In general, non-financial assets like housing, land and small business assets make up a relatively large proportion of household wealth in the developing world and in transition countries. In contrast, financial assets form a large proportion of the household balance sheets in developed countries. Within high level wealth groups, the bulk of wealth is represented by financial assets, while at lower wealth levels real assets tend to dominate. Given the real estate booms across the world before Global Financial Crisis, the fact that 49% of the ultra high net worth individuals are from U.S and 3.67% belong to UK while over 46.5% of millionaires are either American or British (Credit Suisse, Global Wealth Databook 2014) and probably similar ratios before crisis, is easy to understand the misleading data. The rising housing prices during boom closed the gap in composition of world gross wealth between financial and non-financial wealth and according to Atkinson (1989) rising house prices reduce the share of the top wealth percentile in the UK and Wolff (2009) reveals that the ratio of equity prices to house prices has a beneficial effect on the wealth share of the top percentile in U.S or as Yellen (2014) expressed „housing wealth is the most important source of wealth for all but those at the very top", assumption that can be generalized. The 19.55% Compound annual growth rate of Total Wealth of Billionaires (2009-2015) and the growing wealth share of top percentile occurred due to quantitative easing inflating bubbles on stock market and the poor losing their homes for being unable to pay back mortgage loans.

The consequence is clear: 2 simultaneous booms can hide an unequal accumulation of wealth. Practically, the Global Savings Glut (Bernanke, 2005) that was responsible for the large current account deficit of United States was possible because of global wealth and income inequality widening gap between individuals. Inequality developed current account surpluses in emerging markets and deficits in developed economies (especially in U.S) through what I call riskiness channel: high-income groups usually hold riskier financial assets (for evidence see Kennickell, 2009, Figure A3a). The riches from emerging markets with underdeveloped financial markets and other export-led countries invested their wealth in the major financial centers causing large volatilities in current accounts (mean absolute deviation of OECD countries' current account widened from 2.95% in 1995 to 6.76% in 2007, data from UNCTADstat, author's calculations). Their savings provided means for financing imports, the counterpart of a capital account surplus is an increase in current account deficit (Kumhof and Ranciere, 2010).

4) *Inequality is detrimental to human capital. Rising income inequality inhibit human capital formation (a key point in technology evolution) in poor countries, while in rich countries students must get over-indebted in order to pay university fees through student loans.*

Technology is the key factor in economic development of a nation and it is a function of investment (reinvested profit and credit used in production) and human capital. "Children whose parents are in the top quintile of the wealth distribution have a 36 percent chance of also being in the top quintile and a 60 percent chance of being in one of the two top quintiles in their adult years" (ISAACS, SAWHILL and HASKINS 2008, p.9) and 74% of students in the most selective colleges come from families in the top quartile (Carnevale and Rose 2003, p. 141). Only 29% of highscoring students from low socioeconomic backgrounds had completed a bachelor's degree or higher compared to 30% of low-scoring students with high socioeconomic status, 51% middlescoring students with high socioeconomic status and 74% high-scoring students from high socioeconomic backgrounds (Fox, Connolly and Snyder 2005, p. 51). Education is vital to economic mobility: adult children of parents in all five quintiles who achieve a college degree are much more likely to climb up the ladder seeing that 41% of adult children from the bottom quintile make it to the top two quintiles if they earn a college degree and only 14 percent of the adult children without a college degree from the bottom quintile of parental income reach the top two quintiles (ISAACS, SAWHILL and HASKINS 2008, p. 95). Access to education is clearly a factor of the Great Gatsby curve, term coined by Alan B. Krueger (2012) which involves that higher income inequality is associated with less mobility across the generations. Student loans have an uptrend in general and particularly low level income families (see Annex 5). Given the job polarization in U.S Autor (2010), a student loan crisis would be catastrophic for American economic system.

Another framework for typical crises

Business cycle theory has become a fairy tale. The current view is that GDP presents temporary deviations from its "natural rate" or its trend. The Great Recession proved otherwise, there were no small deviations, this time there was a L-shaped recovery. Credit instability is at the core of business cycles. The spiraling debt incurred in financing speculative investments leads to cash flow problems for investors, which are forced to sell their assets in order to pay their debt. This causes a sudden major collapse of asset values named Minsky Moment. We are all Minskyans now. For all that, his masterpiece (financial instability hypothesis) is incomplete without explaining the way economic inequality (economic inequality is a broader concept than income inequality, see Sen, 1997) amplifies financial instability and in what other manners influences economic cycle.

Inequality also depends on structural factors like urbanization and immigration (at national level immigration will have a negative effect on equality of income whilst on global level will have positively affect income distribution) due to increased labor supply. The annual fitted average growth rate of the share of urban population in total population in 1950 – 2010 In U.S is 0.33%, while on 1790 – 1940 is 1.8% (author's calculations, data from World Urbanization Prospects, 2014 Revision and Historical Statistics of the United States 1789 – 1945). Immigrants as Percentage of the U.S. Population reached its maximum in 1890, 14.8% (data from Migration Policy Institute 1850 – 2013). The highest amount of inequality was registered after the Great Recession top 10% Income Share excluding capital gains - 47.76% and including capital gains - 50.6% in 2012 (see The World Top Incomes Database), but immigration reached its top during 1870-1910. Also there was a decline in immigration for 2 decades before the Great Depression and inequality continued to grow. All these point the existence of other forces with high impact on distribution besides structural factors.

We can find clues in Leverage Cycles introduced by Geanakoplos. "Over the cycle inequality can dramatically increase if the leveraged buyers keep getting lucky and dramatically compress if the leveraged buyers lose out." (Geanakoplos, 2010) The reverse is also possible. The distinction between leverage cycle and credit cycle is that the latter has a constant LTV (Geanakoplos & Fostel, 2013). Extreme wealth inequality can reduce margins and transform a credit cycle into a Leverage Cycle.

3. Why Inequality Matters

- Increased inequality may shorten growth duration, as one IMF study indicated that longer growth spells (the interval starting with a growth upbreak and finishing with a downbreak) are correlated with less income inequality (Berg and Ostry, 2011)
- Improving income equality will narrow the saving gap between income groups, thereby tightening conspicuous consumption by the rich and emulation by the less affluent.
- Nassim Nicholas Taleb reveals that "In Extremistan, inequalities are such that one single observation can disproportionately impact the aggregate, or the total" using an example related to net worth "Consider by comparison the net worth of the thousand people you lined up in the stadium. Add to them the wealthiest person to be found on the planet—say, Bill Gates, the founder of Microsoft. Assume his net worth to be close to $80 billion—with the total capital of the others around a few million. How much of the total wealth would he represent? 99.9 percent?" (Taleb 2010, p. 61) The rising income and wealth inequality in the last decades has made our world closer to Extremistan than Mediocristan, making it prone to Black Swans.
- According to Piketty (2012) in the last decades the wealth is inherited
- A more egalitarian approach will improve the health and education of the poor; income redistribution is an investment in human capabilities
- Income inequality and entitlements are the causes behind famine in some parts of the world, not shortage of food, like the Bengal famine of 1943, the Ethiopian famine of 1973, or the Bangladesh famine of 1974. (see Sen, 1988)

In market economies there must be a degree of inequality in order to function, but what is the reason for such great inequalities? There is a competition between capitalists and workers (in fact there is a third type of participant, the managers who get paid with wage and shares, but for simplicity I will use only 2 classes: capitalists and workers). There seems to be a labor market conflict, thus during the economic boom the wage share in G7 countries has fallen, as shown in Annex 7 while during crunch, the share of wages in GDP increased, since profits and output have collapsed and profits are the last paid. A Kaleckian income distribution model is a useful tool for this purpose.

$Y = C+I$ where Y = national income; C = Consumption; I = Investment
$Y = S+P$ where S = Salaries; P = Profits
$C = C_p+C_s$, C_p = capitalists' consumption, C_s = workers' consumption
$C_p = \alpha*P$, α - fraction of consumed profits
$C_s=S$, Workers are presumed to consume all they earn.
$S + P = C+I$, therefore $S + P = S + \alpha*P+I$
$P = I + C_p$

Aggregate investments together with capitalist consumption determine aggregate profits and consequently also the savings that they require, and not the reverse. Also, Investment determines Savings through changes in Income via the multiplier principle developed by Richard Kahn, and via the newly created purchasing power (loans) for the investment to carry on, will eventually become someone's savings.

$P*(1-\alpha) = I$
$P = I/(1-\alpha)$, $Y = S+P$, $Y = S+I/(1-\alpha)$, s = employees' income share in GDP, $S=s*Y$
$Y*(1-s) = I/(1-\alpha)$
$Y = I/(1-s)(1-\alpha)$

The Kahn–Keynes multiplier will be greater as the marginal propensity to consume is higher. The marginal propensity to consume c can be approximated by the share of wages in national income and the Kahn–Keynes multiplier 1/(1-c) can be replaced with the Kaleckian multiplier expressed as 1/(1–marginal distribution towards wages). A greater distribution towards wages implies higher economic growth. While these two models seem to resemble, in fact in the last decades in most developed countries, the consumption of workers was financed by loans not by income, hence the kaleckian model proves to be a sustainable alternative.

Kaleckian multiplier	**Keynesian multiplier**
$\Delta Y = \Delta S + \Delta P$; $P=f(I)$, $P = I + C_p$, $\Delta P \approx \Delta I$	$\Delta Y = \Delta C + \Delta I$
$\Delta Y = \Delta S + \Delta I$	$\Delta Y/\Delta I = K$, K – multiplier
$\Delta Y = g_s{*}\Delta Y + \Delta I$,	$K = \Delta Y/(\Delta Y - \Delta C)$
G_s – distribution of growth to wages, $g_s=\Delta S/\Delta Y$	$K = \Delta Y/(1-\Delta C/\Delta Y)$
$\Delta Y{*}(1 - g_s) = \Delta I$	$K = 1/(1-c)$, c is MPC, marginal propensity to
$\Delta Y/\Delta I = 1/(1 - g_s)$ which means $K \approx 1/(1 - g_s)$	consume

Figure 5. *Kaleckian and Keynesian multipliers*

Blinder (1974) indicates that income inequality variation is greater than MPC's variation. However, Blinder has conducted its research in a period (1947-1972) with low inequality and strong bank regulation. The elasticity of MPC to wage share (% of GDP) for the 1973-2007, period chosen for deregulation and great income inequality variance) is -1.979, whereas the elasticity of Compensation to employees/GDP is for the same period is -4.960. Both Keynes (2009) and Kalecki (Osiatynski 1990, p. 372) were wrong, redistributing income to the less affluent won't reduce propensity to save, at least this wasn't the trend in U.S. A more equal distribution of income will make the contact with higher consumption individuals decrease, resulting a reduced propensity to consumption (Duesenberry 1949, pp. 44-45).

A decline of Kahn multiplier will not follow because less money will be available to speculate and more money will be utilized for purchases of goods and services (wealth to income ratio will also decrease), income and consumption will gain a stronger pace on real terms, while the consumption-income ratio will drop (as the consequence of previous psychological explanation and a smaller wealth effect - an increase in wealth will cause an increase in consumption). I conducted a Granger causality test in order to analyze the relationship between wage share (% of Personal Income) and financialisation in U.S, characterized by the size of financial sector. I used Augmented Dickey-Fuller and Phillips-Perron tests to examine the series (the first difference of logarithms) for stationarity. In both cases and for both series, the test value is less than the critical value for any of the levels of relevance therefore, the null hypothesis is rejected. The data samples match a normal (Gaussian) distribution (Jarque-Bera test).

For autocorrelation of errors I conducted Correlogram of Residuals (Q-Statistics) for a Bivariate AR (one lag) OLS regression with DL_WAGE_SHARE as dependent variable and Breusch-Godfrey Serial Correlation LM Test for DL_VA_FIN as dependent variable. The performed tests indicate that errors are independent. The Correlogram Squared Residuals revealed that error terms don't present heteroskedasticity. The residuals are normally-distributed (Jarque-Bera test). The correlation between wage share and the value added by financial (raw data) is $\approx$ -0.94 and $R^2 = 0.88$.

$$Va\_fin_t = \alpha + \sum\beta_i (Va\_fin_{t-i}) + \sum\psi_j (s_{t-j}) + \varepsilon$$
$$s_t = \Phi + \sum\varphi_i (s_{t-i}) + \sum\omega_j (Va\_fin_{t-j}) + \varepsilon,\ i = 1, n \ \&\ j = 1, n$$

Table 2. *Granger Causality*

Pairwise Granger Causality Tests			
Date: 08/30/15 Time: 20:24			
Sample: 1947 2009			
Lags: 2			
Null Hypothesis:	**Obs**	**F-Statistic**	**Prob.**
DL_WAGE_SHARE does not Granger Cause DL_VA_FIN	60	3.87182	0.0267
DL_VA_FIN does not Granger Cause DL_WAGE_SHARE		3.37679	0.0414

Source: wage share from BEA, author's calculations, VA_FIN from Philippon (2014)

The p – values are under 0.05 (selected significance level) meaning the relationship is mutual and the past values of wage share predict the current level of of value added by the financial sector and viceversa. In export-led countries like Germany the Private Consumption/GDP decreased because the middle class with declining incomes didn't get indebted as the reference group represented by top-end households raised their saving rate indirectly through corporate net saving and thanks to bank lending practices in Germany which are more conservative than in US (Treeck, Treeck and Sturn, 2012). The same goes for China, the share of consumption in GDP depressed (Treck and Sturn, 2012). It seems that rising inequality in debt-led countries leads to declining savings and viceversa for export-led countries.

States are open economies and countries where foreign trade is an important part of the economy, can be profit-led. But, the global economy is a closed economy since exports and imports cancel each other, therefore the global GDP is wage-led (high trade openness of economies leads to greater competition, it should not be a competition between states, but between companies). Mercantilism affects not only the economy that provides global reserve currency, but also global aggregate demand: when reserve accumulation is the result of current account surpluses, there is a reduction in global aggregate demand as highlighted by UN Commission of Experts on Reforms of the International Monetary and Financial System. That's why Keynes Plan involved a system that taxed surplus countries. Plus it is not possible for the majority of the export-seeking countries to grow out of a pro-capital redistribution of income, when this strategy is applied in many other large economies at the same time.

Here we can also add the well-known fact that during and post-recession, current accounts are more balanced because enterprises reduce their production costs and consumers (except the richest, but they do not make up the majority) don't afford anymore high value added products made abroad as result of falling incomes and low credit availability. The concepts „wage-led" and „profit-led" were introduced by Bhaduri and Marglin (1990) and their model measures the impact of 1 per cent point increase in the profit increase over private aggregate demand (private consumption, investment and net exports). The results of researches (Onaran and Galanis, 2012) using this model are paradoxical inasmuch as the private consumption/disposable income ratio in U.S. has grown, despite the upward trend of income inequality. Even more, there can't be permanently wage-led or profit-led economies, as maximum growth would be reached when the wage or the profit share is zero. Clearly, this is a false statement. Logically an economy goes through stages of wage-led and profit-led growth. We can find evidence in this case following the events after The Great Depression. The crisis led to a redistribution policy in favor of wages after World War II, this period was named the Golden Age. This system has exhausted its synergy three decades latter ending in the Great Stagflation. The crisis was a reason for income redistribution in favor of profits that has taken place since and caused the current crisis.

As both regimes have failed, I can conclude that the assumptions made above are correct and because in average growth was more robust over the Golden Age than during the Great Moderation (and due to generally negative net exports), without any calculations we can say that U.S. is wage-led upon long-term. Seeing that two totally different systems had taken place one after the other resulting in different crisis we can draw another set of conclusions:

- the stronger each class becomes, the greater is its capacity to further increase its share of income until a crisis or a political change occurs
- there is no optimum wage share or profit share, because of the never ending war between classes, the distribution of income is unstable and pursuing wage-led growth will make the economic growth less sensitive to wage share growth. Likewise pursuing profit-led growth on long term will undermine GDP growth.

Nevertheless, the long distribution waves are mostly in favor of capitalists. The introduction of managers in this story shows us that top incomes earners today are CEOs or new entrepreneurs, not "rentiers" (Saez, 2013) doubling the pressure for low-income earners. In the same time, bailouts with lack of regulations and punishment (leaders are rewarded for their incompetence) threaten recovery and set the foundations of future crisis and the next long distribution wave in favor of the rich.

4. The Link between Inflation, Wages and Unemployment

The conventional belief is that unemployment is a consequence of high wages, an outcome of downward wage rigidity. This is wrong. Wages don't exhibit rigidity in either direction, they are changed only at fairly long stretch (Leijonhufvud, 2012) and if wages were flexible it would make things much worse during a debt-deflation (Leijonhufvud, 2002) as the fall of wages would exacerbate deflation and real debt, or during a stagflation where rapid increase in wages would amplify inflation. Even in normal times, extreme volatile wages would be detrimental for not providing stability to employees and for reducing the ability of enterprises to adapt to new circumstances.

The classical view that rising unemployment is the result of high wages was reinforced in the 1970s, when the wage share hit record high in developed countries. However, in the subsequent decades, unemployment was on average higher (compared to unemployment recorded during Golden Age of Capitalism) whilst real wages were far behind productivity growth. Wages should not be viewed as an impediment for investment, but as a source of stable demand. Wages would be detrimental to economic growth just in a profit squeeze situation, conjuncture that seems far away from our days. Wage increase could make the transition to a moderate rate of inflation. A moderate inflation can avoid liquidity trap entrance. Minsky argues that if the rate of inflation is high at the time of the crisis, even though the bust causes investment to slump, rising cash flows enable the repayment of debt incurred before the economic collapse. The result is slow growth and high inflation, but few bankruptcies. This is a self-correcting mechanism because prolonged slump is avoided (Keen, 1995).

A moderate inflation may improve economic performance: it can melt away the debt and reduce unemployment (the latter is a consequence of the first one and of the money illusion which holds true at low and moderate inflation). Inflation is influenced by wages and money among other factors. The relationship between inflation and money supply growth is weak when the inflation is low (Stiglitz). Improving income inequality by rising wages could help the transition to moderate inflation and it can be further improved after the completion of this phase without creating inflationary pressures. For reducing income inequality and not giving rise to further inflationary pressures it is required a policy that would encourage faster wage growth for poorly paid jobs relative to growth of wages for highly paid work. This means that at the bottom, wage growth will exceed productivity growth, while at the top, productivity growth will surpass wage growth (Minsky, 1968), in this way repairing the inequalities made during Great Moderation.

5. Fiscal and International Solutions

The following fiscal and international solutions are note-worthy:

- Progressive taxes ameliorate income inequality and reduce the expansion of budget deficit in case of public wage growth
- Increase fiscal pressure and improve redistribution. Post taxes Gini Index (gini_net) is on average lower than Gini before taxes (gini_market) see Solt, 2009. The most important public expenses is education, it will reduce frictional unemployment and it will lessen social immobility. Job matching and public services are crucial, not welfare spending.
- Another idea is the inheritance tax. It is implemented in few states, but in emerging states it could chase away investors
- A better collection of taxes by eliminating loopholes in tax law
- More bargaing power for workers and increase minimum wages. The last measure would also reduce tax evasion since many employers conclude work contracts to the minimum wages (gray tax evasion area).
- Liberalize migration so that poor people can move to richer countries

6. Monetary Solutions

Some of the fiscal solutions have obvious drawbacks and must be doubled by monetary policies who likewise influence wealth and income distribution.

Nassim Nicholas Taleb and Daniel G. Goldstein (2007) showed that the ratio of standard deviation and mean absolute deviation is about 1.25 if the series of variables is Gaussian and greatly increases in a world of fat tails. As we can see in figure 7, the loan impulse in U.S. between 1947M01-2015M03 is highly unstable. The leptokurtotic distribution obtained with an excess kurtosis > 7, exhibit volatility clustering, meaning that "large changes tend to be followed by large changes – of either sign" (Mandelbrot, 1963).

The inexistence of neutrality in the long term entails distributional effects of monetary policy. We must underline that Austrians reject the idea of long-run neutrality of money since credit expansion will always distort the structure of production (Huerta de Soto, 2009, pp. 540-541). The essence of Inequality Fragility Hypothesis is the spiral between financial markets and economic inequality. Finance can quickly degenerate into a rent-seeking activity thanks to the flexibility provided by financial engineering (Zingales, 2015).

Between 1960 and 2009 the financial industry doubled its share in GDP. Besides rent-seeking, there is another reason for this increase in financial industry: GDP grew slower because of more and more money being oriented to asset markets instead of being allocated to business, while financial industry had to grow to support the creation of securities. Aggregate demand (GDP) is formed of basic aggregate demand and the demand generated solely by speculative bubbles (Croitoru, 2015). But, even the bubble before Great Recession could not produce any excess in aggregate demand (Summers, 2013). Inequality has contributed via riskiness channel.

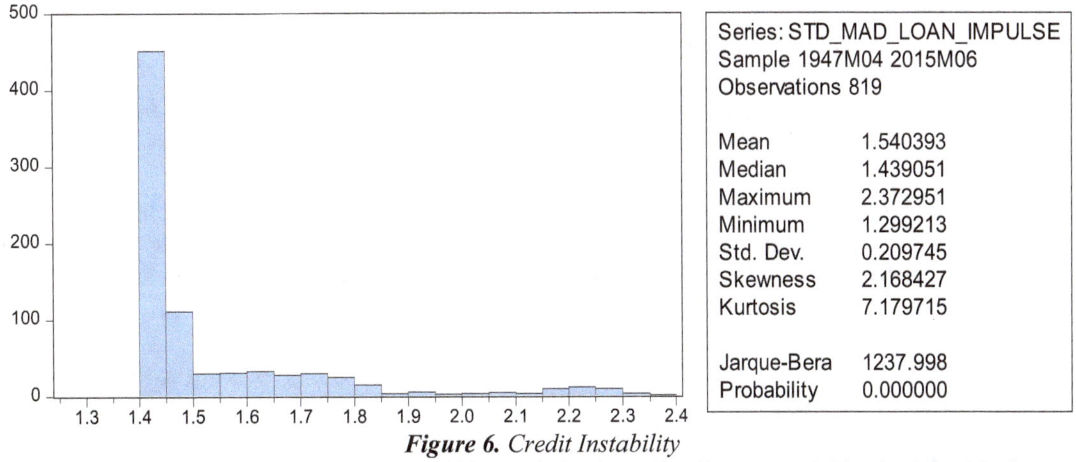

Figure 6. *Credit Instability*

Source: Federal Reserve Board, H8, Loans and leases in bank credit, all commercial banks, Monthly data, not seasonally adjusted

Since 1997Q3 M2 velocity has recorded an almost permanent drop signaling the development of an overtrading economy. If money supply grows faster than nominal GDP, the consequences will be the development of speculative bubbles and decreasing velocity. The upward drift in credit demand came from inequality and the advance in supply of credit was driven by financial innovation (securitization) "in many cases the expansion of credit resulted from the development of substitutes for what previously had been the traditional monies" as asserted by Charles Kindleberger (2005, p. 64). We can test the hypothesis of credit-driven asset prices by using S&P Composite as proxy for financial asset prices. Its dependence on Debt Margin can be plotted with HP filter.

$Y_t = G_t + K_t$, Y_t is the analyzed variable, in this case, debt margin and SP Composite, G_t – growth component (trend) and K_t – cyclical component

$\sum_{t=1}^{T} K_t^2 + \lambda\sum_{t=1}^{T}[(G_t\text{-}G_{t-1}) - (G_{t-1}\text{-}G_{t-2})]^2$ – the minimizing equation to smooth trend, $\lambda = 14400$

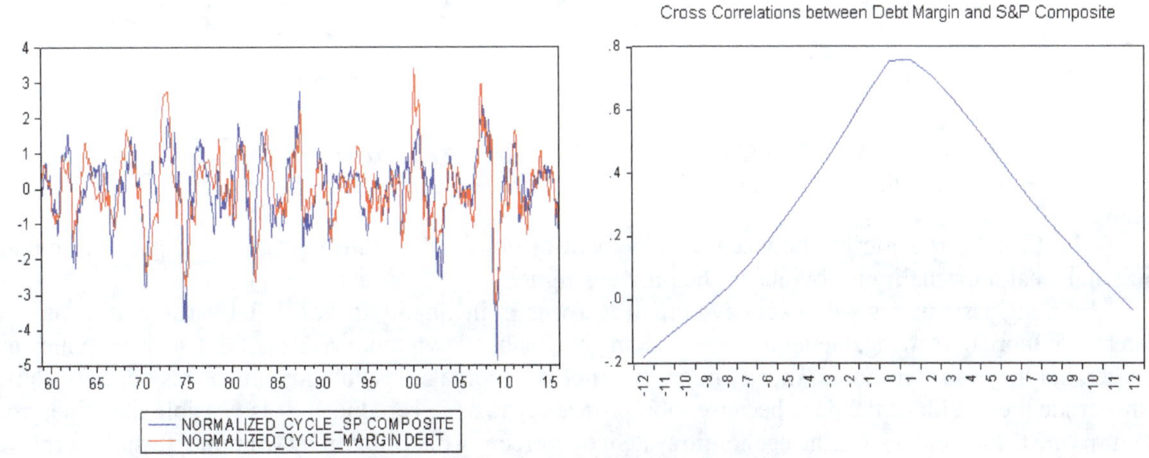

Figure 7. *Credit and financial asset prices*

Source: Margin Debt, Monthly data, New York Stock Exchange, 1951M01 – 2016M01, S&P Comp. P data from Shiller, Robert J., Stock Market Data Used in "Irrational Exuberance" Princeton University Press, 2000, 2005, 2015, updated, Monthly Data

The normalized debt margin log deviations from HP trend are correlated with normalized asset prices log deviations and the mutual causality is obvious it as the correlation with one lag (asset pricing depending on debt margin) is 0.6572 while the correlation with one lead is 0.7589.

Residence property prices are too dependent on debt (see annex 8) in most developed countries except for Germany.

Monetary policy has two main channels that influence economic inequality in contrary sense: the riskiness channel, an expansionary monetary policy will put upward pressure upon equity prices, therefore raising the wealth of the rich and credit channel which benefits the first to get the new injections of money (the poor have higher debt ratios relative to income and wealth), only if inflation is high enough to gain advantage over others and to meltdown their debt without affecting purchasing power (real incomes are rising).

$C_{lih} = a*Y_{lih} + b*W_{lih}$

$C_{hih} = \rho*a*Y_{hih} + \rho*b*W_{hih}$, C_{lih} – consumption of low-income households, C_{hih} – consumption of high – income households, $0 < a < 1$, $0 < b < 1$, $0 < \rho < 1$, $a<b$

$W = W_{lih} + W_{hih}$, W – household wealth

$R_a = \theta*W_{lih} + \rho*\theta*W_{hih}$, R_a – riskless assets (money, T-bills, real assets without mortgage). When inequality rises, R_a/W will drop and credit to money and loans to money ratios will grow. Because money is not neutral, the influence of money and near-monies on distribution can modeled as:

$I = I_0 + MI$, I_0 – inequality independent of monetary evolutions, MI – monetary inequality represented **by capital gains, their distribution** and

$W_t/Y_t = [W_{t-1} * (1 - \text{Depreciation}) + \text{Investment}] * (1+e_t) / Y_{t-1}*g$, e_t **– existing assets price inflation in excess over GDP deflator**, g - real growth, (modified version of Piketty's two-good model wealth accumulation model)

$Y = Y_{ww} + Y_{we}$, Y_{ww} – aggregate demand without wealth effect, Y_{we} – wealth effect

$Y_{we} = b*(W_{lih} + \rho*W_{hih})$, W_{lih} - low income households, W_{hih} – high income households

$W_{lih}/W_{hih} = X$

$Y_{we} = X + Y_{EA}$, Y_{EA} – demand for existing assets, wealth effect is dependent on demand for existing assets and on the distribution of wealth.

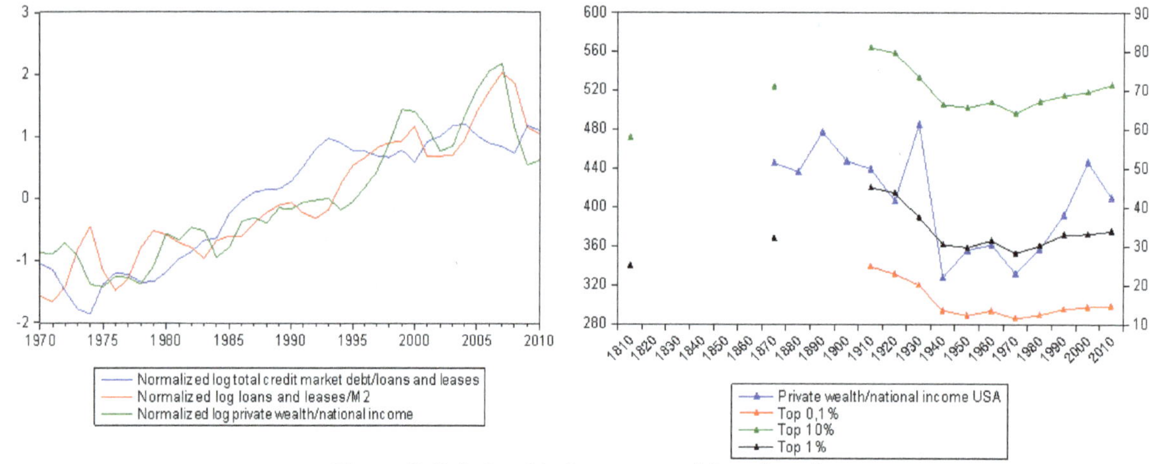

Figure 8. *Relationship between wealth and credit*
Source: Piketty, T., Technical appendix of the book « Capital in the 21st century

The Circular relationship between development of non-bank credit, decoupling loans from money, wealth and wealth inequality is obvious in the previous figure.

Inflating asset prices with excessive credit is a wealth inequality driver. Afterwards wealth supplies collateral for more borrowing. Generally, low income households own more riskless asset such as money and real asset, but they use their homes mostly not as a source of income or speculation, but as residence. Inflation doesn't erode the wealth of the poor because their propensity to save is reduced. It is possible that asset price downturns are the natural way of the economic system of correcting distribution by whipping fortunes achieved through monetary gains without added value, given that during recessions inflation falls less than the relative price of assets, acting as automatic stabilizers against inequality. Debt becomes the income of financial sector. After the Great Recession, the household debt to GDP ratio has shrunk in size, yet financial income and the share of top 10% income share continued their upward trend. These are the results of quantitative easing. Policymakers are trying to cheat the business cycle, but it won't work. The weak economic grow is a by-product of asset gambling and resource misallocation of an overly large financial sector. In general, is believed that credit impulse influences only investment, the stock of credit equals stock of capital (Biggs, Mayer and Pick, 2009). Investment is a flow and is linked to the flow of credit therefore the change in investment and thus, economic growth is dependent on credit impulse.

$\Delta I = \Delta\Delta Cr$, ΔI – change in investment, $\Delta\Delta CR$ – credit impulse

Textbooks describe financial intermediation like this: households save and companies invest their savings. It is wrong. Commercial banks create money (other financial intermediaries perform a transfer of purchasing power) and in the last decades household debt went through the roof. Capital is divided into productive capital and financial capital (existing assets trading). Credit impulse is also related to financial capital. Curbing credit impulse and preserving credit flow at sustainable levels plus targeting a moderate and stable inflation will smooth asset price bubbles and inequality. With these policies it will be less probably that borrowing will be based on the collateral value rather than on expected cash flows.

The actions needed to mitigate credit impulse: use a form of capital requirements (Equity/Total Assets) for all financial institutions to counter credit impulse fluctuations (prohibit securitization because it allows avoidance of capital requirements and decouples credit from money or at least include off balance sheet items in formula and impose restrictions on preferred shares as financial corporations can raise capital without slowing credit creation), impose loan to value ratios and debt thresholds for all borrowers (homeowners, margin buyers and businesses) during boom. This proposal should not be confused with the Basel III regulatory framework. It doesn't involve risk-weighted assets. All Basel Agreements have been procyclical. Another error of Basel regulation structure is that stress testing implies that macroeconomic shocks affect financial institutions. In reality is quite the opposite: the inverted yield curve affects the profitability of financial intermediaries. The future reduction in credit supply will have a negative impact on real activity (see Adrian, Estrella and Shin, 2010).

A greater distribution towards high income households led to a smaller wealth effect in comparison to the period before crisis. This under potential growth has sparked controversy among theorists. The two mechanisms provided by Keynes, 2009 (interest rates) and Kalecki (income distribution) for equilibrating Savings and Investments, can provide an explanation. It is possible that decreasing wage share over long periods of time would contribute among other factors to higher ex-ante savings than ex-ante planned investment because capitalists and corporate sector save more. Corporations are sitting on piles of cash and have become net holders of financial assets, exerting more stress on real interest rates to fall in order to reach equilibrium, which combined with low inflation favored search for yield and build-up of large debt. Anyway, regardless of accepted theory, secular stagnation, global savings glut, debt supercycle or Gordon's headwinds, they all have one common element: increasing inequality.

7. Conclusions

The paper analyzes the main outcomes and determinants of income and wealth inequality at global level and especially in U.S. The vicious circles between economic inequality and financial instability are highlighted by increasing debt-to-income ratios for low income households that borrow in order to adhere to the same living standards with wealthy individuals and by riskiness channel: high-income groups usually hold riskier financial assets. The Global Savings Glut and current account volatilities were the result of increasing inequality. The riches from countries with weak financial markets and export oriented nations invested a great percentage of their wealth in U.S. transforming it in the deficit of last resort. Rising inequality in debt-led countries leads to declining savings and viceversa for export-led countries. Social immobility is yet another negative consequence of high income inequality because access to education is restricted for students from low income families.

One of the main determinants of income and wealth distribution in U.S is financialisation because of asset gambling and resource misallocation. My analysis reveals that human capital is substituted with financialisation in an overtrading economy. Asset prices depend on credit as credit log deviations from HP trend are correlated with normalized asset prices log deviations and precede it and if the leveraged buyers are lucky inequality will rise. Because of non-neutrality of money, inequality can be classified into inequality independent of monetary evolutions and monetary inequality. Central bankers can ameliorate monetary inequality by targeting moderate inflation and curbing credit impulse. This study can be further developed by comparing the actual income and wealth inequality with the results produced by a life cycle model, the difference being identified as monetary inequality and simulating the impact of monetary policy on it.

References

Adrian, T., Estrella, A., Shin, H.S., 2010. Monetary Cycles, Financial Cycles, and the Business Cycle, *Federal Reserve Bank of New York Staff Reports*, Staff Report no. 421

Atkinson, A.B., J. P. F. Gordon and A. J. Harrison, 1989. Trends in the shares of top wealth holders in Britain, 1923-1981, *Oxford Bulletin of Economics and Statistics* 51, pp.315-332.

Autor, D, 2010. The Polarization of Job Opportunities in the U.S. Labor Market, Implications for Employment and Earnings, *MIT Department of Economics and National Bureau of Economic Research*, [online] Available at: http://economics.mit.edu/files/5554 [Accessed on 2 February 2016]

B. B. Mandelbrot, 1963. The variation of certain speculative prices, *Journal of Business, XXXVI,* 1963. pp. 394–419.

Bank for International Settlements, 2016. *Residential property price statistics* [online] Available at: http://www.bis.org/statistics/pp.htm [Accessed on 9 January 2016].

Bernanke, B.S., 2005. *The Global Saving Glut and the U.S. Current Account Deficit - Sandridge Lecture*, Virginia Association of Economists, Richmond, Virginia [online] Available at: http://www.federalreserve.gov/boardDocs/Speeches/2005/200503102/default.htm [Accessed on 2 February 2016]

Biggs, M., Mayer, T. and Pick, A., 2009. Credit and Economic Recovery, *DNB Working Paper*, No. 218

Blinder, A., 1974. Distribution Effects and the Aggregate Consumption Function, *Econometric Research Program Research Memorandum No. 162* [online] Available at: https://www.princeton.edu/~erp/ERParchives/archivepdfs/M162.pdf [Accessed on 2 February 2016]

Bureau of the Census with the Cooperation of the social science research council, 1949. *Historical Statistics of the United States 1789 – 1945, Bureau of the Census Library*, [online] Available at: https://www2.census.gov/prod2/statcomp/documents/HistoricalStatisticsoftheUnitedStates1789-1945.pdf [Accessed on 23 January 2016]

Carnevale, A.P. and Stephen J.R., 2003. *Socioeconomic Status, Race/Ethnicity and* Selective College Admissions, New York: The Century Foundation [online] Available at: https://tcf.org/assets/downloads/tcf-carnrose.pdf [Accessed on 12 March 2016]

Croitoru, L., 2015. 'Stagnarea seculară', ,'bulele salvatoare' şi creşterea economică în România ('Secular Stagnation', 'Saving Bubbles' and Economic Growth in Romania) [online] Available at: http://www.bnro.ro/Studii,-analize,-puncte-de-vedere-4009.aspx [Accessed on 12 March 2016].

Duesenberry, J., 1949. *Income Savings and the Theory of Consumer Behavior*. Cambridge: Harvard University Press

Eurostat, 2016. *Eurostat*. [online] Available at: http://ec.europa.eu/eurostat [Accessed on 9 January 2016].

Federal Reserve, 2016. *Federal Reserve of United States* [online] Available at: www.federalreserve.gov/ [Accessed on 9 January 2016].

Fox, M.A., Connolly, B.A. and Snyder, T.D., 2005. Youth Indicators 2005 Trends in the Well-Being of American Youth [online] Available at: http://nces.ed.gov/pubs2005/2005050.pdf [Accessed on 2 February 2016]

Geanakoplos, J., 2010. The Leverage Cycle, in: D. Acemoglu, K. Rogoff and M. Woodford, eds. *NBER Macroeconomic Annual* 2009, vol 24, pp.1-65

Geanakoplos, J., Fostel, A., 2013. Reviewing the Leverage Cycle, Federal Reserve Bank Dallas, [online] Available at: https://www.dallasfed.org/assets/documents/research/events/2013/uncertainty_geanakoplos2.pdf [Accessed on 12 March 2016].

Huerta de Soto, J., 2009. *Money, Bank Credit and Economic Cycles*, 2nd ed., Auburn, Ala.: Ludwig von Mises Institute.

International Labour Organization, 2016. *ILOSTAT Database* [online] Available at: https://www.ilo.org/ilostat [Accessed on 9 January 2016].

Isaacs, J.B., Sawhill, I.V. and Haskins, R., 2008. Getting ahead or losing ground: Economic mobility in America. The Brookings Institution [online] Available at: http://www.brookings.edu/research/reports/2008/02/economic-mobility-sawhill [Accessed on 2 February 2016]

Keen, S., 1995. Finance and economic breakdown: modeling Minsky's "financial instability hypothesis". *Journal of-Post Keynesian Economics Summer: 995.* Vol. 17, No. 4, pp.607–635

Kennickell, A.B., 2009. Ponds and Streams: Wealth and Income in the U.S., 1989 to 2007, *Finance and Economics Discussion Series Divisions of Research & Statistics and Monetary Affairs,* Washington, D.C.: Federal Reserve Board.

Keynes, J.M., 2009. *Teoria generală a ocupării fortei de muncă, a dobânzii şi a banilor*, Bucureşti: Editura Publica.

Kindleberger, C.P. and Aliber, R., 2005. *Manias, Panics, and Crashes: A History of Financial Crises.* Hoboken, New Jersey: John Wiley & Sons.

Krueger, A.B., 2012. *Speech - The Rise and Consequences of Inequality*, Chairman Council of Economic Advisers

Kumhof, M. and Ranciere, R., 2010. Inequality, Leverage and Crises, *IMF Working Paper 10/268.*

Leijonhufvud, A., 2012. *The Unstable Web of Contracts* Revised, INET - Berlin [online] Available at: http://www3.ucn.cl/SubirDocumentos/upload/repositorio/14802-Articulo.pdf [Accessed on 2 February 2016]

Migration Policy Institute, 2016. *Migration Data Hub* [online] Available at: http://www.migrationpolicy.org/programs/data-hub [Accessed on 9 January 2016].

Milanovic, B. and Lakner, C., 2013. Global Income Distribution From the Fall of the Berlin Wall to the Great Recession, Policy Research Working Paper 6719, *The World Bank Development Research Group Poverty and Inequality Team* [online] Available at: https://openknowledge.worldbank.org/handle/10986/16935 [Accessed on 2 February 2016]

Minsky, H.P., 1982. *Can "It" Happen Again? Essays on Instability and Finance*. Armonk, N.Y.: M.E. Sharpe.

Minsky, Hyman P., 1968. Effects of Shifts of Aggregate Demand upon Income Distribution. *American Journal of Agricultural Economics* Vol. 50, No. 2, pp.328-339

OECD, 2016. *Financial statistics – OECD* [online] Available at: http://www.oecd.org/std/fin-stats/ [Accessed on 9 January 2016].

Onaran, Ö. and Galanis, G., 2012. Is aggregate demand wage-led or profit-led? National and global effects - Geneva: ILO Working Papers 478623, International Labour Organization. [online] Available at: http://www.ilo.org/public/libdoc/nonigo/2012/478623.pdf [Accessed on 23 January 2016]

Osiatynski, J., ed., 1990. Collected Works of Michal Kalecki: Volume I: *Capitalism: Business Cycles and Full Employment*, Oxford: Clarendon Press

Ostry, J.D. and Berg, A.G., 2011. Inequality and Unsustainable Growth: Two Sides of the Same Coin? *IMF Staff Discussion Notes* No. 11/8, [online] Available at: https://www.imf.org/external/pubs/cat/longres.aspx?sk=24686.0 [Accessed on 23 January 2016]

Oxfam, 2015. Wealth: Having It All and Wanting More, Oxfam Issue Briefing January 2015. [online] Available at: https://www.oxfam.org/sites/www.oxfam.org/files/file_attachments/ib-wealth-having-all-wanting-more-190115-en.pdf [Accessed on 2 March 2016]

Palley, T.I., 2014. Effective demand, endogenous money, and debt: a Keynesian critique of Keen and an alternative theoretical framework. *Review of Keynesian Economics*, Edward Elgar Publishing, vol. 2(3), pp. 312-320, July.

Philippon, T., 2014. Has the US Finance Industry Become Less Efficient? On the Theory and Measurement of Financial Intermediation. *American Economic Review, 105(4), pp.1408-1438*

Piketty, T., 2012. *Wealth, Inequality & Taxation*, IMF [online] Available at: http://piketty.pse.ens.fr/files/PikettyIMF27092012(suppl).pdf [Accessed on 2 February 2016]

Piketty, T., 2014. *Capital in the Twenty-First Century*, Cambridge, MA: Belknap Press.

Piketty, T., 2016. *Capital in the 21st century – Figures and Tables from the book* [online] Available at: http://piketty.pse.ens.fr/en/capital21c2 [Accessed on 9 January 2016].

Rajan, R., 2010. *Fault Lines: How Hidden Fractures Still Threaten the World Economy*, N.J:Princeton University Press.

Reserve Bank of Australia, 2016. *Reserve Bank of Australia (RBA)* [online] Available at: www.rba.gov.au/ [Accessed on 9 January 2016].

Saez, E., 2013. Striking it Richer: The Evolution of Top Incomes in the United States, Updated with 2012 preliminary estimates), UC Berkeley [online] Available at: http://eml.berkeley.edu//~saez/saez-UStopincomes-2012.pdf [Accessed on 2 February 2016]

Sen, A., 1997. From income inequality to economic inequality, *Southern Economic Journal,* 64(2), pp.384-397

Sen, A., 1998. *The possibility of social choice - Nobel Lecture*, December 8, 1998 [online] Available at: http://www.nobelprize.org/nobel_prizes/economic-sciences/laureates/1998/sen-lecture.pdf [Accessed on 23 January 2016]

Shiller, R.J., 2016. Robert J. Shiller Sterling Professor of Economics Yale University [online] Available at: http://www.econ.yale.edu/~shiller/ [Accessed on 9 January 2016].

Shorrocks, A., Davies, J. and Lluberas, R., 2014. *Credit Suisse Global Wealth Databook 2014*, [online] Available at: https://publications.credit-suisse.com/tasks/render/file/?fileID=5521F296-D460-2B88-081889DB12817E02 [Accessed on 23 January 2016]

Shorrocks, A., Davies, J. and Lluberas, R., 2015. *Credit Suisse Global Wealth Databook 2015*, [online] Available at: http://publications.credit-suisse.com/tasks/render/file/index.cfm?fileid=C26E3824-E868-56E0-CCA04D4BB9B9ADD5 [Accessed on 23 January 2016]

Snowdon, B., 2002. Outside the mainstream: An interview with Axel Leijonhufvud, Northumbria University, [online] Available at: http://www-ceel.economia.unitn.it/staff/leijonhufvud/interview.pdf [Accessed on 2 February 2016]

Solt, F., 2009. Standardizing the World Income Inequality Database. *Social Science Quarterly*, 90(2), pp.231-242.

Statistics Canada, 2016. *Survey of Financial Security Canada* [online] Available at: www.statcan.gc.ca/imdb-bmdi/2620-eng.htm [Accessed on 9 January 2016].

Stiglitz, J.E., 2012. Is mercantilism doomed to fail? China, Germany, and Japan and the Exhaustion of Debtor Countries, *INET* Berlin

Stiglitz, J.E., 2013. *Preţul Inegalităţii, Cum societatea divizată din ziua de astăzi ne pune în pericol viitorul*, Bucureşti: Editura Publica

Summers, L.H., 2013. *IMF Fourteenth Annual Research Conference in Honor of Stanley Fischer* [online] Available at: http://larrysummers.com/imf-fourteenth-annual-research-conference-in-honor-of-stanley-fischer/ [Accessed on 2 March 2016]

Taleb, N.N. and Goldstein, D.G., We Don't Quite Know What We Are Talking About When We Talk About Volatility, *Journal of Portfolio Management*, Vol. 33, No. 4.

Taleb, N.N., 2010. *Lebăda Neagră: Impactul foarte puţin probabilului*, Ediţia a II-a, Bucuresti, Curtea Veche Publishing

Taleb, N.N., 2013. *Probability, Fat Tails, and Antifragility Elements of Risk Engineering,* [online] Available at: http://gfoix.com/wp-content/uploads/2013/11/textbook.pdf [Accessed on 2 March 2016]

U.S. Bureau of Economic Analysis, 2016. *U.S. Bureau of Economic Analysis (BEA)* [online] Available at: www.bea.gov/ [Accessed on 9 January 2016].

UNCTADstat, 2016. *UNCTADstat Database* [online] Available at: http://unctadstat.unctad.org/EN/ [Accessed on 9 January 2016].

United Nations General Assembly, 2009. Report of the Commission of Experts of the President of the United Nations General Assembly on Reforms of the International Monetary and Financial System, September 21, 2009 [online] Available at: http://www.un.org/ga/econcrisissummit/docs/FinalReport_CoE.pdf [Accessed on 2 February 2016]

United Nations, 2014. World Urbanization Prospects - 2014 Revision [online] Available at: https://esa.un.org/unpd/wup/Publications/Files/WUP2014-Highlights.pdf [Accessed on 2 March 2016]

van Treeck, T. and Sturn S., 2012. Income inequality as a cause of the Great Recession? A survey of current debates, *International Labour Office, Conditions of Work and Employment Branch*. - Geneva: *ILO*

van Treeck, van T., Inequality, the crisis, and stagnation, *Ineteconomics* [online] Available at: *https://ineteconomics.org/uploads/papers/van_Treeck.pdf* [Accessed on 2 March 2016]

Veblen, T., 1909. The limitations of marginal utility, *Journal of Political Economy*, vol. 17 [online] Available at: http://www.elegant-technology.com/resource/MARG_UT.PDF [Accessed on 2 March 2016]

Wolff, E.N., 2009. *Poverty and Income Distribution*, 2nd edition, Chichester, West Sussex: Wiley-Blackwell.

World Wealth and Income Database, 2016. *The World Top Incomes Database* [online] Available at:http://topincomes.parisschoolofeconomics.eu/ [Accessed on 9 January 2016].

Yellen, J.L., 2014. Perspectives on Inequality and Opportunity from the Survey of Consumer Finances, *Conference on Economic Opportunity and Inequality Federal Reserve Bank of Boston,* [online] Available at: http://www.federalreserve.gov/newsevents/speech/yellen20141017a.htm [Accessed on 13 April 2016]

Zingales, L., 2015. DOES FINANCE BENEFIT SOCIETY? NBER Working Paper 20894 [online] Available at: http://faculty.chicagobooth.edu/luigi.zingales/papers/research/finance.pdf [Accessed on 13 April 2016]

Appendices

Annex 1. Financial fragility In Euro Area (2010)

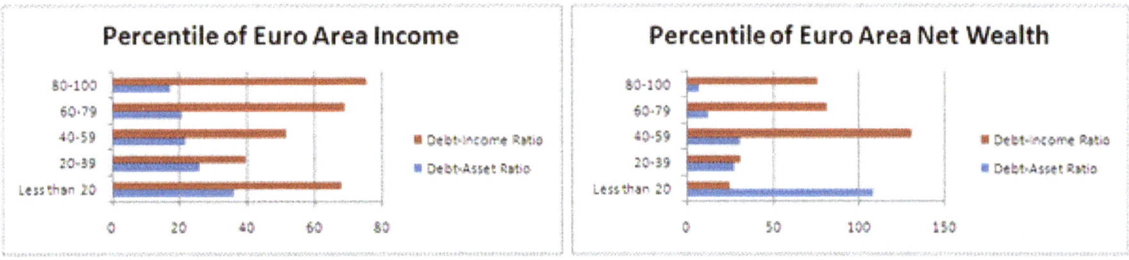

Source: Statistics Paper Series NO 2 / Apri l 2013 The Eurosystem Household Finance and Consumption Survey Results from the first wave, pp. 65, Year of reference 2010 (Belgium (2010), Germany (2010), Greece (2009), Spain (2008), France (2010), Italy (2010), Cyprus (2010), Luxembourg (2010), Malta (2010), Netherlands (2009), Austria (2010), Portugal (2010), Slovenia (2010), Slovakia (2010), Finland (2009))

Annex 2. Debt ratios by percentile of net worth in Australia and Canada

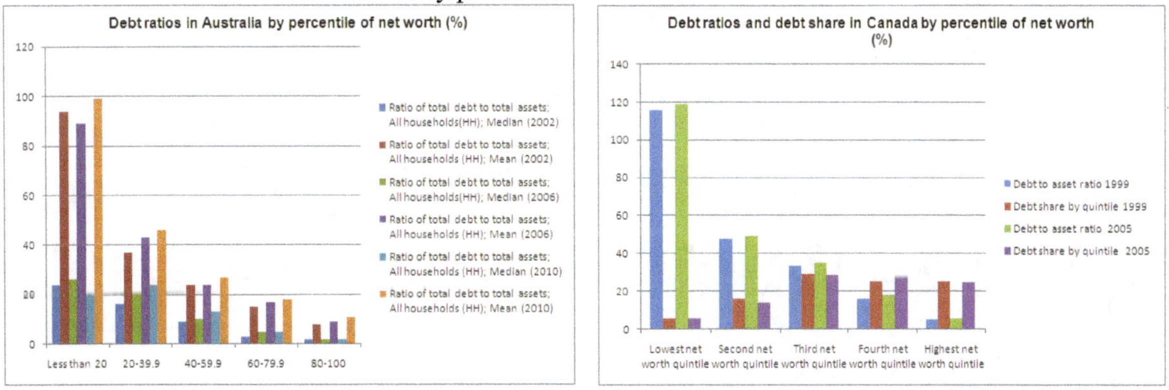

Source: Australia RBA, Publication date 15-mar-2012 and Canada Survey of Financial Security Statistics Canada (2005), author's calculations

Annex 3. Share of labour income in world gross output

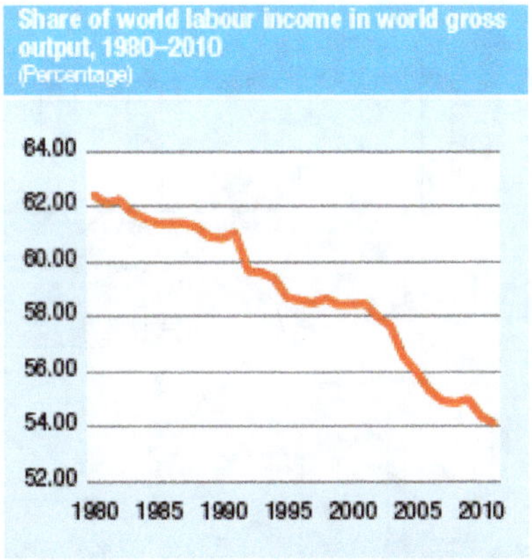

Source: POST-2015 POLICY BRIEF, No.02, 29 NOVEMBER 2013, GROWTH AND POVERTY ERADICATION: WHY ADDRESSING INEQUALITY MATTERS

Annex 4. Wealth share of top percentile in the world, 2000–15 (%)

2200 1	2200 2	2200 3	2200 4	2200 5	2200 6	2200 7	2200 8	2200 9	2201 0	2201 1	2201 2	2201 3	2201 4	2201 5
448. 4	446. 9	446. 3	446. 3	446. 9	446. 1	444. 7	444. 2	444. 0	444. 4	445. 0	446. 0	447. 1	448. 2	550. 0

Global Wealth Databook 2014, 2015, Credit Suisse

Annex 5. Evolution of Education Loans in U.S (1989-2013)

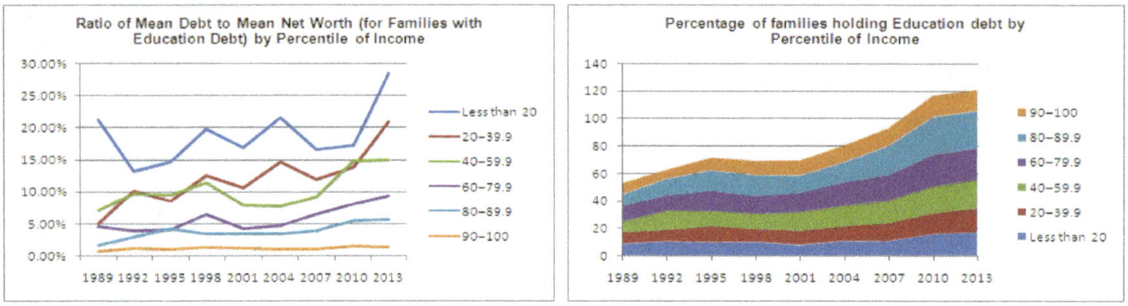

Source: Survey of Consumer Finances 2013, author's calculations

Annex 6. Growth of inequality in U.S

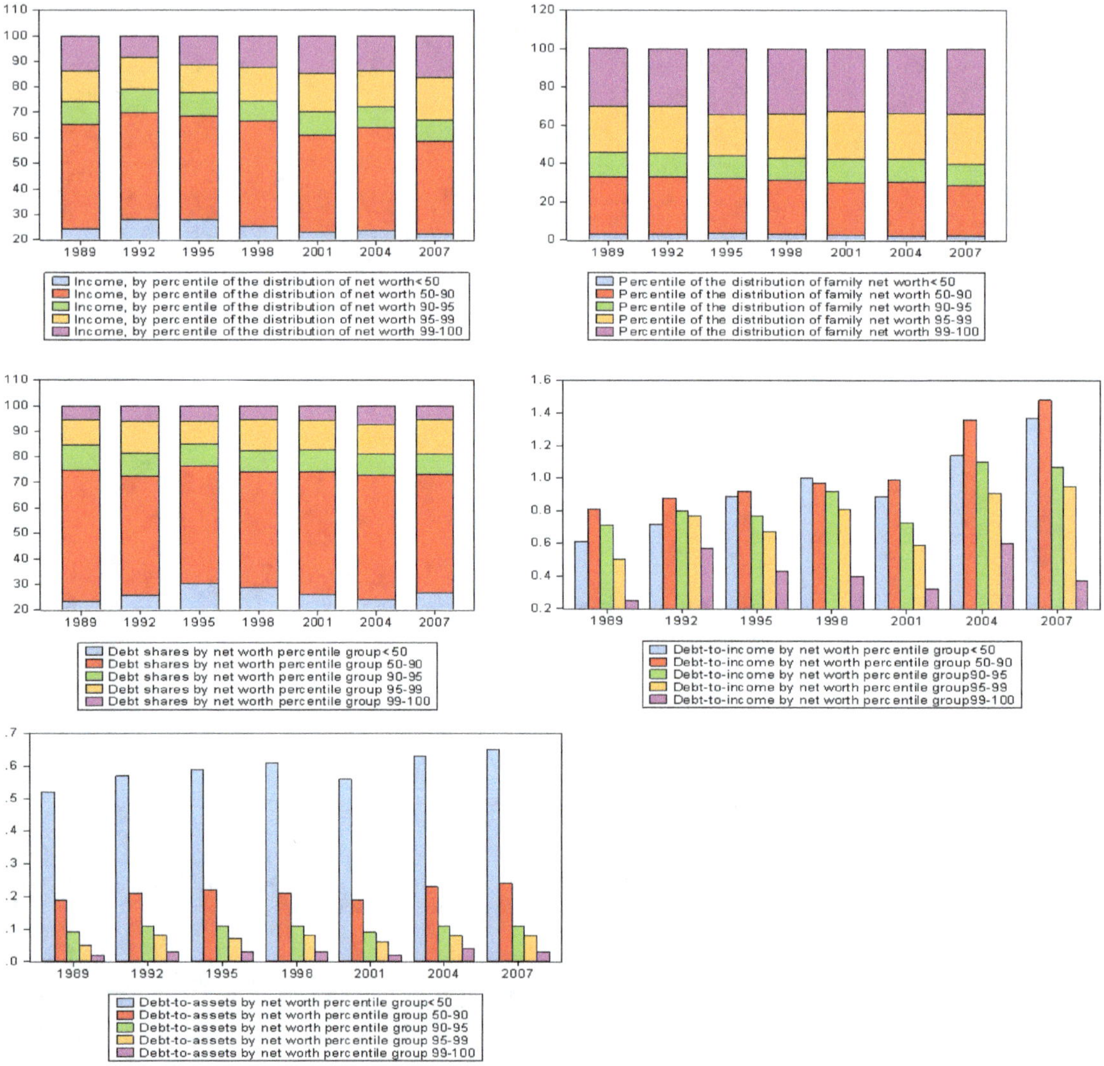

Source: Kennickell (2009), author's calculations

Annex 7. Labour income share in Gross Domestic Product (GDP) - adjusted

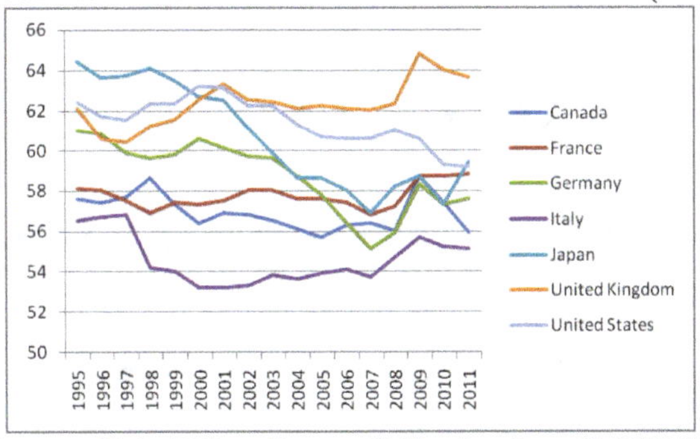

Source: Global Wage Report Collection from ILOSTAT

Annex 8. Residential property prices and Household debt/GDI

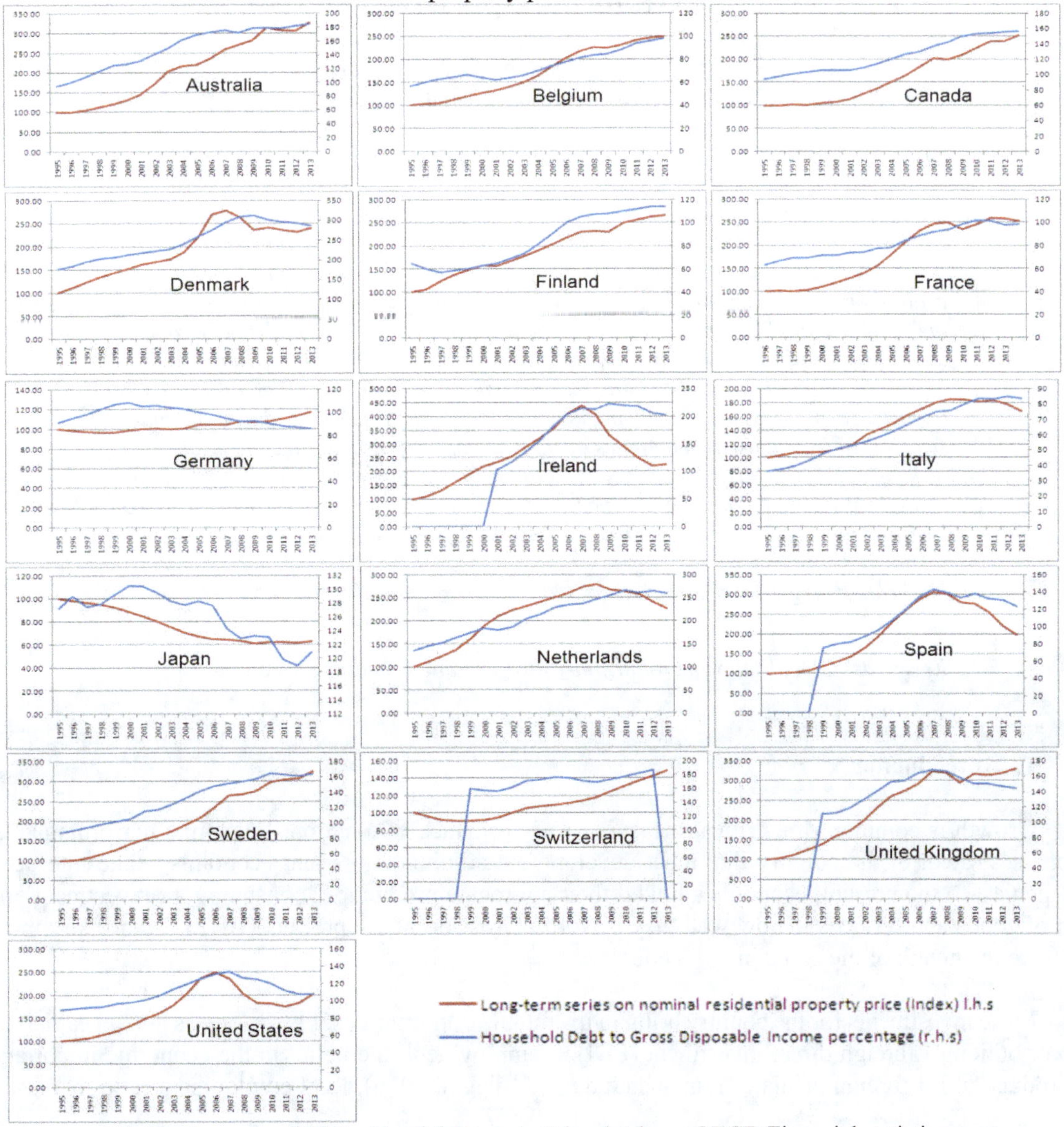

National sources, BIS Residential Property Price database, OECD Financial statistics

8

Truth Behind Economic Performance, Natural Resources and Attracting Foreign Direct Investment

Arthelo P. PALMA*

University of Southeastern Philippines, Philippines
Davao Central College, Philippines

Using a preliminary investigation and analysis on the latest data on GDP (Gross Domestic Product) performance, GOI (Global Opportunity Index), Vulnerability Score, Readiness Score, and the number of resources of economic importance, exploratory or preliminary SEM (structural equation modelling) was prompted on the recent available data of the 131 countries (n=131). The model was robust, addressing concerns about multivariate assumptions and other measures on the goodness of fit. It was found that the number of natural resources of economic importance plays a large role in the GDP performance. Thus, the preliminary symptom of Dutch disease continues to manifest for as long as each country aims for development, with their resources as ultimate enticing factors for foreign direct investment (FDI). In addition, economic growth is so far observed to be associated with the vulnerability of the country to climate change. Finally, economic growth was found to be linked to the negative impacts argued by the dependency theory. Implication on governance was discussed.

***Keywords**: GDP, FDI, vulnerability measure, readiness measure, resources*

1. Introduction

Growth is common or a critical measure of performance of a nation. Economic performance is one area of the growth of the country that most development administrators and economists take into account. From the past to the present, economies linked their aggregate production, consumption, investment and net export of goods and services to how well they perform. Gross domestic product (GDP) is a primary indicator to measure the health of the economy of a country.

More investments for the country bring in irrefutable opportunities. For as long as human capital favors the contribution of foreign direct investment (FDI) to employment, the belief in the economic importance of skill production for foreign affiliates remains (Jude and Silaghi, 2016). Real employment ratio increases real

*Corresponding Author:
Arthelo P. Palma, Davao Central College, Philippines and University of Southeastern Philippines, Davao City, Philippines

GDP in the short run (Ozturk and Acaravci, 2010), as far as human capital could associate itself with regional economic growth (Fleisher, Li and Zhao, 2008). From the standpoint of neoclassical economics, China through inward FDI achieved economic gains in the form of capital formation, export expansion, technology transfer, and transformation of the economic structures and institutions (Lo, Hong and Li, 2016). Looking at it through the lens of neoclassical economics, it makes sense why nations, particularly the developing ones, should attract FDI. It was found that FDI has a greater impact on the welfare of poor countries than the wealthier ones in Africa (Gohou and Soumare, 2012). In Southeast Asia, those with competitive advantages are said to continue to attract investors due to observed pluses of FDI (Diaconu, 2014).

Nevertheless, there are some noted drawbacks in attracting FDI. First, reducing employment protection rules increases FDI, which is a common theme of critique of globalization (Olney, 2013). Although such might not be the general scenario for all, for example in the European case, investment is not affected by stringent employment protection laws, but rather by the level of access to financial markets (Calcagnini, Ferrando and Giombini, 2014). Next, investment at some point may require loss of some natural resources that for instance, are of high value to the rural poor population that could only be counterweighed by gaining employment and opportunities (Baumgartner, Braun, Abebaw, and Muller, 2015). In addition, as far as the environmental issue is concerned, a study asserts that a foreign involvement in ownership in China can haggle with environmental levies associated with pollution control, which gives birth to concession just to attract FDI primarily in developing provinces (Chen, Maung, Shi and Wilson, 2014).

On the other hand, natural resources simply boast economic growth. As noted, since 2002, mineral-rich regions in Russia are richer than other regions (Alexeev and Chernyavskiy, 2015). In Norwegian economy, about 20 percent of the annual GDP per capita increase is associated with endowment of petroleum resources such as oil, natural gas, natural gas liquids, and condensate (Mideksa, 2013). In addition, investing resource revenues in public capital may promote economic growth (Melina, Yang and Zanna, 2016).

However, economic development has substantial drawback when economies forget to produce back-up industries as other industries flourish due to the discovery of natural resources that are of high economic importance. Such is found in the case of the Dutch disease, coined by the *The Economist* in 1977 (Ebrahim-zadeh, 2003; The Economist, 1977). Therefore, managing income from the expected natural resource revenue eliminates the possibility of Dutch disease explained in literature. The productivity and supply responses of spending could be the roots to ensure the realization of the benefits linked to mineral revenue (Go, Robinson and Thierfelder, 2016). Furthermore, countries with greater economic freedom may not be that vulnerable to the negative growth effects of resource rents (Farhadi, Islam and Moslehi, 2015).

The UN Millennium Project (2006) asserts that investing in development is key to a nation's success which makes millennium development (MDG) goals matter. The project simply sees MDGs as the fulcrum of international development policy, that help advance the means to a productive life, and they are critical for global security. The bottom line of this is development. The UN Millennium Project reported that there are four reasons for shortfalls in achieving the goals and could be summarized as governance failures, poverty traps, pockets of poverty and areas of specific policy neglect.

While measuring the growth of the economy is still substantial through the lens of neo-classical growth theory, there are other important things that can be considered in understanding the country's economic growth as implied in the report of the UN Millennium Project. The efficiency of labor, for instance, allows the economy to ignite economic growth for as long as a faster labor-force growth exists. In context, if the government does what it needs to do, investment will pour in, giving everyone a good opportunity to employment, and eventually economic growth, as implied into the GDP. By citing the point of the UN Millennium Project, it is clear that governance issue plays a significant role in making natural resources and attracting foreign direct investment productive, at some point. A good governance allows the achievement of MDGs to their full level, especially in the midst of acquiring sustainability and innovation to national development in the new era, by which the environment, the source of raw materials for development, is at stake. This requires that the economy of the country should be linked to other economies, creating a significant justification of the dependency theory (Ahiakpor, 1985; Ferraro, 2008).

For this paper, to address the combined theoretical foundation of dependency theory and the one stated by the UN Millennium Project about governance failure, it is of importance to measure how these natural resources and the country's ability to attract foreign investment (GOI) affect the GDP performance. Much to understanding this relationship is the interest of conducting an initial exploration of the mediation effect of vulnerability score and readiness score. These are specific measures of level of governance potential of a country, but not specifically addressed in the literature yet as far as their linkage to economic performance is concerned. On the other hand, GOI itself could mark as potential measure of governance level, but it will be brought to a higher stage if mediated by other factors in line with governance, is a particular point of view that this paper investigates. Furthermore, even if the number of natural resources could truly improve a country's investment potential, thus its GDP's performance, government intervention through its level of governance is still a remarkable issue, so as to eliminate the preliminary economic symptom of Dutch disease.

2. Research Methodology

2.1 Data and Sample Size

The study is an initial exploration of testing the associated relationship of variables in the preliminary discussion. Thus, the latest available data for GOI, number of natural resources of economic value per country, readiness score, vulnerability score and GDP in 2016 were gathered for data analysis and exploration purposes.

There were data sets coming from 131 countries, of which at least 80 percent of these nations are developing countries. In the following sections, information of the data sets and variables of the study is presented.

ND-Gain Index Organization (2016) measures every country's vulnerability score and readiness score, which are all specific measures of government's level of performance in governing the negative impact of climate change and ability to leverage investments and convert them to adaptation actions.

Milken Institute (2016), on the other hand, reveals the Global Opportunity Index (GOI) for each country, which measures economic fundamental factors, ease of doing business, quality of regulations and rule of law. Singapore was on top in 2015. The GOI simply measures the ability of a country to attract foreign investments, which clearly is a primary task of the government, prior to economic growth.

Central Intelligence Agency (2016) has a list of every nation's primary natural resources with substantial value to the economy. Furthermore, the organization published the latest data for GDP (PPP, OER, Per Capita) of each country.

2.2 Internal Validity

To ensure that the study measures what it actually wants to measure, everything placed in the model has a corresponding connection to the established theory or proposed theory. For this paper, the fundamental point of view relies on the dependency theory and the UN Millennium Project, with particular reference as to how or why economies fail to achieve their goals. One fundamental concern is failure governance. Each variable in the model, at some point, measures or has link to matters concerning governance.

Furthermore, multivariate assumptions and analysis for the data were preliminary considered and addressed prior to data analysis, to ensure that the model measures the existing reality concerning growth and development of the nation. One particular area of concern is the fitness of the model. The other is on how the entire process of analysis adheres to the assumption stated within the context of the modelling technique of multivariate analysis using Structural Equation Modelling (SEM).

2.3 External Validity (Generalizability)

As part of the limitation of the study, secondary data together with their availability was a primary concern. In fact, around 40 percent of the countries with missing data and were eliminated from the analysis, as a result. However, the data sets include economic and governance information of the remaining 131 countries, which is enough number to suffice the scope or coverage of this study to ensure generalizability.

2.4 Reliability

The study is based on descriptive correlation, aiming to achieve a mathematical model with a high level of credibility. Using SEM technique, as an objective tool, similar results would be obtained if the same data sets and sample size will be generated by other parties aiming to redo the model.

2.5 Objectivity

The sources of data for this study are the ND-Gain Index Organization, Milken Institute and Central Intelligence Agency. These are organizations linked independently to prime academic institutions, and publish their data online for transparency purposes. Thus, they have no other choice but to measure objectively. That alone allows a slim chance for objectivity to be influenced so much by human skill and perception, which in reality might be a common drawback for using survey questionnaires, at some point.

3. Results and Discussion

3.1 Model Fit (Model 1 versus Model 2)

After the preliminary multivariate analysis or testing multivariate assumptions and data screening, there were two models obtained. First, the proposed model and the second one, the modified model for which an excellent model fit was observed.

Under the first model, probability of getting the Chi Square statistics value of 45.04 is .00, but in the second model, probability is .63 for the Chi Square .229. This alone speaks that there is something interesting and conclusive to look forward to in the second model. When the minimum value of discrepancy (CMIN) is divided by the degrees of freedom, with its restriction principle to ensure unbiased probability, a ratio less than 2 signifies good model fit. Again, with CMIN/df = 22.52, the first model is far behind the second model and with CMIN/df = .229 at a probability value of .63. The goodness of fit index (GFI) reveals that the first model might be good with GFI = .895, but the second model is far better with GFI = .999. A value of 1 for GFI indicates perfect fit. The comparative fit index (CFI) shows that the first model might also be a good model with CFI = .916. However, the second model is quite more than good because of CFI = 1, revealing a perfect model fit. The normed fit index (NFI) is another measure of the model's fitness. A value of 1 or closer to it marks a very good fit. Although NFI = .914 for the first model, the NFI for the second model is 1, which remarkably holds the latter model better than the former. The Tucker-Lewis coefficient suggests that a value closer to 1 is a very good fit. Based on this coefficient, the second model is a good fit because TLI = 1.015, compared to the first model with TLI = .582.

The root mean square error (RMSEA) is a measure for the close fit of the model. A RMSEA of .05 or less indicates a close fit of the model in relation to the degrees of freedom. For the first model, the probability of getting a sample as large as RMSEA = .407 is .00. On the other hand, for the second model, the probability of getting a sample as low as RMSEA = .00 is .68.

Overall, with all the statistical tests to measure the goodness-of-fit of the model reveal that the second model is the best model to use for the estimate.

***Table 1**. Model Fit*

Model	$X^{2\,(df)}$	CMIN/df	GFI	CFI	NFI	TLI	RMSEA
1	45.04 (Sig = .00) (df = 2)	22.52 (Sig = .00)	0.895	0.916	0.914	0.582	0.407 (Sig = .00)
2	0.229 (Sig = .63) (df = 1)	0.229 (Sig = .63)	0.999	1.000	1.000	1.015	0.000 (Sig = .68)

By covariating the error estimate for readiness score and vulnerability score, the second model became a better model. Illustration of this covariation is shown in Figure 2.

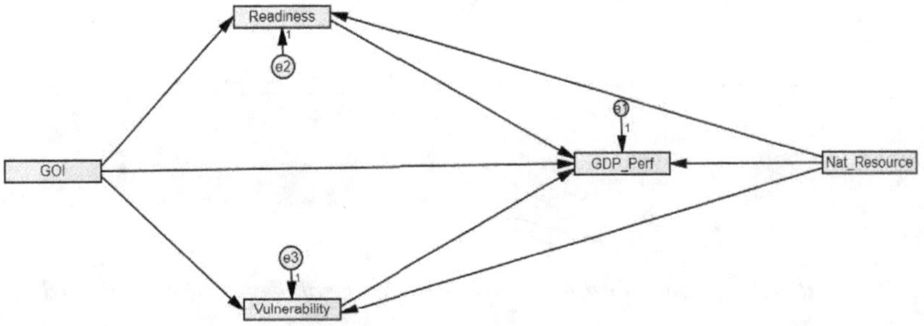

***Figure 1**. The proposed model (Model 1) based on the theoretical framework*

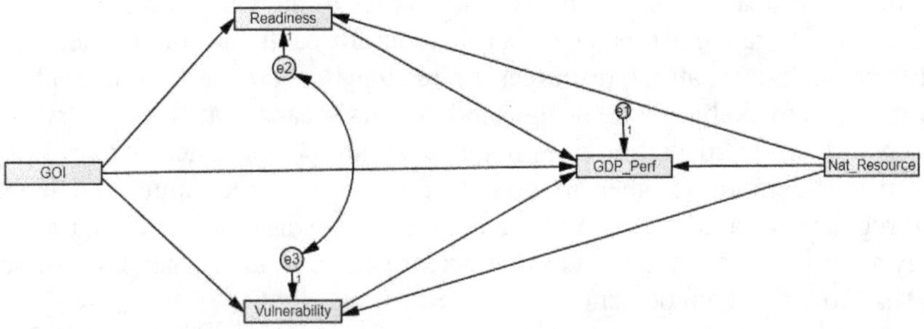

***Figure 2**. Modified model (Model 2) based on modification indices result*

Based on Figure 3, when GOI goes up by 1 standard deviation, the readiness score goes up by .91, standard deviation and vulnerability score goes down by .76. This means that when the ability of the nation to attract foreign investment increases, its ability to leverage investments and convert them to adaption increases as well. On the other hand, there is a downfall for this high dexterity to attracting foreign investment because this can lower the country's exposure, sensitivity and ability to adapt to the negative impact of climate change. This must be the case, knowing that according to UN Millennium Project (2006) only the advanced countries have the ability to initiate good governance as far as sustainability issue is concerned. Considering that most of the countries included in the model are developing countries, they have the tendency to attract foreign investment as priority, but along the way, they might not be quite able at establishing the sustainability issue yet, just as the Philippines for instance, as a sample case. This sounds like an interesting viewpoint, as far as the dependency theory is concerned, knowing that economies of developed countries are enriched at the expense of those developing ones.

When GOI goes up by 1 standard deviation, GDP performance goes up by .37. GDP performance goes up by .13 standard deviation when the number of natural resources of economic values goes up by 1 standard deviation. When the number of natural resources of economic importance goes up by 1 standard deviation, readiness score moves up by .04 standard deviation, and vulnerability score goes down by -.13 deviation. Based on the previous discussion as anchored on the fundamental and implication of dependency theory, the number of natural resources of economic importance, especially among developing countries, reduces the government's level of performance in governing the negative impact of climate change. On the other side, it improves the country's ability to leverage investments and convert them to adaptation actions. However, the small value of readiness score from the path of GDP performance to readiness score implies that the number of natural resources of economic importance creates a low capacity of the country to leverage investments and convert them to adaptation actions. For this reason, it may sound that the Dutch disease generally exists in the world, especially among economies that are largely dependent on natural resources for their economic growth. This also implies that since there was only a relatively small value in the path from natural resources to the readiness score, its statistical significance is of primary importance. It is of interest to find if there is something going on to this this path.

Meanwhile, GOI and natural resources explain 83 percent of the variance of readiness score and 59 percent of the vulnerability score. The combined predictors of GDP performance explain 62 percent of its variance. This means that the predictors are quite good requirements to predict the readiness score, vulnerability score and GDP performance of the country.

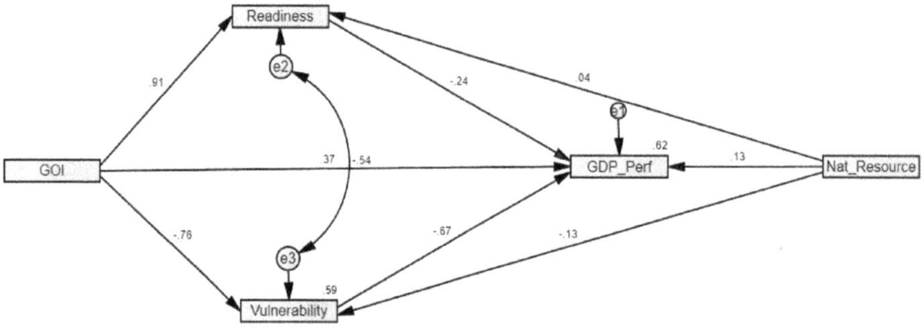

Figure 3. *Standardized estimate of relationship between variables based on standard deviations.*

3.2 Regression Weight

Considering that there was a promising association between the variables, it is of primarily concern to consider their statistical significance with the probability values of their coefficients.

Revealed in Table 2 are the estimates of coefficients for each variable in their respective paths, and the p-values. Only the path for natural resources to readiness score and from readiness score to GDP performance have not-so-remarkable paths in the model. This means that the country's ability to leverage investments and convert them to adaptation does not affect GDP performance. After all, in reality, investors will only invest upon consideration of other important factors such as economic fundamentals, ease of doing business, quality of regulations, and rule of law. This observation was empirically supported by the model as GOI has statistically significant contribution to GDP performance. In fact, when GOI increases by 1 percent, GDP performance rises to around 5.6 percent.

On the other hand, the idea that the number of natural resources affects the ability of the country to leverage investments and convert them to adaptation actions cannot be statistically established. The probability value for this path is more than α =.05, which is .307. This cannot be established, as there are many countries good at governance level in managing their resources so as not to be affected by Dutch disease, and there are also others, especially developing countries or relatively developed ones, which are affected by policies of developed or investing countries, as in line with the evidence of some studies (Calcagnini, Ferrando and Giombini, 2014; Baumgartner, Braun, Abebaw and Muller, 2015; Chen, Maung, Shi and Wilson, 2014).

When GOI increases by 1 percent, an increase of 10.9 percent in the readiness score is statistically significant. This should be the case, knowing that attracting foreign direct investment is associated with ensuring leveraging investments and converting them to adaptation actions. However, as countries attract investment, their vulnerability to some environmental concerns decreases by 5.9 percent when their capacity to attract FDI increases by 1 percent. Much of the implication of this was explained earlier.

Another important evidence to prove the peril of dependency is marked by the decrease of 5.8 percent in the vulnerability score when the natural resources increase by 1 percent. This suggests that economies may overlook governing the negative impact of climate change, while exhausting their natural resources for economic advantage. In reality, and based on dependency theory, advanced economies take advantage of the resources of poor countries to their advantage.

When the number of natural resources of economic importance increases by 1 percent, readiness score increases by 2.6 percent, which is another indication of attracting FDI, which could suggest that Dutch disease may be hampered at some point, even if it exists generally in the economy of the world.

A 1 percent increase in GOI, natural resources and vulnerability leads to 5.6 percent increase, 11.9 percent increase, and 133 percent decrease in GDP performance, respectively. This only proves that the three predictors are significant components of the model that could predict the economic performance of the country. It sounds that attracting foreign direct investment and the number of natural resources are the factors that provide positive contribution to the economic performance. The percentage of natural resources guarantee GDP performance, which is another remarkable proof that the danger for Dutch disease generally is eminent in the world economy, as far as the literature is concerned (Melina, Yang and Zanna, 2016). Furthermore, it sounds that when countries are quite focused or serious about addressing climate change or sensitive to its issues, the GDP performance will be largely and badly affected. Thus, this proves the finding according to which there is a need to somehow sacrifice policies associated with environmental concerns just to ensure economic growth as an exchange (Chen, Maung, Shi and Wilson, 2014).

***Table 2**. Regression weights of the independent variables*

Path			Estimate	S.E.	C.R.	P
Readiness	<---	GOI	.109	.004	25.480	***
Vulnerability	<---	GOI	-.059	.004	-13.601	***
Vulnerability	<---	Nat_Resource	-.058	.026	-2.256	.024
Readiness	<---	Nat_Resource	.026	.026	1.022	.307
GDP_Perf	<---	GOI	.056	.020	2.806	.005
GDP_Perf	<---	Nat_Resource	.119	.050	2.387	.017
GDP_Perf	<---	Readiness	-.308	.198	-1.554	.120
GDP_Perf	<---	Vulnerability	-1.327	.198	-6.710	***

Note: ***The regression weight for predictors in the prediction of dependent variable is significantly different from zero at the 0.001 level (two-tailed).

3.3 Mediation Influence

For the other important part of the study, testing the mediation effect is the main concern of the study.

It shows on Table 3 that readiness score and vulnerability score have only partial mediation effect to the GDP performance. This means that GOI and percentage of natural resources of economic importance have direct effect to GDP performance.

For this reason, the symptom for Dutch disease is evident because of the vulnerability of GDP performance to increase when the percentage of natural resources of economic importance increases. In fact, as stated in Table 2, a 1 percent increase in natural resources adds up around 11.90 percent to the country's GDP performance.

However, GOI, as governance indicator, is another fundamental component to increase GDP performance. Thus, the results of the study add up something to the idea of Ebrahim-zadeh (2003) and *The Economist* (1977). Governance is necessary, and diversification of industries is part of it, due to the consideration of economic fundamentals, ease of doing business, quality of regulations and rule of law.

***Table 3**. The mediation influence of vulnerability score and readiness score to GDP performance*

Relationship	Direct without mediator	Direct with mediator	Remarks
GOI>Read>GDP	0.659 (0.001)	0.408 (0.001)	Partial mediation
GOI>Vul>GDP	0.659 (0.001)	0.415 (0.001)	Partial mediation
Nat>Vul>GDP	0.207 (0.001)	0.131 (0.017)	Partial mediation
Nat>Read>GDP	0.207 (0.001	0.132 (0.015)	Partial mediation

4. Conclusion and Recommendation

The number of natural resources of economic importance plays an important role in the GDP performance. Thus, the preliminary symptom of Dutch disease continuous to manifest for as long as each country aims for development, with their resources as ultimate enticing factors for foreign investment. In addition, economic growth is so far observed to be associated with the vulnerability of the country to climate change. Finally, economic growth was found to be linked to the negative impacts argued by the dependency theory.

The findings imply that in order to ensure growth and not to hamper potential development, good governance is a fundamental factor to directly and partially affect and mediate future economic growth. Good governance is a great contributing factor to the country's GDP performance.

However, future researches are necessary to expand and support the above stated claim to stand conclusive considering that the data in this study consisted of information from developing and developed economies combined in this comprehensive analysis. An insight about focused investigations to be initiated separately for developing and developed countries is a remarkable area of interest for future inquiries.

References

Ahiakpor, J.C.W., 1985. The Success and Failure of Dependency Theory: The Experience of Ghana. *International Organization,* 39(3), pp.535-552. doi:10.1017/S0020818300019172

Alexeev, M. and Chernyavskiy, A., 2015. Taxation of natural resources and economic growth in Russia's regions. *Economic Systems,* 39(2), pp.317-338.

Apostology, M., 2013. Governance and Enterprise Restructuring in Southeast Europe: Gross Domestic Product and Foreign Direct Investments. *Corporate Governance: The International Journal of Business in Society,* 13(4), pp.431-438. doi:10.1108/CG-01-2011-0002.

Baumgartner, P., von Braun, J., Abebaw, D. and Muller, M., 2015. Impacts of Large-scale Lang Investments on Income, Prices, and Employment: Empirical Analysis in Ethiopia. *World Development,* 72, pp.175-190.

Calcagnini, G., Ferrando, A. and Giombini, G., 2014. Does Employment Protection Legislation Affect Firm Investment? The European Case. *Economic Modelling,* 36, pp.658-665. doi:10.1016/j.econmod.2013.06.036.

Central Intelligence Agency, 2016. *The World Factbook: Field listing-Natural Resources.* [online] Available at: https://www.cia.gov/library/publications/the-world-factbook/fields/2111.html [Accessed on 7 February 2016].

Central Intelligence Agency, 2016. *The World Factbook: Country Comparison-GDP (Purchasing Power Parity).* [online] Available at: https://www.cia.gov/library/publications/the-world-factbook/rankorder/2001rank.html [Accessed on 7 February 2016].

Central Intelligence Agency, 2016. *The World Factbook: Country Comparison-GDP Per Capita (PPP).* [online] Available at: https://www.cia.gov/library/publications/the-world-factbook/rankorder/2004rank.html [Accessed on 7 February 2016].

Central Intelligence Agency, 2016. *The World Factbook: Field Listing-GDP (Official Exchange Rate).* [online] Available at: https://www.cia.gov/library/publications/the-world-factbook/rankorder/2004rank.html [Accessed on 7 February 2016].

Chen, O., Maung, M., Shi, Y. and Wilson, C., 2014. Foreign Direct Investment Concessions and Environmental Levies in China. *International Review of Financial Analysis,* 36, pp.241-250. doi:10.1016/j.irfa.2013.12.002.

Diaconu, L., 2014. The Foreign Direct Investments in South-East Asia in the Context of the 1997 and 2007 Crises, *Procedia – Social and Behavioral Sciences,* 109, pp.160-164. doi:10.1016/j.sbspro.2013.12.437.

Ebrahim-zadeh, C., 2003. Back to Basics – Dutch Disease: Too much wealth managed unwisely. *Finance and Development*, A quarterly magazine of the IMF. IMF.

Farhadi, M., Islam, Md. R. and Moslehi, S., 2015. Economic Freedom and Productivity Growth in Resource-rich Economies. *World Development,* 72, pp.109-126.

Ferraro, V., 2008. Dependency Theory: An Introduction. *The Development Economics Reader,* ed. Giorgio Secondi. London: Routledge: pp.58-64.

Fleisher, B., Li, Haizheng, and Zhao, M.Q., 2008. Human Capital, Economic Growth, and Regional Inequality in China. *Econstor.* Available at: http://www.econstor.eu/bitstream/10419/34981/1/573334765.pdf [Accessed on 3 January 2016].

Go, D. S., Robinson, S., and Thierfelder, K., 2016. Natural resource revenue, spending strategies and economic growth in Niger. *Economic Modelling,* 52, pp.564-574.

Gohou, G., and Soumare, I., 2012. Does Foreign Direct Investment Reduce Poverty in Africa and are there Regional Differences? *World Development,* 40(1), pp.75-95. doi:10.1016/j.worlddev.2011.05.014.

Jude, C., and Silaghi, M.I.P., 2016. Employment effect of foreign direct investment: New evidence from Central and Eastern European countries. *International Economics,* 145, pp.32-49. doi:10.1016/j.inteco.2015.02.003

Lo, D., Hong, F., and Li, G., 2016. Assessing the Role of Inward Foreign Direct Investment in Chinese Economic Development, 1990-2007: Towards a Synthesis of Alternative Views. *Structural Change and Economic Dynamics,* 37, pp.107-120. doi:10.1016/j.strueco.2016.01.004.

Melina, G., Yang, S.C.S., and Zanna, L. F., 2016. Debt sustainability, public investment, and natural resources in developing countries: The DIGNAR model. *Economic Modelling,* 52, pp.630-649.

Mideksa, T. K., 2013. The economic impact of natural resources. *Journal of Environmental Economics and Management,* 65(2), pp.277-289.

Milken Institute, 2016. *Global Opportunity Index Ranking.* [online] Available at: http://www.globalopportunityindex.org/opportunity.taf?page=rankings [Accessed on 30 January 2016].

Millennium Development Project, 2006. *Investing Development: A Practical Plan to Achieve the Millennium Development Goals.* London: United Nations Development Program.

Notre Dame Global Adaptation Index (ND-GAIN) Organization, 2016. *Country Rankings.* [online] Available at: http://index.gain.org/ranking [Accessed on 30 January 2016].

Olney, W. W., 2013. A race to the bottom? Employment protection and foreign direct investment. *Journal of International Economics,* 91(2), pp.191-203. doi: 10.1016/j.jinteco.2013.08.003

Olson, M. Jr., Sarna, N., and Swamy, A. V., 2000. Governance and Growth: A Simple Hypothesis Explaining Cross-Country Differences in Productivity Growth. *Public Choice,* 102(3), pp.341-364.

Ozturk, I., and Acaravc, A., 2010. CO2 emissions, energy consumption and economic growth in Turkey. *Renewable and Sustainable Energy Reviews*, 14, pp.3220 – 3225. doi: 10.1016/j.rser.2010.07.005.

Smith, R. J., Muir, R. D. J., Walpole, M. J., Balmford, A., and Williams, N. L., 2003. Governance and the loss of biodiversity. *Nature,* 426, pp.67-70. doi:10.1038/nature02025.

The Economist, 1977. The Dutch Disease (November 26, 1977). *The Economist*, pp.82-83.

Appendices

Annex 1. *Curve estimate between the GDP performance and percentage of nation's resources of economic value*

R Square	F	P-value	Curve estimate
.098	***24.114***	***.000***	***Linear***
-	-	-	Logarithmic
-	-	-	Inverse
.103	12.693	.000	Quadratic
.104	8.553	.000	Cubic
.090	21.944	.000	Compound
-	-	-	Power
-	-	-	S
.090	21.944	.000	Growth
.090	21.944	.000	Exponential
.090	21.944	.000	Logistic

Annex 2. *Curve estimate between the GDP performance and country's global opportunity index (GOI)*

R Square	F	P-value	Curve estimate
.447	***106.765***	***.000***	***Linear***
.440	103.710	.000	Logarithmic

.414	93.193	.000	Inverse
.447	53.037	.000	Quadratic
.449	35.314	.000	Cubic
.406	90.235	.000	Compound
.413	92.950	.000	Power
.403	88.962	.000	S
.406	90.235	.000	Growth
.406	90.235	.000	Exponential
.406	90.235	.000	Logistic

Annex 3. *Curve estimate between the GDP performance and country's vulnerability score*

R Square	F	P-value	Curve estimate
.593	**259.142**	**.000**	**Linear**
.598	264.805	.000	Logarithmic
.575	240.504	.000	Inverse
.600	132.760	.000	Quadratic
.601	88.293	.000	Cubic
.539	208.494	.000	Compound
.519	191.924	.000	Power
.474	160.506	.000	S
.539	208.494	.000	Growth
.539	208.494	.000	Exponential
.539	208.494	.000	Logistic

Annex 4. *Curve estimate between the GDP performance and country's readiness score*

R Square	F	P-value	Curve estimate
.390	***114.861***	***.000***	***Linear***
.363	102.624	.000	Logarithmic
.307	79.854	.000	Inverse
.392	57.595	.000	Quadratic
.395	38.658	.000	Cubic
.280	70.171	.000	Compound
.270	66.651	.000	Power
.239	56.528	.000	S
.280	70.171	.000	Growth
.280	70.171	.000	Exponential
.280	70.171	.000	Logistic

Annex 5. *Relationship between the independent variables*

Test	Pearson r coefficient	P-value	Decision on Ho
Vulnerability vs Readiness	-.824**	.000	Reject
Vulnerability vs GOI	-.762**	.000	Reject
Readiness vs GOI	.908**	.000	Reject

Note: **Correlation is significant at the 0.01 level (2-tailed)

Annex 6. *Collinearity statistics among the independent variables*

Variables	Tolerance	VIF
Vulnerability score	.296	3.383
Readiness	.124	8.057
Global Opportunity Index	.176	5.679

Annex 7. *Collinearity statistics after dropping "readiness" from the independent variables*

Variables	Tolerance	VIF
Vulnerability score	.419	2.385
Global Opportunity Index	.419	2.385

Annex 8. *Scatterplot between the standardized residual and the standardized predicted value*

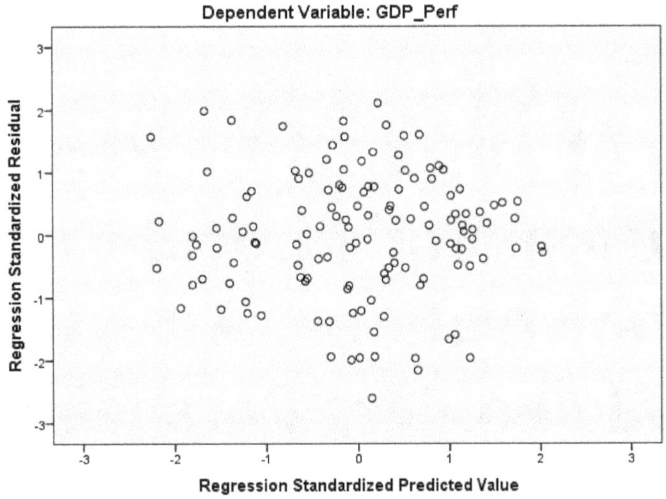

Annex 9. Normal P-P plot of regression standardize residual

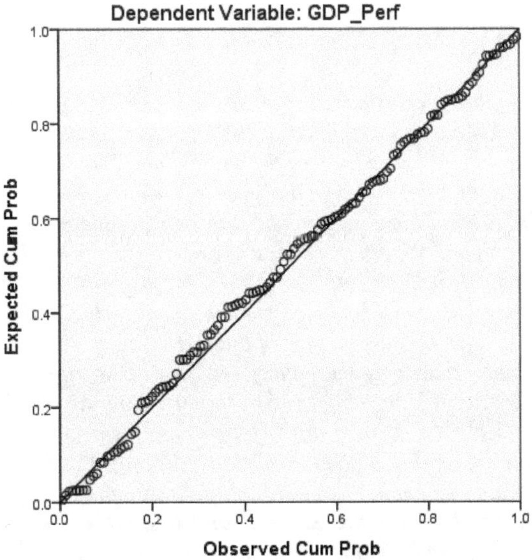

Annex 10. Normality statistics of unstandardized and standardized residuals

Descriptive	Unstandardized Residuals	Standardized Residuals
Skewness	-.230	-.230
Standard error (Skewness)	.210	.210
z value Skewness	***-1.09***	***-1.09***
Kurtosis	-.220	-.220
Standard error (Kurtosis)	.417	.417
z value Kurtosis	***-.53***	***-.53***

Annex 11. The Skewness and Kurtosis of distribution for each variable

Variables	Skewness	Standard Error	Skw z-value	Kurtosis	Standard Error	Kurt z-value
GDP_Perf	-0.233	0.210	1.11	-0.985	0.420	-2.34
Resources	0.683	0.212	3.22	-0.077	0.420	-0.18
GOI	0.141	0.210	0.67	-0.828	0.420	-1.97
Vulnerability	0.402	0.212	1.89	-0.608	0.420	-1.45
Readiness	0.504	0.210	2.40	-0.693	0.420	-1.65

9

Analysis of Sustainable Performance in Romania's Local Public Administrations: An External Stakeholders Perspective

Diana MIHAIU*

Lucian Blaga University of Sibiu, Romania

Building a sustainable performance system at the level of the local public administrations must have as starting point the local public administration's (LPA) mission and must go down to the level of the individual. This system must follow the external performance that it delivers to the citizens, the outcomes generated, but also the internal performance which suggests how to achieve the external performance. We propose in this regard the simultaneous use of the Balanced Scorecard tool for managing the internal performance and the Public Service Value Model for measuring the external performance measurement which derives from the organization's mission. In the second part of the work we analyzed comparatively the external performance created by the county capitals of Romania in the year 2013 using the Public Service Value Model (PSVM). Based on this analysis, the county capitals of Romania can be divided in the following categories: high performance organizations (value driven), budget conscious organizations, low performance organizations (sleeping giants) and quality conscious organizations. This classification is useful both for the external and internal stakeholders because it shows the efficiency of public money spending and the areas in which the LPA is performing well, and also the ones that need to be improved.

Keywords: *performance, Balanced Scorecard, sustainable performance*

1. Introduction

The objective of this article is to analyze the sustainable performance of the local public administrations from Romania, from the external stakeholders' perspective. The sustainable performance of the public organizations is given by the value created by the organization for the concerned stakeholders by its

* Corresponding Author:
Diana Mihaiu, Faculty of Economic Studies, Lucian Blaga University of Sibiu, Romania

mission. I propose in this regard the simultaneous use of the Balanced Scorecard tool for managing the internal performance and the Public Service Value Model for measuring the external performance measurement which derives from the organization's mission. The combined use of the Balanced Scorecard tool with the Public Service Value Model creates a solid basis in order to implement a coherent system for obtaining the sustainable performance at the local administrations level.

2. Literature Review

The concept of performance has no universally accepted definition. But in the public sector where the central objective has a side that is preponderant social namely meeting the collective needs of the society in order to ensure the economic and social balance, defining the performance concept involves ensuring the economics (economy), the efficiency and the effectiveness of a project, program, action together with ensuring fairness (equity), the environmental requirements (environment) and the integrity (integrity) (Schacter, 2002).

Implementing a system for obtaining, monitoring and measuring the performance is a necessary requirement for a public administration which is financed from taxpayer's money and which must satisfy public needs. But any attempt of targeting performance turns into a double-edged blade: it can generate favorable aspects or it may be counterproductive and generate false performance, speculative behavioral (De Bruijn, 2007). That is why thinking and implementing such a system requires accountability, rigor, analytical and anticipatory capacity of those involved.

Most systems for measuring performance in the public sector are designed and imposed by external political factors to the organization which do not fully know the specifics of the activities, which generates opposition from employees. Another essential condition for the success of the initiative is that the system must be known and accepted by everyone involved in the activity of the organization: managers, employees. Otherwise, employees will focus only on facile activities that yield results measured by the key performance indicators (tunnel vision), thereby determining a degradation of their professional activity and cases of performance paradoxes (Van Thiel and Leeuw, 2002, pp.269). Also, the public organization manager must realize that only fulfilling certain financial performance indicators can harm the quality of the public services; if he does not realize this aspect then he will not invest much effort in implementing an integrated system for obtaining and measuring performance (Modell, 2004). This means that it should exist at the individual level the honest feeling of being truly performing. If this mentality does not exist then any system can be speculated to some degree by employees, managers who do not share the organization's mission and who serve other interests. Bernard Marr emphasizes that the starting point in implementing a successful performance management is to create a "performance driven culture" (Marr, 2008, p.241).

The objectives targeted by the management and measuring the performance in the public sector have changed over time as the ideologies of the state interventionism have changed and depending on the phase of the economic cycle faced by the economy. In periods when the budget deficits are high and the objective of the state is to reduce them, the performance can mean public spending cuts and increased efficiency on the account of costs. This model is known as the "input-output model for measuring performance." This model is considered insufficient for analyzing the fulfillment achievement degree of the mission by the public organization because it must analyze the impact of the inputs and outputs over the society. Therefore, the model must be supplemented with the analysis of the outcome-flows generated by the public program / organization with the social environmental impact, meaning the model must enable the analysis of achieving a sustainable performance (Bovaird and Loffler, 2009, pp.152-154). Nan Chai also states that a system of management and performance measurement in the public sector should allow an integrated approach to social, economic and environmental objectives in a balanced way (Chai, 2009, p.4). Christopher Pollitt and Geert Bouckaert developed a logic model for measuring the performance in the public sector having as starting point the socio-economic situation, the needs of the citizens, and finally the analysis of the outcome-flows generated and their impact on the stakeholders concerned (Pollitt and Geert, 2011, p.16).

The sustainable performance of the public organizations is given by the value created by the organization for the concerned stakeholders by its mission. Public value does not just represent obtaining outcome or cost reductions, it means achieving both aspects in a balanced manner and understanding the strategic compromises that need to be addressed in this process (Cole and Parston, 2006, p.63-64; Mihaiu, 2014).

Building a system for obtaining sustainable performance at the level of the public organizations must take have as starting point the local public administration's (LPA) mission and must go down to the level of the individual. It must follow the external performance that it delivers to the citizens, the outcomes generated, and also the method of obtaining the respective performance.

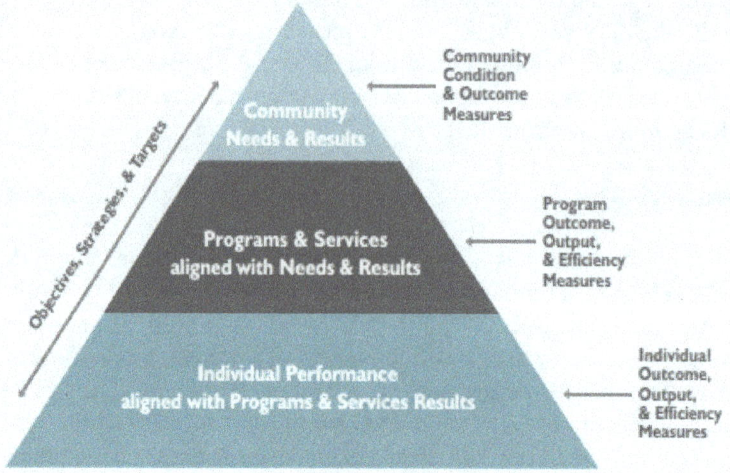

Figure 1. *Performance Management System: alining mission - objectives – measurement at all levels*
Source: National Performance Management Advisory Commssion, 2010, pp.13.

I propose in this regard the simultaneous use of the Balanced Scorecard tool for managing the internal performance and the Public Service Value Model for measuring the external performance derived from the organization's mission.

Balanced Scorecard is a performance management tool developed by *Kaplan and Norton* that seeks the transformation of the organization's vision and strategy into objectives, measures, results. It was originally built to serve the performance management in private companies and in this respect it combines the financial indicators with those of non-financial nature divided into four strategic perspectives for the company's success (Kaplan and Norton, 1996):

- *Financial perspective*, in which it is aimed at the financial performance of the organisation. It is the perspective in which is found the main objective of the private organizations, namely the profit.
- *Customer perspective*, which aims to customer satisfaction.
- *Internal process perspective*, which aims at the quality of the products / services, improving the processes.
- *Learning and growth perspective*, which follow the intangible assets of the organization: employees and knowhow; improving the employees' knowledge in order to provide increased support for the internal process.

Balanced Scorecard was also adapted to the public sector specific that has other goals than the private sector. In the public sector, the focus and the main objective is the organization's mission. From the mission derive the wanted outcomes and must be delivered to the stakeholders. Therefore in the public sector the focus is set on the mission and on the impact over the citizens opposed to the private sector where the focus is set on the financial perspective.

The four perspectives of the Balanced Scorecard defined by *Kladogeni Anthoula, Hatzigeorgiou Alexandros* for a LPA are:

- *stakeholders perspectives*, in which it is examined how the LPA has fulfilled its mission, the local community development.
- *financial resources management perspective*, in which is analyzed the procurement and allocation of the financial resources in the purpose of achieving the mission.
- *internal process perspective*, in which it is analyzed the operational efficiency; adapting and implementing processes that would comply with legal regulations that would respond to the internal and external informational needs; implementing control systems and internal audit, etc.
- *training perspective*, in which it is analyzed the efficiency of the employees; the human resource contributing directly to improving the internal processes.

Each perspective must be associated with a strategic goal, a set of objectives and some performance indicators related to each objective that would enable the measurement of the achievement degree of the defined objectives (Kladogeni and Hatzigeorgiou, 2001, p.71). The schematic representation of the Balanced Scorecard for a LPA in general, is shown in the figure below.

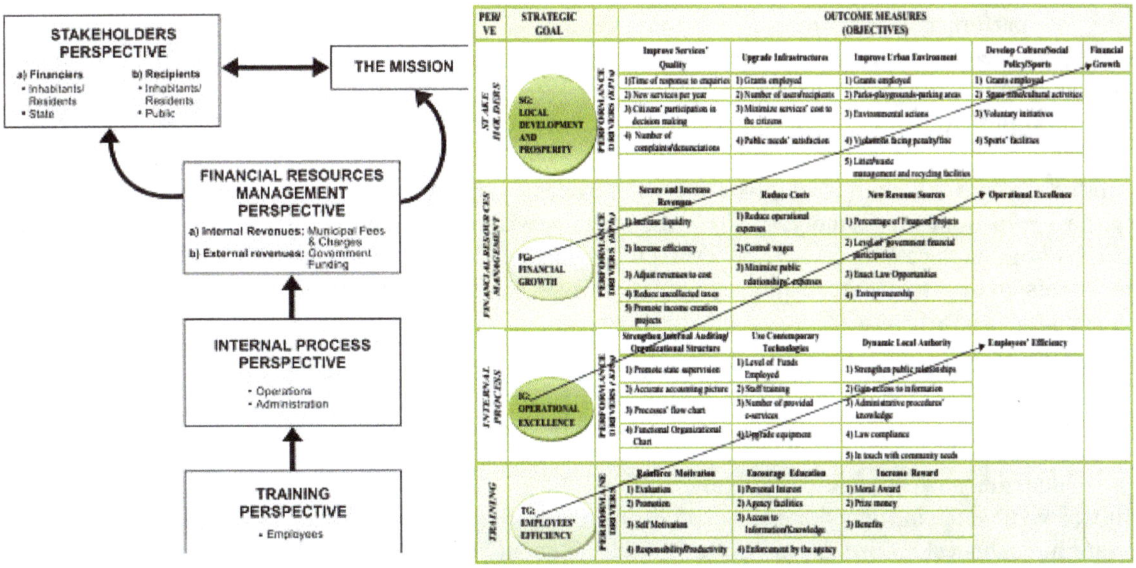

Figure 2. Balanced Scorecard perspectives for a Local Public Authority
Source: Kladogeni and Hatzigeorgiou, 2011

Public Service Value Model is a model developed by Martin Cole and Greg Parston which introduces a new way to measure performance in the public sector, namely through public value created by the public organization analyzed. The public value delivered by the organization is given by the size of the outcomes generated by it and is derived from the organization's mission, coupled with the financial effort involved, according to the following formula (Cole and Parston, 2006):

Public Service Value = Outcomes/Cost Effectiveness

This model facilitates the definition and measurement of the value created by the public organizations for external stakeholders (e.g. citizens, in general). In other words, this model allows measuring the degree of fulfillment of the mission of the organization among citizens.

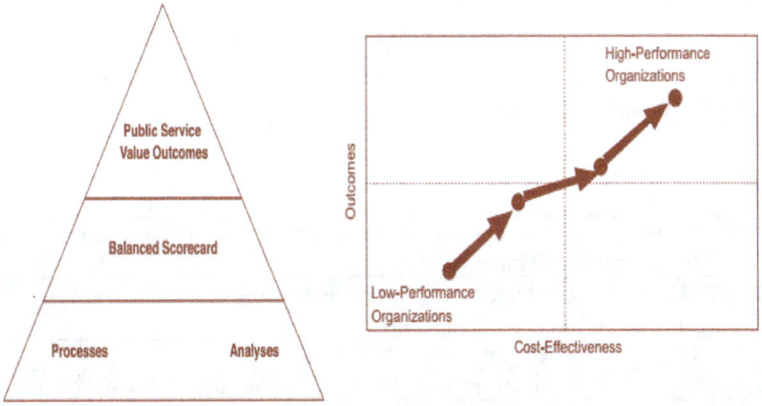

Figure 3. Balanced Scorecard and Public Service Value Model for obtaining a sustainable performance and its measurement in the public sector
Source: Cole and Parston, 2006

The combined use of the Balanced Scorecard tool with the Public Service Value Model creates solid basis in order to implement a coherent system for obtaining the sustainable performance at the level of the local administrations. Balanced Scorecard accompanied by strategy maps offers logical support for organizing and transforming the mission and APL strategy in objectives, actions and internal performance measurement indicators. Also one should not lose sight of how the LPA contributes to the local community development, meaning its external performance. In order to analyze this, the Public Service Value Model is particularly useful because it balances the outcomes obtained with the LPA financial effort involved and divides the LPA into four categories:

- high performance organizations (value driven);
- budget conscious organizations;

- low performance organizations (sleeping giants);
- quality conscious organizations.

3. Methodology

In this part we will analyze comparatively the external performance created by the county residence municipalities from Romania in the year 2013, the latest year for which there are present reporting. In this endeavor the Public Service Value Model (PSVM) will be used. The outcomes indicators were divided into 7 categories corresponding to the areas of responsibility of the LPA analyzed:

- culture and art;
- workforce;
- preparing the territory;
- population;
- health;
- education and economic development.

It was wanted the introduction of two additional categories: safety and public order, social protection, but there are no statistical reporting units for all of the 39 county residence municipalities analyzed, and for this reason they have been abolished. The primary data were taken from the National Statistics Institute reports in Romania (Romania's National Informational System, 2016, available online at http://edemos.insse.ro).

The Cost Effectiveness Indicator is calculated reporting the outcomes score at the LPA public expenditure/inhabitant score. The outcomes score is obtained by summing up the standardized values of all the indicators related to the 7 categories, weighted equally because we consider all the responsibility fields of the LPA have equal importance. The LPA public expenditure score is given by the standardized value through minimum amount of the public expenditure for each LPA.

Considering that the indicators are expressed in different measurement units it was imposed standardization of data, a process that was done after the following process:

- For indicators that optimize through maximum, the standardized value (Sv) of the indicator was calculated as follows:

$$Sv = (v_i - v_{min}) / (v_{max} - v_{min})$$

- For indicators that optimize through minimum, the standardized value (Sv) of the indicator was calculated as follows:

$$Sv = (v_{max} - v_i) / (v_{max} - v_{min})$$

The outcomes indicators used in the analysis of the external performance through the public value created by the county residence municipalities in Romania are presented in the table below:

Table 1. *The outcomes indicators of county residence municipalities of Romania*

Area of Responsibility	Outcomes indicator
1. Culture and art (C&A)	I1: Providing local communities with publicly available volumes (volumes existent in the library per 1,000 inhabitants)
	I2: The degree of access of the population to mass media and culture information (libraries / 100,000 inhabitants)
	I3: Active readers per 1,000 inhabitants
	I4: Visitors in museums and public collections per 1,000 inhabitants
2. Workforce (W)	I5: The number of registered unemployments whith an averages for 100 employees
3. The territory equipment (TE)	I6: The capacity of the drinking water production facilities per capita (cubic meters per day / capita)
	I7: Existing living space at the end of the year which lies on average per inhabitant (square meters / inhabitant)
	I8: The amount of drinking water supplied to the domestic consumers which would be appropriate per capita
	I9: The amount of natural gas distributed for households who returns in average per capita
	I10: The share of modernized urban roads
	I11: The share of urban roads with water network
	I12: The level of housing renewal
	I13: The level of housing renewal
	I14: The share of urban roads with gas network
	I15: The area covered with green areas per capita

4. Population (P)	I16: Infant mortality rate (deaths under 1 year / 1000 live births)
	I17: The natural growth rate of population (inhabitants)
5. Health (H)	I18: Population access to family medicine (medical offices per 1,000 inhabitants)
	I19: Population access to dental care / dental medicine services (dental offices per 1,000 inhabitants)
	I20: Population access to a doctor (excluding dentist) (residents / doctor)
	I21: Population access to the dentist (inhabitants / dentist)
6. Education (E)	I22: Number of pupils in primary and secondary education (including special education) which averages to a teacher (students / teacher)
	I23: Gross enrollment rate of children in pre-school (%)
	I24: Workload of a teacher (preschool / kindergarten)
	I25: Share of population of age 10 years and older without education (0 years of schooling) (%)
7. Economic development (ED)	I26: The number of tourist arrivals which corresponds in average per resident
	I27: The density of enterprises (companies / 1,000 inhabitants)
	I28: The density of non-commerce enterprises (enterprises / 1000 inhabitants)
	I29: The average number of employees in active non-agricultural enterprises per 1,000 inhabitants
	I30: The average number of employees in active non-commerce enterprises per 1,000 inhabitants
	I31: The entrepreneurial Capacity (‰)
	I32: The natural growth rate of enterprises (‰)

Source: Indicators proposed by the National Institute of Statistics for evaluating the public local administration's performance

4. Results and Discussions

Based on indicators in the table above the score of the outcomes was calculated that allows visualizing the results and the impact achieved by LPA following its actions. The results of this outcome score are presented in table and graph below.

Table 2. *The standardized level of the outcomes score obtained by LPA in Romania, in 2013*

Municipality	Total Outcome Scores	C&A Score	W Score	TE Score	P Score	H Score	E Score	ED Score
Oradea	17.20	0.64	0.92	3.88	1.40	3.33	2.64	4.39
Bistrita	15.70	0.89	0.64	5.00	1.62	1.80	2.74	3.01
Cluj-Napoca	23.36	2.76	0.93	6.26	1.24	3.14	3.44	5.59
Baia Mare	13.71	1.44	0.71	3.59	1.50	1.85	1.69	2.93
Satu Mare	15.61	1.12	1.00	4.38	1.37	2.17	2.75	2.82
Zalau	13.51	1.33	0.56	2.81	1.63	2.08	2.95	2.16
Alba Iulia	15.47	1.73	0.25	3.31	1.35	2.60	2.89	3.34
Brasov	15.58	0.55	0.88	3.95	1.40	2.19	2.60	4.02
Sfintu Gheorghe	12.97	1.25	0.66	4.10	1.40	1.41	2.53	1.61
Miercurea Ciuc	17.01	2.06	0.55	4.40	1.36	2.08	3.26	3.29
Tirgu Mures	18.99	1.54	0.83	5.38	1.56	2.96	3.45	3.26
Sibiu	21.16	2.78	0.92	4.98	1.33	3.27	3.20	4.69
Bacau	13.40	1.19	0.62	4.34	1.29	2.01	2.37	1.58
Botosani	9.96	1.56	0.35	3.26	1.43	1.36	1.12	0.88
Iasi	14.86	1.57	0.90	3.12	1.92	2.94	1.81	2.59
Piatra Neamt	12.92	1.17	0.37	4.07	1.01	2.53	2.03	1.75
Suceava	15.37	1.70	0.61	4.20	1.64	2.85	2.33	2.03
Vaslui	10.24	1.12	0.42	3.28	1.79	0.69	2.56	0.37
Braila	7.85	0.39	0.46	3.48	0.21	0.72	1.57	1.03
Buzau	10.99	0.88	0.70	3.76	1.16	1.57	1.27	1.66
Galati	9.74	0.71	0.61	2.76	0.96	0.91	2.19	1.61
Tulcea	10.12	1.29	0.59	2.30	0.91	1.04	1.92	2.05
Focsani	9.75	0.87	0.75	2.55	1.23	1.51	1.73	1.12
Pitesti	15.93	1.23	0.59	4.43	1.73	2.57	2.56	2.82
Calarasi	7.73	1.02	0.46	3.52	0.99	0.14	0.65	0.95

Tirgoviste	13.86	2.17	0.60	3.95	1.61	1.98	1.87	1.69
Slobozia	12.35	0.96	0.42	4.78	1.26	1.32	1.88	1.73
Ploiesti	11.90	0.76	0.70	4.17	1.11	1.62	1.02	2.52
Alexandria	13.09	1.66	0.12	5.01	1.57	1.61	1.73	1.39
Bucuresti	17.79	1.22	0.82	4.60	0.78	2.61	1.48	6.28
Craiova	14.06	0.79	0.45	5.24	1.41	2.47	1.66	2.04
Tirgu Jiu	13.68	1.05	0.00	4.63	1.62	1.87	1.85	2.65
Drobeta-Turnu Severin	9.37	0.89	0.02	2.89	1.23	1.89	2.08	0.37
Slatina	13.60	0.98	0.62	4.68	1.62	1.30	2.03	2.38
Ramnicu Valcea	13.37	1.16	0.14	3.69	1.31	2.08	2.43	2.56
Arad	18.35	1.45	0.88	5.21	1.05	3.20	2.40	4.16
Resita	11.69	1.38	0.44	4.40	0.58	1.92	2.03	0.95
Deva	15.39	1.32	0.61	5.10	0.69	2.33	1.70	3.64
Timisoara	18.65	1.32	0.96	4.53	1.37	3.68	2.45	4.33

Source: Author's own calculations

It can be seen that the first place is occupied by Cluj Napoca with the highest level of the outcomes achieved. On the second position is Sibiu, the sixth position is Bucharest, and the last positions are occupied by Botosani, Focsani, Galati, Drobeta Turnu Severin, Calarasi and Braila.

In terms of the outcomes obtained in the *culture field* the first position is occupied by Sibiu, followed by Cluj Napoca, Miercurea Ciuc, Targoviste, Alba Iulia and Suceava. The worst results in the culture field were recorded in the municipalities of Craiova, Ploiesti, Galati, Oradea, Brasov, Braila.

In the field of *employment*, good results were obtained by Satu Mare, Timisoara, Cluj Napoca, Sibiu, Oradea, the municipality Iasi recording the lowest number of unemployed. The municipality most disadvantaged in terms of unemployment is Targu Jiu.

In terms of *territory equipment*, the top municipalities are: Cluj Napoca, Tirgu Mures, Craiova, Arad, Deva.

Regarding the *population*, the results obtained in the infant mortality and natural growth domains are favorable for cities: Iasi, Vaslui, Pitesti, Suceava and less favorable in Resita, Braila.

In the *health field*, the first position is occupied by the Timişoara municipality and the last position by Calarasi city. Bucharest municipality ranks 10.

In the *education field*, favorable results were obtained in Targu Mures, Cluj Napoca, Miercurea Ciuc, Sibiu. Calarasi city is on the last position.

From the perspective of the *economic development*, the first three places are occupied by Bucharest, Cluj Napoca and Sibiu. However, problems in this regard are recorded by Drobeta Turnu Severin and Vaslui.

Further, in the graph and table below, we analyze the results obtained by the LPA analyzed in comparison with the financial effort undertaken. The financial effort we considered as a local public expenditure per capita, taking into account the standardized value of the indicator.

Table 3. *Public Service Value Score of Romanian local public administration*

County residence	Total outcomes score	Public expenditure/inhabitant score	Cost Effectiveness Score
Cluj-Napoca	23.36	0.86	30.31
Sibiu	21.16	0.75	22.74
Tirgu Mures	18.99	0.71	19.27
Timisoara	18.65	0.59	16.03
Arad	18.35	0.67	17.66
Bucuresti	17.79	0.63	16.17
Oradea	17.20	0.35	11.36
Miercurea Ciuc	17.01	0.46	12.53
Pitesti	15.93	0.80	18.71
Bistrita	15.70	0.67	15.05
Satu Mare	15.61	0.94	24.14
Brasov	15.58	0.78	17.46
Alba Iulia	15.47	0.77	17.26
Deva	15.39	0.71	15.50
Suceava	15.37	0.64	14.16
Iasi	14.86	0.58	12.58
Craiova	14.06	0.68	13.56

Tirgoviste	13.86	0.00	6.86
Baia Mare	13.71	0.69	13.51
Tirgu Jiu	13.68	0.72	14.08
Slatina	13.60	0.42	9.66
Zalau	13.51	0.79	15.56
Bacau	13.40	0.86	17.28
Ramnicu Valcea	13.37	0.82	16.21
Alexandria	13.09	0.89	18.15
Sfintu Gheorghe	12.97	0.71	13.21
Piatra Neamt	12.92	0.84	16.04
Slobozia	12.35	0.83	15.32
Ploiesti	11.90	0.88	16.16
Resita	11.69	0.98	19.59
Buzau	10.99	0.90	15.37
Vaslui	10.24	0.07	5.34
Botosani	9.96	1.00	17.59
Focsani	9.75	0.09	5.16
Galati	9.74	0.73	10.18
Drobeta-Turnu Severin	9.37	0.94	14.41
Braila	7.85	0.96	12.60
Calarasi	7.73	0.93	11.58

Source: Author's calculations based on the centralized primary data from the portal http://edemos.insse.ro and from each LPA websites; *Country residence Tulcea was not taken into consideration due to lack of information

We can notice that in terms of the outcomes generated, the Cluj Napoca municipality is ranked first, followed by Sibiu. The Bucharest municipality ranks in position no. 6. The last positions in the ranking are occupied by Botosani, Focsani, Galati, Drobeta Turnu Severin, Calarasi and Braila.

Analyzing the financial effort of LPA, materialized in public expenditure per capita it is observed that the municipalities that have spent the most money per capita are: Targoviste, Vaslui, and Focsani. At the other end the municipalities with the lowest allocated expenditure per capita are Botosani, Resita, Braila, Satu Mare and Drobeta Turnu Severin.

From these comparisons it is observed that municipalities Targoviste, Vaslui and Focsani received the highest per capita financial allocations, but failed to create results and impact at the level of the financial effort, they being on the last position in the ranking of outcomes generated.

In the chart below are represented the county capital cities of Romania according to the public value created based on the Public Sector Value Model methodology.

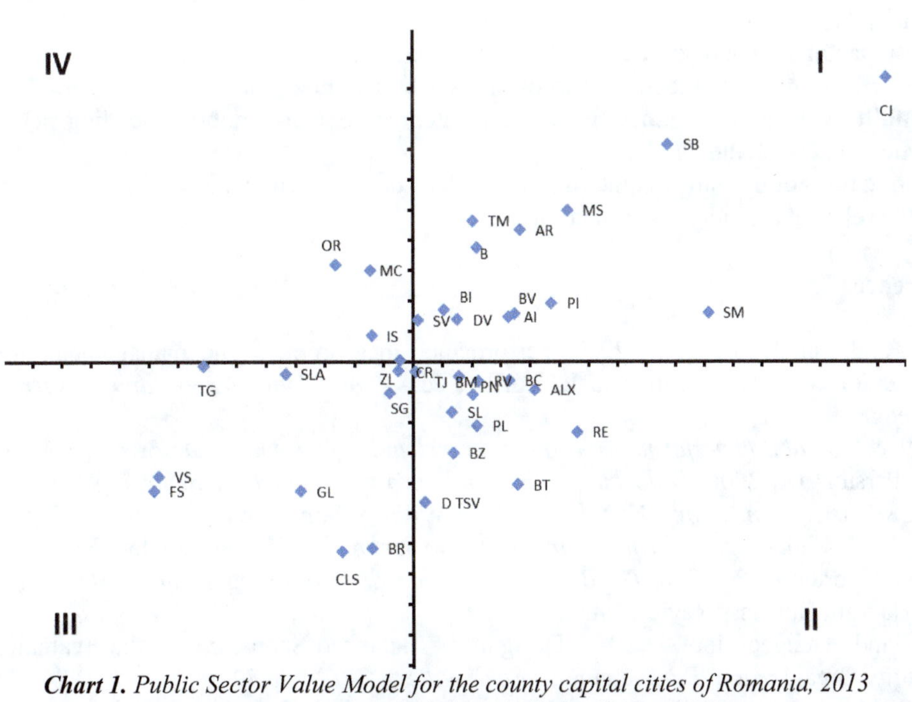

Chart 1. *Public Sector Value Model for the county capital cities of Romania, 2013*
Source: Author's calculations (Mihaiu, 2015, p.135)

From the chart above, realized based on the Public Sector Value Model methodology, we can see that there are outlined four categories of municipalities in terms of sustainable performance, namely:

- ***Quadrant I - municipalities highly performing***, are those who record a sustainable performance because they obtained high levels of the outcomes delivered to society under the conditions of ensuring cost efficiency: Cluj (the best performing municipality), Sibiu, Targu Mures, Arad, Timisoara, Bucharest, Bistrita Brasov, Deva, Suceava, Alba Iulia, Pitesti, Satu Mare;
- ***Quadrant II – buget concerned municipalities***, are those municipalities that have a high cost efficiency, but which is obtained based on some low public spending per capita, not on generating high results. The level of the outcome-flows generated is below average. From this category we mention: Craiova, Targu Jiu, Baia Mare, Piatra Neamt, forthe Bacau, Alexandria, Slobozia, Ploiesti Resita, Buzau, Botosani, Drobeta Turnu Severin;
- ***Quadrant III - non-performing municipalities*** are those municipalities that record outcomes below average and a low cost efficiency, meaning they consume high public funds without generating value with those financial allocations. This category includes: Calarasi, Braila, Galati, Focsani, Vaslui, St. George, Zalau, Slatina, Târgovişte;
- ***Quadrant IV - municipalities focused on high quality***, are those municipalities that record really high costs, but above average and the outcome-generated are above average. Or in other words, are the municipalities who score above average but with high financial efforts. This category includes: Oradea, Miercurea Ciuc, Iasi.

5. Conclusions

In this paper I proposed using the Balanced Scorecard and Public Service Value Model for obtaining a sustainable performance and its measurement in the public sector. The combined use of the Balanced Scorecard tool with the Public Service Value Model creates solid basis in order to implement a coherent system for obtaining the sustainable performance at the level of the local administrations.

Implementation of the Balanced Scorecard as a tool for internal performance involves obtaining support and acceptance from employees. Use of the Public Service Value Model provides a tool for measuring public value created by LPA for external stakeholders. This model was applied to municipalities of Romania. Based on the results, the cities analyzed can be divided into the following categories:

- **high performance organizations (value driven)**, those that registered above average outcomes and public expenditure per capita below average: Satu Mare, Bistrita,Pitesti, Bucuresti, Arad, Timisoara, Targu Mures, Sibiu and Cluj Napoca.
- **budget conscious organizations**, those that have public spending / capita below average but lower outcomes: Baia Mare, Targu Jiu, Zalau, Bacau, Ramnicu Valcea, Alexandria, Sfantu Gheorghe, Piatra Neamt, Slobozia, etc.
- **low performance organizations (sleeping giants)**, public expenditure per capita above average and below average outcomes: Targoviste, Vaslui and Focsani.
- **quality conscious organizations**, high outcomes but also public spending per capita higher: Miercurea Ciuc and Oradea.

The limitations of this study come from the lack of data needed to study all Romania's county capital cities and all the relevant areas for a LPA activity.

References

Bouckaert, G. and Van Dooren, W., 2009. Performance measurement and management in public sector organizations. In: T. Bovaird and E. Loffler, ed., *Public Management and Governance*. London: Routledge.

Chai, N., 2009. *Sustainability performance evaluation system in government*. Dordrecht: Springer.

Cole, M. and Parston, G., 2006. *Unlocking Public Value: a new model for achieving high performance in public service organizations,* New Jersey: John Wiley & Sons, Inc.

De Bruijn H., 2007. *Managing Performance in the Public Sector*, 2nd Edition. London: Routledge

Kaplan, R.S. and Norton, D.P., 1996. *The Balanced Scorecard: Translating Strategy into Action.* Cambridge, MA: Harvard Business Review Press.

Kladogeni, A. and Hatzigeorgiou A., 2011. Designing a Balanced Scorecard for the Evaluation of a Local Authority Organization. *European Research Studies, XIV(2),* pp.72-77.

Marr, B., 2008. *Managing and delivering performance*. Oxford, UK: Butterworth-Heinemann.

Mihaiu, D.M., 2014. Sustainable Performance Of Public Organizations: Shaping A Coherent System For Implementing And Measuring The Concept. *Studies In Business And Economics, 9(3),* pp.50-56.

Mihaiu, D., 2015. *Proiectarea unui sistem coerent de asigurare a performantei sustenabile in sectorul public.* Sibiu: Lucian Blaga University Publishing House.

Modell, S., 2004, Performance Measurement Myths in the Public Sector: a Research Note. *Financial Accountability and Management, 20(1),* pp. 39–55.

National Performance Management Advisory Commission, 2010. *A Performance Management Framework for State and Local Government: From Measurement and Reporting to Management and Improving* [online] Available at: http://www.gfoa.org/sites/default/files/APerformanceManagementFramework.pdf [Accessed on 12 July 2016].

Pollitt C. and Bouckaert, G., 2011. *Public Management Reform. A Comparative Analysis - New Public Management, Governance and the Neo-Weberian State*, 3rd Edition. Oxford: Oxford University Press.

Romania's National Informational System, 2016. Sistemul Informational National Statistic [online] Available at: edemos.insse.ro/portal [Accessed on 12 May 2016].

Schacter, M., 2002. *Practitioner's Guide to Measuring the Performance of Public Programs*. Ottawa: Institute on Governance.

Van Thiel, S. and Leeuw, F.L., 2002. The Performance Paradox in the Public Sector. *Public Performance and Management Review,* 25(3), pp.267-281.

10

Problems Encountered during the Transition to Market Economy in Azerbaijan and Solution Attempts

Elchin SULEYMANOV* and Sabuhi YUSIFOV

Qafqaz University, Azerbaijan

After re-gaining its independence on 18 October 1991, the Republic of Azerbaijan started the transformation to the market-based economy and the integration into the world economy. The country's oil and natural gas reserves have been considered the main source for financing a range of government programs for reforms. On the one hand, these reserves had to be used effectively; on the other hand, there was a huge demand for foreign investment for extraction. To this end, Azerbaijan has signed "Contract of the Century" in 1994. Although Azerbaijan has wide oil and natural gas reserves, it has faced a number of difficulties in its transition path. This study analyzes these problems and reforms for solving them. One of the types of the problems related to the economic structure of the former Soviet Union: disruption of the economic ties between the republics resulted in a decline of production, high levels of unemployment and prices and consequently led to an economic recession in all of the republics. Another set of problems related to the lack of sufficient institutional bases to transform to the market economy. Moreover, internal conflicts between the political parties and groups for having authority as well as political chaos in the republic can be considered other serious problems during the transition period. Furthermore, Karabakh war and occupation of 20 percent of the Azerbaijani territory by the Armenian military forces had made the situation extremely complicated. Despite all of these extremes, Azerbaijan transformed to the market-based economy decidedly and even became one of the fast growing countries of the world. Even in 2013, with the GDP growth rate of 5.6 percent, Azerbaijan was a leader among growing economies. In parallel with this significant economic development, there is still a need for some socio-economic and institutional reforms in order to get a well-functioning market-based economy in Azerbaijan.

Keywords: *Azerbaijan, oil, natural gas, informal sector, energy resources, oil dependency*

1. Introduction

After gaining its independence in October 18th 1991, Azerbaijan has launched a number of reforms to liberalize it economy and realize a smooth transition to market economy. Energy sources such as gas and oil

* Corresponding Author:
Elchin Suleymanov, PhD, Qafqaz University, Faculty of Economics and Administration, Khirdalan city, 120 Hasan Aliyev, Baku, Absheron, Azerbaijan Republic

reserves in the basin of the Caspian Sea were main instruments in achieving these targets. Efficient utilization of these resources served as a pre-requisite of these economic goals and hopefully Azerbaijan succeeded in that. Since 1994 Azerbaijan has started extensive utilization of Caspian energy resource in the name of economic, political and social reformation, regeneration, growth and independence. A number of resolutions were made and followed by contracts and project in order to produce oil and gas and distribute them to world market (Suleymanov, Zeynalov, 2012).

Other newly independent countries of Caspian Basin, Kazakhstan and Turkmenistan also decided to join this process by utilizing their potential oil and gas reserves with the aim of relieving pains of transition period to reorganize their economies. However existing pipelines had limited capacity and did not coincide with new routes to open up to world energy market, because they were set according to Soviet Union's planned economy and covered only Union countries. The Caspian Basin gained great importance immediately after the collapse of the Soviet Union and proclamation of independence by Caspian coastal countries, namely Azerbaijan, Kazakhstan, and Turkmenistan. Improvements in energy resources of the Caspian Sea became unavoidable for these countries for reformation of their economies and achieving integration to world economy. Especially foreign capital know-how were needed for efficient development of resources. In this regard, the three states invited western firms to invest in the region for energy resource extraction.

Azerbaijan and Kazakhstan wanted their oil revenues to flow rapidly to the country (Aras, 2005). Being one of the world's most important energy sources oil has a wider field of use among other sources of energy. Expenditure on extraction, transportation and distribution of oil comprise the biggest cost of petroleum products.

For all three countries methods for efficient use of the oil proceeds need to be worked out in order to improve non-oil sector and decrease the risk of oil dependency in the long run and achieve rapid economic growth and improvements in real income (Aras, 2008). Some of the macroeconomic indicators of Azerbaijan are displayed in the following table.

Table 1. *Main socio-economic indicators of Azerbaijan*

	2000	2008	2009	2010	2011	2012
Population (thousand)	8 114.3	8 897.0	8 997.6	9 111.1	9 235.1	9 305.1
Total GDP (mln $)	5 272.8	48 852.5	44 297.0	52909.3	63402.5	64412.5
GDP per capita ($)	662.9	5 603.3	5 018.2	5922.0	7 003.4	7 206.5
Total investments (mln AZN)	967.8	9 944.2	7 724.9	9905.7	12 776.4	13 776.4
Foreign trade volume (mln $)	2 917.3	54 926.0	20 824.5	27960.8	36 326.9	36 529.9
Exports (mln $)	1 745.2	47 756.0	14 701.4	21360.2	26 570.9	26 670.9
Imports (mln $)	1 172.1	7 170.0	6 123.1	6600.6	9 756.0	9 859.0
State budget revenues (mln AZN)	714.6	10 762.7	10 325.9	11403.0	15 700.7	17 360.7
State budget expenditure (mln AZN)	764	10 774.2	10503.9	11765.9	15 396.2	17 796.2
Personal income (mln AZN)	4 047.3	20 735.4	22 601.1	25607.0	30 633.5	32 633.5
Average salary (mln AZN)	44.3	274.4	298	331.5	363.1	423.1
Official unemployment	43 739	44 481	41 100	38 966	38 330	37 330
CPI (ratio to the previous year)	101.8	120.8	101.5	105.7	107.9	105.9
PPI (ratio to the previous year)	129.7	123.4	80.6	130.5	133.5	123.5

Source: NSCAR 2012

Caspian energy resources were a motivating factor and in parallel with foreign capital inflows to the country, the international financial institutions started to increase the loans to Azerbaijan. During the last period of the Soviet Union, the process of collapse caused chaotic environment where distribution of state property and social wealth for the purposes of personal use was commonplace. From this point, bribery and corruption inherited from the Soviet system of society was one of the severe social issues. Although some changes were made to deal with bribery and corruption, the presence was long felt widely in the general population. Formal and informal tax systems were available. The regulatory role of informal taxes, was greater than the regulatory role of official duties (Aras, 2005).

2. Overview of the Azerbaijani Economy after Independence

After the declaration of independence most important resources in reforms to achieve Azerbaijan's economic objectives for the realization of the country's free market economy were energy resources of the Caspian Sea consisting of oil and natural gas reserves.

Since 1994, Azerbaijan's oil and natural gas agreements with international companies and common activities in this context have allowed the re-establishment of the infrastructure in the energy sector through the introduction of advanced modern technologies. For example, with the realization of the first stage of the "Contract of the Century" not only the problem of the evaluation of oil stocks in Azeri - Chirag - Guneshli project was successfully solved, but also Azerbaijan has benefited from new oil production technology in the Caspian Sea and modern systems for export of Caspian oil to world markets were established. Azerbaijan has gained the opportunity to renew its energy industry assets by transferring the modern technology to the country and has established institutions and organizations that contribute to the development of oil and gas industry worldwide. Thus, modern research, oil and gas extraction, processing and transportation technologies have been exploited extensively.

In this regard, projects and agreements related to the production and export of Caspian energy resources opened a new page in the history of Azerbaijan's energy industry. In today's global competitive environment, the new state administration of Azerbaijan determined variety of economic development programs, development policies and strategies in order to realize the transition to market economy. It is of strategic importance to make a conscious and systematic analysis of the country's resources and potential opportunities and make a SWOT Analysis in order to develop a new strategy and use the resources in the best way. From the perspective of investing in different sectors, a preliminary strategic step must be to conduct a non-empirical analysis of the country's economy in terms on the macroeconomic, sectorial and non-economy spheres. (Aras, 2005)

Strengths of Azerbaijan's economy in terms of macroeconomics can be listed as following:

- Presence of stable macroeconomic environment in general and especially in terms of price stability: The last 20 years have seen a single digit inflation rate. Prices have remained very stable.
- Low proportion of external debt to GNP: macroeconomic instability was observed in the first years of its independence in the country, namely until 1995 due to the political, economic instability, as well as Nagorno-Karabakh conflict with Armenia. However after the political stability was reached in the country in 1996, and after implementation of certain economic policies, instability left itself to stable growth. Thus, favorable macroeconomic indicators have dominated in the country for nearly 20 years (Suleymanov, Zeynalov, 2010). The following is public debt as a percentage of GDP:

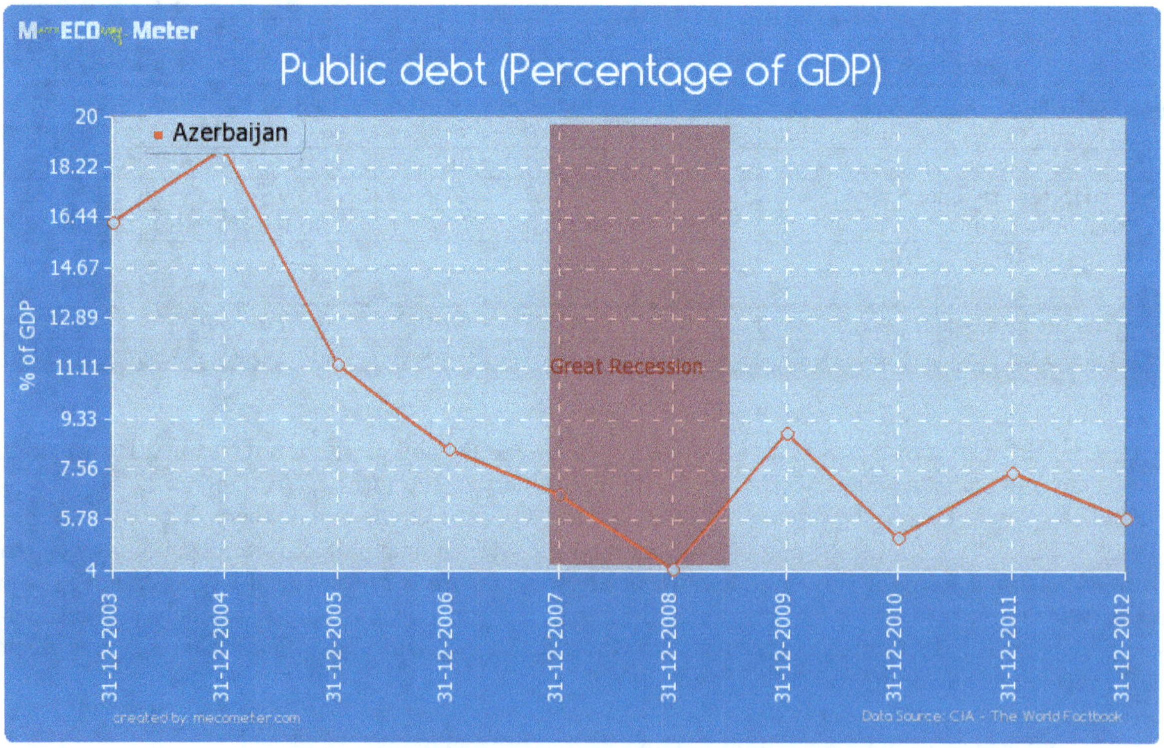

Figure 1. *Public debt as a percentage of GDP (2003-2012)*
Source: http://mecometer.com/whats/azerbaijan/public-debt/

- Stable exchange rate: Although, from time to time Manat appreciated against the dollar and euro, in the long run it showed a stable trend. Azerbaijan left "Ruble Zone" in 1992, and since then the national currency, Manat, was put in circulation. In the first stage, the Manat circulated together with Russian ruble in the country until 1994 when Manat has become the only official currency. As significant portion of the imports were made with ruble, Manat began to lose value against the ruble in 1993 when prices in importing countries, especially in Russia began to rise as a result of price liberalization. On the other hand, the crisis in the banking sector in 1993-94 and negative expectations regarding the value of Manat caused Manat to depreciate against the currencies of other countries. Manat has displayed stable a trend since 2000. On 1st January 2006, as a result the denomination, nominal value of Manat was reduced 5000 times. One Manat was determined to be worth about 1.2 U.S. (Aras, Suleymanov, 2010). The rate of Manat has not changed much for nearly seven years except for very short exchange rate volatility and at times Manat has gained value compared to the dollar. Exchange rates remained stable as economic and political stability provided in the country. According to the World Bank data exchange rates (AZN to USD) were on average 0.80 between 1994 – 2003 and 0.79 between 2009 – 2013

Table 3. *Official exchange rate (US$ per AZN, period average).*

	1994-1998	1999-2003	2004-2008	2009-2013
Azerbaijan	0.80	0.80	0.79	0.79

Source: http://data.worldbank.org/indicator/PA.NUS.FCRF/countries/1W-AZ?display=default

- Presence of cheap labor: Due to the high rate of unemployment in the country, wages are low. According to data of 2013, the minimum wage in the country is 105 Manat, the average wage is around 360 Manats. Payment for labor as a factor of production is advantageous in terms of total cost. This is another factor that encouraged investment in the country.
- Non-economic Strengths can be listed as follows:
- Education level of the population: Despite difficult conditions preceded by decline in the economic situation, people's interest in education was still unchanged as a continuation of the Soviet tradition. Literacy rate in the country is 98%, of which 60 % is highly educated. In each country, primarily for economic development, political stability and this stability will continue to be the managers. Beyond doubt that, each country needs primarily political stability for economic development and strong-willed administrators to pursue these goals. Political stability will serve as an indicator of uninterrupted execution of the economic programs and give confidence to the markets.
- There was still need for continued political stability in Azerbaijan gained when Heydar Aliyev came to power. Uncertainties were drawn to the minimum level with election of President Ilham Aliyev and it increased positive expectations.
- Strategic location: Asian countries are important for the U.S. and European countries because of their strategic location in the corridor to Europe and as well as their bordering with Iran and Russia. Azerbaijan added a new link to the chain of global economic relations with the agreement signed in 1998 in Baku which envisaged transfer of historical Silk Road to 21st century as a communication, transportation and energy transport corridor. Silk Raod served as a historical route for caravans carrying the riches of the East to the West for centuries passed by, Tajikistan, Georgia and Armenia, as well as five of the Turkish Republic. The weaknesses of the national economy from macroeconomic perspective are as follows:
- The unemployment problem: Official statistics in Azerbaijan express that the unemployment rate is around 1.5%, but with different calculations and information provided by international organizations, and in the opinion of experts, the ratio is between 16-25%. Therefore, unemployment in the country is high. One of the reasons for high unemployment level, is that around 1 million people were exposed to forced migration after the occupation of Karabakh by Armenians. On the other hand, closure of many companies which were not competitive enough and compatible with modern production, constitute the most important ratio in the number of unemployed.
- Migration of educated and skilled workers abroad: Due to lack of employment opportunities for educated and skilled workforce, many of them emigrated overseas. The majority of skilled and educated workforce moved to Russia, Turkey, Iran. It is noteworthy that among those who left the country in this way, the higher proportion is made up of young and middle-aged people. This "Brain drain" process has increased more in recent years.
- The share of oil and oil revenue in exports is around 90%. On the other hand, the 75% of budget revenues are derived from petroleum and petroleum-related fields. Thus, as the budget is dependent on the oil revenues and oil revenues in turn are dependent on the world market conjuncture, Azerbaijan has confronted with danger of the 'Dutch Disease' (Sabiroglu, 2001). The following table displays the

dynamics of transfers from State Oil Fund to state budget between 2003-2012.

Table 2. *Transfers from SOFAZ to state budget (2003-2012).*

Year	Transfers from State Oil Fund (mln AZN)	Share of the transfers from State Oil Fund in total budget revenues, %	Share of the transfers from State Oil Fund in GDP, %
2003	100.0	8.2	1.3
2004	130.0	8.8	1.5
2005	150.0	7.2	1.2
2006	585.0	1.1	3.2
2007	585.0	9.7	2.1
2008	3800.0	35.3	9.5
2009	4915.0	47.6	14.2
2010	5915.0	51.9	14.3
2011	9000.0	57.3	18.0
2012	9905.0	58.1	19.8

Source: htttp://budget.az/budget/en/main?content=526

- Slow processing in the privatization of large enterprises.
- Although bureaucracy and corruption declined each year, it is still important problem of the transition process. On the other hand, there is injustice in the distribution of income. In particular, the economic situation of workers in oil and petroleum-based sector is very good while income level of workers in other sectors is very low. Consequently, certain proportion of the population is headed for luxury consumption. The middle layer is not yet formed in the country.
- Monopoly and unfair environment for competition: One of the major problems faced by businesses in the country is the existence of monopoly or unfair competition environment. The existence of monopolies in certain areas of the private sector hampers the development and efficient use of resources. It also causes chaotic increase in the prices from time to time.
- Fluctuations in exchange rates due to lack of confidence in the domestic currency. In the first years of independence, the inflationary process and devaluations in Manat, as a result of the political and economic crises caused people's distrust against the domestic currency.
- The informal economy: the ratio of informal economy in the country's GNP is high. In fact, Azerbaijan ranks high among CIS states the volume of the informal economy. According to official data of the informal economy corresponds to somewhat 18%-20 of GDP. However, in some evaluations, the informal economy is calculated to be greater than the economic activity. According to World Bank experts, the volume of the informal economy is more than 60% of GDP. This ratio which is considered to be off the record corresponds to 8-10 billion dollars. Some experts argue that this ratio is 80%. Despite different figures, in general, high informal economic activities are observed.
- Lack of adequate infrastructure and old technology: Agriculture and livestock watering systems are inadequate. On the other hand, technology needed for agriculture and animal husbandry is both old and inadequate. Facilities essential for tourism, such as transportation and accommodation are incomplete and outdated too. Also, on the industrial sector, inadequate and outdated technology infrastructure is observed. This does not allow producing and manufacturing good quality and cheap products for export to the world market. High dependency on oil and natural gas production cause lack of interest in the development of other sectors. After the banking crisis in the first years of independence, banking sector located in the center of the financial sector has not developed yet. Failure to carry out the privatization of large-scale enterprises has been the most important factor in the underdevelopment of the securities market. Due to low levels of income, the development of the insurance sector has been hampered.
- Existence of sectored monopoly: Presence of monopoly in some sectors has an adverse effect on the price and the quality of the products produced in those sectors, and is an obstacle to the efficient use of production recourses.
- Dutch Disease Hazard: Since exports and foreign investments are oriented towards oil and natural gas production, export products comprise mainly oil and natural gas and budget is also oil revenue dependent, it is obvious that the country's economy is reliant on oil and gas industry. This dependency has further increased since 2006, with the boom in the oil exports.
- Imbalance in regional development: On the other hand, as most economic operations and tax revenues are collected in or around Baku, most of firms and companies agglomerated in Baku, the regional economic

structure displays dependence from Baku.

- After independence in relation to the production of oil and natural gas, the energy sector has been at the center of attention of foreign and domestic investors. Again, skilled labor was also trying to find more jobs in this sector. As a result of accumulation of both investment and skilled labor in a single sector, serious progress has not been made in other sectors.
- Following are non-economic weaknesses:
  - Regional transport barrier: after the Armenian invasion, 130 km of railway transportation that joined Nakhchivan and other regions of the country has been occupied. Therefore the road and rail transportation between Nakhchivan Autonomous Republic of Azerbaijan and other regions cannot be made due to Nagorno-Karabakh territory, occupied by the Armenians. Today passenger and freight transportation to Nakhchivan can be done through Iran.
  - Mindset change: In the process of transition from the Soviet regime to democracy and free market economy, change of mentality has not yet finished and is rather incomplete. The problems are still evaluated with a view similar to the Soviet system. This in turn implies settlement of market economy in the country. Mindset change is a long process, of course and requires time.
- Threats to economy:
  - Oil price fluctuations. Fluctuations in oil prices are the most economically significant threat.
  - Continuation of the problem of Nagorno-Karabakh: Nagorno-Karabakh has not escaped from Armenian occupation yet. There are still conflicts at times in borders. If the problem is not resolved with dialogue there is a tendency to get the occupied lands by force which means the country is likely to be faced with war. This problem is causing a deterrent effect from the point of foreign investors, especially to invest in non-oil sector. Up to 2012, 70% of investments comprising a total of 100 billion dollars are foreign investment. From foreign investments, only 30% of the direct investments were invested in non-oil sector. There were no serious investments in non-oil sector by domestic entrepreneurs.

    Border countries: Occasional political and social problems in Georgia, problems in Dagestan Autonomous Republic arising from Chechnya and Iran's political structure and its tough relation with international community has also had an adverse effect on foreign and domestic investors. Investment held in Azerbaijan, especially large-scale investments, will be made taking into account not only domestic market potential, but also other countries in the region. When Azerbaijan's border countries experience some problems from time to time, it leads to problems at the border and negatively impact foreign trade. Tense relations in the region and sensitive policies led by the country also adversely affect the foreign trade (Aras, 2005).
  - -The status of the Caspian Sea: Inability to determine the status of the Caspian Sea caused negative effects on the country's economic development. Because of this controversy, some of the oil companies do not want to invest in oil production in these beds. Along with petroleum and natural gas reserves, very important fish and caviar resources of the Caspian Sea cannot be used efficiently and involved in economy. On the other hand, the problem of environmental pollution in the Caspian sea and harmful externalities have their negative effects on the economy. Caspian Sea status issue is the obstacle to the development of sea transport.
  - The absence of outlet to seas and oceans: In the absence of the country's outlet to seas and oceans it is not possible to integrate into intercontinental transport and this deprives country form benefitting from maritime transport.

3. Problems Encountered during the Transition to Market Economy in Azerbaijan and Solution Attempts

Within the framework of SWOT analysis of Azerbaijan's economy, both internal strengths and weaknesses of economy and external opportunities and threats faced by the country economy were listed.

The first strategic step by foreign and domestic investors on investment decisions will be made by looking into strengths and weaknesses of the domestic economy and by taking into account the opportunities and threats of economy seen from outside.

It would be appropriate to invest in the area where strengths are in alignment with the opportunity. Only after this step they will be able to decide whether to further invest in terms of sub-sector, products and regions. After the first step it is necessary to get legal and diplomatic support and assurance, as well as build up individual relationships.

The strengths and weaknesses mentioned in the analysis above are important to determine which sectors, how and in what manner to invest in order to achieve economic development of the country. On the other hand, threats and opportunities of the country economy are important for political forces to decide on which programs, projects to implement in order to achieve economic development and integration into the world economy (Aslanlı, 2004)

State administration should make and implement right decisions by harmonization of strengths and opportunities. On the other hand, strategic decisions and policies should be developed by transforming weaknesses into strengths and threats to opportunities. (Bağırzade, 2009)

The government should take more realistic, steady and reassuring steps and provide incentives in the creation of the necessary investment climate. It should identify factors threatening economic activities, adversely affecting the investment climate, should determine political and social policies to relieve weaknesses and take actual steps in accordance with the policies. Azerbaijan has trading partnership with more than 150 countries, is a member of many international and some regional organizations. The oil contracts and international support to these contracts, that support, the oil companies investing in the country give confidence and establishes high investment environment in the country.

- Early transition to a free market compared to other countries in the region. Azerbaijan is much ahead of the newly independent republics in terms of the transition to a free market economy in and carrying out the legal and institutional infrastructure.
- The country which attracted most investments among newly independent countries. Most foreign investments in the region among other countries gained independence is seen in Azerbaijan. This would be a positive indicator for investors in other sectors.
- Being among petroleum and natural gas exporter countries. As a result of work done after the discovery of the new oilfields work done; Azerbaijan joined the chain of oil exporting countries since 2005 and gas exporting countries since 2006. This was the most important opportunity for attracting foreign investment and integrating to world economy.

Non-economic Opportunities are:

- Being on the trade routes and historical intersection: Azerbaijan is geographically located on very important historical New Silk Rode transit route which links the two continents and three sea basins.
- Progress made in the transition to democracy: Azerbaijan is much ahead of the newly independent countries in the region in terms of transition to democracy. This feature allows the country to become a main market for investments in the region.
- Existence of a more stable and democratic government among the countries of the region.
- The political stability and the government's democratic attitude gained after Heydar Aliyev came to power, was an effective factor for investors to prefer Azerbaijan in the region.

Imperfections on Investment Climate:

In terms of the availability of investment climate in Azerbaijan, number of negative factors such as the lack of the necessary legal arrangements, the high rate of tax, bribery, corruption and the presence of monopoly are among the issues of concern for entrepreneurs. Competition policy is considered as one of the essential elements in countries in transition. Lack of the same conditions in the economy hinders the activities of businessmen, thus preventing economic development. Some measures have been taken by the government of Azerbaijan for the removal of inequality in the economy. The adoption of the program to fight against corruption is such an example. Because of high tax rates, the private sector tends to hide economic activities. A large part of private enterprises are giving wages to the majority of their staff unofficially. In fact, informal economy is perceived as illegal production and sales of weapons, narcotics and pornographic products. However in Azerbaijan, informal economic activities are carried out mainly in the areas of the simple production, trade and services. (Bağırzade, 2007). In some evaluations made, the informal economy is recorded to be greater than legal economic activities. 80% of foreign investment in Azerbaijan's seems to be in oil sector. It is worrying to observe that sectoral investments also mainly fall under this category and a significant part of GDP is formed from oil revenues. Price changes in the world market due to the one-sided development of the petroleum sector also cause fluctuations in GDP. This situation was clearly seen in the 1998 Russian crisis.

Briefly, Azerbaijan is faced with a hazard of "Dutch syndrome," which is expressed as the collapse of the other regions or sectors as a result of rapid development of a specific region or a sector.

When economic development is based on the export of natural resources alone, this means only a small group of the population benefit from them, and depletion of these reserves result in a decrease in the living standards of the majority which contradicts to the principles of social justice. Therefore, when the economy relies only on natural resources sector, this would undermine the independency of the countries in both internal and external relations.

High dependency of economy on energy sector will cause negative results on the socio-economic situation. Circulation of potential and skilled labor in the energy sector will adversely affect the development of other sectors. Spending of oil revenues in the purchase of imported goods, especially if consumer goods are imported rather than capital goods, the country's trade balance will turn to negative. In order to defeat the risk of "Dutch syndrome", policies such as strengthening foreign investment flows to Azerbaijani economy, and provision of all necessary conditions for fulfillment of these investments must be among the main objectives for the government. (Bulut, Suleymanov, 2012) The first step should be provision of favorable climate for investments. To realize this first of all non-commercial risks must be eliminated, and regulations on the tax rates, the tax collection system and ethics, and necessary arrangements for administrative and legal regulations for securing foreign capital and for optimization of the tax and customs systems should be made. Besides the Dutch Disease, there are several other caused by foreign capital: the country's increased external debt; diversion of foreign investment into fast revenue-generating activities such as raw material and service areas; presence of very little investment in the country's manufacturing industry; aggregation of almost all investment in Absheron; negligibly small amount of foreign capital in other regions. Despite the fact that the advice and borrowings from international financial institutions played a major role in macroeconomic stabilization in the country, very little progress is observed in the increase in efficiency, levels and yields of production in the real sector and also in socio-economic problems such as social security. One of the major problems faced by operators in the country is tendency to monopoly. Monopolization of certain areas by companies or businessmen hinders the development of private entrepreneurship and even leads to closure of some companies. Monopoly and unfair competition is hampering the development of the private sector in Azerbaijan. The existence of monopoly results in chaotic rises in prices.

4. Conclusion

Briefly, Azerbaijan is facing a hazard of "Dutch syndrome," which is expressed as the collapse of the other regions or sectors as a result of rapid development of a specific region or a sector. Even beyond dependence on one sector, Azerbaijan is facing with the danger of dependency on one region. The conclusion drown from analyses of Azerbaijan's economic development after independence is that, in the 1991-1996 period there was significant progress in almost all parameters. Starting from 1996 stability was ensured and there were positive developments further with the exception of negative effects of Russian (1998) and (2008) world economic crisis.

In particular, with the rapid development of oil and natural gas industry in the 2000s, a very large improvement in basic economic parameters were recorded, and it is expected to continue in the coming years. Thus, despite all the positive and negative processes in economy after independence, between 1991-2013 GDP volume (in other words, Azerbaijan Economy size) increased about 120 times, per capita GDP volume raised 400 times, state budget expenditures 280 times, the total foreign trade volume 30 times, exports 10 time, while imports increased 10 times. Today with all the basic quantitative parameters on the economy, Azerbaijan is a leader in the South Caucasus. Azerbaijan's foreign debt was U.S. $ 5.688 billion at the beginning of 2013. This amount corresponds to 13.6% of GDP. By the amount of external debt per capita, Azerbaijan is ranking in the middle compared with the CIS countries. But despite all the positive developments and government strategies and policies implemented after independence in Azerbaijan, there are still certain problems experienced in the economy. The most important problems can be listed as follows:

- High dependency of the economy on the oil sector,
- Absence of economic growth model generating employment,
- Regional inequalities, inefficiency of the agricultural sector,
- Socio-economic problems endangered by the occupation of Nagorno-Karabakh and the surrounding regions by Armenia,
- High interest rates, high tax burden, underdeveloped public services,
- The low rate of incorporation, weak corporate governance tradition,
- "Cash economy" is common, artificial monopoly, informality, corruption and various infrastructure problems exist.

The following policy measures may be effective for the solution of the current problems in the economy:

- Sustainable economic development, increasing employment, poverty reduction, reducing injustice in income distribution, reducing regional inequalities and ensuring horizontal balance between regions, following government policies in the framework of government's 2008-2012 and 2013-2015 regional development programs which aim development of non-oil sector.

- The applicability of the laws and in the process of transition to market economy and benefiting from the experience of developed countries of the world. The country should transform from natural resources-based economic growth model to high technology and efficiency-based model of economic growth. In order for this, it is important to promote the new technology transfer to the country, to build and develop techno-parks, to implement most perfect models of science and economics cooperation, to establish optimal sized economic agents and apply modern production and management systems that lead to improved efficiency in resource allocation and productivity, to improve quality of education, particularly in technical fields.
- Efficient utilization of approximately $ 50 billion accumulated in the Oil Fund in 2013. These resources must be used effectively and efficiently in both local and offshore investments in order to further increase and guarantee post petrol period.
- In order to reduce poverty and income inequality, existing policy mechanisms for poverty alleviation need to be developed and fiscal policy instruments in reducing income inequality should be used in an active way.
- To ensure the continuity of policies against inflation and minimize its negative impact on the economic system.
- Influence of Interest policies must be promoted in order to divert informal savings into investment in formal sector. From this point the gap between average interest rates on deposits and average return of capital in informal sector must be minimized. Interest on investment loans must be low enough in order to encourage investment activities in the formal sector.
- It is essential to ensure continuity of foreign exchange earnings in the long run which are important elements of macroeconomic stability in the country. Policy measures need to be taken, with the purpose of reducing dependency of export incomes on oil, by increasing the export potential of non-oil sector.
- In order to ensure budget balance sustainability and increase effectiveness of socio-economic functions of budget, there is a need to reduce its dependency on oil revenues and raise the ratio of continuous source of income such as taxes in budget.
- Policies that encourage foreign investment in the non-oil sector should be developed. These policies will boost economic development and limit the effects of informal sector.
- State incentive mechanisms need to be developed for entrepreneurs. In this regard, promoting the expansion of cheap lending mechanisms of National Fund of Support for Entrepreneurship for new entrepreneurs, the development of the incentives mechanism to the agricultural sector to increase the efficiency, the expansion of the state support for entrepreneurs in terms of science and know-how, development of the mechanism of awarding entrepreneurs by the state will be some of effective measures.
- Entrepreneurship infrastructure should be developed. In that regard, the development of the capital and insurance markets, the creation of specific industrial zones, developing necessary infrastructure for consulting services and exhibition industry is important.
- Ensuring the rights and interests of entrepreneurs in the country should be raised further. It is mandatory to raise the level of entrepreneurs' unification, to prevent delays in formal procedures and to protect copyright and intellectual property.
- Necessary policies should be developed to fight against informal economy. In this aspect preparation of state programs to fight against the informal economy, creation of official central institutions, the development of statistical data, stiffening of penalties, removal of legal gaps are important measures to take.

References

Aras, O.N., Suleymanov, E., and Zeynalov, A., 2012. *Azerbaijan's Energy Source Revenues and Their Effect on the Economy of the Country*. Working Paper, Available online at: http://dx.doi.org/10.2139/ssrn.2194173

Bulut, C., and Suleymanov, E., 2012. Importance of Economic Collaboration between Azerbaijan and Turkey in Preventing Dutch Disease in Azerbaijan. *International Symposium on Regional Cooperation and Development,* Erzurum, Turkey, October 17-20, 2012. Available at:

http://dx.doi.org/10.2139/ssrn.2172960

Suleymanov, E., and Zeynalov, A., 2009. The General Assessment of Macroeconomic Indicators of Azerbaijan Economy after Independence from the Economic Stability Point of View. *Journal of Qafquaz University*, Available at SSRN: http://ssrn.com/abstract=2167943

Aras, O. N., 2005. *Azerbaycan Ekonomisi ve Yatırım İmkanları*. Bakü: TÜSİAB Yayın No: 2005-001.

AR Merkezi Bankı. 2012. *2011 İllik Hesabat*. Bakı.

Aras, O.N., 2008. *Azerbaycanın Hazar Ekonomisi ve Stratejisi*. İstanbul: Derin Yayınları.

Aras, O.N., and Süleymanov, E., 2010. *Azerbaycan Ekonomisi*. Baku: Şark-Garb Matbaası.

Aslanlı, A., 2004. *Bakü-Tiflis-Ceyhan: Petrolün Ötesinde Önem Taşıyan Hat*. TUSAM Ulusal Güvenlik Stratejileri Araştırma Merkezi. Available online at: http://www.tusam.net/makaleler.asp?id=48&sayfa=53.

Atakıshıyev. M., 2007. *New Oil Policiy and Economic Development in Azerbaijan*. Baku: Aspoligraf.

Bağırzade, E.R., 2007. Kayıtdışı Ekonominin Temel Özendirici Faktörlerinden Biri Gibi Yolsuzluk ve Onunla Mücadelenin Azerbaycan Girişimleri. *Akademik Bakış, Uluslararası Hakemli Sosyal Bilimler E-Dergisi, Ocak*, 11(5), Available online at: http://www.akademikbakis.org/sayi11/makale/kayitdisi.pdf

Bağırzade, E.R., 2009. Müstegil Azerbaycanda Reallaşdırılan İktisadi Siyasetin Leqallaşdırma Aspektleri. *"Heyder Eliyev Iktisadi Inkişaf Strategiyasının Tentenesi" Mövzusunda Keçirilmiş Elmi-Praktiki Konfransın Tezisleri*, Bakı: İktisad Universiteti, pp. 141-145

Bağırov, S., 1996. Azerbaijan Oil: Glimpses of a Long History. *Journal of International Affair*, 1(2), p.28.

BP.com. BP Statistical Review of World Energy 2011, Available online at: http://www.bp.com/centres/energy,

Cornell Svante E. - Ismaılzade Fariz, (2005) "The Baku-Tbilisi-Ceyhan Pipeline: Implications for Azerbaijan", *The Baku-Tbilisi-Ceyhan Pipeline: Oil Window to the West*, (Edited by S. Frederick Starr and Svante E. Cornell)

Baker & McKenzie. 2012. Doing Business in Azerbaijan

Eldaroğlu, E., 2001. Neft Fondunun Vesaitleri Hansı İstiqamete Yöneldilmelidir? *Azerbaycan Milli Demokratiya Fondu, "Azerbaycan" Bülleteni,* 25 (145).

Sabiroğlu, İ., 2001. Neft Böhranları ve Holland Sindromu. *Azerbaycan Milli Demokratiya Fondu Azerbaycan Bülleteni,* No: 19 (139).

Süleymanov, E., Zeynalov, A., 2010. Azərbaycan Respublikasının Xalis İxrac Funksiyası və Xarici Ticarət Multipikatoru", *Azərbaycan, Qloballaşma Prosesində Qafqaz və Mərkəzi Asya III beynəlxalq Konfrans,* Qafqaz Universiteti, səhifə/səhifə aralığı: 124-125.

11

Post Inflation Targeting Monetary Policy: A Study of Britain, Japan and the United States

Mehdi MONADJEMI* and John LODEWIJKS

Australian School of Business,
University of New South Wales, Sydney, Australia

There is now considerable disquiet about the appropriate monetary strategy that central banks should follow in the aftermath of the global financial crisis. Several influential commentators have called for the abandonment of inflation targeting. Empirical research examining three major economies demonstrates that inflation targeting was effective prior to the crisis and a more flexible form of targeting may still be appropriate after the crisis.

***Keywords**: Inflation targeting, monetary policy, comparative study*

1. Introduction

In the January 31, 2013 issue of Financial Times, Charles Goodhart argued that the recovery from the Great Recession (GR) of 2007-2008 has been slow and disappointing. There are indications that central banks of major industrial countries are using different monetary policy strategy. For example, suggestion that Bank of England is moving towards targeting nominal income, Bank of Japan emphasising employment growth and the Federal Reserve setting a limit for unemployment are all indications of central banks direction monetary policy towards output and employment. Taking Goodhart's suggestion further, it is imperative to see how different types of targeting evolved prior to the GR.

Inflation targeting as a strategy for conducting monetary policy became popular among the industrial and developing countries during the decade of 1990s. The strategy for conducting monetary policy in the 1970s, 1980s and the 1990 respectively changed from money supply targeting, inflation control and central bank independence and inflation targeting. It is interesting to note that the change in the strategy occurred at the same time for the countries that followed the above monetary policy strategies.

Oechsle (2013) argues that "Krugmanite" is a strategy under which the central bank has the mandate to target some growth rate of nominal GDP. The central bank attempts to maintain the actual growth rate of nominal GDP within the target through the use of monetary instruments. Under this strategy, if because of some unexpected negative shocks, the target is missed, the central bank uses its instrument to maintain a higher future rate of growth.

The purpose of this paper is to examine the extent to which real sector targeting has replaced other forms of targeting in three major industrial countries. In Sections 2-4 the concept of targeting and different

* Corresponding Author:
Mehdi Monadjemi, Australian School of Business, University of New South Wales, Sydney, Australia

forms of targeting are examined. Theoretical discussions and empirical results are presented in Section 5, and summary and concluding results are offered in Section 6.

2. Monetary Targeting

In conducting monetary policy some variables such as inflation, rate of growth output and unemployment rate are called final targets and some such as money supply, interest rate and exchange rate are called intermediate targets. The central bank attempts to influence the final targets by setting the intermediate targets.

For a successful targeting, an intermediate target must meet the following conditions:

i. The relationship between intermediate and final targets must be stable. If this condition is not met, changes in the intermediate target may not influence the final target or it may change the final target in an undesirable direction.
ii. Data on the intermediate target must be available prior to the data on the final target. This condition allows the central bank to forecast the future changes in the final target by observing the behaviour of the intermediate target.
iii. The intermediate target must be under the control of the central bank.

Monetary targeting was exercised during the 1970s for controlling inflation in Britain, United States, Canada, Australia and New Zealand. This procedure relied on Friedman Schwartz (1963) where the authors showed a long run close relationship between money and prices in the United States.

Monetary targeting adds to the credibility of the central bank and prevents inflationary consequences of a discretionary policy based on the choice between growth and inflation. Moreover, the existence of a target creates transparency in implementation of monetary policy and allows the privates sector to anticipate the direction of monetary policy.

The central bank cannot control both money and interest rate simultaneously. If money is controlled interest rate is left free and vice versa. Poole (1970) proposed conditions for choosing money or interest rate as an intermediate target. Poole assumed that the objective of the central bank is to minimize the deviation of output from its desired level.

Monetary targeting is preferable if the economy is subject to a real sector shock such as changes in consumption, investment or exports. Interest rate targeting is preferable if the source of instability is from the financial sector.

Monadjemi and Kearney (1990) showed that in the 1970s in the United States, United Kingdom, Canada, Germany and Australia monetary targeting was successful in reducing inflation. During the 1980s, financial innovations and financial deregulations caused a considerable instability in the velocity of money. Fluctuations in the velocity of money introduced several problems in conducting monetary targeting. For example, financial deregulations led to a significant expansion of bank deposits and the supply of money (money supply include bank deposits). An increase in the supply of money without a corresponding rise in nominal GDP led to a fall in velocity of money. Most of the above-mentioned countries suspended monetary targeting in the 1980s.

3. Exchange Rate Targeting

During the 1980s, several countries conducted monetary policy by targeting the exchange rate. Stability of the exchange rate is important particularly for countries that international trade comprises a large proportion of their aggregate economic activity.

In 1979, in the context of the European Monetary System (EMS), eight European countries decided to limit fluctuations of their exchange rates within ± 2.5 percent relative to the German Mark. EMS was successful in keeping the inflation rates of the member countries in line with the rate of inflation in Germany, which was the lowest in Europe. EMS actively continued operation until 1992 when a significant depreciation of the British Pound and an increasing limit of fluctuations to ± 15 percent automatically caused the breakdown of the system. Eventually the European Monetary Union and the single currency were introduced in 1999 and the European Central Bank (ECB) was assigned the task of managing euro's liquidity.

In the commodity producing countries, the exchange rate is highly correlated with the commodity prices. In these countries exchange rate targeting may cause problems that are similar to the Argentine (2001), Mexico, (1994) and Britain (1992). In these cases eventually the central bank floated the exchange rate.

4. Inflation Targeting

During the 1990s, some countries such as Australia, Brazil, Britain, Canada, Chilli, Norway, South Africa, Korea, and New Zealand commenced conducting monetary policy base on inflation targeting. In this procedure, the central bank attempts to conduct monetary policy such that the expected rate of inflation remains within a specified range. Countries that exercised inflation targeting were successful in keeping their rate of inflation within the targeted range.

The preference of price stability against growth and employment was demonstrated in Rogoff (1985). Rogoff argued that the society is better-off if the objective function of the central bank is different than the objective function of the society. In other words the monetary authorities must be conservative with an objective function that assigns higher weight to price stability than employment. Decisions made by a conservative central bank must be independent of the expansionary policies of the government. Alesina and Summers (1993) showed that over a decade, Germany and Switzerland with most independent central banks experienced lowest possible rate of inflation.

Preference of price stability over employment follows separate articles by Friedman (1968) and Phelps (1968). Both studies showed that an expansionary monetary policy increases employment in the short run but in the long run employment returns to the natural rate and inflation remains at a higher level. In other words, in the long run an expansionary monetary policy increases inflation without affecting unemployment. Kyland and Prescott (1977) society's welfare is improved if in conducting monetary policy the central bank follows a rule rather than discretion. The authors showed that conducting monetary policy based on a rule generates no inflation whereas a discretionary monetary policy produces positive inflation. Rogoff (1985) argues that in the absence of productivity shocks, inflation targeting is the best strategy because it has no trade-off between inflation and unemployment.

In Argentine one unit of local currency was set to one US dollar. This procedure reduced inflation but created banking crises. In 1994 Mexico attempted to limit fluctuations of peso against the US dollar. However, political turmoil and the loss of foreign exchange reserves forced the government to devalue the peso. In 1992 Britain was forced to leave the EMS fixed exchange rate system when Bank of England experienced heavy losses.

Inflation targeting is not suitable in the presence of a supply shock. In this case control of inflation is associated with a large drop in output and employment.

In inflation targeting by publicly announcing targets and monetary policy strategy the central bank becomes more transparent and responsible. Mishkin and Posen (1997) argued that those countries that implement inflation targeting must have developed financial markets, macroeconomic stability, an independent monetary policy and a credible monetary policy. Moreover, the central bank must not be committed to maintain the exchange rate.

The logic behind the inflation targeting is based on the long run policy ineffectiveness of monetary policy. In the long run monetary policy affects prices but not output.

The importance of maintaining an inflation target varies among different countries. At the top of the list is New Zealand where the governor of the central bank's job depends on the maintenance of the inflation targets. Inflation targeting is not sensitive to the terms of trade shocks because generally prices of food, energy and interest rate on mortgages are excluded from the consumer price index. Prices of these items are very volatile and cause changes in the aggregate supply curve.

Those economists who are against the inflation targeting such as Debelle and Fischer (1994) and Posen (1995) argue that in Germany and Switzerland inflation targeting was successful enforced at the cost of high unemployment. Recently most of the macroeconomists and central bankers believe that maintaining a low inflation target leads to macroeconomic stability in the long run. Supporters of inflation targeting are not in favour of zero inflation. They argue that since nominal wages are rigid downward, having a positive inflation is the only way to reduce real wages and create employment. Moreover, maintenance of a very low inflation target may lead to the dander of deflation. Bernanke and Mishkin (1997) argue that similar situation existed in Japan in the late 1990s.

Svensson (1999) identifies three features for inflation targeting:

i. Existence of a clear numerical target for inflation,
ii. Forecasts of inflation as a framework for conduction monetary policy,
iii. High level of transparency and responsibility.

McCallum (1996) examined the success of inflation targeting in Canada, Britain, Sweden and New Zealand that conducted monetary policy in the context of inflation targeting in 199o to 1993. All of these countries used consumer price index, excluding food and energy prices, as a measure of price level. McCallum argues that inflation targeting is preferable to the discretionary policy because in the latter method more attention is paid to the benefits of an expansionary policy than the costs of the policy.

McCallum showed that high rates of inflation that existed in the above mentioned countries in the 1970s and the 1980s, declined to 2 to 4 percent in the 1990s.

Among the developed and developing countries respectively New Zealand and Chilli were the first countries that commenced inflation targeting. Bosede (2004) showed that before the implementation of inflation targeting the average rate of inflation in the developed and the developing countries were 3.72 and 13.11 percent respectively. 12 months after the implementation both rates declined to 2.71 and 8.3 percent respectively.

5. Real Sector Targeting: Empirical Evidence

The choice between inflation targeting and real sector targeting is similar to the choice between fixing the price and letting the quantity be determined in the market or setting the quantity and letting the price to be freely determined. The authorities cannot set the price and quantity together at the same time. Historically, real sector targeting rather than inflation targeting became important when the economy was far away from the potential output and inflation is not a serious problem. Notable examples of real sector targeting are during the Great Depression of 1930s and the GR of 2007-2008.

Figures 1 and 2 show quarterly data on inflation and growth of real GDP for Japan, United Kingdom and United States, 1990- 2013.

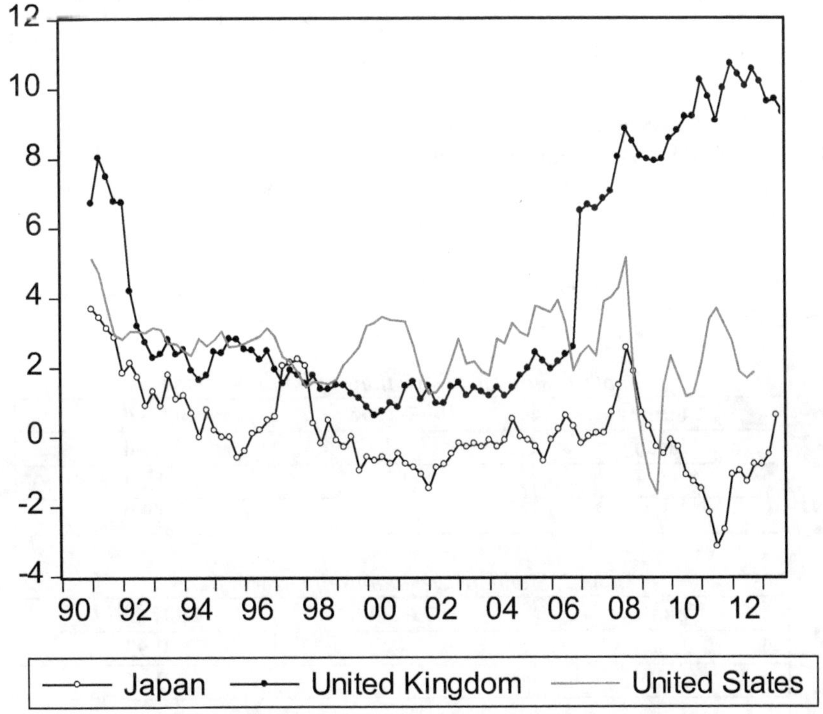

***Figure 1**. Inflation Rates: Japan, United Kingdom, and United States*

Source: All of the series in this study including CPI, growth rates, government expenditure and nominal GDP for Japan, UK and US were collected from the OECD website under quarterly national income account.

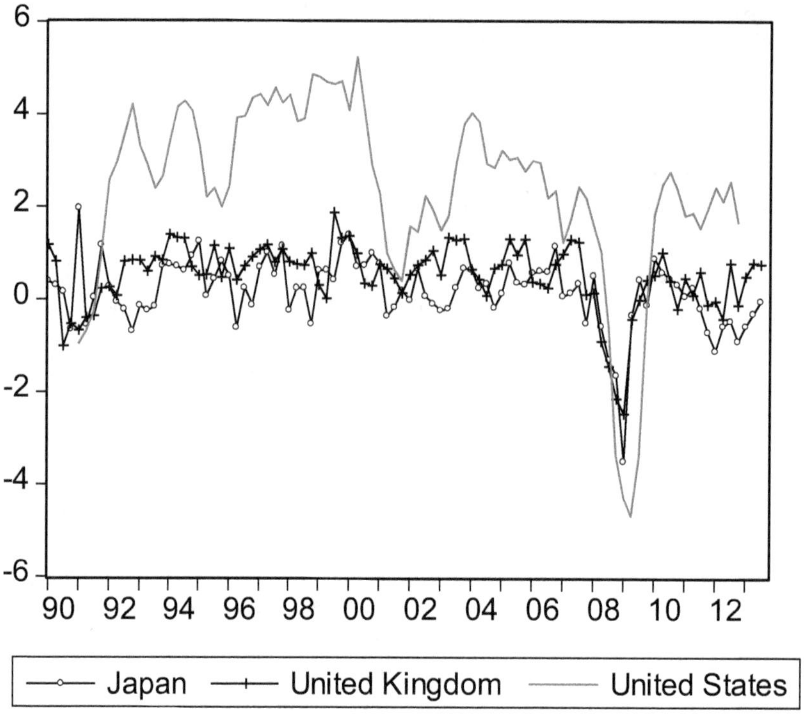

Figure 2. *Growth Rates: Japan, United Kingdom, and United States*

Figure 1 indicates stability of the inflation rates in three countries over roughly about 14 years (1992 to 2006). This period coincides with the period of inflation targeting in all of the three countries. However, the prolong period of tranquil inflation stability did not continue as inflation rates behaved erotically after 2006.

Figure 2 also shows a prolong period of about 17 to 18 years growth for three countries prior to the GR of 2007-2008. All of the three countries experienced a dramatic fall in their growth rates in 2008. Subsequently the fall of growth rates were reversed as governments' macroeconomic policies and rescue packages attempted to restore output and employment. The primary emphasis was placed on growth rather than inflation.

Further information regarding volatility of inflation and growth rates in three selected countries prior and after 2007 are reported in Tables 1and 2.

Table 1. *Standard Deviations of Inflation Rates*

Country	1992-2006	2007-2012
Japan	0.91	1.34
UK	0.93	1.33
USA	0.66	1.60

Table 2. *Standard Deviations of Growth Rates*

Country	1992-2006	2007-2012
Japan	0.49	0.93
UK	0.40	0.96
USA	1.12	2.31

Both tables show more volatile inflation and growth in the latter sub-period. Stability of the inflation rates during the earlier period is indicative of the inflation targeting which was less emphasised as output and employment significantly dropped during the GR in most of the affected countries.

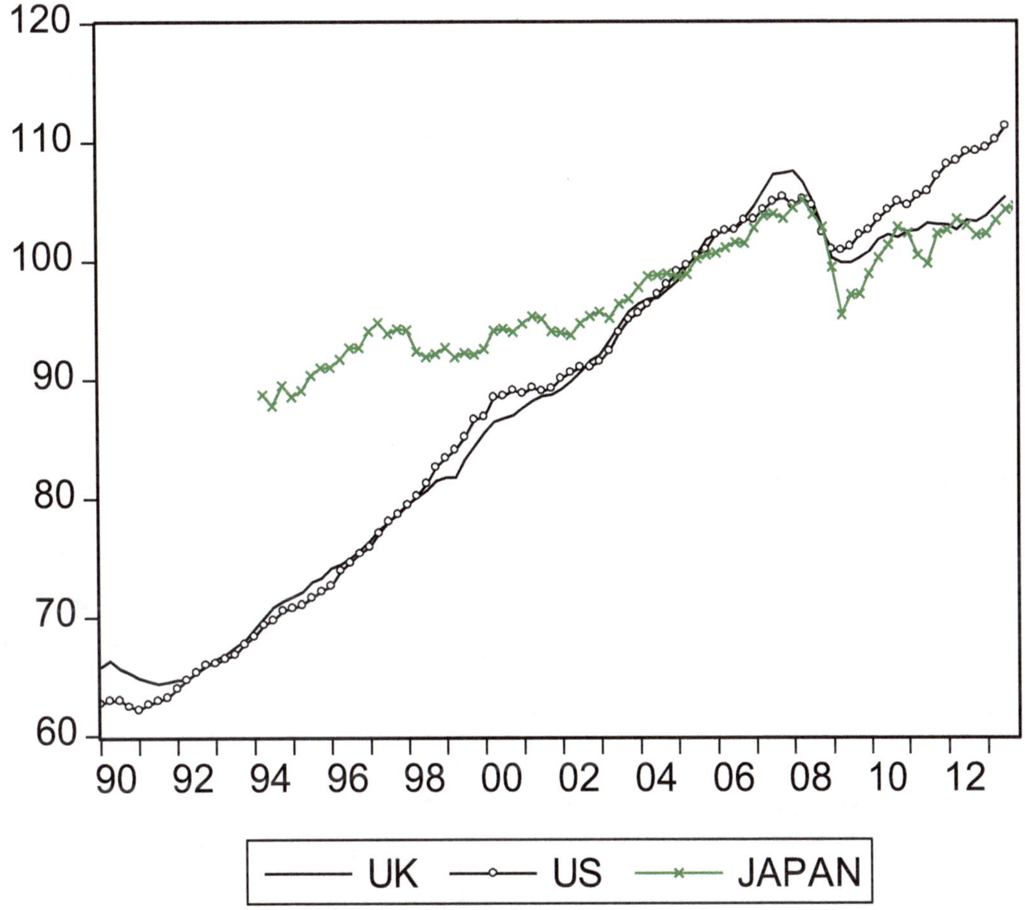

Figure 3*. General Government Expenditure: Japan, UK and USA*

Figure 3 shows that government expenditure in three countries rose steadily until beginning of the financial crises and then after a sharp fall started to rise again indicating fiscal authorities intention to compensate for the decline in output and employment. Figure 3 also suggests that falling government expenditure around 2007 may have contributed to the recession in three selected counties. Monadjemi (2011) argues that rising oil prices coupled with falling government expenditure contributed to the recession in the United States in 2008.

Further evidence on inflation targeting is provided using Hodrick-Prescott (1997) (HP) filter. HP method divides a time series into growth and cyclical components. Using a statistical filter, the growth component can be removed, leaving the cyclical component as deviations around a smooth trend line. Assume Y is a time series on real GDP or CPI.

$$Y = y_c + y_g$$

where y_c *and* y_g respectively are cyclical and growth components of Y. Assuming that inflation targeting was in effect 1990 – 2006, the cyclical component of CPI is not expected to deviate substantially from the trend line. However, with the abolition of inflation targeting after 2006, price level is uncontrolled and is expected to deviate from the trend line.

Applications of HP method for US, UK and Japan are presented in Figures 4 to 9.

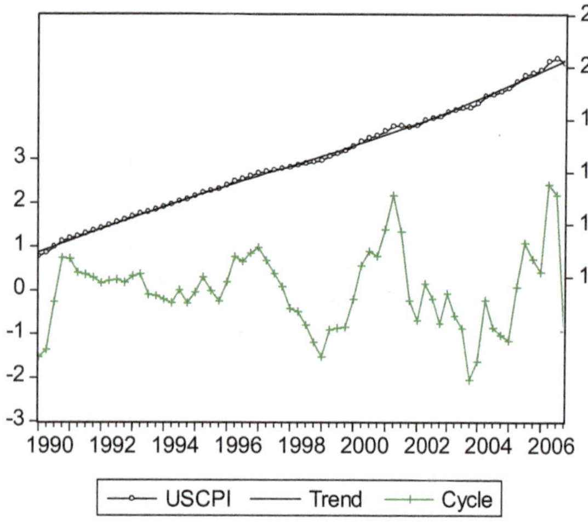

***Figure 4**. Hodrick-Prescott Filter US CPI 1990-2006*

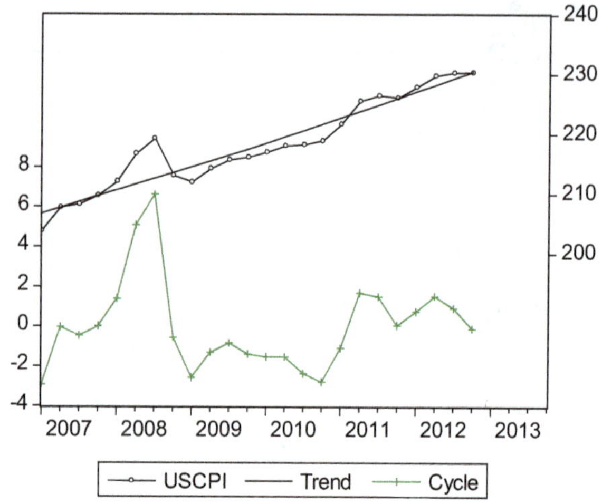

***Figure 5**. Hodrick-Prescott Filter US CPI 2007-2013*

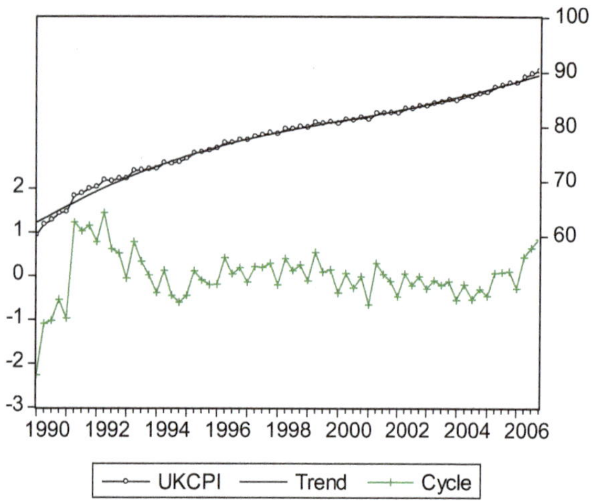

***Figure 6**. Hodrick-Prescott Filter UK CPI 1990-2006*

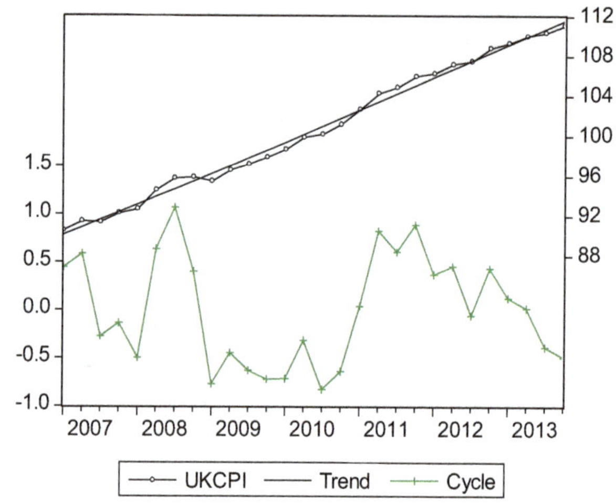

***Figure 7**. Hodrick-Prescott Filter UK CPI 2007-2013*

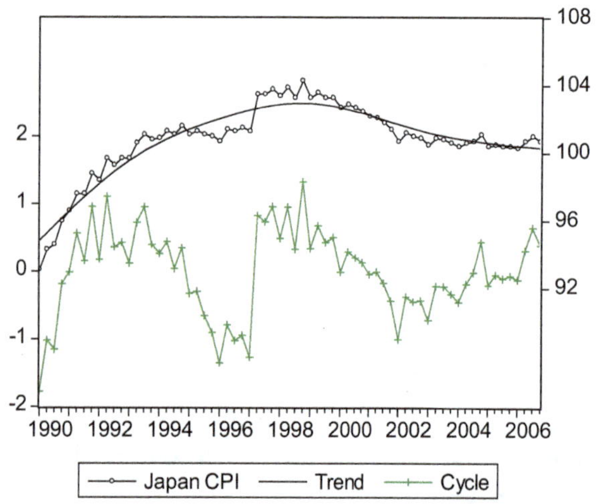

***Figure 8**. Hodrick-Prescott Filter Japan CPI 1990-2006*

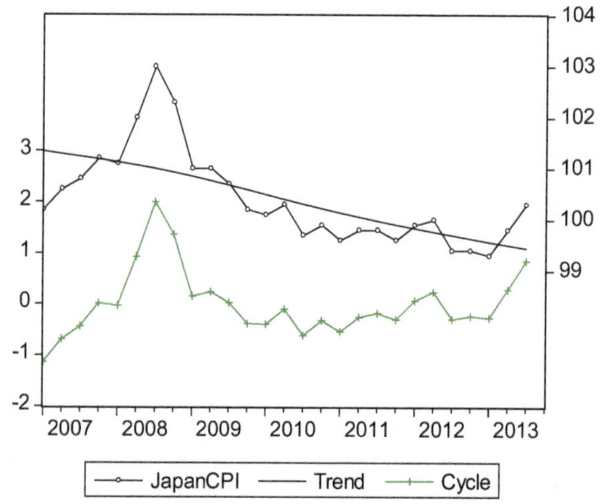

***Figure 9**. Hodrick-Prescott Filter Japan CPI 2007-2013*

All of the figures indicate that prices moved much more closely along the trend lines in 1990 – 2006 than they did in the latter period after 2006. In cases of UK and US in the earlier period, CPIs moved almost completely on the trend lines. These figures provide further evidence on the stability of the prices in three countries enforced by the existence of inflation targeting prior to the GR.

6. Conclusions

Macroeconomic Policy is under review after the harrowing experiences with the global financial crisis and its lingering effects, especially in Europe. The International Monetary Fund, for example, is sponsoring several conferences on 'Rethinking Macro Policy'. There is considerable divergence of views about what the appropriate monetary targets should be after the crisis. A pivotal statement in this respect is the paper by Blanchard et al (2010). This study looks at "what we thought we knew" about the benefits of having just one target of inflation and how "we were wrong" and that "what we have learned from the crisis" is that central banks aimed for too low a level of inflation. The target should be raised to provide liquidity more broadly and to reduce the value of real debt when extensive financial deleveraging is occurring. Coming from an institution such as the International Monetary Fund, which had been a champion of inflation targeting in the past, really does indicate how much central bank behaviour has been transformed.

Michael Woodford (2012, 2013) suggests caution before we discard the conventional wisdom. Our empirical results support this proposition. Inflation targeting has provided stability for medium-run inflation expectations before the crisis and has prevented a deflationary spiral, during and after the crisis. What the profession has learned is that inflation stabilization, in itself, does not guarantee macroeconomic stability. A more flexible form of inflation targeting is called for. For example, a central bank may target nominal GDP in such a way that it hits an inflation target over a medium-run rather than in the short-run. Official interest rates might be lowered even if inflation targets are not being met at that point in time as long as nominal GDP is below or is trending below a nominal GDP target. Similarly, interest rates may be raised even if inflation targets are being met if there are indications of excessive debt accumulations, property bubbles and fear of financial crises. Monetary policy needs to be cognisant of not only inflation and real activity forecasts but also the spectre of financial crises.

References

Alesina, A. and Summers, L., 1993. Central Bank Independence and Macroeconomic Performance: Some Comparative Evidence. *Journal of Money Credit and Banking*, 25, pp. 151-162

Bernanke, B. and Mishkin, F., 1997. Inflation Targeting: A New Framework for Monetary Policy, *Journal of Economic Perspectives*, spring, 11(2), pp. 97-116

Blanchard, O, DellAriccia, G & Mauro, P., 2010. Rethinking Macroeconomic Policy. *Journal of Money, Credit and Banking*, 42(6), supplement, pp. 199 - 215

Bosede, ND. 2004. Inflation Targeting Framework for Jamaica: An Empirical Exploration, *Research Discussion Paper, Bank of Jamaica*, July

Debelle, G. and Fischer, S., 1995. How Independent Should a Central Bank Be?, in *Goals, Guidelines and Constrains Facing Monetary Policymakers, edited by Fuhrer, J., Federal Reserve Bank of Boston*, pp. 195-221

Friedman, M., 1968. The Role of Monetary Policy. *American Economic Review*, 58(1), March, pp. 1-17

Friedman, M. and Jacobson Schwartz, A., 1963. *A Monetary History of the United States 1867- 1960.* Princeton University Press, Princeton

Goodhart, C., 2013. Central Banks Asked to Walk Inflations Razor Edge. *Financial Times,* 31 January

Hordick, R. J. And Prescott, E. C., 1997. Post-War US Business Cycles: An Empirical Investigation. *Journal of Money, Credit and Banking*, 29, pp. 1-16

Kydland, F. and Prescott, E., 1977. Rules Rather than Discretion: The Inconsistency of Optimal Plans. *Journal of Political Economy*, 85, June, pp. 473-491

McCullum, B., 1996. Inflation Targeting in Canada, New Zealand, Sweden, the United Kingdom, and in General, *NBER working Paper*, 5579

Mishkin, F. and Posen, A., 1997. Inflation Targeting: Lessons from Four Countries, *Economic Policy Review, Federal Reserve Bank of New York*, 3(3), August

Monadjemi, M. S., 2011. Monetary Policy and Oil Prices. *Global Economy Journal*, 11(3), pp. 1-16

Monadjemi, M. and Kearney, C., 1990. Deregulation and the Conduct of Monetary Policy. *Economic and Labour Relation Review*, December, pp. 18-33

Oechsle, T., 2013. A Monetary and Fiscal Framework for Macroeconomic Stability in the European Monetary Union. *Real World Economics Review*, 65, pp. 51-64

Phelps, E., 1968. Money Wage Dynamics and Labour Market Equilibrium. *Journal of Political Economy*, 76(4), July/August, pp. 678-711

Poole, W., 1970. Optimal Choice of Monetary Instruments in a Simple Stochastic Macro Model. *Quarterly Journal of Economics*, 84, May, pp. 197-216

Posen, A., 1995. Declaration Are Not Enough: Financial Sector sources of Central Bank Independence. *NBER Macroeconomic Annual*, pp. 253-274

Rogoff, K., 1985. The Optimal Degree of Commitment to an Intermediate Monetary Target. *Quarterly Journal of Economics*, 100, November, pp. 1169-1189

Svensson, L., 1999. Inflation Targeting as a Monetary Policy Rule. *Journal of Monetary Economics*, 43, pp. 607-654

Woodford, M., 2012. Inflation Targeting and Financial Stability. *NBER Working Paper Series*, Working Paper 17967, April

Woodford, M., 2013. Monetary Policy Targets after the Crisis, *in IMF Rethinking Macro Policy II: First Steps and Early Lessons Conference, April 16-17, 2013*, Washington, DC

12

Achieving the Renewable Energy Target for Jamaica

Abdullahi Olabode ABDULKADRI*

The University of the West Indies, Mona Campus, Jamaica

The high cost of energy in Jamaica, one of the highest in the Caribbean region, is usually cited as a hindrance to industrial development and efficiency, especially in the manufacturing sector. High energy cost is also considered to be a national energy security issue and the government is taking steps to ensure adequate supply of energy at affordable prices. In the current National Development Plan, the government has set a target for renewable energy sources to supply 20% of the country's energy need by the year 2030. Using a linear programing model of energy planning, we examine how realistically this target could be achieved. Our findings indicate that the 20% renewable energy target is technically achievable with the optimal plan showing a mixture of wind power, hydropower and bagasse power but no solar power. However, when the timeline for investment in new generating capacities that will ensure the attainment of the target is considered, it becomes highly improbable that the target will be met. This study fills the gap that exists in evidence-based analysis of energy policy in Jamaica.

Keywords: *energy planning; energy policy; renewable energy; linear programming; evidence-based policy analysis; Jamaica*

1. Introduction

Energy issues have dominated national discuss in Jamaica in recent times. Since the Government of Jamaica (GOJ) announced a plan in 2004 to introduce liquefied natural gas (LNG) into the country's energy mix as a way to diversify energy sources and reduce the price of energy, there has been a lot of excitement on energy-related issues in the island. With a population of about 2.7 million people, Jamaica is the largest English-speaking country in the Caribbean. The economy has been on the decline with negative growth in GDP for most of the last decade. Between 2008 and 2012, GDP value added declined, ranging from a low of 0.5% in 2012 to a high of 3.4% in 2009. The only growth (1.4%) recorded in that interval occurred in 2011. During this period, the manufacturing and construction sectors, both energy-intensive, recorded greater declines in GDP value added than the economy as a whole (BOJ, 2013). The potential for the manufacturing sector to drive economic growth and provide employment opportunities has always been sounded by the Jamaica Manufacturer's Association (JMA). Given that imports of manufactured goods constitute about 10% of all goods imported to the country compared to just 1% of exported goods (BOJ, 2013), the argument for import-substitution sounds tenable. However, JMA and other stakeholders have consistently cited high energy prices as a detrimental factor to industrialization in Jamaica. For example, industrial rate for electricity in

* Corresponding Author:
Abdullahi Olabode Abdulkadri, Department of Economics, The University of the West Indies, Mona Campus, Jamaica

Jamaica is US$0.31 per kWh compared to US$0.06 in Trinidad and Tobago (Makhijani et al., 2013), its major regional trading partner.

The energy issue has been paramount on the agenda of the GOJ and a number of initiatives have been floated and policy measures taken to tackle it. The government adopted a national energy policy in 2009 with the vision to attain "a modern, efficient, diversified and environmentally sustainable energy sector providing affordable and accessible energy supplies with long-term energy security and supported by informed public behaviour on energy issues and an appropriate policy, regulatory and institutional framework" (Ministry of Energy and Mining, 2009, p. 1). The national energy policy also feeds into the broader national development plan, Vision 2030 Jamaica, with the vision to make Jamaica, by the year 2030, "the place of choice to live, work, raise families, and do business" (Planning Institute of Jamaica, 2009, p. 1). Both the Vision 2030 Jamaica and the national energy policy have set specific goals for renewable energy (RE) sources to form an increasing share of the country's energy mix, reaching 20% by 2030. Although the government remains committed to this goal as outlined in policy statements, it remains uncertain if the targets will be achieved by the deadlines.

Lack of substantial progress towards energy diversification has called to question the reliability of the targets for renewables set by the government. In this paper, focusing on the electricity sub-sector, we examine the progress made so far in incorporating RE sources in the generation of electricity in Jamaica vis-à-vis the required progress that is needed if the targets are to be met. Using a linear programming model, we developed an energy plan that specifies the amount of electricity generation required to meet expected future demands, disaggregated by source. Our model suggests that a rather rapid investment in RE sources is necessary if the targets are to be met. Based on the optimal least-cost plan, only wind, hydro and bagasse power are the recommended RE sources that should be considered over the next 16 years. The results have implications for policy. Although Jamaica has abundant solar energy potential, based on current costs and already installed fossil-fuel generating capacity, solar power is not an economic investment for the country. Therefore, if the targets for renewable energy are to be achieved in the electricity sub-sector, greater emphasis should be placed on wind power and bagasse power as energy sources.

In the next section, an overview of the energy sector in Jamaica is presented. This is followed by the methodology section in which the linear programming (LP) model used to generate the optimal energy plan for Jamaica is presented and a description of the data and sources of data is provided. The results are then presented followed by a discussion of the findings. The paper concludes with implications for policy.

2. The Energy Sector in Jamaica

Petroleum is the major source of energy in Jamaica, accounting for 90% of the country's energy needs (Ministry of Mining, 2009). Electricity generation constitute the largest share of petroleum consumption (31% in 2010) and oil accounted for 95.3% of 4214 GWh of electricity generated in 2009 (Makhijani et al., 2013). The Petroleum Corporation of Jamaica, an executive agency of GOJ, has the sole authority for oil importation. In 2011, the government spent more on oil importation (US$2.2 billion) than the country's total export receipts (US$1.65 billion) (Makhijani et al., 2013). For a country experiencing a stagnant economy, such a mismatch erodes foreign reserves and further aggravates the domestic economic situation. Understandably, energy security and affordability are key goals of Jamaica's national energy policy and the introduction of renewable energy is seen as a critical factor in achieving these goals. To that end, the GOJ has set targets to increase the share of RE sources from 5% in 2008 to 12.5%, 15% and 20% by 2015, 2020 and 2030, respectively.

Diversification initiatives in the energy sector have mainly been focused on the electricity sub-sector, except for the introduction of ethanol fuel (E-10), in the earlier years, in the road transportation sub-sector. The energy mix diversification drive has been slow and hampered by many factors, including regulatory, financial and technical issues. The Jamaica Public Service Company Limited (JPSCo) is the dominant player in electricity generation in the country and has an exclusive right to power transmission and distribution. A private company with 20% government ownership, JPSCo accounts for about 70% of installed generating capacity of 925 MW. Four independent power producers (IPPs) account for the remaining capacity. One of the IPPs, Wigton Windfarm has a capacity of 38.7MW exclusively from wind. This and a 3 MW wind turbine operated by JPSCo represent all the wind power energy on the national grid and account for 1.4% of total energy generated in 2009. The only other renewable source of energy on the national grid is hydropower accounting for 3.3% of energy generated in the same year. The rest was generated from fuel-powered plants (Makhijani et al., 2013).

As a monopoly in power transmission and distribution, and a dominant player in power generation, the Office of Utilities Regulation (OUR) regulates JPSCo. The OUR Act of 1995 (amended in 2000), among others, stipulates that the office will encourage competition and the development and use of indigenous resources. However, the OUR has taken a lukewarm attitude towards, if not stymied, the development of RE sources in accordance with the national energy policy and its mandate. The office prepared an energy generation expansion plan for the country in 2010, a year after the national energy policy was adopted and the Vision 2030 Jamaica was implemented. The Generation Expansion Plan (OUR, 2010) provided three future energy demand forecasts (base, low and high) for the country. It also included three cases (scenarios) for energy expansion strategy. These involve natural gas, natural gas/coal and business-as-usual cases. Surprisingly, no case or strategy was provided for renewable sources. Instead, the plan included a brief narrative on the obstacles confronting RE projects in the country and indicated that the mid-term RE penetration target set by the national energy policy will not likely be achieved. As the government agency with the regulatory power and responsibility to effect energy diversification, the plan falls far short of a forward-looking strategy. At the minimum, the plan should have included a renewable energy case if only to indicate to the policy makers the magnitude of investment or the incentives needed to make the RE policy of the GOJ attainable.

Notwithstanding, international partners have conducted major studies on RE in Jamaica. In 2005, the United Nations' Economic Commission for Latin America and the Caribbean (ECLAC) sponsored a study on the RE potential in Jamaica (Loy and Coviello, 2005). The study concluded that there is an abundance of RE sources in the country and singled out the sugar processing industry as one of the largest sources of RE through the use of biomass for electricity generation. The study also indicated the need for better identification of existing potentials and on-site assessments and measurements as precursors for the achievement of long-term renewable energy goals.

The recommendations made by the ECLAC study were addressed in a recent study by the Worldwatch Institute (Makhijani et al, 2013). The study entailed a more comprehensive mapping of the RE potentials of Jamaica and provided scenarios for incorporating renewable energy sources in the country's energy mix. The study showed that not only is the 20% RE target achievable by 2030, a much higher target of 93% renewables by 2030 is also possible. That feat will entail investing in 3,500 MW of new renewable capacity, predominantly solar and wind power, over a period of 18 years. However, in a business-as-usual scenario, petroleum continues to dominate the energy source in a proportion similar to that of 2012.

On the practical side, the GOJ has been engaged in a protracted process of introducing LNG as an energy source in Jamaica. After signing a Memorandum of Understanding with the government of Trinidad and Tobago in 2004 to supply 1.15 million of metric tonnes annually, it was expected that two new combined cycle power plants will be built to run on LNG (Loy and Coviello, 2005). Ever since, the LNG project tender process has been mired in controversy resulting in numerous cancellations, with the most recent occurring in May 2014. A new process for selecting the preferred company to build a 380 MW plant that will run on LNG is now underway. Ten years after the idea was first floated as the ideal opportunity to cut the cost of electricity in Jamaica, a company to build and operate the proposed plant is yet to be determined. Meanwhile, consumers continue to endure high electricity price. Had the last tender process been successful, the winning bid would have guaranteed a price of US$0.13 per kWh which is just a third of the price currently paid by residential consumers. Delays in bringing the LNG project to reality has not only resulted in a jump in the projected investment cost, it has also progressively pushed the cost of electricity up as old and inefficient plants, a high proportion of which have outlived their useful economic life (OUR, 2010), continue to be operated and the cost passed on to the consumers.

Against this background, it is useful to determine what it will take to achieve a 20% target for renewable sources in the country's energy mix. Such information will be helpful to investors, regulators and policy makers in objectively and realistically assessing the renewable energy targets set in the national energy policy.

3. Methodology

3.1 Analytical Model

Linear Programming (LP) is an optimization model that has been used extensively for energy planning. Zeng et al. (2011) provided a review of an extensive list of studies using optimization models for energy systems planning. These studies include those using LP and other forms of optimization models for planning energy systems (Kavrakoglu, 1980; Smith, 1980; Beck et al., 2008), incorporating renewables in the energy mix (Cormio et al., 2003), and assessing decarbonisation targets (Kannan, 2009; Kannan and Strachan, 2009).

In the present study, we apply LP to generate optimal combination of energy sources for Jamaica that will ensure that the RE targets for 2015, 2020 and 2030 are met. The model is specified as follows:

$$\underset{\Delta X}{\text{Min}}\, Z = \sum_{i}^{k}\sum_{t}^{T} c_i \Delta X_{it}$$

Subject to:

$$\sum_i^k \bar{X}_i = \overline{GC}$$
$$\bar{X}_i + \sum_t^T \Delta X_{it} \le maxX_i \qquad \forall\, i$$
$$\sum_i^k \Delta X_{it} \ge \Delta D_t \qquad \forall\, t$$
$$\overline{GC} + \sum_t^T \Delta D_t = D_T$$
$$\sum_i^k \bar{X}_i + \sum_i^k \Delta X_{it} \ge 0.125 \times (\overline{GC} + \Delta D_t), when\ t = 2015\ \&\ k \in RE$$
$$\sum_i^k \bar{X}_i + \sum_t^{T-1}\sum_i^k \Delta X_{it} \ge 0.15 \times (\overline{GC} + \sum_t^{T-1} \Delta D_t), when\ t = 2015, 2020\ \&\ k \in RE$$
$$\sum_i^k \bar{X}_i + \sum_t^T\sum_i^k \Delta X_{it} \ge 0.20 \times (\overline{GC} + \sum_t^T \Delta D_t) \qquad \forall\, t\ \&\ i \in RE$$
$$\Delta X_{it} = 0 \qquad where\ applicable$$
$$x \ge 0$$

Where, ΔX_{it} is the change in electricity generation from energy source *i* by period *t*;
c_i is the unit cost of capital for generating a kWh of electricity from energy source *i*;
$\bar{X}_i$ is the initial generating capacity of energy source *i* in year 2009;
$\overline{GC}$ is the total generating capacity from all sources in year 2009;
ΔX_{it} is the change in generating capacity of energy source *i* in year *t*;
$maxX_i$ is generating potential of energy source *i*;
ΔD_t is the additional demand for electricity in year *t* from the previous period;
D_T is the forecast for electricity demand in year 2030;
$i = 1, \ldots, k$ represents k different sources of electricity generation;
$t = 1, \ldots, T$ represents time periods 2015, 2020 and 2030;
x represents any variable in the model;
RE is the set of renewable energy sources; and
Z is the minimum aggregate cost of investment.

The objective function represents the capital portion of the levelized costs of electricity generation (LCOE) in Jamaica as a proxy for the investment cost needed to build new generating capacities to meet future energy demands. This "investment cost" is minimized while ensuring that the target for renewable energy in the energy mix for each of the three time periods (2015, 2020 and 2030) is satisfied. This is done with due cognizance of the capacity limit for each energy source in the country and electricity demand forecast. Other timeline restrictions are incorporated to provide for realistic results that ensure that only technically feasible options are included in the optimal results for any time period. For example, since LNG is not a feasible option for 2015, a restriction is placed in the model not to generate electricity from natural gas in 2015. Other accounting restrictions are included to ensure model consistency. The optimal result from the LP model will indicate additional electricity generated for each period to meet the demand requirement and the source.

For ease of modelling and to normalize the variability in efficiency inherent in the different RE sources, energy capacity is modelled in GWh and not in MW. This will ensure that the renewable energy target is measured against the amount of electricity generated and not just in terms of capacity installed.

3.2 Data

The National Energy Policy (Ministry of Energy and Mining, 2009), OUR (2010) and Worldwatch (2013) were the main sources of data. The National Energy Policy served as the source for renewable energy targets for Jamaica. OUR (2010)'s base forecast for future electricity demand in Jamaica was used to set the minimum requirement for additional electricity generation by the three timelines. The existing capacity for oil-powered plants and potential capacities for RE sources were derived from Makhijani et al. (2013). The capacity for natural gas-fired plants was set at the original total capacity of 480 MW tendered by the OUR for the LNG project. Makhijani et al. (2013) reported a system loss (technical and non-technical) of 22.3% in 2011. To accommodate this reality in the optimal plan, a system loss of 20% was provided for in the input data. The capital portion of the levelized cost of electricity generation reported by Makhijani et al. (2013) represents the per unit cost of electricity generation attributable to the initial capital invested in the generation capacity. This value was used as a proxy for the unit cost of investment. Therefore, while it provides a realistic measure of the relative costs of investment for different energy sources, it does not represent the actual cost of upfront investment needed to build the new capacities.

4. Results

Current estimate from the Ministry of Science, Technology, Energy and Mining (formerly Ministry of Energy and Mining) indicates that the renewable energy share has increased from 5% in 2008 to about 8% in 2014. Using trend analysis, a linear and an exponential projection of the trend were compared to the policy targets (Figure 1). The analysis shows that if the current trend continues on a linear path, the renewable energy target will not be met for any of the timeline years. However, in the case of an exponential growth in renewable energy sources, the target will be met only for 2030, after investment in renewables would have been ratcheted up between now and 2025, at which time the growth in accelerated investment will be equivalent to the required growth in investment had the target been met all along.

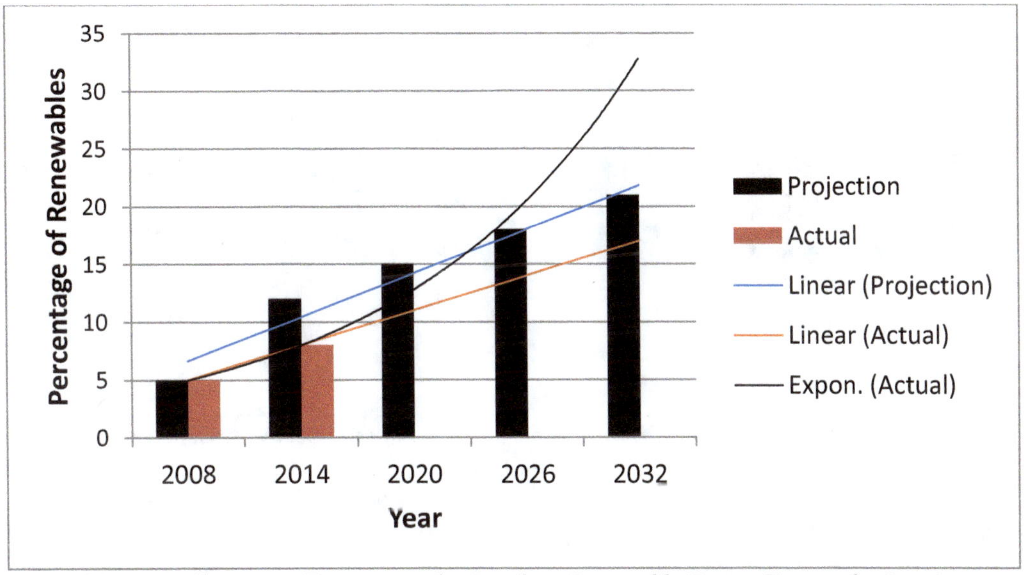

Figure 1. *Alternative Trajectories for Reaching Renewable Energy Targets for Jamaica*

The optimal LP result for achieving the renewable energy target for 2015, 2020 and 2030 is presented in Table 1. The result shows the optimal combination of renewable sources to include wind power, hydropower and bagasse power, but not solar power. By 2015, additional fuel-based capacity needs to be installed to produce 201 GWh of electricity. By the same year, major investments in wind power capacity must be made to produce 971 GWh of electricity. The only additional investment required between 2015 and 2020 is in natural gas plant(s) that have enough capacity to generate 1574 GWh of electricity. A more diversified energy-mix would be attained by 2030 with new investments in wind power (374 GWh), hydropower (126 GWh), bagasse power (596 GWh) and natural gas power (2631 GWh). Overall, the renewable energy target will be surpassed for 2015 and 2020, and met for 2030. In 2030, natural gas will account for one-third of electricity generation in addition to 20% produced from renewable sources.

Table 1. *Historical and Required New Electricity Generation to Meet Future Electricity Demand in Jamaica (2009-2030)*[1]

Historical (2009) Generation		Recommended Additional Generation			
Source	Electricity (GWh)	Source	Electricity (GWh) by Year		
			2015	2020	2030
Petroleum	4819	Petroleum	201		
Wind	71	Wind	971		375
Hydro	167	Hydro			126
		Solar			
		Bagasse			596
		Natural Gas		1574	2631
Total	**5057**		**1172**	**1574**	**3728**

[1] *Results incorporate a 20% system loss due to technical and non-technical losses.*

The composition of the different RE sources in the renewable energy share is shown in Figure 2. Wind power is the dominant RE source in the optimal mix for the three timelines accounting for at least 60% of renewables at any point in time. Hydropower remains fairly stable at about 13% across the periods while bagasse power accounts for about a quarter in 2030. The result provides evidence that the renewable energy targets are technically feasible and the attainment of the targets will facilitate the diversification of energy sources in Jamaica.

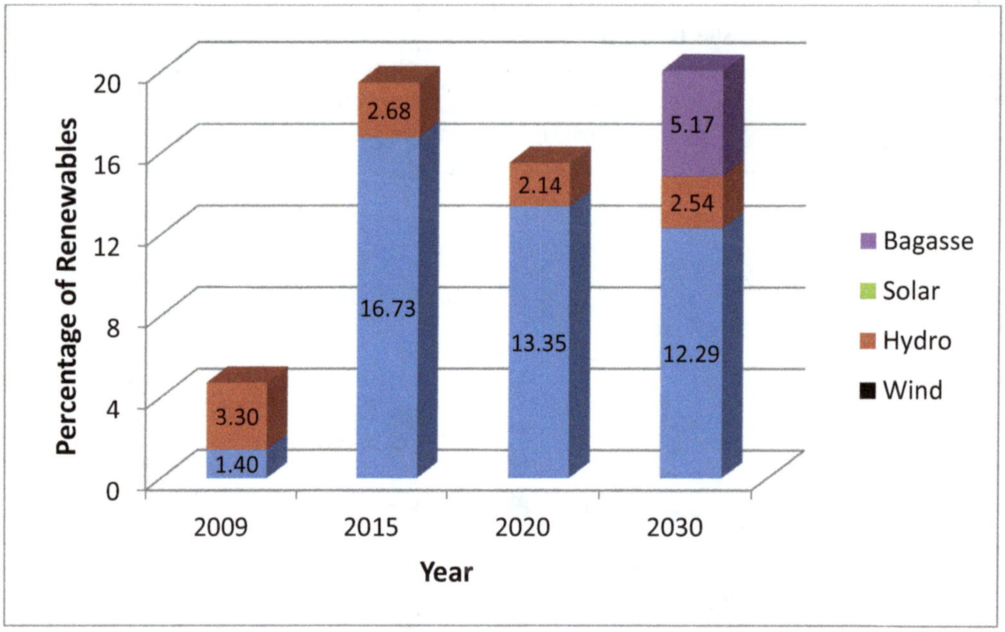

***Figure 2**. Share of Renewable Sources of Energy in the Optimal Plan for Electricity Generation in Jamaica (2009-2030)*

5. Discussion

Although the optimal result shows technical feasibility, the practicality of this happening is highly improbable. For this to be a reality, major investments in wind farms need to be made in a period of a year and a half. At the moment, more attention is devoted to introducing LNG in the energy mix and that process has taken 10 years without any practical results. JPSCo has not shown any interest to invest in wind farms or any other forms of RE on a massive scale. The OUR has either shown lack of interest in pushing for RE or not offered any encouragement to JPSCo and other IPPs to invest in RE. This is against the backdrop of increasing public displeasure with high electricity prices and a more recent pronouncement by the government that the target for RE by 2030 is no longer 20% but 30%. This apparent discordant in the policy of the government on one hand and the action or inaction of the regulator and power generating companies on the other is troubling and brings to question the evidence-base for energy policy promulgation in Jamaica.

Although no real analysis has ever been provided as the evidence for setting the renewable energy target in Jamaica, anecdotal evidence suggests that the target is technically achievable. The recent report by Worldwatch Institute (Makhijani et al., 2013) showing that Jamaica could attain 93% RE in its energy mix by 2030 would have validated that perception and the recent shift in the target from 20% to 30% may not have been unconnected to that study. What will be more useful for policy makers and energy stakeholders in Jamaica, however, is an indicative plan or plans of what sort of investments need to happen and when for these targets to be achieved. To our knowledge, no such study has been done despite the need for it.

The current study fills the gap in evidence-based economic analysis that is required to inform practical energy planning, as it relates to RE, in Jamaica. Our findings indicate that the 20% RE target is technically achievable. Our study also reveals a rather surprising finding that investing in solar energy is not optimal for the country. Contrary to increasing popularity of solar panels in Jamaica, given current investment climate and costs, solar energy is not recommended as an energy option for electricity generation for the national grid. At first glance, this finding appears contrary to that reported in Makhijani et al. (2013) that showed solar energy as the major source of RE for a 93% RE penetration. A closer look at their results will show that a higher percentage of wind energy is indicated at lower RE penetration and the share of solar energy only increases at higher penetration. The current study provides evidence that at lower RE penetration target, solar power will not be an optimal choice. The inclusion of solar energy at lower levels of RE penetration, as shown by Makhijani et al. (2013), will only be economically justified if there are expectations and future plans to expand on solar energy, in which case early investments will drive down costs on future units as the scale of installation is increased significantly. A market for RE that is 73% larger will provide such an incentive and hence the reason for the difference in the results between this study and Makhijani et al. (2013).

The findings of this study should provide a basis for serious dialog in the energy sector of Jamaica on the reality of GOJ's RE target. As at present, this target is stated more conveniently as a slogan than pursued as a policy objective. It is high time the government realises that the target will not be achieved unless meaningful actions needed to actualize it take place. The first step in that line of actions is to know how the target can be achieved and what it will take to achieve it. This study has shown one of possibly several ways in which the target can be achieved. As more information is provided by stakeholders, the model can be applied to generate alternative plans under different scenarios. However, until such a time, this study provides a good starting point for instigating a much needed debate on the RE target policy in Jamaica.

6. Conclusions

Vision 2030 Jamaica, the national development plan for Jamaica, and the country's national energy policy have set a renewable energy target of 20% for the country by 2030. Previous studies (Loy and Coviello, 2005; Makhijani et al., 2013) have shown that Jamaica has great potentials for renewable energy and the government is now mulling a 30% target for renewables by 2030. Meanwhile, RE penetration in Jamaica remains at about 8% and is far short of 12% that it should have been had the country been on track to achieving the policy target. Many observers consider electricity prices to be too high in Jamaica and the introduction of renewable energy, among other benefits, is expected to lower cost of energy in the medium to long term. However, there are renewable energy sceptics within the energy sector and concrete large scale investments to actualize the target are yet to be made. Also, until this study, no economic analysis has been done to guide policy implementation in relation to the attainment of the RE target.

The results of this study indicate that the RE target is technically achievable. This will be done through investment in additional wind power, hydropower and bagasse power generating capacities between now and 2030. Surprisingly, solar power is not competitive and not recommended for the national grid for a 20% RE penetration. When the required investment for the target to be achieved is measured against actual growth in RE sources in Jamaica, it becomes highly improbable that the 20% target will be achieved talk less of a 30% target. Therefore, this study provides the much needed evidence-base analysis that is lacking in policy analysis in relation to the RE target in Jamaica. Unless the government gets serious about promoting RE, the prospects for a sustainable low-carbon feature for Jamaica are bleak and public concerns about high electricity prices and anaemic economic growth, in the face of government's inaction to meaningfully facilitate RE, may actually lead to popular support for using coal, a high CO_2-emitting energy source. This scenario is becoming increasingly likely as the government moves forward on its plan to engage the China Habour Engineering Company (CHEC) to build a logistic hub in Jamaica. The project is expected to result in a US$1.5 billion investment in Jamaica and create 10,000 new jobs. CHEC has signified its plan to generate its own energy using coal as it considers the price of electricity in Jamaica to be too high for its planned investment. This and other realities of the local setting suggest that a low-carbon future for Jamaica is, for the moment, unsustainable.

References

Bank of Jamaica, 2013. *Quarterly Statistical Digest, July-September, 2013*. Kingston, Jamaica: Bank of Jamaica (BOJ).

Beck, J., Kempener, R., Cohen, B., and Petrie, J., 2008. A complex systems approach to planning, optimization and decision making for energy networks. *Energy Policy*, 36, pp. 2795–2805.

Cormio, C., Dicorato, M., Minoia, A., and Trovato, M., 2003. A regional energy planning methodology including renewable energy sources and environmental constraints. *Renewable and Sustainable Energy Reviews*, 7, pp. 99–130.

Kannan, R., 2009. Uncertainties in key low carbon power generation technologies—Implication for UK decarbonisation targets. *Applied Energy*, 86, pp. 1873–1886.

Kannan, R., and Strachan, N., 2009. Modelling the UK residential energy sector under long-term decarbonisation scenarios: Comparison between energy systems and sectoral modelling approaches. *Applied Energy*, 86, pp. 416–428.

Kavrakoglu, I., 1980. Decision analysis in the energy sector. *Applied Mathematical Modelling*, 4, pp. 456–462.

Loy, D. and Coviello, M., 2005. *Renewable energies potential in Jamaica*. Santiago, Chile: United Nations.

Makhijani, S., Ochs, A., Weber, M., Konold, M., Lucky, M., and Ahmed, A., 2013. *Jamaica Sustainable Energy Roadmap: Pathways to an Affordable, Reliable, Low-Emission Electricity System.* Washington, DC: Worldwatch Institute.

Ministry of Energy and Mining, 2009. *National Energy Policy 2009-2030*. Kingston, Jamaica: Ministry of Energy and Mining (now Ministry of Science, Technology, Energy and Mining).

Office of Utilities Regulation, 2010. Generation Expansion Plan 2010. Kingston, Jamaica: Office of Utilities Regulation (OUR).

Planning Institute of Jamaica, 2009. *Vision 2030 Jamaica: National Development Plan*. Kingston, Jamaica: Planning Institute of Jamaica.

Smith, B.R., 1980. Modelling New Zealand's energy system." *European Journal of Operations Research*, 4, pp. 173–184.

Zeng, Y., Cai, Y., Huang, G. and Jing, D., 2011. A Review of Optimization Modeling of Energy Systems Planning and GHG Emission Mitigation under Uncertainty. *Energies*, 4, pp. 1642-1656.

13

Human Capital, Wealth, and Renewable Resources

Wei-Bin ZHANG*

Ritsumeikan Asia Pacific University, Japan

This paper studies dynamic interdependence among physical capital, resource and human capital. We integrate the Solow one-sector growth, Uzawa-Lucas two-sector and some neoclassical growth models with renewable resource models. The economic system consists of the households, production sector, resource sector and education sector. We take account of three ways of improving human capital: Arrow's learning by producing (Arrow, 1962), Uzawa's learning by education (Uzawa, 1965), and Zhang's learning by consuming (Zhang, 2007). The model describes a dynamic interdependence among wealth accumulation, human capital accumulation, resource change, and division of labor under perfect competition. We simulate the model to demonstrate existence of equilibrium points and motion of the dynamic system. We also examine effects of changes in the productivity of the resource sector, the utilization efficiency of human capital, the propensity to receive education, and the propensity to save upon dynamic paths of the system.

***Keywords**: education; physical capital; renewable resource; human capital; propensities to save and to learn; time distribution among study, work and leisure*

1. Introduction

Three kinds of "capital" - physical capital such as machines, human capital such as skills, and renewable resources such as forests - are important for economic growth and development. As human capital, resources and physical capital are scarce resources and play different roles in production and consumption, it is significant to study how these resources are allocated in different activities. Moreover, these stock variables change according to different mechanisms. Physical capital changes due to, for instance, depreciation and wealth accumulation. Savings by households, firms, or nations are essential for physical capital accumulation. Human capital is accumulated through human capital in learning. Education and learning by doing are common sources of human capital accumulation. Stock of renewable resources is also changeable according how fast agents utilize resources and how fast renewable resources grow. This paper studies dynamic interdependence among physical capital, resource and human capital. We integrate the Solow one-sector growth, Uzawa-Lucas two-sector and some neoclassical growth models with renewable resource models. The economic system consists of the households, production sector, resource sector and education sector. We take account of three ways of improving human capital: Arrow's learning by producing (1962), Uzawa's learning by education (Uzawa, 1965), and Zhang's learning by consuming (2007). The model describes a dynamic interdependence among wealth accumulation, human capital accumulation, resource change, and division of labor under perfect competition.

* Correspondence:
Wei-Bin Zhang, Ritsumeikan Asia Pacific University, 1-1 Jumonjibaru, Beppu-Shi, Oita-ken, 874-8577 Japan

As far as physical capital and wealth accumulation are concerned, the model in this study is based on the neoclassical growth theory. Most of the models in the neoclassical growth theory are extensions and generalizations of the pioneering works of Solow in 1956. The model has played an important role in the development of economic growth theory by using the neoclassical production function and neoclassical production theory. The Solow model has been extended and generalized in numerous directions (e.g., Uzawa, 1961; Kurz, 1963; Diamond, 1965; Stiglitz, 1967; Drugeon and Venditti, 2001; Erceg *et al.* 2005). An important direction of extending the traditional neoclassical one-sector growth model was carried out by Uzawa (1965), who proposed a formal dynamic growth model with education. But with regards to formal modeling of education and economic growth, the work by Lucas (1988) has recently caused a great interest in the issue among economists. Dynamic interdependence between education and economic growth is currently a main topic in the literature of economic theory and economic empirical studies (e.g., Hanushek and Kimko, 2000; Barro, 2001; Krueger and Lindahl, 2001; Fleisher *et al.* 2011; Li *et al.*, 2012; Castelló-Climent and Hidalgo-Cabrillana, 2012). In the Uzawa-Lucas model and many of their extensions and generalizations, it is implicitly assumes that all skills and human capital is formed due to formal schooling. Common sense tells us that much of the so-called human capital may be accumulated through parents' influences, family and other social environment, and other social and economic activities, not to say learning by producing (and professional training). If these non-school factors are neglected in modelling human capital and economic growth, we may not be able to properly understand the role of formal education in economic development. Chen and Chevalier (2008) point out: "Making and exploiting an investment in human capital requires individuals to sacrifice not only consumption, but also leisure. When estimating the returns to education, existing studies typically weigh the monetary costs of schooling (tuition and forgone wages) against increased wages, neglecting the associated labor/leisure tradeoff." This study will generalize the Uzawa-Lucas two-sector growth model by taking account of leisure activities, learning by producing and learning by consuming.

Natural resources are incorporated into the neoclassical growth theory in the 1970s (e.g., Plourde, 1970, 1971; Stiglitz, 1974; Clark, 1976; Dasgupta and Heal, 1979). In fact, economists were aware of the necessity of modeling resources with dynamic theory long before. For instance, Gordon (1956) emphasized the need for a dynamic approach to fisheries economics as one finds in capital theory in economics: "The conservation problem is essentially one which requires a dynamic formulation… The economic justification of conservation is the same as that of any capital investment – by postponing utilization we hope to increase the quantity available for use at a future date. In the fishing industry we may allow our fish to grow and to reproduce so that the stock at a future date will be greater than it would be if we attempted to catch as much as possible at the present time. … [I]t is necessary to arrive at an optimum which is a catch per unit of time, and one must reach this objective through consideration of the interaction between the rate of catch, the dynamics of fish population, and the economic time-preference schedule of the community or the interest rate on invested capital. His is a very complicated problem and I suspect that we will have to look to the mathematical economists for assistance in clarifying it." As pointed out by Munro and Scott (1985), in the 1950s it was quite difficult to develop workable dynamic models of resources. Solow (1999) also argues for the necessity of taking account of natural resources in the neoclassical growth theory. According to Solow if the resource good is used as one of the inputs in the production, then it is easy to incorporate the use of renewable resources into the neoclassical growth model. Nevertheless, Solow does not show how to incorporate possible consumption of renewable resource into the growth model. There are only a few models of growth and renewable resources which treat the renewable resource as both input of production and a source of utility (see, Beltratti, *et al.*, 1994, Ayong Le Kama, 2001). Our model contains the renewable resource as a source of utility and input of production. It should be noted that there are also studies on dynamic interactions among economic growth, renewable resources and elastic labor supply on the basis of the neoclassical growth theory with capital accumulation and renewable resource (e.g., Eliasson and Turnovsky, 2004, Alvarez-Cuadrado and van Long, 2011). Our model differs from these studies not only in that we use an alternative utility function, but also in that we introduce human capital and education sector into the growth theory with capital and resource.

Another important variable in dynamic analysis is time distribution among various activities. The allocation of time has been explicit introduced into economic theory since Becker (1965) published his seminal work in 1965. There is an immense body of empirical and theoretical literature on economic growth with time distribution between home and non-home economic and leisure activities (e.g., Benhabib and Perli, 1994; Ladrón-de-Guevara *et al.* 1997; Jones and Manuelli, 1995; Turnovsky, 1999; Greenwood and Hercowitz, 1991; Rupert *et al.* 1995; Cambell and Ludvigson, 2001). Nevertheless, only a few theoretical economic growth models with renewable resource and human capital explicitly treat work time as an endogenous variable. This paper introduces endogenous time into the neoclassical growth theory with renewable resource. This paper is to integrate two papers by Zhang (2007, 2011). The former paper deals with education and capital accumulation, while the latter studies dynamic interactions between resource and physical capital. This paper integrates the two models to examine dynamic interactions among human capital, physical capital and renewable resources. Our model is also a synthesis of three main growth models – Solow's one-sector growth model, Arrow's learning by doing model, and the Uzawa-Lucas's growth model with education - in the growth literature. We integrate the main mechanisms of economic growth in these three models in a comprehensive framework. The remainder of the paper is organized as follows. Section 2 defines the economic model with endogenous human capital accumulation, resource dynamics and wealth accumulation. Section 3 shows that the motion of the economic system is described by three differential equations and simulates the model. Section 4 carries out comparative dynamics analysis. Section 5 concludes the study.

2. The Basic Model

The economy has three - production, education and renewable resource - sectors. Most aspects of the production sector are similar to the standard one-sector growth model in the neoclassical growth theory (Burmeister and Dobell, 1970; Barro and Sala-i-Martin, 1995). It is assumed that there is only one (durable) good in the economy under consideration. Households own assets of the economy and distribute their incomes to consume and save. Production sectors or firms use inputs such as labor with varied levels of human capital, different kinds of capital, knowledge and natural resources to produce material goods or services. Exchanges take place in perfectly competitive markets. Factor markets work well; factors are inelastically supplied and the available factors are fully utilized at every moment. Saving is undertaken only by households. All earnings of firms are distributed in the form of payments to factors of production, labor, managerial skill and capital ownership. We assume a homogenous and fixed population $\overline{N}$. The labor force is employed the three sectors. We select commodity to serve as numeraire, with all the other prices being measured relative to its price. We assume that wage rate is identical among all professions.

2.1. The production sector

We assume that production is to combine labor force, $N_i(t)$, and physical capital, $K_i(t)$, and renewable resource, $X_i(t)$. We use the conventional production function to describe a relationship between inputs and output. Let $F_i(t)$ stand for output level of the production sector at time t. The production function is specified as follows

$$F_i(t) = A_i K_i^{\alpha_i}(t) N_i^{\beta_i}(t) X_i^{\gamma_i}(t), \quad A_i, \alpha_i, \beta_i, \gamma_i > 0, \quad \alpha_i + \beta_i + \gamma_i = 1, \tag{1}$$

where A_i, α_i, β_i and γ_i are positive parameters. Markets are competitive; thus labor and capital earn their marginal products. The rate of interest, $r(t)$, and wage rate, $w(t)$, the price of the resource, $p_x(t)$, are determined by markets. The marginal conditions are given by

$$r(t) + \delta_k = \frac{\alpha_i F_i(t)}{K_i(t)}, \quad w(t) = \frac{\beta_i F_i(t)}{N_i(t)}, \quad p_x(t) = \frac{\gamma_i F_i(t)}{X_i(t)}, \tag{2}$$

where δ_k is the given depreciation rate of physical capital.

2.2. Resource sector and change of renewable resources

We use $X(t)$ to represent the stock of the resource. We assume that the natural growth rate of the resource is a logistic function of the existing stock (e.g., Brander and Taylor, 1998; Brown, 2000; Hannesson, 2000; Cairns and Tian, 2010, Farmer and Bednar-Friedl, 2011). It should be noted that there are some alternative approaches to renewable resources in the literature (Tornell and Velasco, 1992; Long and Wang, 2009; Fujiwara, 2011). The logistic function is

$$\phi_0 X(t)\left(1 - \frac{X(t)}{\phi}\right),$$

where the variable, ϕ, is the maximum possible size for the resource stock, called the carrying capacity of the resource, and , the variable, ϕ_0, is "uncongested" or "intrinsic" growth rate of the renewable resource. If the stock is equal to ϕ, then the growth rate should equal zero. If the carrying capacity is much larger than the current stock, then the growth rate per unit of the stock is approximately equal to the intrinsic growth rate. In this case, the congestion effect is negligible. It should be noted that according Jinni (2006), the carrying capacity changes as a function of the stock of a renewable resource. Also in Benchekroun (2003), an inversed-V shaped dynamics of resource accumulation is accepted. The resource decreases if its stock is sufficiently large. There are also models which introduce human efforts and other factors to the dynamics of resources (e.g., Long, 1977; Berck, 1981; Levhari and Withagen, 1992; Ayong Le Kama, 2001; Wirl, 2004).

We use $F_x(t)$ to stand for the harvest rate of the resource. The change rate in the stock is then equal to the natural growth rate minus the harvest rate, that is

$$\dot{X}(t) = \phi_0 X(t)\left(1 - \frac{X(t)}{\phi}\right) - F_x(t). \tag{3}$$

We assume a nationally owned open-access renewable resource. The open-access case was initially examined by Gordon (1954). There are different approaches to growth with renewable resources with different property-rights regimes (e.g., Bulter and Barbier, 2005; Copeland and Taylor, 2009; Alvarez-Guadrado and Von Long, 2011; Tajibaeva, 2012). With open access, harvesting occurs up to the point at which the current return to a representative entrant equals the entrant's cost. We use $N_x(t)$ and $K_x(t)$ to respectively stand for the labor force and capital stocks employed by the resource sector. We assume that harvesting of the resource is carried out according to the following harvesting production function

$$F_x(t) = A_x X^b(t) K_x^{\alpha_x}(t) N_x^{\beta_x}(t), \quad A_x, b \ge 0, \quad \alpha_x, \beta_x > 0, \quad \alpha_x + \beta_x = 1, \tag{4}$$

where A_x, b, α_x and β_x are parameters. It should be noted that the Schaefer harvesting production function which is taken on the following form

$$F_x(t) = A_x X(t) N_x(t),$$

is a special case of (4). The Schaefer production function does not take account of capital (or with capital being fixed, see Schaefer, 1957). The function with fixed capital and technology is widely applied to fishing (see also, Paterson and Wilen, 1977; Milner-Gulland and Leader-Williams, 1992; Bulter and van Kooten, 1999). As machines are important inputs in harvesting, we explicitly take account of capital input.

Harvesting is carried out by competitive profit-maximizing firms under conditions of free entry. The marginal conditions are given as follows

$$r(t) + \delta_k = \frac{\alpha_x p_x(t) F_x(t)}{K_x(t)}, \quad w(t) = \frac{\beta_x p_x(t) F_x(t)}{N_x(t)}. \tag{5}$$

2.3. The education sector and accumulation of human capital

We assume that the education sector is also characterized of perfect competition. Students are supposed to pay the education fee $p_e(t)$ per unity time. The education sector pays teachers and capital with the market rates. Let $N_e(t)$ and $K_e(t)$ stand for respectively the labor force and capital stocks employed by the education sector. The cost of the education sector is given by $w(t)N_e(t) + r(t)K_e(t)$. The total education service is measured by the total (qualified) education time received by the population. The production function of the education sector is assumed to be a function of $K_e(t)$ and $N_e(t)$. We specify the production function of the education sector as follows

$$F_e(t) = A_e K_e^{\alpha_e}(t) N_e^{\beta_e}(t), \ \alpha_e, \beta_e > 0, \ \alpha_e + \beta_e = 1, \tag{6}$$

where A_e, α_e and β_e are positive parameters. Empirical studies on education production functions are referred to, for instance, Krueger (1999). For given $p_e(t)$, $H(t)$, $r(t)$, and $w(t)$, the education sector chooses $K_e(t)$ and $N_e(t)$ to maximize profit. The optimal solution is given by

$$r(t) + \delta_k = \frac{\alpha_e p_e(t) F_e(t)}{K_e(t)}, \ w(t) = \frac{\beta_e p_e(t) F_e(t)}{N_e(t)}. \tag{7}$$

Following Zhang (2007), we assume that there are three sources of improving human capital, through education, "learning by producing", and "learning by leisure". Arrow (1962) first introduced learning by doing into growth theory; Uzawa (1965) took account of trade-offs between investment in education and capital accumulation, and Zhang (2007) introduced impact of consumption on human capital accumulation (via the so-called creative leisure) into growth theory. We use $H(t)$ to stand for the level of human capital. We propose that human capital dynamics is given by

$$\dot{H}(t) = \frac{\upsilon_e F_e^{a_e}(t)\left(H^m(t) T_e(t) \bar{N}\right)^{b_e}}{H^{\pi_e}(t)\bar{N}} + \frac{\upsilon_i F_i^{a_i}(t)}{H^{\pi_i}(t)\bar{N}} + \frac{\upsilon_x F_x^{a_x}(t)}{H^{\pi_x}(t)\bar{N}} + \frac{\upsilon_h C^{a_h}(t) T_h^{b_h}(t)}{H^{\pi_h}(t)\bar{N}} - \delta_h H(t), \tag{8}$$

where δ_h (> 0) is the depreciation rate of human capital, υ_e, υ_i, υ_h, a_e, b_e, a_i, a_h and b_h are non-negative parameters. The signs of the parameters π_e, π_i, and π_h are not specified as they can be either negative or positive. The above equation is a synthesis and generalization of Arrow's, Uzawa's, and Zhang's ideas about human capital accumulation. The term, $\upsilon_e F_e^{a_e}\left(H^m T_e \bar{N}\right)^{b_e} / H^{\pi_e} \bar{N}$, describes the contribution to human capital improvement through education. Human capital tends to increase with an increase in the level of education service, F_e, and in the (qualified) total study time, $H^m T_e \bar{N}$. The population $\bar{N}$ in the denominator measures the contribution in terms of per capita. The term H^{π_e} indicates that as the level of human capital of the population increases, it may be more difficult (in the case of $\pi_e > 0$) or easier, for instance, due to learning externalities as in Choi (2011) (in the case of $\pi_e < 0$) to accumulate more human capital via formal education. We refer the literature on human capital externalities to Rauch (1993) and Liu (2007), and on economies of scale and scope in education to Cohn and Cooper (2004). It should be noted that this unique formation of human capital is important to explore complexity of human capital accumulation, division of time and economic growth. For instance, the formation implies that if a society can enable people to learning through work experiences and through non-higher-education activities, national economic growth can be sustainable if its higher education is not efficient.

We take account of learning by doing effects in human capital accumulation by the term $\upsilon_i F_i^{a_i} / H^{\pi_i}$. This term implies that contribution of the production sector to human capital improvement is positively related to its production scale F_i and is dependent on the level of human capital. The term H^{π_i} takes account of returns to scale effects in human capital accumulation. The case of $\pi_i > (<)\ 0$ implies that as human capital is increased it is more difficult (easier) to further improve the level of human capital. We take account of learning by consuming by the term $\upsilon_c C^{a_h} T_h^{b_h} / H^{\pi_h} N_0$. This term can be interpreted similarly as the term for learning by producing. It should be noted that in the literature on education and economic growth, it is assumed that human capital evolves according to the following equation (see Barro and Sala-i-Martin, 1995)

$$\dot{H}(t) = H^{\eta}(t) G(T_e(t)),$$

where the function G is increasing as the effort rises with $G(0) = 0$. In the case of $\eta < 1$, there is diminishing return to the human capital accumulation. This formation is due to Lucas (1988). As $\dot{H}/H < H^{\eta - 1} G(1)$, we conclude that the growth rate of human capital must eventually tend to zero no matter how much effort is devoted to accumulating human capital. Uzawa's model may be considered a special case of the Lucas model with $\gamma = 0$, $U(c) = c$, and the assumption that the right-hand side of the above equation is linear in the effort. Solow adapts the Uzawa formation to the following form

$$\dot{H}(t) = H(t)\kappa T_e(t).$$

This is a special case of the above equation. The new formation implies that if no effort is devoted to human capital accumulation, then $\dot{H}(0) = 0$ (human capital does not vary as time passes; this results from depreciation of human capital being ignored); if all effort is devoted to human capital accumulation, then $g_H(t) = \kappa$ (human capital grows at its maximum rate; this results from the assumption of potentially unlimited growth of human capital). Between the two extremes, there is no diminishing return to the stock $H(t)$. To achieve a given percentage increase in $H(t)$ requires the same effort. As remarked by Solow (2000), the above formulation is very far from a plausible relationship. If we consider the above equation as a production for new human capital (i.e., $\dot{H}(t)$), and if the inputs are already accumulated human capital and study time, then this production function is homogenous of degree two. It has strong increasing returns to scale and constant returns to $H(t)$ itself. It can be seen that our approach is more general to the traditional formation with regard to education. Moreover, we treat teaching also as a significant factor in human capital accumulation. Efforts in teaching are neglected in Uzawa-Lucas model. Choi (2011) proposes the following human capital accumulation equation

$$\dot{H}(t) = B(t)[u(t)H(t)]^{\phi}\,\overline{H}^{\theta}(t) - \delta_H\,H(t),$$

where $B(t)$ is productivity of human capital production and $u(t)$ is the fraction of human capital devoted to human capital accumulation. Here $\overline{H}(t)$, is the average human capital stock in the economy. The term, $\overline{H}^{\theta}(t)$, measures learning externalities. As for a homogenous population, $\overline{H}(t)$ is $H(t)$. We see that Choi's learning equation is a special case of (3).

2.4. Consumer behaviors

Consumers make decisions on choice of consumption levels of goods, services, and education (which is services), as well as on how much to save. It should also be remarked that neither Uzawa nor Lucas took account of leisure in their growth models with education. Hahn (1990) takes account of leisure in generalizing the Lucas model, altering model to the case that each member of the population can use his available – nevertheless fixed - time for working, for leisure, or for studying. Like Hahn, this study also introduces leisure into the growth model with leisure, but in an alternative approach to household proposed by Zhang (1993). We denote per capita wealth by $\bar{k}(t)$, where $\bar{k}(t) \equiv K(t)/\overline{N}$. Per capita current income from the interest payment $r(t)\bar{k}(t)$ and the wage payment $w(t)T(t)$ is given by

$$y(t) = r(t)\bar{k}(t) + w(t)H^{m}(t)T(t).$$

We call $y(t)$ the current income in the sense that it comes from consumers' work and current earnings from ownership of wealth. The total value of wealth that consumers can sell to purchase goods and to save is equal to $p_0(t)\bar{k}(t)$, where $p_0(t)\ (= 1)$ is the price of the capital good (which is unity). Here, we assume that selling and buying wealth can be conducted instantaneously without any transaction cost. The per capita disposable income is given by

$$\hat{y}(t) = y(t) + \bar{k}(t) = (1 + r(t))\bar{k}(t) + w(t)H^{m}(t)T(t). \tag{9}$$

The disposable income is used for saving and consumption. At each point of time, a consumer would distribute the total available budget among saving, $s(t)$, consumption of the commodity, $c(t)$, education, $T_e(t)$, and consumption of the resource good, $c_x(t)$. The budget constraint is given by

$$c(t) + s(t) + p_e(t)T_e(t) + p_x(t)c_x(t) = \hat{y}(t) = (1 + r(t))\bar{k}(t) + w(t)H^m(t)T(t). \tag{10}$$

The total available time is allocated among working, receiving education, and leisure. The consumer is faced with the following time constraint

$$T(t) + T_e(t) + T_h(t) = T_0, \tag{11}$$

where T_0 is the total available time. Substituting (10) into the budget constraint (7) yields

$$c(t) + s(t) + w(t)H^m(t)T_h(t) + \bar{p}(t)T_e(t) + p_x(t)c_x(t) = \bar{y}(t) = (1 + r(t))\bar{k}(t) + w(t)H^m(t),$$
$$\bar{p}(t) \equiv p_e(t) + w(t)H^m(t). \tag{12}$$

At each point of time, consumers have four variables, the consumption level of consumption good $c(t)$, the consumption level of resource $c_x(t)$, the level of saving $s(t)$, the leisure time $T_h(t)$, and the education time $T_e(t)$, to decide. For simplicity of analysis, we specify the utility function as follows

$$U(t) = T_h^{\sigma_0}(t)\, T_e^{\eta_0}(t) c^{\xi_0}(t) s^{\lambda_0}(t) c_x^{\chi_0}(t), \quad \sigma_0, \eta_0, \xi_0, \lambda_0, \chi_0 > 0, \tag{13}$$

where σ_0 is called the propensity to use leisure time, ξ_0 the propensity to consume the good, λ_0 the propensity to own wealth, σ_0 the propensity to use leisure time, and η_0 the propensity to get education, and χ_0 the propensity to consume the resource good. It should be noted that we enter the time that the household spends on education into the utility. In traditional economic growth theory with endogenous human capital, education is mainly modeled by assuming that it positively affects earnings through enhanced productivity. Nevertheless, common sense tells us that one chooses education not only for higher wages, but also for social status, for social network buildings, signaling, or other purposes. In the literature of education and economics, the signaling view of education was initially formally presented by Spence (1973), Arrow (1973), and Stiglitz (1975). This implies that in addition to wages there are many other factors which we should take account of when analyzing decision on education decision. For instance, Lee (2007) holds that signaling explains why American students study more in college than in high school while the opposite is true for East Asian students. Hussey (2012) empirically distinguish human capital augmentation and the signaling value of MBA education using U.S. data. Hussey shows that signaling plays a large role in producing post-graduation earnings. Applying the idea that money burning (such as some advertising activities by firms, e.g., Nelson, 1974; Kihlstrom and Riordian, 1984; Milgrom and Roberts, 1986) may convey credible information, with a model of higher education as money burning activities Ishida (2004) shows: "this money burning activity can actually be welfare-improving under certain conditions. This result indicates that, even when education is simply a way to waste resources, it can still be meaningful and even socially desirable under certain conditions."

For the representative consumer, the wage rate $w(t)$, the rate of interest $r(t)$, the fee of education $p_e(t)$, and the price of resource $p_x(t)$ are given in markets. Maximizing $U(t)$ subject to the budget constraint yields

$$w(t)\, \mathrm{H}^{\mathrm{m}}(t)T_h(t) = \sigma\, \bar{y}(t), \quad \bar{p}(t)T_e(t) = \eta\, \bar{y}(t), \quad c(t) = \xi\, \bar{y}(t), \quad s(t) = \lambda\, \bar{y}(t), \quad p_x(t)c_x(t) = \chi\, \bar{y}(t), \tag{14}$$

where $\sigma \equiv \rho\sigma_0$, $\eta \equiv \rho\eta_0$, $\xi \equiv \rho\xi_0$, $\lambda \equiv \rho\lambda_0$, $\chi \equiv \rho\chi_0$, $\rho \equiv \dfrac{1}{\sigma_0 + \eta_0 + \xi_0 + \lambda_0 + \chi_0}$.

The demand for resource is given by $c_x = \chi \bar{y} / p_x$. The demand decreases in its price and increases in the disposable income. An increase in the propensity to consume the resource good increases the consumption when the other conditions are fixed. As any factor is related to all the other factors over time, it is difficult to see how one factor affects any other variables over time in the dynamic system.

We now find dynamics of capital accumulation. According to the definition of $s(t)$, the change in the household's wealth is given by

$$\dot{\bar{k}}(t) = s(t) - \bar{k}(t) = \lambda \bar{y}(t) - \bar{k}(t). \tag{15}$$

For the education sector, the demand and supply balances at any point of time

$$T_e(t)\bar{N} = F_e(t). \tag{16}$$

"The research indicates that literacy scores, as a direct measure of human capital, perform better in growth regressions than indicators of schooling. A country able to attain literacy scores 1% higher than the international average will achieve levels of labour productivity and GDP per capita that are 2.5 and 1.5% higher, respectively, than those of other countries." (OECD, Education at a Glance, 2006: 155). This implies that when modeling education and economic growth, it is necessary to take quantity and quality aspects of education. Equation (16) accounts for quantity balance of education. The quality aspect of education is reflected in the term of human capital accumulation associated with education in equation (3).

2.5. Full employment of the production factors

The labor force and capital are allocated among the three sectors. Let $N(t)$ and $K(t)$ stand for respectively the labor supply and total capital stock. The total labor force and the total capital are given by

$$N(t) = H^m(t)T(t)\bar{N}, \quad K(t) = \bar{N}\bar{k}(t), \tag{17}$$

where the parameter, m, measures of the efficiency that the population applies human capital. The conditions of full employment of labor and capital are

$$K_i(t) + K_e(t) + K_x(t) = K(t), \quad N_i(t) + N_e(t) + N_x(t) = N(t). \tag{18}$$

As output of the production sector is equal to the sum of the level of consumption, the depreciation of capital stock and the net savings, we have

$$C(t) + S(t) - K(t) + \delta_k K(t) = F_i(t), \tag{19}$$

where $C(t)$ is the total consumption, $S(t) - K(t) + \delta_k K(t)$ is the sum of saving and depreciation, and

$$C(t) = c(t)\bar{N}, \quad S(t) = s(t)\bar{N}.$$

As the resource output is used up by the production sector and the households, we have

$$c_x(t)\bar{N} + X_i(t) = F_x(t). \tag{20}$$

We completed the model. The model is based on some strict assumptions. Nevertheless, from the structural point of view our model is general in the sense that it synthesizes a few well-known models in economics. For instance, if we neglect resource and assume human capital constant, then the model is the one-sector neoclassical growth model by Solow (1956). If we neglect resources, then the model is structurally similar to the well-known Uzawa-Lucas two-sector model (Uzawa, 1965; Lucas, 1988). As mentioned before, our approach is also based on some growth models in the literature of resource economics.

3. The Dynamics and Its Properties

The dynamic system consists of three differential equations for wealth (or physical capital), human capital and resource stock. As the three differential equations contain other variables, we need to find three differential equations which contain only three variables. The following lemma shows how to obtain the three differential equations which contain only three variables. We also provide a computational procedure for calculating all the variables in the system at any point of time. This section examines dynamics of the model. The following lemma provides the procedure about how to determine the motion of all the variables in the dynamic system. We first introduce a variable

$$z(t) \equiv \frac{r(t) + \delta_k}{w(t)}.$$

3.1. Lemma

The dynamics of the economic system is governed by the following three differential equations with three variables, $z(t)$, $X(t)$, and $H(t)$

$$\begin{aligned}\dot{z}(t) &= \Lambda_z(z(t),\, X(t),\, H(t)),\\ \dot{X}(t) &= \Lambda_X(z(t),\, X(t),\, H(t)),\\ \dot{H}(t) &= \Lambda_H(z(t),\, X(t),\, H(t)),\end{aligned} \tag{21}$$

where Λ_z, Λ_X and Λ_H are $z(t)$, $X(t)$, and $H(t)$ given in the appendix. Moreover, all the other variables are determined as functions of $z(t)$, $X(t)$, and $H(t)$ at any point of time by the following procedure: $x_i(t)$ by (A6) $\rightarrow p_x(t)$ by (A5) $\rightarrow r(t)$ by (A3) $\rightarrow w(t)$ by (A3) $\rightarrow \bar{k}(t)$ by (A20) $\rightarrow K(t) = \bar{k}(t)\bar{N} \rightarrow N(t)$ by (A18) $\rightarrow T(t) = N(t)/H^m(t)\bar{N} \rightarrow T_h(t)$ and $T_e(t)$ by (A16) $\rightarrow p_w(t)$ by the definition $\rightarrow p_e(t)$ by (A16) $\rightarrow K_i(t)$ and $K_e(t)$ by (A13) $\rightarrow K_x(t)$ by (A11) $\rightarrow N_i(t)$, $N_e(t)$, and $N_x(t)$ by (A1) $\rightarrow \bar{y}(t)$ by (A15) $\rightarrow$ $c_x(t)$, $c(t)$, $s(t)$ by (14) $\rightarrow X_i(t) = x_i(t)N_i(t) \rightarrow F_i(t)$ by (1) $\rightarrow F_x(t)$ by (4) $\rightarrow F_e(t)$ by (6) $\rightarrow U(t)$ by (11).

The lemma provides a computational procedure for following the motion of the economic system with initial conditions. As it is difficult to interpret the analytical results, to study properties of the system we simulate the model. In the remainder of this study, we specify the depreciation rates by $\delta_k = 0.05$, $\delta_h = 0.03$, and let $T_0 = 1$. We specify the other parameters as follows

$$\begin{aligned}&\alpha_i = 0.33,\ \gamma_i = 0.08,\ \alpha_e = 0.45,\ \alpha_x = 0.3,\ \phi_0 = 5,\ \phi = 8,\ \lambda_0 = 0.6,\ \xi_0 = 0.08,\\ &\sigma_0 = 0.2,\ \eta_0 = 0.01,\ \chi_0 = 0.01,\ N_0 = 5,\ A_i = 1,\ A_e = 0.9,\ A_x = 0.3,\ b = 0.5,\\ &m = 0.8,\ v_e = 1,\ v_i = 2,\ v_h = 1.2,\ v_x = 1.5,\ a_e = 0.3,\ b_e = 0.4,\ a_i = 0.4,\\ &a_x = 0.1,\ a_h = 0.2,\ b_h = 0.1,\ \pi_e = 0.3,\ \pi_i = 0.7,\ \pi_x = 0.7,\ \pi_h = 0.6.\end{aligned} \tag{22}$$

The propensity to save is 0.6 and the propensities to consume education and resource are 0.01. We specify the values of the parameters, α_i and α_x in the Cobb-Douglas productions approximately 0.3. The propensity to enjoy leisure is 0.2. The total productivities of the production sector, education sector, and resource sector are respectively 1, 0.9 and 0.3. The conditions $\pi_e = 0.2$, $\pi_i = 0.7$ and $\pi_h = 0.1$ mean respectively that the learning by education, learning by producing, and learning by consuming exhibits (weak) increasing effects in human capital. We plot the motion of the system under (22) with the following initial conditions

$$z(0) = 0.08, \quad X(0) = 7, \quad H(0) = 12.$$

The motion of the variables is plotted in Figure 1. In Figure 1, the national output is

$$Y = F_i + p_x F_x + p_e F_e .$$

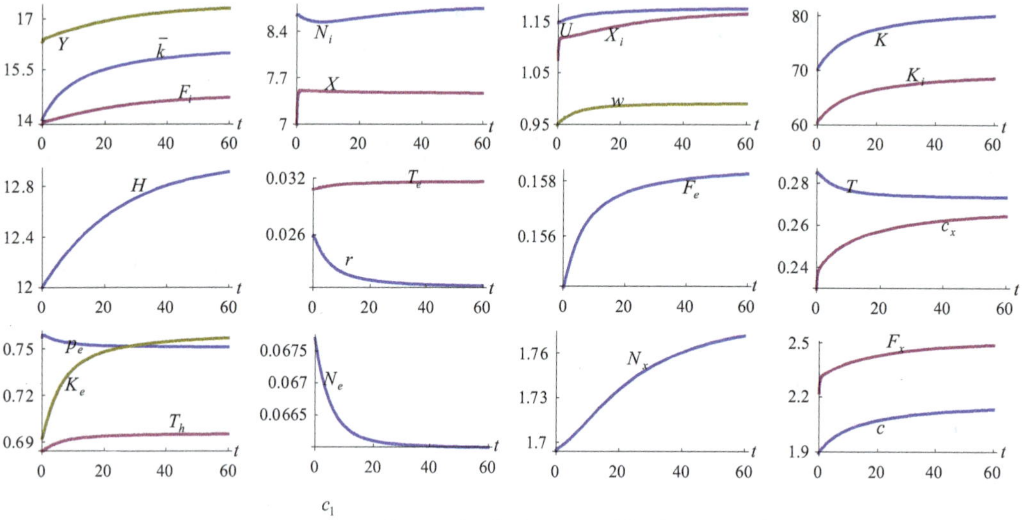

Figure 1. The Motion of the Economic System

As the initial level of human capital is lower than its equilibrium value, human capital rises over time. In association with rises in human capital, the wage rate rises and rate of interest falls over time. The equilibrium values of the variables are listed as follows

$$Y = 17.33, \quad K = 80.16, \quad H = 12.93, \quad N = 10.53, \quad X = 7.47, \quad F_i = 14.70,$$
$$F_x = 2.49, \quad F_e = 0.16, \quad N_i = 8.74, \quad N_x = 1.77, \quad N_e = 0.066, \quad K_i = 68.72,$$
$$K_x = 10.68, \quad K_e = 0.76, \quad r = 0.021, \quad p_e = 0.75, \quad p_x = 1.01, \quad W = 7.69, \quad T = 0.27,$$
$$T_h = 0.70, \quad T_e = 0.032, \quad c = 2.14, \quad c_x = 0.27, \quad s = 16.03, \quad U = 1.18.$$

It is straightforward to calculate the three eigenvalues at the equilibrium point as follows

-4.50, -0.18, -0.04.

As the eigenvalues are negative, the equilibrium point is locally stable. Hence, if the system is near the equilibrium, it will approach the equilibrium in the long term. This conclusion is important as it guarantees that we can effectively carry out comparative dynamic analysis.

4. Comparative dynamic analysis

We simulated the motion of the national economy under (22). We now study how the economic system reacts to exogenous changes, for instance, in resource capacity and preference. As the lemma gives a computational procedure to calibrate the motion of all the variables, we can conduct analysis on effects of change in any parameter on transitory processes as well stationary states of all the variables. In the rest of this study we use $\overline{\Delta} x(t)$ to stand for the change rate of the variable, $x(t)$, in percentage due to changes in the parameter value.

4.1. A rise in the carrying capacity of the renewable resource

We first study the case when the carrying capacity of renewable resource is increased as follows: $\phi : 8 \Rightarrow 8.2$. The simulation result is plotted in Figure 2. When he capacity is expanded, from equation (3) we see that the level of renewable resource stock tends to increase. The old development path is disturbed. The level of resource stock is augmented. In association of rises in the stock, both the production sector and households use more resources. The price of resource stock is lowered due to the expansion of supply. The education time and leisure time are initially reduced and work time is initially reduced; in the long term the time distribution is slightly affected. It should be noted that education time is augmented in the long term. The level of human capital is initially increased faster than the total labor force; in the long term the level of human capital is increased less than the total labor force. The total physical stock is also increased in association with rises in the consumption level of goods and the wealth. The education sector's output and its inputs are slightly affected. The other two sectors' output levels and inputs are increased. The utility level and national output are enhanced.

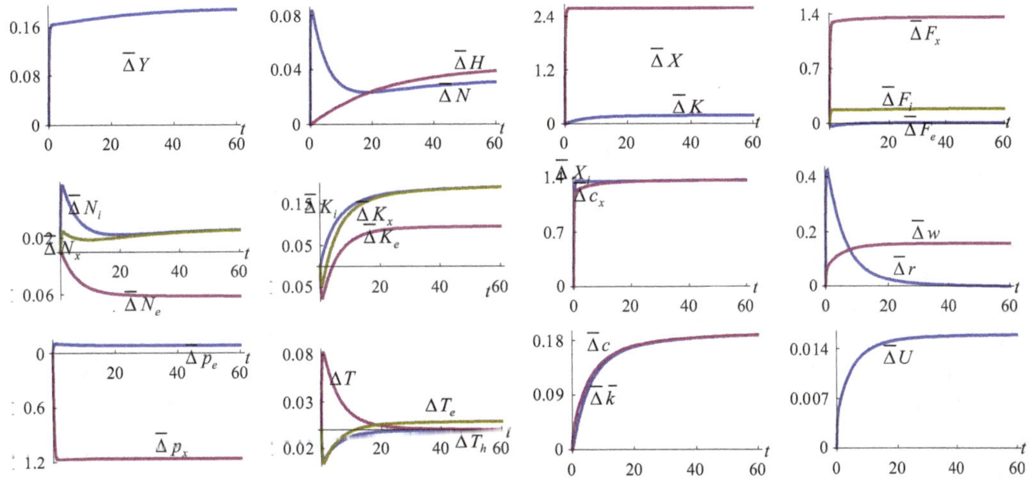

Figure 2. A Rise in the Capacity of Resources

Our simulation shows that if the economic system functions effectively, an economy with richer natural resources should have faster economic growth and better steady state. It should be mentioned that the impact of natural resources on economic as well as human development has caused attention of economists for a long time. Debates about whether natural resources are a blessing or a curse for human development are still a hot topic in the literature of economic development. It is well-known that the in the 1990s Sachs and Warner (1999, 2001) demonstrated a negative relationship between resource dependence and economic growth over the period 1970-1990. Since then, the curse of natural resource hypothesis has been theoretically re-examined and empirically tested in many studies. In a recent comprehensive study on natural resources and economic development, Daniele (2011: 568) concludes: "Natural resources can be a blessing for countries, but the blessing can turn into a curse when rents serve to fund conflicts, to corrupt institutions or are simply wasted. So, the effects that resources produce on people's welfare do not appear to depend on the resources themselves, as much as on the social and institutional ability to manage them. In this respect, the concept of resource curse appears misleading, as it tends to hide the real pathology affecting some nations: poor governance of natural resources." In fact, It has been empirically demonstrated that natural resources may have either an adverse or positive effect on the equilibrium growth rate (for instance, Gylfason, *et al.* 1999, Barbier, 1999, Chen and Lu, 2009).

4.2. An enhancement in efficiency of the education sector

We now increase the total productivity of the education sector as follows: $A_e : 0.8 \Rightarrow 0.92$. When A_e is increased, by $T_e N_0 = F_e$ the education time is increased initially. In the association of rise in the productivity, the price of education tends to fall and the education sector employs less labor and capital inputs. The households spend more time on education and less time on work and leisure. The three sectors' output levels are all increased. The national output and wealth initially fall slightly and increases but very small in the long term. The total labor is reduced and the level of human capital and the wage rate are increased. The rate of interest falls and the utility level is enhanced.

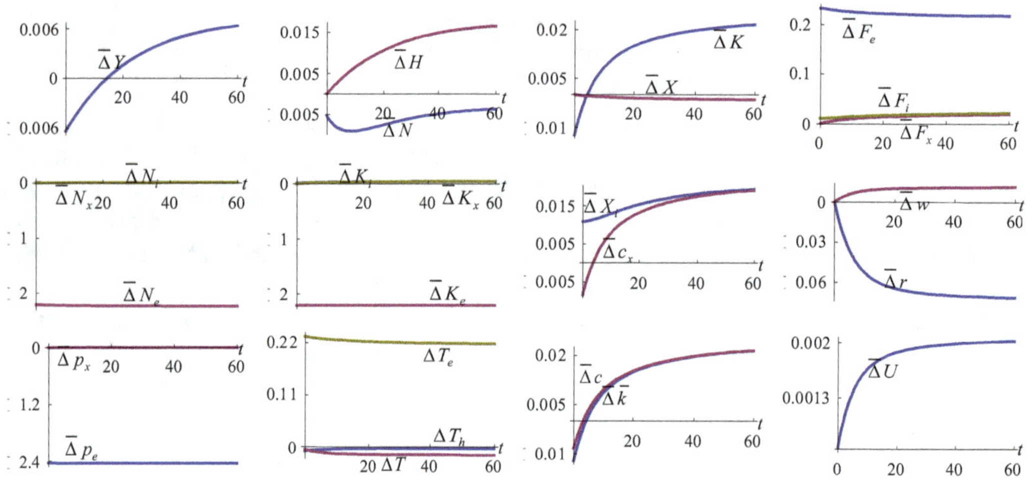

Figure 3. An Enhancement in Efficiency of the Education Sector

4.3. Human capital being more effectively utilized

We now study what will happen to the economic system if workers more effectively utilize human capital as follows: $m: 0.8 \Rightarrow 0.82$. The total labor is increased. The increase in the total labor is mostly absorbed by the production and resource sectors. The output levels and capital inputs of the production and resource sectors are increased. The output level and two inputs of the education sector are slightly affected. The economy has lower level of the resource, even though the resource input and consumption levels are increased. The rate of interest is initially increased and reduced in the long term. The wage rate is reduced. The education price is initially slightly increased, but reduced in the long term. The price of the resource is increased. The households spend more time on education and less time on leisure. The work time is slightly affected. The national output and utility level are enhanced.

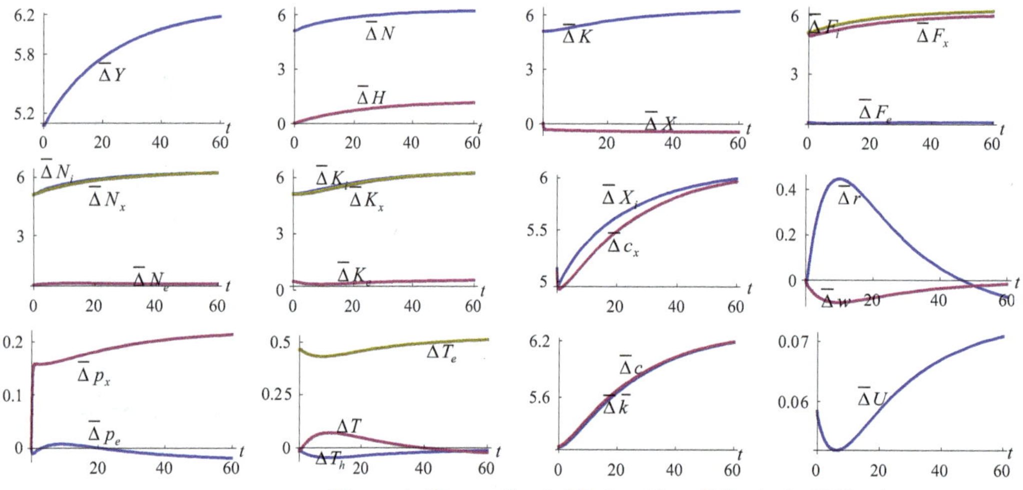

Figure 4. Human Capital Being More Effectively Utilized

4.4. The propensity to receive education being strengthened

We increase the propensity to receive education as follows: $\eta_0 : 0.01 \Rightarrow 0.012$. The simulation result is plotted in Figure 5. As the preference for education is strengthened, the education time is increased. Both leisure time and work time are reduced. The level of human capital is increased. The total labor supply is initially reduced and increased in the long term. The fall in the total labor is due to the reduction the work time. Correspondingly, the national output falls initially and rises in the long term. The rise in the demand for education drives up the price of education. The output level and capital and labor inputs of the education sector are increased. The total wealth is slightly changed. The stock of renewable resource is reduced first and then increased. The price of resources is reduced. The consumption and input levels of the resources are initially reduced and enhanced in the long term. The output levels and input levels of the production and resource sectors are slightly reduced. The rate of interest and utility level are increased.

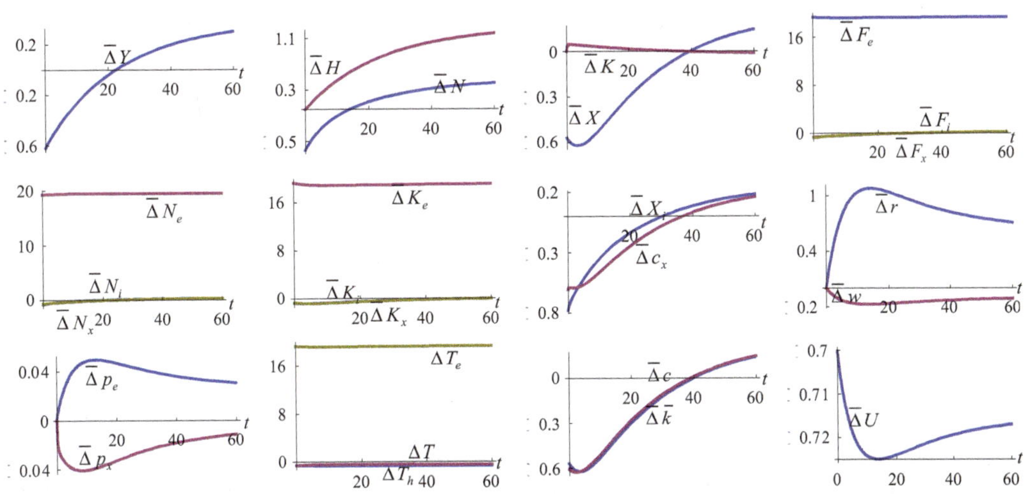

Figure 5. The Propensity to Receive Education Being Strengthened

4.5. The propensity to save being augmented

We increase the propensity to save as follows: $\lambda_0 : 0.6 \Rightarrow 0.62$. The simulation result is plotted in Figure 6. As the propensity to save is increased, the national wealth is increased. The increase in the total wealth enables the three sectors employs more capital inputs in the long term. The rise in the total physical wealth is association with a slight fall in the stock of the renewable resource. The price of the resource is increased, while the price of education is reduced. The rate of interest is reduced, while the wage rate is increased. The households work longer hours and have less leisure time and education time. The consumption level of resource by the households is initially reduced, and increased in the long term. The output levels of the production and resource sectors are increased, while the output level of the education sector is slightly reduced in association with falling in the price of education.

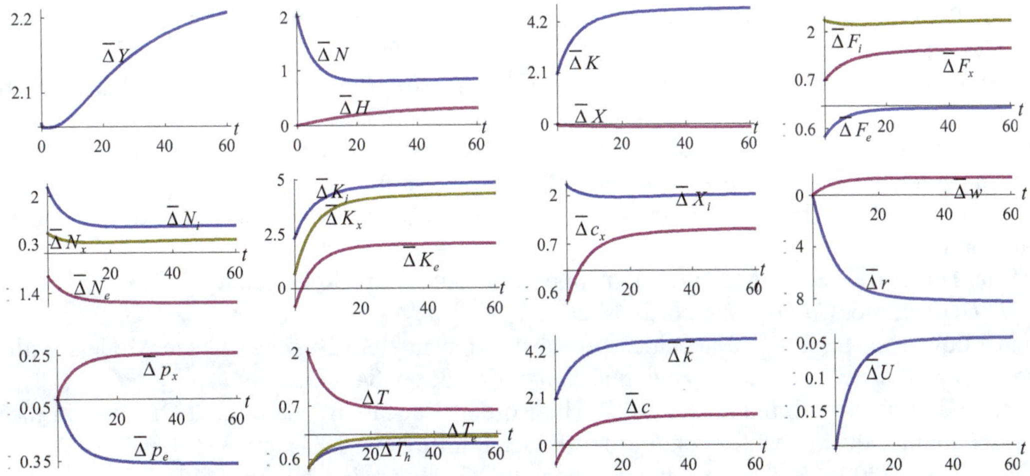

Figure 6. The Propensity to Save Being Augmented

5. Concluding Remarks

The main concern of this paper is dynamic interdependence among physical capital, resource and human capital. We modelled the dynamics of the three variables in an economic system with production, resource and education sectors. We took account of three ways of improving human capital: learning by producing, learning by education, and learning by consuming. The model describes a dynamic interdependence among wealth accumulation, human capital accumulation, resource change, and division of labor under perfect competition. We simulated the model to demonstrate existence of equilibrium points and motion of the dynamic system. We also examined effects of changes in the productivity of the resource sector, the utilization efficiency of human capital, the propensity to receive education, and the propensity to save upon dynamic paths of the system. We may extend the model in some directions. For instance, we may introduce some kind of government intervention in education into the model. Ownership of resources is a complicated issue. Another interesting extension is to examine how human capital and education may interact with population dynamics.

References

Arrow, K.J., 1962. The Economic Implications of Learning by Doing. *Review of Economic Studies*, 29, pp.155-173.

Arrow, K., 1973. *Higher Education as a Filter. Journal of Public Economics*, 2, 193-216.

Ayong Le Kama, A.D., 2001. *Sustainable Growth, Renewable Resources and Pollution. Journal of Economic Dynamics and Control*, 25, 1911-1918.

Alvarez-Guadrado, F. and von Long, N., 2011. Consumption and Renewable Resource Extraction under Alternative Property-Rights Regimes. *Resource and Energy Economics*, 33(4), pp. 1028-1053.

Barbier, E.B., 1999. Endogenous Growth and Natural Resource Scarcity. *Environmental and Resource Economics*, 14, pp. 51-74.

Barro, R.J., 2001. Human Capital and Growth. *American Economic Review, Papers and Proceedings*, 91, pp. 12-17.

Barro, R.J. and Sala-i-Martin, X., 1995. Economic Growth. New York: McGraw-Hill, Inc.

Beltratti, A., Chichilnisky, G., and Heal, G.M., 1994. Sustainable Growth and the Golden Rule. In *The Economics of Sustainable Development*, edited by Goldin, I. and Winters, I.A. Cambridge: Cambridge University Press.

Benchekroun, H., 2003. Unilateral Production Restrictions in a Dynamic Duopoly. *Journal of Economic Theory*, 111, pp. 237-261.

Benhabib, J. and Perli, R., 1994. *Uniqueness and Indeterminacy: On the Dynamics of Endogenous Growth. Journal of Economic Theory*, 63, pp. 113-142.

Berck, P., 1981. Optimal Management of Renewable Resources with Growing Demand and Stock Externalities. *Journal of Environmental Economics and Management*, 11, pp.101-118.

Brander, J.A. and Taylor, M.S., 1998. The Simple Economics of Easter Island: A Ricardo-Malthus Model of Renewable Resource Use. *American Economic Review*, 81, pp. 119-138.

Brown, G.M., 2000. Renewable Natural Resource Management and Use without Markets. *Journal of Economic Literature*, 38, pp. 875-914.

Bulter, E.H. and Barbier, E.B., 2005. *Trade and Renewable Resources in a Second Best World: An Overview. Environmental and Resource Economics*, 30, pp. 423-463.

Bulter, E.H. and Van Kooten, G.C., 1999. Economics of Antipoaching Enforcement and the Ivory Trade Ban. *American Journal of Agricultural Economics*, 81, pp. 453-466.

Burmeister, E. and Dobell, A.R., 1970. *Mathematical Theories of Economic Growth*. London: Collier Macmillan Publishers.

Cairns, D.R. and Tian, H.L., 2010. Sustained Development of a Society with a Renewable Resource. *Journal of Economic Dynamics & Control*, 24, pp. 2048-2061.

Campbell, J.Y. and Ludvigson, S., 2001. Elasticities of Substitution in Real Business Cycle Models with Home Production. *Journal of Money, Credit and Bankings*, 33, pp. 847-875.

Castelló-Climent, A. and Hidalgo-Cabrillana, A., 2012. The Role of Education Quality and Quantity in the Process of Economic Development. Economics of Education Review, 31(4), pp. 391-409.

Chen, C.H. and Lu, Z.N., 2009. *Analysis of the Economical Growth Model with Limited Renewable Resource*. International Journal of Nonlinear Science, 7, pp. 90-94.

Chen, M.K. and Chevalier, J.A., 2008. The Taste for Leisure, Career Choice, and the Returns to Education. *Economics Letters*, 99, pp. 353-356.

Choi, S.M., 2011. How Large Are Learning Externalities? *International Economic Review*, 52, pp. 1077-1103.

Clark, C.W., 1976. *Mathematical Bioeconomics: The Optimal Management of Renewable Resources*. New York: Wiley.

Cohn, E. and Cooper, S.T., 2004. Multi-product Cost Functions for Universities: Economies of Scale and Scope. In *International Handbook on the Economics of Education*, edited by Johnes, G. and Johnes, J., Cheltenham: Edward Elgar.

Copeland, B.R. and Taylor, M.S., 2009. Trade, Tragedy, and the Commons. *American Economic Review*, 99, pp. 725-749.

Dasgupta, P.S. and Heal, G.E., 1979. *The Economics of Exhaustible Resources*. Cambridge: Cambridge University Press.

Drugeon, J.P. and Venditti, A., 2001. Intersectoral External Effects, Multiplicities & Indeterminacies. *Journal of Economic Dynamics & Control*, 25, pp. 765-787.

Eliasson, L. and Turnovsky, S.J., 2004. Renewable Resources in an Endogenously Growing Economy: Balanced Growth and Transitional Dynamics. *Journal of Environmental Economics and Management*, 48, pp. 1018-1049.

Erceg, C., Guerrieri, L. and Gust, C., 2005. Can Long-Run Restrictions Identify Technology Shocks? *Journal of European Economic Association*, 3, pp. 1237-1278.

Farmer, K. and Bednar-Friedl, B., 2010. *Intertemporal Resource Economics – An Introduction to the Overlapping Generations Approach*. New York: Springer.

Fleisher, B., Hu, Y.F., Li, H.Z., and Kim, S.H., 2011. Economic Transition, Higher Education and Worker Productivity in China. *Journal of Development Economics*, 94, pp. 86-94.

Fujiwara, K., 2011. Losses from Competition in a Dynamic Game Model of a Renewable Resource Oligopoly. *Resource and Energy Economics*, 33, pp. 1-11.

Gordon, H.S., 1954. The Economic Theory of a Common Property Resource: The Fishery. *Journal of Political Economy*, 62, pp. 124-142.

Greenwood, J. and Hercowitz, Z., 1991. The Allocation of Capital and Time over the Business Cycle. *The Journal of Political Economy*, 99, 1188-1214.

Gylfason, T., Herbertsson, T., and Zoega, G., 1999. A Mixed Blessing: Natural Resources and Economic Growth. *Macroeconomic Dynamics*, 3, pp. 204-25.

Hahn, F.H., 1990. *Solowian Growth Models, in Growth, Productivity, Unemployment*, edited by P. Diamond. Mass., Cambridge: The MIT Press.

Hannesson, R., 2000. Renewable resources and the gains from trade. *Canadian Journal of Economics*, 33, pp. 122-132.

Hanushek, E. and Kimko, D., 2000. Schooling, Labor-Force Quality and the Growth of Nations. *American Economic Review*, 90, pp. 1194-1204.

Hussey, A., 2012. Human Capital Augmentation versus the Signaling Value of MBA. *Economics of Education Review*, 31, 442-451.

Ishida, J., 2004. Education as Advertisement. *Economics Bulletin*, 10, pp. 1-8.

Jones, L. and Manuelli, R.E., 1997. The Sources of Growth. *Journal of Economic Dynamics and Control*, 21, pp. 75-114.

Kihlstrom, R.E. and Riordan, M.H., 1984. Advertising as a Signal. *Journal of Political Economy*, 92, pp. 427-450.

Krueger, A.B., 1999. Experimental Estimates of Education Production Functions. *Quarterly Journal of Economics*, 114, pp. 497-532.

Krueger, A.B. and Lindahl, M., 2001. Education for Growth: Why and for Whom. *Journal of Economic Literature*, 39, pp. 1101-1136.

Kurz, M., 1963. The Two Sector Extension of Swan's Model of Economic Growth: The Case of No Technical Change. *International Economic Review*, 4, pp. 1-12.

Ladrón-de-Guevara, A., Ortigueira, S., and Santos, M.S., 1999. A Two Sector Model of Endogenous Growth with Leisure. *The Review of Economic Studies*, 66, pp. 609-631.

Lee, S., 2007. The Timing of Signaling: To Study in High School or in College? *International Economic Review*, 48, pp. 785-807.

Levhari, D. and Withagen, C., 1992. Optimal Management of the Growth Potential of Renewable Resources. *Journal of Economics*, 56, pp. 297-309.

Li, H.B., Liu, P.W., and Zhang, J.S., 2012. Estimating Returns to Education Using Twins in Urban China. *Journal of Development Economics*, 97, pp. 494-504.

Liu, Z.Q., 2007. The External Returns to Education: Evidence from Chinese Cities. *Journal of Urban Economics*, 61, pp. 542-564.

Long, N.V. and Wang, S., 2009. Resource-grabbing by Status-conscious Agents. *Journal of Development Economics*, 89, pp. 39-50.

Lucas, R.E., 1988. On the Mechanics of Economic Development. *Journal of Monetary Economics*, 22, pp. 3-42.

Milgrom, P. and Roberts, J., 1986. Price and Advertising Signals of Product Quality. Journal of Political Economy, 94, pp. 796-821.

Milner-Gulland, E.J. and Leader-Williams, N., 1992. A Model of Incentives for the Illegal Exploitation of Black Rhinos and Elephants. *Journal of Applied Ecology*, 29, pp. 388-401.
Munro, G.R. and Scott, A.D., 1985. The Economics of Fisheries Management. In *Handbook of Natural Resource and Energy Economics, vol. II*, edited by Kneese, A.V. and Sweeney, J.L., Amsterdam: Elsevier.
Nelson, P., 1974. Advertising as Information. *Journal of Political Economy*, 82, pp. 729-754.
Paterson, D.G. and Wilen, J.E., 1977. Depletion and Diplomacy: The North-Pacific Seal Hunt, 1880-1910. In *Research in Economic History*, edited by Uselding, P. JAI Press.
Plourde, G.C., 1970. A Simple Model of Replenishable Resource Exploitation. *American Economic Review*, 60, pp. 518-522.
Plourde, G.C., 1971. Exploitation of Common-Property Replenishable Resources. *Western Economic Journal*, 9, pp. 256-266.
Rauch, J., 1993. Productivity Gains from Geographic Concentration of Human Capital: Evidence from the Cities. *Journal of Urban Economics*, 34, pp. 380-400.
Rupert, P., Rogerson, R., and Wright, R., 1995. Estimating Substitution Elasticities in Household Production Models. *Economic Theory*, 6, 179-193.
Sachs, J.D. and Warner, A.M., 2001. The Curse of Natural Resources. *European Economic Review*, 45, pp. 827-838.
Schaefer, M.B., 1957. Some Considerations of Population Dynamics and Economics in Relation to the Management of Marine Fisheries. *Journal of Fisheries Research Board of Canada*, 14, pp. 669-681.
Solow, R., 1956. *A Contribution to the Theory of Growth. Quarterly Journal of Economics*, 70, pp. 65-94.
Solow, R., 1999. Neoclassical Growth Theory. In *Handbook of Macroeconomics*, edited by Taylor, J.B. and Woodford, M. North-Holland.
Solow, R., 2000. *Growth Theory – An Exposition*. New York: Oxford University Press.
Spence, M., 1973. Job Market Signaling. *Quarterly Journal of Economics*, 87, pp. 355-374.
Stiglitz, J.E., 1967. A Two Sector Two Class Model of Economic Growth. *Review of Economic Studies*, 34, pp. 227-238.
Stiglitz, J.E., 1974. Growth with Exhaustible Natural Resources: Efficient and Optimal Growth Paths. *Review of Economic Studies, Symposium on the Economics of Exhaustible Resources*, 123-138.
Stiglitz, J.E., 1975. The Theory of Screening, Education, and the Distribution of Income. *American Economic Review*, 65, pp. 283-300.
Tajibaeva, L.S., 2011. Property Rights, Renewable Resources and Economic Development. *Environmental and Resource Economics*, 51, pp. 23-41.
Tornell, A. and Velasco, A., 1992. The Tragedy of the Commons and Economic Growth: Why does Capital Flow from Poor to Rich Countries?, *Journal of Political Economy*, 100, 1208-1231.
Turnovsky, S.J., 1999. Fiscal Policy and Growth in a Small Open Economy with Elastic Labor Supply. *The Canadian Journal of Economics*, 32, 1191-1214.
Uzawa, H., 1961. On A Two-Sector Model of Economic Growth I. *Review of Economic Studies*, 29, pp. 47-70.
Uzawa, H., 1965. Optimal Technical Change in an Aggregative Model of Economic Growth. *International Economic Review*, 6, pp. 18-31.
Wirl, F., 2004. Sustainable Growth, Renewable Resources and Pollution: Thresholds and Cycles. *Journal of Economic Dynamics & Control*, 28, pp. 1149-1157.
Zhang, W.B., 1993. Woman's Labor Participation and Economic Growth - Creativity, Knowledge Utilization and Family Preference. *Economics Letters*, 42, pp. 105-110.
Zhang, W.B., 2007. Economic Growth with Learning by Producing, Learning by Education, and Learning by Consuming. *Interdisciplinary Description of Complex Systems*, 5, pp. 21-38.
Zhang, W.B., 2011. Renewable Resources, Capital Accumulation, and Economic Growth. *Business Systems Research*, 1, pp. 24-35.

7. Appendix: Proving Lemma 1

The appendix shows that the dynamics can be expressed by three dimensional differential equations. From (2), (5) and (7), we obtain

$$z \equiv \frac{r+\delta_k}{w} = \frac{\tilde{\alpha}_i N_i}{K_i} = \frac{\tilde{\alpha}_e N_e}{K_e} = \frac{\tilde{\alpha}_x N_x}{K_x}, \tag{A1}$$

where we omit time index and $\tilde{\alpha}_j \equiv \dfrac{\alpha_j}{\beta_j}$, $j = i, e, x$.

By (1), we have

$$f_i(z, x_i) \equiv \frac{F_i}{N_i} = A_i x_i^{\gamma_i} \left(\frac{\tilde{\alpha}_i}{z}\right)^{\alpha_i}, \tag{A2}$$

where we also use (A1) and $x_i \equiv X_i / N_i$. By (2), (A1) and (A2), we have

$$r+\delta_k = \frac{\alpha_i z f_i}{\tilde{\alpha}_i}, \quad w = \beta_i f_i, \quad p_x = \frac{\gamma_i f_i}{x_i}. \tag{A3}$$

We can express w, r and p_x as functions of z and x_i. From (5) and (A1), we solve

$$r+\delta_k = \frac{\alpha_x p_x A_x X^b z^{\beta_x}}{\tilde{\alpha}_x^{\beta_x}}, \quad w = \frac{\beta_x p_x A_x X^b \tilde{\alpha}_x^{\alpha_x}}{z^{\alpha_x}}. \tag{A4}$$

From (A2) and the marginal conditions for labor in (A3) and (A4), we have

$$p_x = \frac{\beta_0 x_i^{\gamma_i} z^{\alpha_x - \alpha_i}}{X^b}, \tag{A5}$$

where $\beta_0 \equiv \dfrac{\beta_i A_i \tilde{\alpha}_i^{\alpha_i}}{\beta_x A_x \tilde{\alpha}_x^{\alpha_x}}$.

From (A5) and (A3), we solve

$$x_i = \frac{\gamma_i \beta_x A_x \tilde{\alpha}_x^{\alpha_x}}{\beta_i} \frac{X^b}{z^{\alpha_x}}. \tag{A6}$$

From the above analyses, we express w, f_i, r, p_x and x_i as functions of z and X. From (6) and (7), we have

$$p_e = \frac{w z^{\alpha_e}}{\beta_e A_e \tilde{\alpha}_e^{\alpha_e}}. \tag{A7}$$

where we also use (A1). Hence, we can express p_e and $\bar{p}$ as functions of z, X, and H.

From (20), (2) and $p_x c_x = \chi \bar{y}$ in (14), we get $\chi \bar{N} \bar{y} + \gamma_i F_i = p_x F_x$.

From $T_e = \eta \bar{y} / \bar{p}$ in (14) and (16), we have $\bar{y} = \dfrac{\bar{p} F_e}{\bar{N} \eta}$.

Insert this equation in $\chi \bar{N} \bar{y} + \gamma_i F_i = p_x F_x$

$$\frac{\chi \bar{p} F_e}{\eta} + \gamma_i F_i = p_x F_x. \tag{A8}$$

From (2), (5) and (7), we have

$$r + \delta_k = \frac{\alpha_i F_i}{K_i} = \frac{\alpha_x p_x F_x}{K_x} = \frac{\alpha_e p_e F_e}{K_e}. \tag{A9}$$

Substituting (A9) into (A8) yields

$$K_x = \bar{p}_e K_e + \bar{\gamma}_i K_i, \tag{A10}$$

where $\bar{p}_e(z, X, H) \equiv \frac{\alpha_x \chi \bar{p}}{\eta \alpha_e p_e}$, $\bar{\gamma}_i \equiv \frac{\alpha_x \gamma_i}{\alpha_i}$,

Insert (A1) in $N_i + N_e + N_x = N$

$$\frac{K_i}{\tilde{\alpha}_i} + \frac{K_e}{\tilde{\alpha}_e} + \frac{K_x}{\tilde{\alpha}_x} = \frac{N}{z}. \tag{A11}$$

Insert (A10) in $K_i + K_e + K_x = K$ and (A11)

$$\varepsilon_{1i} K_i + \varepsilon_{1e} K_e = \frac{N}{z},$$
$$\varepsilon_{2i} K_i + \varepsilon_{2e} K_e = K, \tag{A12}$$

where $\varepsilon_{1i} \equiv \frac{1}{\tilde{\alpha}_i} + \frac{\bar{\gamma}_i}{\tilde{\alpha}_x}$, $\varepsilon_{1e}(z, X, H) \equiv \frac{1}{\tilde{\alpha}_e} + \frac{\bar{p}_e}{\tilde{\alpha}_x}$, $\varepsilon_{2i} \equiv 1 + \bar{\gamma}_i$, $\varepsilon_{2e}(z, X, H) \equiv 1 + \bar{p}_e$.

Solve (A12) with K_i and K_e as variables

$$K_i = \left(\frac{\varepsilon_{2e} N}{z} - \varepsilon_{1e} \bar{k} \bar{N}\right)\varepsilon, \quad K_e = \left(\varepsilon_{1i} \bar{k} \bar{N} - \frac{\varepsilon_{2i} N}{z}\right)\varepsilon, \tag{A13}$$

where we use $K = \bar{k} \bar{N}$ and $\varepsilon(z, X, H) \equiv \frac{1}{\varepsilon_{1i} \varepsilon_{2e} - \varepsilon_{2i} \varepsilon_{1e}}$.

By (A13) and (A10), we solve the capital distribution, K_i, K_e and K_x, as functions of z, X, N, H, and $\bar{k}$. By (A1), we solve the labor distribution, N_i, N_e and N_x, as functions of z, X, N, H, and $\bar{k}$.

From (2), (5) and (7), we have

$$F_i = \frac{w N_i}{\beta_i}, \quad X_i = \frac{\gamma_i F_i}{p_x}, \quad F_x = \frac{w N_x}{\beta_x p_x}, \quad F_e = \frac{w N_e}{\beta_x p_e}. \tag{A14}$$

We express F_i, X_i, F_x, and F_e as functions of z, X, N, and $\bar{k}$. From (7) and $\bar{y} = \bar{p} F_e / \bar{N} \eta$, we have

$$\bar{y} = p_w N_e, \tag{A15}$$

where $p_w(z, X, H) \equiv \frac{\bar{p} w}{\beta_e \bar{N} \eta p_e}$.

From (A15) and $p_x c_x = \chi \bar{y}$ in (14), we express $\bar{y}$ and c_x as functions of z, X, N, H, and $\bar{k}$. From $w H^m T_h = \sigma \bar{y}$, $\bar{p} T_e = \eta \bar{y}$, and the definition of $\bar{y}$, we have

$$T_h = \left(\frac{1+r}{H^m w}\right) \sigma \bar{k} + \sigma T_0,$$

$$T_e = \frac{(1+r)\eta \bar{k}}{\bar{p}} + \frac{T_0 \eta H^m w}{\bar{p}}. \tag{A16}$$

From $T + T_e + T_h = T_0$ and (A16), we have

$$T = h_1 - h_2 \bar{k}, \tag{A17}$$

where $h_1(z, X, H) \equiv T_0 - \sigma T_0 - \frac{T_0 \eta H^m w}{p}$, $h_2(z, X, H) \equiv \left(\frac{\sigma}{H^m w} + \frac{\eta}{\bar{p}}\right)(1+r)$.

From $N = H^m T \bar{N}$, and (A17), we have

$$N = \left(h_1 - h_2 \bar{k}\right) \bar{N} H^m. \tag{A18}$$

From (19) and $K = \bar{k} \bar{N}$, we have

$$(\xi + \lambda)\bar{y} - \delta \bar{k} = \frac{w N_i}{\beta_i \bar{N}}, \tag{A19}$$

where we also use (14) and (A14). Substituting the definition of $\bar{y}$ and $N_i = z K_i / \tilde{\alpha}_i$ into (A19) yields

$$\left[\tilde{\xi}(1+r) - \delta\right]\bar{k} + \tilde{\xi} T_0 H^m w = \frac{\tilde{\varepsilon}_2 N}{z} - \tilde{\varepsilon}_1 \bar{k} \bar{N},$$

where we also use (A13) and $\tilde{\xi} \equiv \xi + \lambda$, $\tilde{\varepsilon}_j(z, X, H) \equiv \frac{\varepsilon \varepsilon_{je} z w}{\beta_i \tilde{\alpha}_i \bar{N}}$, $j = 1, 2$.

Insert (A18) into the above equation

$$\bar{k} = \Psi(z, X, H) \equiv H^m \left[\frac{\tilde{\varepsilon}_2 h_1 \bar{N}}{z} - \tilde{\xi} T_0 w\right]\left[\tilde{\xi}(1+r) + \tilde{\varepsilon}_1 \bar{N} + \frac{\tilde{\varepsilon}_2 h_2 \bar{N} H^m}{z} - \delta\right]^{-1}. \tag{A20}$$

From (A20), we solve $\bar{k}$ as a function of z, X and H.

It is straightforward to check that all the variables can be expressed as functions of z, X and H at any point of time by the following procedure: x_i by (A6) $\rightarrow p_x$ by (A5) $\rightarrow r$ by (A3) $\rightarrow w$ by (A3) $\rightarrow \bar{k}$ by (A20) $\rightarrow K = \bar{k}\,\bar{N}$ $\rightarrow N$ by (A18) $\rightarrow T = N / H^m \bar{N}$ $\rightarrow T_h$ and T_e by (A16) $\rightarrow p_w$ by the definition $\rightarrow p_e$ by (A16) $\rightarrow K_i$ and K_e by (A13) $\rightarrow K_x$ by (A11) $\rightarrow N_i$, N_e, and N_x by (A1) $\rightarrow \bar{y}$ by (A15) $\rightarrow c_x$, c, s by (14) $\rightarrow X_i = x_i N_i$ $\rightarrow F_i$ by (1) $\rightarrow F_x$ by (4) $\rightarrow F_e$ by (6) $\rightarrow U$ by (11).

We note that the right-hand sides of (3) and (8) are functions of z, X and H. Hence, we have

$$\dot{X}(t) = \Lambda_X(z, X, H),$$
$$\dot{H}(t) = \Lambda_H(z, X, H), \tag{A21}$$

where we do explicitly express Λ_X and Λ_H as it straightforward but their expressions are tedious.

Taking derivatives of (A20) with respect to t yields

$$\dot{\bar{k}} = \frac{\partial \Psi}{\partial z}\dot{z} + \Lambda_X \frac{\partial \Psi}{\partial X} + \Lambda_H \frac{\partial \Psi}{\partial H}, \tag{A22}$$

where we also use (A21). From (15), we have

$$\dot{\bar{k}} = \lambda\,\bar{y}(z, X, H) - \bar{k}. \tag{A23}$$

From (A22) and (A23), we solve

$$\dot{z} = \Lambda_z(z, X, H) \equiv \left(\lambda\,\bar{y} - \Psi - \Lambda_X \frac{\partial \Psi}{\partial X} - \Lambda_H \frac{\partial \Psi}{\partial H}\right)\left(\frac{\partial \Psi}{\partial z}\right)^{-1}. \tag{A24}$$

We thus proved the lemma.

14

Analysis of European Union Economy in Terms of GDP Components

Simona VINEREAN*

The Bucharest University of Economic Studies

The impact of the crises on national economies represented a subject of analysis and interest for a wide variety of research studies. Thus, starting from the GDP composition, the present research exhibits an analysis of the impact of European economies, at an EU level, of the events that followed the crisis of 2007 – 2008. Firstly, the research highlighted the existence of two groups of countries in 2012 in European Union, namely segments that were compiled in relation to the structure of the GDP's components. In the second stage of the research, a factor analysis was performed on the resulted segments, that showed that the economies of cluster A are based more on personal consumption compared to the economies of cluster B, and in terms of government consumption, the situation is reversed. Thus, between the two groups of countries, a different approach regarding the role of fiscal policy in the economy can be noted, with a greater emphasis on savings in cluster B. Moreover, besides the two groups of countries resulted, Ireland and Luxembourg stood out because these two countries did not fit in either of the resulted segments and their economies are based, to a large extent, on the positive balance of the external balance.

Keywords: *GDP, consumption expenditure, consumption expenditure of general government, Gross capital formation, External balance of goods and services*

1. Introduction

Keynes placed the consumption function at the center of his theory regarding the economic fluctuations that plays a major role in the subsequent development of macroeconomic analysis. Mankiw analyzed the consumption function starting with Keynes's main ideas from his timeframe, and then he examined it from the perspective of the obtained results when Keynes's ideas were confronted with empirical data (Mankiw, 2010, p. 496).

The relationship between society income and that which is expected that will be spent for consumption depends on the psychological characteristics of society, characteristics that are named 'propensity to consume'. Thus, consumption depends on aggregated income and consequently on employment level, with the exception of the case when there are changes in relation to propensity to consume (Keynes, 1936, p.88). Also, Keynes (1936, p.62) stated that the expenditure on consumption during any period must mean the value of goods sold to consumers during that period, which throws us back to the question of what is meant by a consumer-purchaser. Expenditure on consumption can be defined as $-A_1$ where A is the total sales made during the period and A_1 is the total sales made by one entrepreneur to another.

* Correspondence:
Simona Vinerean, The Bucharest University of Economic Studies, E-mail address: simonavinerean@yahoo.com

Starting from the definition of income, we can define current investment as "the current addition to the value of the capital equipment which has resulted from the productive activity of the period... this addition is equal to what we have just defined as saving, for it is that part of the income of the period which has not passed into consumption (Keynes, 1936, p.63).

Macroeconomic equilibrium occurs when aggregate demand of goods and services is equal to aggregate supply of goods and services, which leads to the equation of macroeconomic equilibrium:

$$Y = C + G + I + En$$

where Y represents national income, C - Household and NPISH final consumption expenditure; G - Final consumption expenditure of general government; I - Gross capital formation; En - External balance of goods and services.

This equation is valid for the situation of an open economy which has economic relations with the rest of the world. Moreover, a simplified form of the equation is used for the analysis of macroeconomic equilibrium in a closed economy. In this case, the following expression arises:

$$Y = C + G + I$$

Macroeconomic equilibrium can be rewritten starting from the equality that has to exist between outputs and inputs of money:

$$C + S + T = C + I + G + En$$

Where T represents taxes.

The above relationship becomes:

$$(S - I) + (T - G) = En$$

Where (S – I) represents the net saving from the private sector, (T – G) represents government budget surplus, En represents trade balance surplus.

2. Research Methodology

In this section, the current situation in the EU is analyzed based on empirical data, in terms of GDP components: C - Household and NPISH final consumption expenditure; G - Final consumption expenditure of general government; I - Gross capital formation; En - External balance of goods and services.

In this analysis, we will consider as exogenous variables the following four components that characterize the economic situation in the European Union household and NPISH final consumption expenditure (C), final consumption expenditure of general government (G), gross capital formation (I) and external balance of goods and services (En). All four variables are expressed as a percentage of GDP and the data were provided by Eurostat.

The current analysis of this study includes the following two steps:

1. Segmentation of EU countries in groups of countries, according to C, G, I and En.
2. Factor analysis of the segment results.

3. Analysis and Results

3.1. Segmentation of the European Union

In this first stage of the analysis, several segments were attained, which include groups of countries characterized by similar results of the four variables taken into account (C, G, I and En). To achieve this research objective, we use the Two-Step Cluster method and we obtained the following results regarding the relevancy of the clusters formed:

Algorithm	TwoStep
Inputs	4
Clusters	3

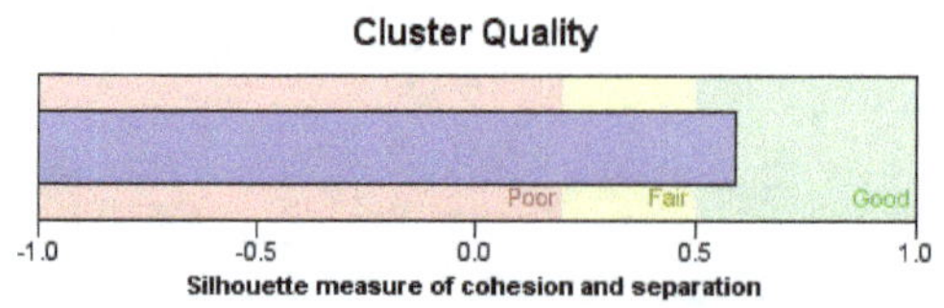

Figure 1. *Segmentation Model Summary*

From the figure above (Figure 1), it can be observed that the three clusters resulted, with their forming variables, and the segmentation has a high relevance in terms of the quality of clusters obtained.

Further, the relative and absolute proportions of clusters and the countries that form each segment are presented.

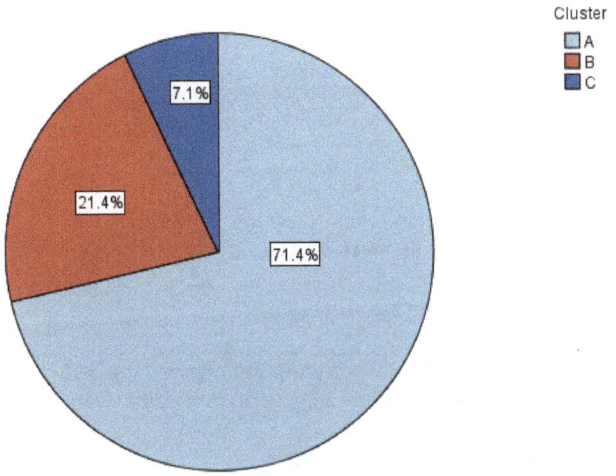

Input (Predictor) Importance

1.0 0.8 0.6 0.4 0.2 0.0

Cluster	1	2	3
Label	A	B	C
Description	Austria; Bulgaria; Cyprus; Czech Republic; Estonia; Germany; Greece; Hungary; Italy; Latvia; Lithuania; Malta; Poland; Portugal; Romania; Slovakia; Slovenia; Spain, UK	Belgium; Denmark; Finland; France; Netherlands; Sweden	Ireland; Luxembourg
Size	71.4% (20)	21.4% (6)	7.1% (2)
Inputs	g 18.88	g 26.45	g 17.75
	en 0.95	en 2.88	en 26.70
	c 60.55	c 51.68	c 39.95
	i 19.45	i 19.07	i 16.10

Figure 2. *Clusters of EU Countries*

Thus, the analysis displays three segments with following composition:

Table 1. *Clusters of EU Countries*

Cluster	Features	Countries
A	**60.55%** Household and NPISH final consumption expenditure **18.88%** Final consumption expenditure of general government **19.45%** Gross capital formation **0.95%** External balance of goods and services	Austria, Bulgaria Cyprus, Czech Republic Estonia, Germany Greece, Hungary Italy, Latvia Lithuania, Malta Poland, Portugal Romania, Slovakia Slovenia, Spain United Kingdom
B	**51.68%** Household and NPISH final consumption expenditure **26.45%** Final consumption expenditure of general government **19.07%** Gross capital formation **2.88%** External balance of goods and services	Belgium Denmark Finland France Netherlands Sweden
C	**39.95%** Household and NPISH final consumption expenditure **17.75%** Final consumption expenditure of general government **16.10%** Gross capital formation **26.70%** External balance of goods and services	Ireland Luxembourg

Next, Table 2 presents a descriptive analysis of the 3 clusters, as an intermediate stage of transition to the second stage of analysis.

***Table 2.** Descriptive Statistics*

Descriptive statistics		N	Minimum	Maximum	Mean	Std. Deviation
A	C	20	50.6	73.7	60.550	5.5687
	G	20	15.5	21.8	18.885	1.8196
	I	20	12.8	28.2	19.450	4.4687
	En	20	-5.2	7.4	.950	3.9501
	Valid N	20				
B	C	6	45.6	57.7	51.683	4.7831
	G	6	24.7	28.5	26.450	1.7661
	I	6	17.4	21.0	19.067	1.4194
	En	6	-2.3	8.4	2.883	4.1825
	Valid N	6				
C	C	2	32.1	47.8	39.950	11.1016
	G	2	17.5	18.0	17.750	.3536
	I	2	10.9	21.3	16.100	7.3539
	En	2	24.2	29.2	26.700	3.5355
	Valid N	2				

3.2. Factor Analysis of the Resulted Segments

Further, the study aims to achieve factorial analysis using the Principal Component Analysis as the extraction method and Varimax with Kaizer normalization as the rotation method, for the 2 of the 3 resulted segments. Thus, cluster C is excluded from the analysis because it includes only two countries characterized by contextual circumstances in respect of the indicators of the analysis, and cannot be integrated into a broader analysis of the situation in the EU.

Factor Analysis of Cluster A

Regarding the results obtained from factor analysis for cluster A, they are represented in the following tables (Tables 3 and 4):

Table 3. Total Variance Explained for Cluster A

Component	Initial Eigenvalues			Extraction Sums of Squared Loadings			Rotation Sums of Squared Loadings		
	Total	% of Variance	Cumulative %	Total	% of Variance	Cumulative %	Total	% of Variance	Cumulative %
1	2.123	53.078	53.078	2.123	53.078	53.078	2.080	52.010	52.010
2	1.552	38.793	91.871	1.552	38.793	91.871	1.594	39.860	91.871
3	.319	7.983	99.854						
4	.006	.146	100.000						

Table 4. Rotated Component Matrix for Cluster A

	Component	
	1	2
C	-0.902	0.427
G	0.654	0.637
I	0.073	-0.981
En	0.914	0.209

It is observed that cluster A is influenced by two main factors: consumption and investment. Thus, consumption (expressed in C, G and En) explains 52.01% of the cases, and investments explain 32.86% of the cases.

Factor Analysis of Cluster B

Regarding the results obtained from factor analysis for cluster B, they are represented in the following tables (Tables 5 and 6):

Table 5. Total Variance Explained for Cluster B

Component	Initial Eigenvalues			Extraction Sums of Squared Loadings			Rotation Sums of Squared Loadings		
	Total	% of Variance	Cumulative %	Total	% of Variance	Cumulative %	Total	% of Variance	Cumulative %
1	3.624	90.602	90.602	3.624	90.602	90.602	2.183	54.579	54.579
2	.359	8.971	99.573	.359	8.971	99.573	1.800	44.994	99.573
3	.016	.405	99.978						
4	.001	.022	100.000						

Table 6. Rotated Component Matrix for Cluster B

	Component	
	1	2
C	-0.914	0.406
G	0.645	-0.757
I	-0.384	0.922
En	0.886	-0.460

It is observed that cluster B is influenced by two main factors: consumption and investment. Thus, final consumption expenditure (C) and external balance (En) explain 54.579% of the analysis' situations, and investment (I) and government consumption (G) explain 44.994% of the situations.

4. Conclusion

In this conducted study, we main analysis methods were used: Two-Step Cluster in the first stage (for an EU segmentation) and Principal Component Analysis as the extraction method and Varimax with Kaizer normalization as the rotation method, in the second stage of the analysis (for a factor analysis of the segments resulted in the first stage). Thus, through the process of segmentation via Two-Step Cluster, the following the situation at EU level was identified:

***Table 1.** Clusters of EU Countries*

Cluster	Countries	C	G	I	En
A	Austria	55.1	19.0	22.7	3.2
	Bulgaria	64.3	15.5	23.8	-3.7
	Croatia	60.2	19.8	19.4	0.7
	Cyprus	67.6	19.2	13.1	-2.6
	Czech Republic	50.6	20.5	23.3	5.6
	Estonia	51.2	19.2	28.2	0.3
	Germany	57.5	19.3	17.3	5.9
	Greece	73.7	17.8	13.6	-5.0
	Hungary	54.8	20.4	17.5	7.4
	Italy	60.9	20.1	17.9	1.1
	Latvia	62.4	16.0	25.5	-3.9
	Lithuania	63.3	17.6	18.3	0.8
	Malta	60.0	21.2	12.8	6.1
	Poland	61.5	17.8	20.4	0.3
	Portugal	65.7	18.2	16.7	-0.6
	Romania	62.4	15.7	27.0	-5.2
	Slovakia	57.7	17.6	19.4	5.2
	Slovenia	56.9	20.8	17.5	4.8
	Spain	59.3	20.2	19.8	0.8
	United Kingdom	65.9	21.8	14.8	-2.2
	Mean	**60.55**	**18.88**	**19.45**	**0.95**
B	Belgium	52.9	25.0	21.0	1.1
	Denmark	49.1	28.5	17.4	5.1
	Finland	56.4	25.1	19.8	-0.8
	France	57.7	24.7	19.8	-2.3
	Netherlands	45.6	28.5	17.5	8.4
	Sweden	48.4	26.9	18.9	5.8
	Mean	**51.68**	**26.45**	**19.07**	**2.88**
C	Ireland	47.8	18.0	10.9	24.2
	Luxembourg	32.1	17.5	21.3	29.2
	Mean	**39.95**	**17.75**	**16.10**	**26.70**

From the results of the analysis, it is observed that the economies of cluster A are based more on personal consumption (60.55% of GDP) compared to the economies of cluster B (51.68% of GDP), and in terms of government consumption, the situation is reversed (26.45% of GDP for cluster B compared to 18.88% for cluster A). Thus, between the two groups of countries, a different approach regarding the role of fiscal policy in the economy can be noted, with a greater emphasis on savings in cluster B. Regarding Ireland and Luxembourg, it is apparent that the savings of these countries are based, to a very large extent, on the positive balance of the external balance.

References

Mankiw, G., 2010. Macroeconomics, ed.a 7-a, Worth Publishers

Keynes, J. M., 1936. *The General Theory of Employment, Interest, and Money.* London: MacMillan

15

Effects of Measurement Errors on Population Estimates from Samples Generated from a Stratified Population through Systematic Sampling Technique

Abel OUKO[1*], Cheruiyot W. KIPKOECH[2], Emily KIRIMI[3]

[1]The East African University, Kenya
[2]Maasai Mara University, Kenya
[3]Technical University of Kenya

In various surveys, presence of measurement errors has led to misleading results in estimation of various population parameters. This study indicates the effects of measurement errors on estimates of population total and population variance when samples are drawn using systematic sampling technique from a stratified population. A finite population was generated through simulation. The population was then stratified into four strata followed by generation of ten samples in each of them using systematic sampling technique. In each stratum a sample was picked at random. The findings of this work indicated that systematic errors affected the accuracy of the estimates by overestimating both the population total and the population variance. Random errors only added variability to the data but their effect on the estimates of the population total and population variance was not that profound.

Keywords: *Measurement errors, Systematic Errors, Stratified population, Population Total and Population Variance*

1. Introduction

The ultimate goal of each survey is to obtain information about the population under study. The theory of sample survey as developed during the past several decades provides us with various kinds of scientific tools for drawing samples and making valid inference about the population parameters of interest. According to Koninj (1973), in measurement of physical quantities the personnel and devices that we have to use may not give as precise measurements as the best available. Measurement errors cannot be completely eliminated but minimized to an extent which their effects on survey results are not that profound. Basic contributions to the methodology of measurement error models were given by Mahalanobis (1946), Hansen (1946) and Sukhatme and Seth (1952) have examined the question of non sampling errors in census and survey work and they have furnished mathematical models for such errors. The objective of this study was to investigate the effects of measurement errors on the estimates of population total and population variance when samples are drawn from a stratified population using systematic sampling technique. The contribution of this study is to establish more weight as to why systematic errors should be minimized if at all valid results are to be obtained.

Corresponding Author:
Abel Ouko, Department of Mathematics, The East African University, Kenya

2. Systematic sampling

This is a sample selection technique in which sample members are selected from a given population according to a random starting point and a fixed periodic interval. Systematic sampling is still thought of as being random, as long as the periodic interval is determined beforehand and the starting point is random. A common way of selecting members into the sample using systematic sampling is simply by dividing the total number of units in the population by the desired number of units for the sample. The result of the division serves as the marker for selecting sample units from within the given population. Systematic sampling is to be applied only when the given population is logically homogeneous because systematic sample units are uniformly distributed over the population. In some cases systematic sampling is preferred since it spreads the sample more evenly over the population and easier to conduct.

Table 1. *Composition of the k systematic samples.*

Sample no.	1	2	...	i	...	K
	y_1	y_2	...	y_i	...	y_k
	y_{k+1}	y_{k+2}	...	y_{k+i}	...	y_{2k}
	...	...	...	...	...	...
	$y_{(n-1)k+1}$	$y_{(n-1)k+2}$	...	$y_{(n-1)k+3}$	...	y_{nk}
Means	$\bar{y}_1$	$\bar{y}_2$	...	$\bar{y}_i$	...	$\bar{y}_k$

2.1. Stratified Systematic sampling.

This is whereby the finite population under study is divided into relatively homogeneous groups referred to as strata and then systematic sampling is carried out in each stratum to generate samples.

Notations:

N_h - Total number of units in stratum h where {h =1, 2, ..., H}

n_h - Number of units in a sample drawn from stratum h

μ_{hk} - The true value of the kth unit in stratum h.

y_{hk} - is the observed value of the kth in stratum h.

Note that $N = N_1 + N_2 + \text{........} + N_H$

3. Sampling design

In the theory of finite population sampling, a sampling design specifies for every possible sample its probability of being drawn. It is convenient to have special notation for this probability which in this case will be P(s).

In other words we assume there is a function P (.) such that P(s) gives the probability of selecting specified samples under the scheme in use. The function P (.) will be referred to as sampling design.

4. The Simple Measurement Model

In this case we would like to formulate a statistical model for measurements made on elements of a sample from a finite population. Consider a finite population, $U = \{1 \ldots, k, \ldots, N\}$.It is assumed that for each element $k \in U$, there exists a true value μ_k and that the objective is to estimate the population total of these true values,

$$t_\mu = \sum_U \mu_k$$

A sample s of size n_s is selected from U by a given probability sampling design $p(.)$. The idea is to obtain the true value μ_k for each element $k \in s$, but what we actually obtain through the measurement procedure are the observed values y_k for $k \in s$. The observed y_k is composed of the true value μ_k and a random error or both random error and systematic error $y_k - \mu_k$. For lack of better values, y_k is used in the estimation. For a given sample s, the random variables $y_k\,(k \in s)$ are assumed to have a certain joint probability distribution (conditional on s), called a measurement model denoted by m. In this case we consider our survey as a two stage process whereby the first stage involves the sample selection, which results in a selected sample s and the second stage involves the measurement procedure, which generates an observed value y_k for each $k \in s$. When evaluating expectations and variances with respect to the two stages jointly, the conditional argument is useful. As for the expected values,

$$E_{pm}(.) = E_p\left[E_m(./s)\right]$$

Where $E_m(./s)$ denotes conditional expectation with respect to the measurement model m, for a given sample s, $E_p(.)$ denotes expectation with respect to the sample design $p(.)$ and $E_{pm}(.)$ denotes expectation with respect to sampling design and measurement model jointly.
Similarly, for the joint variance, called the *pm-variance* or the *total variance*, we have

$$V_{pm}(.) = E_p\left[V_m(./s)\right] + V_p\left[E_m(./s)\right]$$

Where $V_m(./s)$ denotes conditional variance with respect to the model m, given s, $V_p(.)$ denotes variance with respect to $P(.)$ and $V_{pm}(.)$ denotes variance with respect to $P(.)$ and m jointly.
We specify further the model m. For element k and l belonging to the same sample s, the first and second moments are

$$\mu_k = E_m(y_k / s)$$

$$\sigma_k^2 = V_m(y_k / s)$$

$$\text{And} \quad \sigma_{kl} = C_m(y_k, y_l / s)$$

5. Measurement errors.

Measurement is the basis of any scientific study. All measurements are, however, approximate values (not true values) within the limitation of measuring device, measuring environment, process of measurement and human error. Several measurements of the same quality on the same subject will not in general be the same.

Measurement errors refer to errors in survey responses arising from the method of data collection, the respondent or the questionnaire. They include the errors in a survey response as a result of respondents confusion, ignorance, carelessness, or dishonesty; the errors attributable to the interviewer, perhaps as a consequence of the poor or inadequate training, prior expectations regarding respondents' response etc. These measurement errors end up causing a considerable effect on survey estimates. These errors are broadly classified in two categories which are systematic errors and random errors

Systematic errors are biases in measurement which lead to the situation where the mean of many separate measurements differs significantly from the actual value of the measured attribute. All measurements are prone to systematic errors, often of several different types. The errors of this category are characterized by deviation in one direction from the true value. Systematic errors may result from; Usage of faulty instrument, Usage of faulty measuring process and Personal bias. Clearly this type of error cannot be minimized by repeated measurements. Systematic errors can therefore lead to either overestimation or underestimation of the desired population parameters.

Random errors are errors in measurement that lead to measurable values being inconsistent when repeated measures of a constant attribute or quantity are taken. Random errors unlike systematic errors are not unidirectional i.e. some measurements are higher while some are lower than the true value. Another distinguishing aspect of random errors is that it is not biased. It is normally present because of the limitation of the instrument in hand and the limitation of the part of the human ability. No human being can repeat an action in exactly the same manner. Hence it is likely that the same person reports different values with the same instrument, which measures quality correctly. This error is caused by any factor that randomly affects the sample. Random errors add variability to the data but do not affect the average performance for the group. This is why at times it is regarded as 'noise'.

5.1. Mathematical model for measurement errors.

According to Cochran (1977), we assume a large number of independent repetitions of the measurement on the ith unit are possible. Let $y_{i\alpha}$ be the value obtained in the αth repetition.

Then $\quad y_{i\alpha} = \mu_i + e_{i\alpha}$

Where $\quad \mu_i$ = true value

$e_{i\alpha}$ = measurement error

Where the expectation of e_{ij} is zero and variance is σ_i^2.

$$E[e_{i\alpha}] = 0$$

$$Var[e_{i\alpha}] = \sigma_i^2$$

Therefore,

$$E[y_{i\alpha} / i] = \mu_i$$

$$V[y_{i\alpha} / i] = \sigma_i^2$$

6. Inclusion probability in a stratified population

Suppose we have a stratified population containing H number of strata. If we take one stratum denoted by h, our indicator variable becomes,

$$I_{hk}(s) = \begin{cases} 1 \ \textit{if the } k^{th} \textit{ unit is included in the sample from stratum } h \\ 0 \ \textit{otherwise} \end{cases}$$

Our first order inclusion probability is denoted by π_{hk} which denotes the probability that element k from stratum h is included into the sample. In the case of systematic sampling, because each element k belongs to one of the $'a_h'$ equally probable systematic samples in stratum 'h', (where a_h is the sampling interval in stratum h.)

$$\pi_{hk} = \frac{1}{a_h}$$

The second order inclusion probability is denoted by π_{hkl} which refers to the probability that both elements 'k' and 'l' from stratum h are included into the sample. Under systematic sampling in stratum h

$$\pi_{hkl} = \begin{cases} \frac{1}{a_h} \ \textit{if } k \textit{ and } l \textit{ from stratum } h \textit{ are in same systematic sample} \\ 0 \ \textit{otherwise} \end{cases}$$

The expectation and variance of $I_{hk}(s)$ are obtained as follows,

$$E[I_{hk}(s)] = \pi_{hk}$$
$$V[I_{hk}(s)] = \pi_{hk}(1-\pi_{hk})$$

Covariance

$$\operatorname{cov}[I_{hk}I_{hl}] = \pi_{hkl} - \pi_{hk}\pi_{hl}$$

Since in stratum h our sampling interval is a_h we will have a_h systematic samples in the stratum indicated by s_r where $r = 1,2,\ldots,a_h$

7. Horvitz Thompson estimator in a Stratified Population

According to Horvitz and Thompson (1952), the estimator of the population total is given by

$$\hat{t}_{HT} = \sum_{h=1}^{H}\sum_{k=1}^{n_h}\frac{y_{hk}}{\pi_{hk}}$$

Its variance is given by,

$$V\left(\hat{t}_{HT}\right) = \sum_{h=1}^{H}\sum_{k=1}^{N_h}\frac{y_{hk}^2}{\pi_{hk}}(1-\pi_{hk}) + \sum_{h=1}^{H}\sum_{k=1}^{N_h}\sum_{k\neq l}^{N_h}\frac{y_{hk}y_{hl}}{\pi_{hk}\pi_{hl}}(\pi_{hkl} - \pi_{hk}\pi_{hl})$$

According to Sarndal (1992) there is no unbiased estimator of the variance of estimated population total when a sample is generated using systematic sampling technique. A precise estimator below was then chosen

$$\hat{V}\left(\hat{t}_{HT}\right) = \sum_{h=1}^{H}\hat{V}_h\left(\hat{t}_{hHT}\right)$$
$$\hat{V}\left(\hat{t}_{HT}\right) = \sum_{h=1}^{H}N_h^2\frac{1-f_h}{n_h}S_{hs_r}^2$$
$$where\ \ S_{hs_r}^2 = \frac{1}{n_h - 1}\sum_{hs_r}\left(y_{hk} - \bar{y}_{hs_r}\right)$$

Where $f_h = \dfrac{n_h}{N_h}$ represents the sampling fraction

8. The Mean Square Error (MSE)

The mean square error (MSE) of an estimator is one of the many ways to quantify the difference between values implied by an estimator and the true values of the quantity being estimated. The difference occurs because of randomness or because the estimator does not account for information that could produce a more accurate estimate. In order to compare a biased estimate with unbiased estimate or two estimates that have different amounts of bias, a useful criterion is the 'mean square error' of the estimate measured from the population value that is being estimated. Formally,

$$MSE\left(\hat{\mu}\right) = E\left[\hat{\mu} - \mu\right]^2 = E\left[\left(\hat{\mu} - m\right) + (m-\mu)\right]^2$$
$$= E\left(\hat{\mu} - m\right)^2 + 2(m-\mu)E\left(\hat{\mu} - m\right) + (m-\mu)^2$$
$$= \left(Variance\ of\ \hat{\mu}\right) + (bias)^2$$

The cross product term varnishes since $E\left(\hat{\mu}-m\right)=0$. The use of the MSE as a criterion of the accuracy of an estimate amounts to regarding two estimates that have the same MSE as equivalent. This is not strictly correct because the frequency distribution of errors $\left(\hat{\mu}-\mu\right)$ of different sizes will not be the same for the two estimates if they have different amounts of bias.

9. Total variance of the estimator of the population total in absence of systematic errors

The total variance in the absence of systematic errors is obtained as follows. Since our population is stratified our measurement model is $y_{hk}=\mu_{hk}+e_{hk}$

Where

$$E_m\left(y_{hk}/s\right)=\mu_{hk} \qquad k\in s$$
$$V_m\left(y_{hk}/s\right)=\sigma_{hk}^2 \qquad k\in s$$
$$Cov_m\left(y_{hk}y_{hl}/s\right)=\sigma_{hkl} \qquad k,l\in s$$

The total variance is given by

$$V_{pm}\left(\hat{t}_{HT}\right)=V_p\left[E_m\left(\hat{t}_{HT}/s\right)\right]+E_p\left[V_m\left(\hat{t}_{HT}/s\right)\right]$$

Where

$$E_p\left[V_m\left(\hat{t}_{HT}\right)\right]=E_p\left[V_m\left(\sum_{h=1}^{H}\sum_{k=1}^{n_h}\frac{y_{hk}}{\pi_{hk}}\right)\right]$$

$$=E_p\left(\sum_{h=1}^{H}\sum_{k=1}^{n_h}\frac{\sigma_{hk}^2}{\pi_{hk}^2}+\sum_{h=1}^{H}\sum_{k,l\in s_{r=1}}^{s_{a_h}}\sum_{k=1}^{n_h}\sum_{k\neq l}^{n_h}\frac{\sigma_{hkl}}{\pi_{hk}\pi_{hl}}\right)$$

$$=\sum_{h=1}^{H}\sum_{k=1}^{N_h}\frac{\sigma_{hk}^2}{\pi_{hk}}+\sum_{h=1}^{H}\sum_{k,l\in s_{r=1}}^{s_{a_h}}\sum_{k=1}^{N_h}\sum_{k\neq l}^{N_h}\frac{\sigma_{hkl}\pi_{hkl}}{\pi_{hk}\pi_{hl}}$$

$$V_p\left[E_m\left(\hat{t}_{HT}\right)\right]=V_p\left[E_m\left(\sum_{h=1}^{H}\sum_{k=1}^{n_h}\frac{y_{hk}}{\pi_{hk}}\right)\right]$$

$$=V_p\left[\sum_{h=1}^{H}\sum_{k=1}^{n_h}\frac{\mu_{hk}}{\pi_{hk}}\right]$$

$$=\sum_{h=1}^{H}\sum_{k=1}^{N_h}\frac{\mu_{hk}^2}{\pi_{hk}}\left(1-\pi_{hk}\right)+\sum_{h=1}^{H}\sum_{k,l\in s_{r=1}}^{s_{a_h}}\sum_{k=1}^{N_h}\sum_{k\neq l}^{N_h}\frac{\left(\pi_{hkl}-\pi_{hk}\pi_{hl}\right)}{\pi_{hk}\pi_{hl}}\mu_{hk}\mu_{hl}$$

Therefore the total variance in absence of systematic errors is given by

$$V_{pm}\left(\hat{t}_{HT}\right)=\sum_{h=1}^{H}\sum_{k=1}^{N_h}\frac{\sigma_{hk}^2}{\pi_{hk}}+\sum_{h=1}^{H}\sum_{k,l\in s_{r=1}}^{s_{a_h}}\sum_{k=1}^{N_h}\sum_{k\neq l}^{N_h}\frac{\sigma_{hkl}\pi_{hkl}}{\pi_{hk}\pi_{hl}}+\sum_{h=1}^{H}\sum_{k=1}^{N_h}\frac{\mu_{hk}^2}{\pi_{hk}}\left(1-\pi_{hk}\right)+\sum_{h=1}^{H}\sum_{k,l\in s_{r=1}}^{s_{a_h}}\sum_{k=1}^{N_h}\sum_{k\neq l}^{N_h}\frac{\left(\pi_{hkl}-\pi_{hk}\pi_{hl}\right)}{\pi_{hk}\pi_{hl}}\mu_{hk}\mu_{hl}$$

By replacing both first and second order inclusion probabilities with $\frac{1}{a_h}$ the variance becomes

$$V_{pm}\left(\hat{t}_{HT}\right)=\sum_{h=1}^{H}\sum_{k=1}^{N_h}a_h\sigma_{hk}^2+\sum_{h=1}^{H}\sum_{k,l\in s_{r-1}}^{s_{a_h}}\sum_{h=1}^{N_h}\sum_{k\neq l}^{N_h}a_h\sigma_{hkl}+\sum_{h=1}^{H}\sum_{k=1}^{N_h}(a_h-1)\mu_{hk}^2+\sum_{h=1}^{H}\sum_{k,l\in s_{r-1}}^{s_{a_h}}\sum_{k=1}^{N_h}\sum_{k\neq l}^{N_h}(a_h-1)\mu_{hk}\mu_{hl}$$

10. The mathematical model for measurement of errors in stratified population

Since our population is stratified, the model becomes

$$y_{hk}=\mu_{hk}+e_{hk}$$

μ_{hk} - represents the true value of unit k in stratum h

e_{hk} - represents the measurement error term of unit k in stratum h

$$\therefore E_m\left(y_{hk}/s\right)=b_{hk}+\mu_{hk} \qquad k\in s$$

Where b_{hk} refers to the bias term

$$V_m\left(y_{hk}/s\right)=\sigma_{hk}^2 \qquad k\in s$$

The covariance between k^{th} and l^{th} unit is

$$Cov_m\left(y_{hk}y_{hl}/k,l\in s\right)=E\left[y_{hk}-E(Y_{hk})\right]\left[y_{hk}-E\left(y_{hk}\right)\right]$$

$$=E\left(e_{hk}-b_{hk}\right)\left(e_{hl}-b_{hl}\right)$$

$$=Cov\left(e_{hk}e_{hl}\right)$$

$$\therefore Cov_m\left(y_{hk}y_{hl}/k,l\in s\right)=\sigma_{hkl}$$

11. Decomposition of the mean square error.

In this case we will consider the Horvitz Thompson estimator and the effect of measurement errors on its accuracy. We will decompose the mean square error into components, assuming that the measurements obey the simple measurement model 'm' as stated before. The mean square error of $\hat{t}_{HT}$ can be written as the sum of the total variance and squared bias.

$$MSE_{pm}\left(\hat{t}_{HT}\right)=V_{pm}\left(\hat{t}_{HT}\right)+\left[B_{pm}\left(\hat{t}_{HT}\right)\right]^2$$

The total variance is given by $V_{pm}\left(\hat{t}_{HT}\right)=E_{pm}\left[\hat{t}_{HT}-E_{pm}\left(\hat{t}_{HT}\right)\right]^2$

The bias is given by $B_{pm}\left(\hat{t}_{HT}\right)=E_{pm}\left(\hat{t}_{HT}\right)-t_{\mu}$

This is called the measurement bias, which arises when expected measurement values on elements do not agree with true values. Variance term can be decomposed as follows

$$V_{pm}\left(\hat{t}_{HT}\right)=V_p\left[E_m\left(\hat{t}_{HT}/s\right)\right]+E_p\left[V_m\left(\hat{t}_{HT}/s\right)\right]=V_1+V_2$$

The first component V_1 is referred to as the sampling variance which is zero in the case of complete enumeration whereas the second component V_2 is referred to as the measurement variance. The Horvitz Thompson estimator for the population total in this case will be

$$\hat{t}_{HT} = \sum_{h=1}^{H}\sum_{k=1}^{n_h}\frac{y_{hk}}{\pi_{hk}}$$

But,

$$E_{pm}\left(\hat{t}_{HT}\right) = E_p\left[E_m\left(\sum_{h=1}^{H}\sum_{k=1}^{n_h}\frac{y_{hk}}{\pi_{hk}}\right)\right]$$

$$= E_p\left(\sum_{h=1}^{H}\sum_{k=1}^{n_h}\frac{g_{hk}}{\pi_{hk}}\right) \quad where \quad g_{hk} = \mu_{hk} + b_{hk}$$

$$= \sum_{h=1}^{H}\sum_{k=1}^{N_h}\frac{g_{hk}}{\pi_{hk}}E_p\left[I_{hk}\right]$$

$$= \sum_{h=1}^{H}\sum_{k=1}^{N_h} g_{hk} \qquad since \quad E_p\left[I_{hk}\right] = \pi_{hk}$$

$$= \sum_{h=1}^{H}\sum_{k=1}^{N_h}\mu_{hk} + \sum_{h=1}^{H}\sum_{k=1}^{N_h} b_{hk}$$

From the decomposition of the variance term, we have V_1 & V_2 where

$$V_1 = V_p\left[E_m\left(\hat{t}_{HT}\right)\right] \qquad V_2 = E_p\left[V_m\left(\hat{t}_{HT}\right)\right]$$

$$\therefore V_1 = V_p\left[E_m\left(\hat{t}_{HT}\right)\right] = V_p\left[E_m\left(\sum_{h=1}^{H}\sum_{k=1}^{n_h}\frac{y_{hk}}{\pi_{hk}}\right)\right]$$

$$= V_p\left[\sum_{h=1}^{H}\sum_{k=1}^{n_h}\frac{g_{hk}}{\pi_{hk}}\right]$$

$$= \sum_{h=1}^{H}\sum_{k=1}^{N_h}\frac{g_{hk}^2}{\pi_{hk}^2}V\left[I_{hk}\right] + \sum_{h=1}^{H}\sum_{k,l\in s_{r=1}}^{s_{a_h}}\sum_{k=1}^{N_h}\sum_{k\neq l}^{N_h}\frac{g_{hk}}{\pi_{hk}}\frac{g_{hl}}{\pi_{hl}}\operatorname{cov}\left(I_{hk}I_{hl}\right)$$

$$But \quad V\left[I_{hk}\right] = \pi_{hk}\left(1-\pi_{hk}\right) \qquad and \qquad \operatorname{cov}\left(I_{hk}I_{hl}\right) = \left(\pi_{hkl} - \pi_{hk}\pi_{hl}\right)$$

$$\therefore V_1 = \sum_{h=1}^{H}\sum_{k=1}^{N_h}\frac{g_{hk}^2}{\pi_{hk}^2}\pi_{hk}\left(1-\pi_{hk}\right) + \sum_{h=1}^{H}\sum_{k,l\in s_{r=1}}^{s_{a_h}}\sum_{k=1}^{N_h}\sum_{k\neq l}^{N_h}\frac{g_{hk}}{\pi_{hk}}\frac{g_{hl}}{\pi_{hl}}\left(\pi_{hkl} - \pi_{hk}\pi_{hl}\right)$$

$$= \sum_{h=1}^{H}\sum_{k=1}^{N_h}\frac{g_{hk}^2}{\pi_{hk}}\left(1-\pi_{hk}\right) + \sum_{h=1}^{H}\sum_{k,l\in s_{r=1}}^{s_{a_h}}\sum_{k=1}^{N_h}\sum_{k\neq l}^{N_h}\frac{\left(\pi_{hkl} - \pi_{hk}\pi_{hl}\right)}{\pi_{hk}\pi_{hl}}g_{hk}g_{hl}$$

$$but \quad g_{hk} = \mu_{hk} + b_{hk} \qquad and \qquad g_{hl} = \mu_{hl} + b_{hl}$$

$$V_1=\sum_{h=1}^{H}\sum_{k=1}^{N_h}\frac{(1-\pi_{hk})}{\pi_{hk}}(\mu_{hk}+b_{hk})^2+\sum_{h=1}^{H}\sum_{k,l\in s_{r=1}}^{s_{a_h}}\sum_{k=1}^{N_h}\sum_{k\neq l}^{N_h}\frac{(\pi_{hkl}-\pi_{hk}\pi_{hl})}{\pi_{hk}\pi_{hl}}(\mu_{hk}+b_{hk})(\mu_{hl}+b_{hl})$$

$$=\sum_{h=1}^{H}\sum_{k=1}^{N_h}\frac{(1-\pi_{hk})}{\pi_{hk}}(\mu_{hk}^2+2\mu_{hk}b_{hk}+b_{hk}^2)+\sum_{h=1}^{H}\sum_{k,l\in s_{r=1}}^{s_{a_h}}\sum_{k=1}^{N_h}\sum_{k\neq l}^{N_h}\frac{(\pi_{hkl}-\pi_{hk}\pi_{hl})}{\pi_{hk}\pi_{hl}}(\mu_{hk}\mu_{hl}+\mu_{hk}b_{hl}+\mu_{hl}b_{hk}+b_{hk}b_{hl})$$

$$\begin{aligned}V_1=&\sum_{h=1}^{H}\sum_{k=1}^{N_h}\frac{(1-\pi_{hk})}{\pi_{hk}}\mu_{hk}^2+\sum_{h=1}^{H}\sum_{k,l\in s_{r=1}}^{s_{a_h}}\sum_{k=1}^{N_h}\sum_{k\neq l}^{N_h}\frac{(\pi_{hkl}-\pi_{hk}\pi_{hl})}{\pi_{hk}\pi_{hl}}\mu_{hk}\mu_{hl}\\&+\sum_{h=1}^{H}\sum_{k=1}^{N_h}\frac{(1-\pi_{hk})}{\pi_{hk}}b_{hk}^2+\sum_{h=1}^{H}\sum_{k,l\in s_{r=1}}^{s_{a_h}}\sum_{k=1}^{N_h}\sum_{k\neq l}^{N_h}\frac{(\pi_{hkl}-\pi_{hk}\pi_{hl})}{\pi_{hk}\pi_{hl}}b_{hk}b_{hl}\\&+2\left[\sum_{h=1}^{H}\sum_{k=1}^{N_h}\frac{(1-\pi_{hk})}{\pi_{hk}}\mu_{hk}b_{hl}+\sum_{h=1}^{H}\sum_{k,l\in s_{r=1}}^{s_{a_h}}\sum_{k=1}^{N_h}\sum_{k\neq l}^{N_h}\frac{(\pi_{hkl}-\pi_{hk}\pi_{hl})}{\pi_{hk}\pi_{hl}}\mu_{hk}b_{hl}\right]\end{aligned}$$

$$\begin{aligned}V_2&=E_p\left[V_m\left(\hat{t}_{HT}\right)\right]\\&=E_p\left[V_m\left(\sum_{h=1}^{H}\sum_{k=1}^{n_h}\frac{y_{hk}}{\pi_{hk}}\right)\right]\\&=\sum_{h=1}^{H}\sum_{k=1}^{N_h}\frac{\sigma_{hk}^2}{\pi_{hk}}+\sum_{h=1}^{H}\sum_{k,l\in s_{r=1}}^{s_{a_h}}\sum_{k=1}^{N_h}\sum_{k\neq l}^{N_h}\frac{\sigma_{hkl}\pi_{hkl}}{\pi_{hk}\pi_{hl}}\end{aligned}$$

Thus the total variance in presence of measurement errors is

$$V_{pm}\left(\hat{t}_{HT}\right)=V_p\left[E_m\left(\hat{t}_{HT}/s\right)\right]+E_p\left[V_m\left(\hat{t}_{HT}/s\right)\right]=V_1+V_2$$

$$\begin{aligned}&=\sum_{h=1}^{H}\sum_{k=1}^{N_h}\frac{\sigma_{hk}^2}{\pi_{hk}}+\sum_{h=1}^{H}\sum_{k,l\in s_{r=1}}^{s_{a_h}}\sum_{k=1}^{N_h}\sum_{k\neq l}^{N_h}\frac{\sigma_{hkl}\pi_{hkl}}{\pi_{hk}\pi_{hl}}\\&+\sum_{h=1}^{H}\sum_{k=1}^{N_h}\frac{(1-\pi_{hk})}{\pi_{hk}}\mu_{hk}^2+\sum_{h=1}^{H}\sum_{k,l\in s_{r=1}}^{s_{a_h}}\sum_{k=1}^{N_h}\sum_{k\neq l}^{N_h}\frac{\pi_{hkl}-\pi_{hk}\pi_{hl}}{\pi_{hk}\pi_{hl}}\mu_{hk}\mu_{hl}\end{aligned}$$

$$+\sum_{h=1}^{H}\sum_{k=1}^{N_h}\frac{(1-\pi_{hk})}{\pi_{hk}}b_{hk}^2+\sum_{h=1}^{H}\sum_{k,l\in s_{r=1}}^{s_{a_h}}\sum_{k=1}^{N_h}\sum_{k\neq l}^{N_h}\frac{\pi_{hkl}-\pi_{hk}\pi_{hl}}{\pi_{hk}\pi_{hl}}b_{hk}b_{hl}$$

$$+2\left(\sum_{h=1}^{H}\sum_{k=1}^{N_h}\frac{(1-\pi_{hk})}{\pi_{hk}}\mu_{hk}b_{hk}+\sum_{h=1}^{H}\sum_{k,l\in s_{r=1}}^{s_{a_h}}\sum_{k=1}^{N_h}\sum_{k\neq l}^{N_h}\frac{\pi_{hkl}-\pi_{hk}\pi_{hl}}{\pi_{hk}\pi_{hl}}\mu_{hk}b_{hl}\right)$$

Under systematic sampling in populations with stratification as previously obtained the inclusion probabilities are:

$$\pi_{hk}=\frac{1}{a_h}$$

$$\pi_{hkl}=\begin{cases}\frac{1}{a_h} & \textit{if } k \textit{ and } l \textit{ from stratum } h \textit{ are in same systematic sample}\\[2ex] 0 & \textit{if } k \textit{ and } l \textit{ from stratum } h \textit{ are in different systematic samples}\end{cases}$$

We then substitute these probabilities in

$$V_{pm}\left(\hat{t}_{HT}\right)=V_p\left[E_m\left(\hat{t}_{HT}/s\right)\right]+E_p\left[V_m\left(\hat{t}_{HT}/s\right)\right]$$

$$=\sum_{h=1}^{H}\sum_{k=1}^{N_h}\frac{\sigma_{hk}^2}{\pi_{hk}}+\sum_{h=1}^{H}\sum_{k,l\in s_{r=1}}^{s_{a_h}}\sum_{k=1}^{N_h}\sum_{k\neq l}^{N_h}\frac{\sigma_{hkl}\pi_{hkl}}{\pi_{hk}\pi_{hl}}$$

$$+\sum_{h=1}^{H}\sum_{k=1}^{N_h}\frac{(1-\pi_{hk})}{\pi_{hk}}\mu_{hk}^2+\sum_{h=1}^{H}\sum_{k,l\in s_{r=1}}^{s_{a_h}}\sum_{k=1}^{N_h}\sum_{k\neq l}^{N_h}\frac{\pi_{hkl}-\pi_{hk}\pi_{hl}}{\pi_{hk}\pi_{hl}}\mu_{hk}\mu_{hl}$$

$$+\sum_{h=1}^{H}\sum_{k=1}^{N_h}\frac{(1-\pi_{hk})}{\pi_{hk}}b_{hk}^2+\sum_{h=1}^{H}\sum_{k,l\in s_{r=1}}^{s_{a_h}}\sum_{k=1}^{N_h}\sum_{k\neq l}^{N_h}\frac{\pi_{hkl}-\pi_{hk}\pi_{hl}}{\pi_{hk}\pi_{hl}}b_{hk}b_{hl}$$

$$+2\left(\sum_{h=1}^{H}\sum_{k=1}^{N_h}\frac{(1-\pi_{hk})}{\pi_{hk}}\mu_{hk}b_{hk}+\sum_{h=1}^{H}\sum_{k,l\in s_{r=1}}^{s_{a_h}}\sum_{k=1}^{N_h}\sum_{k\neq l}^{N_h}\frac{\pi_{hkl}-\pi_{hk}\pi_{hl}}{\pi_{hk}\pi_{hl}}\mu_{hk}b_{hl}\right)$$

We then replace both the first and second order inclusion probabilities with $\frac{1}{a_h}$ to obtain

$$V_{pm}\left[\hat{t}_{HT}\right]=\sum_{h=1}^{H}\sum_{k=1}^{N_h}\frac{\sigma_{hk}^2}{\left[\frac{1}{a_h}\right]}+\sum_{h=1}^{H}\sum_{k,l\in s_{r=1}}^{s_{a_h}}\sum_{k=1}^{N_h}\sum_{k\neq l}^{N_h}\frac{\sigma_{hkl}\left[\frac{1}{a_h}\right]}{\left[\frac{1}{a_h}\right]\left[\frac{1}{a_h}\right]}$$

$$+\sum_{h=1}^{H}\sum_{k=1}^{N_h}\frac{\left[1-\frac{1}{a_h}\right]}{\left[\frac{1}{a_h}\right]}\mu_{hk}^2+\sum_{h=1}^{H}\sum_{k,l\in s_{r=1}}^{s_{a_h}}\sum_{k=1}^{N_h}\sum_{k\neq l}^{N_h}\frac{\left[\left[\frac{1}{a_h}\right]-\left[\frac{1}{a_h}\right]\left[\frac{1}{a_h}\right]\right]}{\left[\frac{1}{a_h}\right]\left[\frac{1}{a_h}\right]}\mu_{hk}\mu_{hl}$$

$$+\sum_{h=1}^{H}\sum_{k=1}^{N_h}\frac{\left[1-\frac{1}{a_h}\right]}{\left[\frac{1}{a_h}\right]}b_{hk}^2+\sum_{h=1}^{H}\sum_{k,l\in s_{r=1}}^{s_{a_h}}\sum_{k=1}^{N_h}\sum_{k\neq l}^{N_h}\frac{\left[\left[\frac{1}{a_h}\right]-\left[\frac{1}{a_h}\right]\left[\frac{1}{a_h}\right]\right]}{\left[\frac{1}{a_h}\right]\left[\frac{1}{a_h}\right]}b_{hk}b_{hl}$$

$$+2\left[\sum_{h=1}^{H}\sum_{k=1}^{N_h}\frac{\left(1-\frac{1}{a_h}\right)}{\frac{1}{a_h}}\mu_{hk}b_{hk}+\sum_{h=1}^{H}\sum_{k,l\in s_{r=1}}^{s_{a_h}}\sum_{k=1}^{N_h}\sum_{k\neq l}^{N_h}\frac{\left(\frac{1}{a_h}-\frac{1}{a_h}\frac{1}{a_h}\right)}{\frac{1}{a_h}\frac{1}{a_h}}\mu_{hk}b_{hk}\right]$$

This then simplifies to

$$V_{pm}\left(\hat{t}_{HT}\right)=\sum_{h=1}^{H}\sum_{k=1}^{N_h}a_h\sigma_{hk}^2+\sum_{h=1}^{H}\sum_{k,l\in s_{r=1}}^{s_{a_h}}\sum_{k=1}^{N_h}\sum_{k\neq l}^{N_h}a_h\sigma_{hkl}$$

$$+\sum_{h=1}^{H}\sum_{k=1}^{N_h}(a_h-1)\mu_{hk}^2+\sum_{h=1}^{H}\sum_{k,l\in s_{r=1}}^{s_{a_h}}\sum_{k=1}^{N_h}\sum_{k\neq l}^{N_h}(a_h-1)\mu_{hk}\mu_{hl}$$

$$+\sum_{h=1}^{H}\sum_{k=1}^{N_h}(a_h-1)b_{hk}^2+\sum_{h=1}^{H}\sum_{k,l\in s_{r=1}}^{s_{a_h}}\sum_{k=1}^{N_h}\sum_{k\neq l}^{N_h}(a_h-1)b_{hk}b_{hl}$$

$$+2\left[\sum_{h=1}^{H}\sum_{k=1}^{N_h}(a_h-1)\mu_{hk}b_{hk}+\sum_{h=1}^{H}\sum_{k,l\in s_{r=1}}^{s_{a_h}}\sum_{k=1}^{N_h}\sum_{k\neq l}^{N_h}(a_h-1)\mu_{hk}b_{hl}\right]$$

12. Simulation of a finite population

Visual basic programming language along with Microsoft access were used to generate a finite population of size N=1000. A population was simulated containing true values ranging from 20 to 90 inclusive. The true values had a normal distribution with a mean of 55 and a variance of 100. The population was then subdivided into four strata. This was done by first arranging all the population units in ascending order. The first 300 units were selected to constitute the first stratum and the following 250 units were selected to constitute the second stratum. The third and fourth strata were also selected to contain 250 and 200 units respectively. A sampling interval of 10 was used in each stratum resulting to 10 systematic samples in each stratum. In each stratum a sample was selected at random. In this case an assumption was made that systematic error b_{hk} is proportional to the true value $b_{hk}=d\mu_{hk}$

13. Results

Table 2. *Estimated population total subjected to systematic errors with proportions of size 'd'*

PARAMETER: POPULATION TOTAL AND POPULATION VARIANCE								
		TRUE VALUES	ESTIMATES WITH SYSTEMATIC ERROR					
			d=0.05	d=0.10	d=0.15	d=0.20	d=0.25	d=0.30
STRATUM	1	13320	14215	14881	15547	16213	16879	17545
	2	13350	14030.5	14698	15365.5	16033	16700.5	17368
	3	15050	16034.5	16787	17539.5	18292	19044.5	19797
	4	13840	14369	15061	15723	16445	17137	17829
Estimated pop Total		55560	58649	61427	64205	66983	69761	72539
population Total		55000	57865.3	60615.3	63365.3	66115.3	68865.3	71615.3
Variance of estimator of population Total		1343800	2462003	2620951	2786619	2959005	3138111	3323935
Estimate of the Variance of pop Total		99688.7	188425	199168	210410	222151	234390	247127

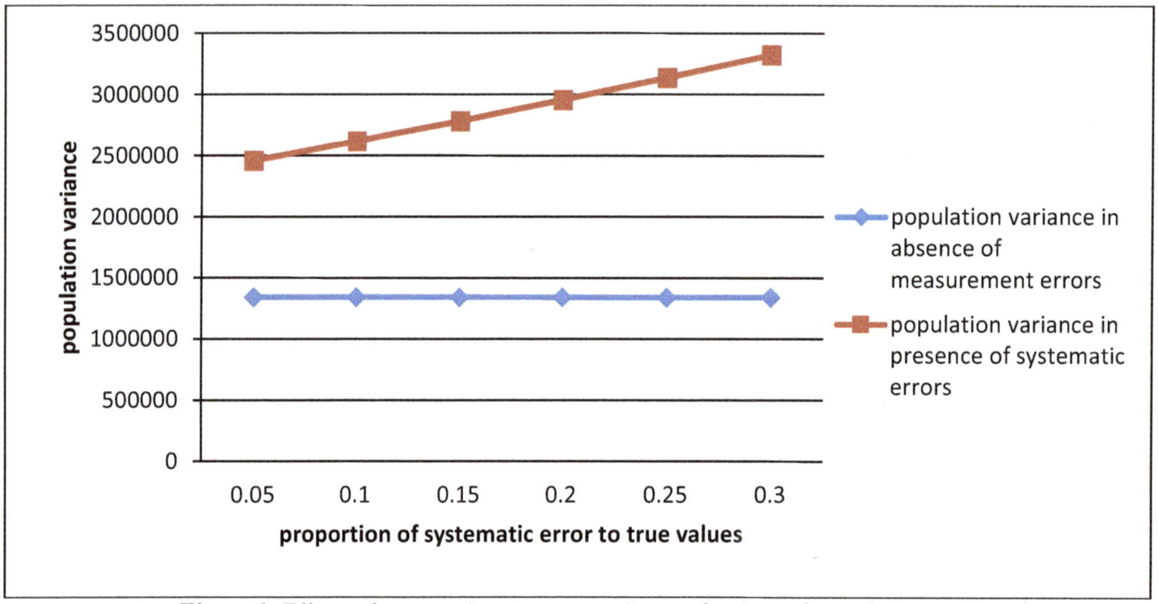

Figure 1. *Effects of systematic errors on variance of estimated population total*

14. Conclusion

The table 2 and figure 1 indicated that there was an increase in population total and population variance with increase in systematic error. The findings of the study indicated that systematic errors had a significant impact on the accuracy of the estimates of both population total and population variance.

References

Cochran, W.G., 1977. *Sampling techniques*. 3rd Edition, John Willey and Sons, New York.

Hansen, M. H., and Hurwitz, W. N., 1946. The problem of non-response in sample surveys. *Journal of the American Statistical Association*, 41, pp.517-529

Horvitz D. G. and Thompson D. J, 1952. A Generalization of sampling without replacement from a finite universe. *Journal of the American Statistical Association*, 47(260), pp.663-685

Koninj H.S., 1973. *Statistical theory of sample survey design and analysis*. North Holland Publishing Company, Amsterdam.

Mahalanobis, P.C., 1946. Recent experiments in statistical sampling in the Indian statistical institute. *Journal of the Royal Statistical Society*, 325-370.

Sarndal, C.E., Swensson, B., and Wretman, J., 1992. *Model assisted survey sampling*. New York, Springer Verlag.

Suhkatme, P.V., and Seth, G.R., 1952. Non-sampling errors in surveys. *Journal of Indian Society of Agricultural Statistics*, 5-41.

16

Effect of Financial Liberalization on the Probability of Occurrence of Banking Crises

Ramzi FARHANI, Ghrissi MHAMDI*,
Abdelkader AGUIR, Mounir SMIDA

University of Sousse, Tunisia
MO²FID Research Unit

This study examines the relationship between financial liberalization and the advent probability of banking crises because of institutional quality. We used a logit panel data for a sample of fifty developing countries during the period (1990-2014). The results show that there is a positive relationship between financial liberalization and banking crises and the strengthening of institutional quality overcomes the problem of banking crises.

Keywords: *banking crises, financial liberalization, institutional quality.*

1. Introduction

Recently, several economies have undergone major transformations, regulatory and institutional in nature. These changes have altered the functioning of institutions and capital markets. The origin of these changes comes mainly from financial liberalization in the 1980s and which affected almost all emerging countries. McKinnon and Shaw (1973) analyzed the phenomenon of "financial repression" which is characterized by excessive government intervention in financial activity. Financial liberalization has been proposed as a response to this situation because it improves the efficiency of investment and eventually economic growth. Overall, financial liberalization has been broken down into three major reforms. This is the liberalization of the movement of capital, the opening of financial markets to international operators and deregulation in lending and deposit rates to increase interbank competition. The proliferation of crises in countries such as Mexico (1995), Asian countries (1997), Brazil (1998), and Turkey (2001) opened the debate on the benefits of deregulation of financial activity.

It is generally accepted that the economic theory of liberalization opposes school financial repression to that of neo-structuralisms. The first finds its theoretical origins in the work of two economists from Stanford McKinnon and Shaw School (1973). Both authors present financial liberalization as an effective and simple strategy to accelerate economic growth. This financial liberalization has been proposed as a response to what

---

* Corresponding Author:
Ghrissi Mhamdi, University of Sousse, MO2FID Research Unit, Faculty of Economic Sciences and Management, Department of Economics, 4023 Tunisia

the authors called "Financial Repression". However, Taylor (1983) and Van Wijnbergen (1983) challenged the validity of this analysis. Starting from a structural view of the economy, they felt that a policy of financial liberalization rather leads to slower economic growth.

In this context, Roubini and Sala-i-Martin (1992) were the first to prove empirically that there's a negative effect between financial repression and economic growth. For them, a liberalized economy is growing faster than so-called repressed economy. For his part, Honing (2008) showed that the mobility of capital has major benefits for the economies concerned, particularly when it comes to the efficient allocation of resources. The new funds represent a new source of financing for domestic investment. It provides new opportunities for these countries to diversify risk and promote subsequent financial development. These words are affirmed by Emran and Stiglitz (2009), which stipulate that a liberalized and competitive market is seen as a necessary condition for the success of the private sector promoting financial development.

As regards the effects of crises, Caprio and Klinderberger (1996) identified 117 crises since the seventies decade in ninety-three countries. These authors confirm that banking crises in developing countries have been tougher and more expensive than those that have affected more advanced economies. In contrast to the latter, the cost of crisis resolution in less developed countries exceeded 10% of GDP (Venezuela 18%, Mexico 15%, Bulgaria 14%). Incidentally, Plihon and Miotti (2001) state that *"The emerging countries of Latin America and Asia have been particularly affected by the banking crisis, the cost was often considerable."*Confirming the point of view of Caprio and Klinderberger, they reported estimates of the cost to the taxpayer to rescue the banking systems involved. Thus, these costs have been estimated at 15% of GDP for Mexico (Peso crisis in 1994-1995) and Venezuela. Compared to the crises of US savings banks in the 1980s (3.5% of GDP) and banking crises in Scandinavia (5-7% of GDP), these costs are relatively high. In the same vein, a study by Honohan and Klingebiel (2000) on a group of thirty four countries with economies in transition in the period 1970-2000 confirms that banking crises emerge additional losses to the economy as , reduced investment and consumption mainly due to credit rationing.

Contrary to the prevailing theory in the 1980s, the proliferation of banking and financial crises, particularly in Asia and Latin America, has led some researchers to review the effects of this liberalization or even question it. Indeed, the number of such attacks has increased significantly and even quadrupled from 1970 as well as a large number of banking crises was preceded by measures that promoted economic liberalization (Kaminsky and Reinhart 1996) , (Caprio and Klingebiel 1996).

Miotti (2001) Kunt and Detragiache (1998) have demonstrated the existence of a close relationship between the banking and financial crises and financial liberalization policies in emerging countries. Alfaro and Hammel (2007), Kim and Kenny (2007), believe that in developing countries, financial liberalization is a vital and necessary step to abandon financial repression and lead to a situation of sustainable growth.

However, Ranciere et al. (2006) conclude that the literature has spawned two completely divergent currents. The first considers that it strengthens the financial development and contributes to sustainable economic growth. The second states that financial liberalization leads to excessive risk-taking. It increases the volatility of macroeconomic indicators and is responsible for the recurrence of banking crises.

It is in this context that lies our empirical investigation test. We will try and verify empirically whether financial liberalization, in its three dimensions (of the domestic financial sector, financial markets and capital account) helped trigger banking crises. In addition, our study is whether the strengthening of the institutional framework mitigates the likelihood of banking crises in developing countries. We studied a panel composed of fifty developing countries (the countries of Asia, Latin America, Africa and the Middle East) that have experience more or less successful in terms of financial openness. Our study spans the period from 1980 to 2014. The choice of this period is justified by the fact that it represents the episodes of financial deregulation and banking crises movements that affected many developing countries and the availability of data for some of these countries.

2. Empirical Methodology

In order to identify the impact of the liberalization of the domestic financial sector, stock markets and the capital account and the effect of institutional quality on the probability of occurrence of banking crises in developing countries, we have resorted to estimates by modeling logit panel data.

The dependent variable in our model represents the banking crises defined as follows:

$$y_{it} = \begin{cases} 1 \; if \; crises \\ 0 \; otherwise \end{cases}$$

with i = {1, ..., N}; t = {1, ..., T}

This type of regression investigates the relationship between a binary response variable and several explanatory variables. She returns to test the probability of occurrence of crises by encoding (0,1). This coding choice (0.1) is traditionally held by the dichotomous models.

Thus, the holding pattern, in this case, is the following:

$$y_{it} = \hat{\beta} X_{it} + \varepsilon_{it}$$

with i = {1, ..., N}, t = {1, ..., T}

and

$$y_{it} = \begin{cases} 1 \; if \; crises \\ 0 \; otherwise \end{cases}$$

y is the vector of dummies variables of banking crises, $\hat{\beta}$ represents the vector of unknown N coefficients to estimate, X is the matrix of explanatory variables and ε residue matrix. y_{it} denotes the vector of binary variables taking the value of a banking crisis in the country i in year(t) and the zero otherwise, we can write:

$$P_i = \Pr ob(Y_{it} = \frac{1}{X_i}) = F(\beta X_i)$$

or

$$E(Y_{it}) = \Pr ob(Y_{it} = 1) * 1 + \Pr ob(Y_{it} = 0) * 0 = \Pr ob(Y_{it} + 1) = Pi$$

"i = 1,..., N

The function F is, the repair function of the logistic:

$$F(\theta) = \frac{e^{\theta}}{1 + e^{\theta}} = \frac{1}{1 + e^{-\theta}} = \cap(\theta)$$

According Hurlin (2003), the logit model defines the probability associated with the event $Y_i = 1(p(Y_{it} = 1))$: Probability of occurrence of banking crises or even high bank fragility in country i in year (t)

$$Modèle \log it P_i = \cap(\beta X_{it}) = \frac{1}{1 + \exp(-\beta X_{it})}; \forall i = 1, ..., N$$

The most commonly used to estimate the parameters of the logistic regression method, consists of the maximum likelihood method. The latter provides estimators good statistical properties.

More concretely, a logistic coefficient indicates that for each additional unit of Xi, the logit increases β. From a practical point of view, the likelihood of the dichotomous logit model is written as follows:

$$L(y, \beta) = \prod_{i=1}^{N} \prod_{t=1}^{T} P_i^{y_{it}} * (1 - P_i)^{1 - y_{it}}$$

The logarithm of the likelihood and given by the following relationship:

$$LnL(y, \beta) = \sum_{i=1}^{N} \sum_{t=1}^{T} \{ y_{it} * Ln[F(X_i \beta)] + (1 - y_{it}) * Ln[1 - F(X_i \beta)] \}$$

It is the function of the multi-variable logit model.

The purpose of these econometric models is to explain the birth of an event with the help of a number of explanatory variables.

3. Data Description

Financial liberalization is identified because of three elements: the deregulation of the domestic financial sector, liberalization of stock markets and the opening of the capital account. As part of our study, we will remember these three dimensions of financial liberalization. Thus, financial liberalization indicator is a composite index of three aspects of financial deregulation.

$$LF = \frac{1}{3}LSFI + \frac{1}{3}LMF + \frac{1}{3}LCC$$

$$SI.\begin{cases} = 1, & financial\ repression \\ = 2, & partial\ liberalization \\ = 3, & total\ liberalization \end{cases}$$

For measuring variables of internal and external financial liberalization we will use in our study, Kaopen indicator developed by Chinn and Ito (2005) to measure the degree of restrictions on capital account. In fact, the last update made in 2011, provides an indicator for more than 180 countries over the period (1970-2011).

This indicator mainly constructed by the method of principal component analysis, has the advantage that it seeks to measure the intensity of restrictions on capital account, not its presence or not. In addition, it covers a growing number of countries (170 countries) for a long period (1970 to 2011). It varies between 1.7 and 2.6. The higher the value, the greater the country in question the capital account is liberalized. In other words, this index takes higher values when that country is more open to international transactions.

To measure the degree of liberalization of stock markets, we retain, a result, the ratio:

$$\frac{portfolio\ flows\ as\ shares + portfolio\ flows\ as\ bonds}{GDP}$$

By definition, portfolio flows in shares representing the sum of the representative of Foreign Action Certificates and national securities held by foreign investors. While portfolio flows in bonds represent bonds purchased by foreign investors.

Theoretically there are two effects of liberalization of financial markets. The first has a positive and significant effect on the probability of occurrence of banking crises, as Miotti and Plihon shows (2001).

The second one, the market liberalization reduces the probability of banking crises by encouraging the development of monetary and financial instruments allowing banks greater diversification of their risks.

To measure the degree of domestic financial liberalization, we had reference to the study by Hamdi Khalfaoui that uses two key indicators to assess the level of development of indirect finance through the degree of channeling capital to the private sector and efficiency of financial intermediation. These indicators are:

- Credits granted to the private sector as a percentage of GDP (CSP) expressed in logarithm. The expected sign is negative justified by the fact this ratio and more, the banking sector is less developed and this can create a banking crisis. It indicates the ability of banks to mobilize and improve its allocation.
- The broad money as a percentage of GDP (M2) e é expressed in logarithms: it represents resents payment methods which is added to almost liquidity.

This indicator reflects the liquidity of the economy and it is supposed to have a positive sign. Thus, if the economy recorded a significant growth rate of the money supply in the sense of M2, it may cause a banking crisis. This variable was extracted from the database of the World Bank.

About banking variables, we used to study Kibritcioglu (2002), to identify a monthly index, similar to that of the pressure on the foreign exchange market. The purpose of the adoption of this index is to measure and predict episodes of fragile banking sector.

In particular, the author has shown that there are three main greatness in the consolidated balance sheet of banks that may be useful in the construction of the index of fragility of the banking sector, namely, bank deposits, loans to the private sector, and external liabilities of domestic banks.

Fluctuations of indicators and likely to prove the fragility of the banking sector in a country. These variables were extracted from the database "Financial Statistics International "from the IMF.

However, deflated nominal series, we used the GDP deflator extracted from the World Bank database and this because of the unavailability of data for the entire sample price indices in the database IMF data. Once deflated series, the index of banking sector fragility (FSB) can be calculated as follows:

$$FSB_t = \frac{\left(\frac{DB_t - \mu_{db}}{\sigma db}\right) + \left(\frac{CBSP_t - \mu_{cbsp}}{\sigma_{cbsp}}\right) + \left(\frac{EEB_t - \mu_{eeb}}{\sigma eeb}\right)}{3}$$

where:

FSB_t = fragility of the banking sector

DB_t = annual variation of banking deposits year t

$\mu et \sigma$ = represents respectively the arithmetic mean and the standard deviation of variables.

$CBSP_t$ = annual change in bank credits to the private sector

EEB_t = annual change in commitments exteriors domestic banks

If the FSB index is between -0.5 and 0, so the banking system is considered in average period of fragility. But, if FSB is less than -0.5, so the banking sector is considered highly vulnerable to systemic crises. To arrive at a base in binary form, we have transformed the FBS values so that gives the value 1 at any FSB and 0 at any FSB . In total, an index of banking sector fragility (FSB) is constructed and transformed for the entire sample consists of forty developing countries over the period (1980-2011).

To assess the impact of institutional variables on the probability of banking crises and empirically test whether the quality of the institutional structure is a determinant of banking crises in developing countries, we have used as a measure of degree of institutional quality, the 'legal systems and property rights "indicator. This indicator is composed of five variables which are: the rules of law, judicial independence, legal system integrity, the existence of objective being and protection of intellectual property. This variable was extracted from the database of "The International Country Risk Guide" (2009). However, and given that this variable is available only for frequencies during the five-year period (1980-2000) and the institutional quality variable does not change in the short term but it changes very slowly, it was considered the value corresponding to the year (t) remains the same until the year (t + 4). This method was proposed by Chinn and Ito (2005), whose objective is to annually exploit available data on five years.

The variable is between 0 and 10, the higher its value, the higher the institutional framework of the country in question is solid, and vice versa.

We selected four macroeconomic and financial variables that are likely to capture the effect of macroeconomic shocks and financial situation on the occurrence of banking crises. As a macroeconomic variable, we basically chose two indicators Knowledge:

- Inflation (The expected sign of this variable is positive.
- The level of ctivityreport economic (the expected sign of this variable is negative.
- Financial variables used in this study are:
- The ratio M2/international exchange reserves expressed in logarithm: This indicator represents the ability of banks to face its External commitments. Thus, more the ratio is high, more the economy is vulnerable to investor confidence crisis. From where the expected sign should be positive.

$$\frac{M_2}{international\ exchange\ reserves}$$

4. Empirical Results

This study draws on studies and Lukkarila Komulainen (2003) and Eichengreen and Arteta (2002), Wyplosz (2001) and Williamson and Mahar (1998) focused on the impact of internal and external liberalization of banking instability. The proposed model is as follows:

$$Prob(CB_{it} = 1) = F(\alpha X_{it-1} + \beta LF_{it})$$

As stated above, the Kaopen indicator constructed by Chinn and Ito (2005), which varies between 1.7 and 2.6 is a liberalization indicator. Thus the higher its value, the greater the country's capital account in question is liberalized. Estimating the effect of liberalization of the capital account on the probability of banking crises give the following results:

Table 1. *The effect of liberalization of the capital account on the probability of banking crises*

Variable	Coefficient	Std Error	Z-Statistic	P > | z |
Kaopen	-0 .11325	0.04426	-2.55	0.010
M2\Reserve	0.07030	0.02141	3.28	0.015
GDP	-0.07846	0.01671	-4.96	0.000
GDC	-0.01421	0.06144	-0.23	0.818
IR	0.00211	0.00832	0.25	0.800
Constant	-0.86126	0.20028	-4.30	0.000
Log likelihood	-584.247			
No. of obs.	880			
Waldchi2 (5)	26.50			

The results presented in this table show that the opening of the capital account negatively affects the probability of banking crises. Thus, liberalization of the capital account is not the main cause of banking crises. This has been validated by Komulainen and Lukkarila (2003), which suggest that the opening of the capital account is not the cause of crises in emerging markets, but the current crisis because of these can probably be deteriorating fundamentals. This result corroborates those of Shehzad and De Haan (2009). They have actually found that some aspects of financial liberalization reduce the likelihood of systemic crises, conditional on adequate banking supervision. Eichengreen and Arteta (2002), the opening of the capital account does not contribute to a banking crisis. While the liberalization of domestic financial sector can lead to banking crises. In addition, Bonfiglioli and Mendicino (2004) have shown, following a dynamic panel study of a sample of 90 developed and developing countries, the countries that have liberalized their capital accounts are less confronted with the advent of crises that the savings bank financially repressed. Both authors justify this by the fact that economic agents appeal to international capital markets for financing in times of banking crises.

However, our results contradict those of the study by Ranciere et al. (2006), which examines the relationship between financial liberalization, financial crises and economic growth. They broke down the impact of financial deregulation on economic growth in two effects: a direct effect on growth and an indirect effect that reflects the growth costs associated with a high frequency of financial crises. They consider that financial openness does not promote the growth of the economy because of the emergence of crises. According to them, financial deregulation has a positive effect on economic growth and also increases significantly the probability of the twin crises (banking crises and currency crises). Financial control variables, the ratio "M2 / Foreign Reserves" are statistically significant and positive (+2.32). This ratio is positively related to the probability of a banking crisis. This finding has been confirmed by Cartapanis (2002). The variable "domestic credit growth" is not significant. Thus, in our study, this variable has no effect on the probability of banking crises in developing countries in line with our predictions.

The variable "economic growth" is statistically significant and negatively related to the probability of occurrence of banking crises. A decrease in the growth of the economy is strongly associated with the likelihood of the emergence of banking crises. The test results of the impact of financial liberalization on the probability of banking crises and illustrated in the following table:

Table 2. *The impact of financial liberalization on the probability of banking crises*

Variable	coefficient	Std Error	Z-statistic	P> | Z |
LMB	-0.12535	0.04126	-3.03	0010
M2\Reserve	0.06030	2810.02	2. 64	0.021
GDP	-0.06846	0.01871	-3.65	0.003
GDC	-0.01321	0.05134	-0.25	0.806
IR	1210.00	7120.00	0.169	0.868
Constant	-0.76126	0370.20	3.799	0.002

Log likelihood	- 611.325			
No. of obs.	880			
Waldchi2 (5)	58.36			

With LMB is the effect of market liberalization as measured by the sum of portfolio flows in equities and flows of portfolio in bonds to GDP, the probability of banking crises during the period (1990-2011) in developing countries.

The liberalization of financial markets is affected by a negative and statistically significant sign (-3.03). These results reject the null hypothesis of our study suggests that market liberalization helps to increase the probability of banking crises. The finding that the opening of financial markets exerts significant negative effects on the probability of occurrence of banking crises can be explained by the fact that the deregulation of financial markets leads to the creation of new monetary and financial instruments best suited to the management of risk (derivatives). It allows banks to diversify better the best risk and minimize their losses later.

5. Concluding Remarks

This study showed that the probability of banking crises is negatively correlated with the opening of the capital account. This has been validated by Komulainen and Lukkarila (2003) have shown that the liberalization of the capital account is not the cause of the crises, but the main reason probably lies in the deteriorating fundamentals. On the other hand, market liberalization negatively affects the frequency of banking crises in emerging countries.

On the other hand, the effect of the internal financial deregulation of financial markets and the capital account on the probability of banking crises is negligible when it is accompanied by an adequate supervisory system and a strong institutional environment.

Finally, we can conclude that the results we have reached throughout this paper show the existence of a negative relationship between external financial liberalization and banking crises. In addition, the results clearly suggest that strengthening the institutional framework could weaken the likelihood of banking crises especially in periods of financial deregulation. In other words, it tends to stimulate banking instability or if the institutional environment is fragile.

References

Alfaro, L., Hammel, E., 2007. Capital flows and capital goods, *Journal of International Economics,* 72 (1), pp.128-150

Arestis, P., 2003. Financial Sector Reforms in Developing Countries with Special Reference to Egypt. *SSRN Journal*, Levy Economics Institute Working Paper No. 383 [online] Available online: http://papers.ssrn.com/sol3/papers.cfm?abstract_id=425821 [Accessed on 10 Jan. 2015]

Arestis, P., Demetriades, P., 1999. Financial Liberalization: The experience of developing countries, *Eastern Economic Journal*, 25(4), pp.441-457.

Bonfiglioli A., Mendicino, C., 2004. *Financial Liberalization, Bank Crises and Growth: Assessing the Links*, Economics and Finance, Working Paper no. 567, [online] Available online: http://papers.ssrn.com/sol3/papers.cfm?abstract_id=1002285 [Accessed on 13 Dec. 2014]

Caprio, G.Jr., Klingebiel, D., 1996. Bank Insolvencies: Cross-country experience, World Bank Policy Research Working Paper, no. 1620, [online] Available online: http://papers.ssrn.com/sol3/papers.cfm?abstract_id=636119 [Accessed on 13 Dec. 2014]

Cartapanis, A., 2003. Vers une prévention macro-prudentielle des crises financières internationales. *Revue d'économie financière*, 70(1), pp.89-100.

Chinn, M.D., Ito, H., 2005. *What matters for financial development? Capital controls, Institutions, and Interactions*, National Bureau of Economic Research, Working Paper, no. 11370, [online] Available online: http://www.nber.org/papers/w11370 [Accessed on 13 Oct. 2014]

Daniel, B., Jones, J., 2007. Financial Liberalization and Banking Crises in emerging economies, *Journal of International Economics,* 72(1), pp.202-221.

Eichengreen, B., Arteta, C., 2000. Banking Crises in Emerging Markets: Presumptions and Evidence, *Financial Policies in Emerging Markets*, pp 47-94.

Fisher, K.P., Smaoui, H., 1997, *From financial to banking failure Liberalization: Starting on the wrong foot?*, University of Laval Canada, Working Paper, no. 3, [online] Available online: http://128.118.178.162/eps/fin/papers/9706/9706005.pdf [Accessed on 27 Oct. 2014]

Honig, A., 2008. Addressing causality in the effect of capital account liberalization on growth, *Journal of Macroeconomics*, 30 (4), pp.1602-1616.

Honohan, P., 1997. *Banking System Failures in Developing and Transition Countries: Diagnosis and Prediction*, Bank for International Settlements, Working Paper no. 39, [online] Monetary and Economic Department – BASLE, Available online: http://www.bis.org/publ/work39.pdf [Accessed on 13 Dec. 2014]

Icard, A., 2002. *Stabilité financière et contrôle prudentiel*. BIS symposium at the BEAC Colloqium "Rôle et fonction d'une banque centrale à l'ère de la globalisation" [online] Bis.org Available at: http://www.bis.org/speeches/sp021121.htm [Accessed on 10 Nov. 2014].

Kaminsky, G., Reinhart, C., 1999. The Twin Crises: the Causes of Banking and Balance-of-Payment Problems, *American Economic Review*, 89(3), pp.473-500.

Kaminsky G., Schmukler, S.L., 2003. Short-Run Pain, Long - Run Gain: The Effects of Financial Liberalization, International Monetary Fund - Working Paper WP / 03/34, [online] IMF.org Available at: http://www.imf.org/external/pubs/ft/wp/2003/wp0334.pdf [Accessed on 10 Nov. 2014]

Kibritcioglu, A., 2002. Excessive Risk-Taking, Banking Sector Fragility, and Banking Crises, University of Illinois at Urbana-Champaign, [online] Available at: http://business.illinois.edu/working_papers/papers/02-0114.pdf [Accessed on 21 Oct. 2014]

Komulainen, T., Lukkarila, J., 2003. What drives financial crises in Emerging Markets?, *Emerging Markets Review*, 4(3), pp.248-272.

McKinnon, R., 1973. *Money and Capital in Economic Development*, Washington: Brookings Institution

Plihon, D., Miotti, L., 2001. Libéralisation Financière, Spéculation et Crises Bancaires, *Économie Internationale*, 85, pp 3-36

Ranciere, R., Tornell, A., Westermann, F., 2006. Decomposing the effects of financial Liberalization: Crisis vs. growth, *Journal of Banking and Finance*, 30(12), pp.3331-3348.

Shehzad, C.T., De Haan, J., 2009. *Financial Liberalization and Banking Crises*, [online] Available online: http://www.finance-innovation.org/risk09/work/6450490.pdf [Accessed on 9 Nov. 2014]

Williamson, J., Mahar, M., 1998. A survey of Financial Liberalization, *Essays in International Finance* no. 211, International Finance Section, Department of Economics and Princeton University, Princeton, New Jersey: Princeton Universtity

Wyplosz, C., 2001. *How Risky is Financial Liberalization in the Developing Countries?*, Discussion Paper Series No. 14., [online] Available online: https://faculty.fuqua.duke.edu/~charvey/Spur/Wyplosz_How_risky_is.pdf [Accessed on 17 Nov. 2014]

17

Analysis of the Economic Research Context after the Outbreak of the Economic Crisis of 2007-2009

Alin OPREANA[1]* and Simona VINEREAN[2]

[1]Lucian Blaga University of Sibiu
[2]The Bucharest University of Economic Studies

In this paper it, we have conducted a factor analysis which implied determining the international research directions that have characterized the period following the outbreak of the crisis in 2007 and 2008-2011. In this research, we used secondary data that were extracted from 342 articles, which were based on 665 individual researches. Following this research, we have identified three main research in the macroeconomic areas which explained 56% of all the analyzed research. Also, the results showed the trends in macroeconomic research after the start of the crisis in 2007.

***Keywords**: macroeconomics, meta-analysis, factor analysis, economic models, economic literature*

1. Introduction

Since 2007, the global economy has been going through an experience that showed the limits of prevailing economic models and that led to the destruction of the sense of confidence in the economic paradigm. From solving the models, there were several prescriptions that were obtained for the most of the economic downturns that have followed in the last century until the outbreak of the economic crisis of 2007-2009, which through its extent and magnitude has represented an event that cannot be compared to anything that has ever happened before, yet it contains all of them together, as Krugman previously stated (2008).

The new global economic mutations that occurred in 2007 after the outbreak of the crisis have had inevitable repercussions on the scientific activity in the macroeconomic study area. Starting from this aspect, we are interested in what the new trends of research in macroeconomics and how the scientific activity was influenced by the economic events of after 2007.

In this context, we use the factor analysis method to achieve the objectives that will be presented in the following section.

* Corresponding Author:
Alin Opreana, Lucian Blaga University of Sibiu, Romania

Thus, in the first stage of this research, we will establish the main research questions, the purpose of the research, and its related objectives and hypotheses. Thus the main research question identified for this analysis is to provide detailed knowledge of the state of scientific research in the aftermath of the 2007-2008 crisis in macroeconomic theory.

2. Research Methodology

The purpose of research is to determine the research directions that have characterized the period following the crisis that broke in 2007, more specifically in the 2008-2011 timeframe. From this global purpose of the research the following objectives and their related hypotheses are derived:

Objective 1: Description of the research state based on descriptive statistics

Hypothesis 1: The core of the research state is concentrated mainly in the United States and Europe

Objective 2: Establishing a factor analysis of the research state in 2008-2011

Hypothesis 2: There are at least two main directions in terms of macroeconomic research in 2008-2011

Objective 3: Analysis of the main research directions resulted from factor analysis

Hypothesis 3: The main research directions resulted from the factor analysis are in a direct relationship with the events that followed the outbreak of the 2007-2008 crisis

In the next stage, we designed the study by identifying the necessary information sources and by establishing the methods used in compiling the information and the systematization of these information.

By identifying the sources of information for this research, we chose five international journals (American Economic Review, European Economic Review, Journal of Economic Theory, The Journal of Economic Literature and the Journal of Economic Perspectives). These sources of information were the basis of the information collection methods necessary to answer the research question, more precisely by to investigate of secondary sources from which we have extracted the studies that examined topics related to macroeconomic theory and monetary economics in the period 2008-2011.

***Table 1**. The secondary sources used in researching the theoretical context*

Journal	Volumes considered for *researching the* theoretical context
American Economic Review	Vol. 98 (2008) – Vol. 101 (2011)
European Economic Review	Vol. 52 (2008) – Vol. 55 (2011)
Journal of Economic Theory	Vol. 139 (2008) – Vol. 146 (2011)
The Journal of Economic Literature	Vol. 46 (2008) – Vol. 49 (2011)
The Journal of Economic Perspectives	Vol. 22 (2008) – Vol. 25 (2011)

In order to obtain importance factors, each journal was evaluated based on six criteria for evaluation and classification used by ISI Thomson:

C1 - Total Citations
C2 - 5-year Impact Factor
C3 - Immediacy Index
C4 - Number of articles
C5 - Eigenfactor score
C6 – Article Influence score

Thus, for the five journals under investigation, the following data were extracted:

***Table 2**. Classification criteria for journal importance*

Journal	JCR Data				Eigenfactor Metrics	
	Total Citations	**5-year Impact Factor**	**Immediacy Index**	**Number of articles**	**Eigenfactor score**	**Article Influence score**
Journal of Economic Theory	5.052	1.519	0.358	109	0.02628	2.421

European Economic Review	3.629	1.860	0.229	70	0.01212	1.774
American Economic Review	26.525	4.076	0.793	237	0.10039	5.662
Journal of Economic Literature	4.715	9.426	0.850	20	0.01696	9.820
Journal of Economic Perspectives	5.626	5.865	0.512	43	0.02773	6.799

For linearization, we calculated the relative values of the criteria based on the maximum identified amount for each criterion:

***Table 3**. Linearization of the journals' classification criteria*

Journal	Total Citations	5-year Impact Factor	Immediacy Index	Number of articles	Eigenfactor score	Article Influence score
Journal of Economic Theory	0.19	0.16	0.42	0.46	0.26	0.25
European Economic Review	0.14	0.2	0.27	0.3	0.12	0.18
American Economic Review	1	0.43	0.93	1	1	0.58
Journal of Economic Literature	0.18	1	1	0.08	0.17	1
Journal of Economic Perspectives	0.21	0.62	0.6	0.18	0.28	0.69

To obtain weighted coefficients related to each criterion we used the FRISCO formula:

$$\beta = \frac{p + \Delta p + m + 0{,}5}{-\Delta p' + \frac{Ncrt}{2}}$$

where: p = the sum of points obtained for each line by a certain criterion

Δp = the difference between the considered score criterion and the score of the last criterion

m = the number of criteria that have a lower number of points than the considered criterion

Ncrt = the number of considered criteria

Δp' = the difference between the considered score criterion and the score of the first criterion

Table 4 shows the weighted coefficients for each criterion, taking into consideration the importance of each criterion in relation to the other criteria. Thus, the C_1 (Total Citations) and C_2 (5-year Impact Factor) were considered to have a primary importance, whereas the other criteria have a secondary importance.

***Table 4**. Determining the coefficients related to the importance criteria of the journals*

Criteria	C_1	C_2	C_3	C_4	C_5	C_6	Points	Level	Weight
C_1	0.5	0.5	1	1	1	1	**5**	**1**	**5.0**
C_2	0.5	0.5	1	1	1	1	**5**	**1**	**5.0**
C_3	0	0	0.5	0.5	0.5	0.5	**2**	**3**	**0.5**
C_4	0	0	0.5	0.5	0.5	0.5	**2**	**3**	**0.5**
C_5	0	0	0.5	0.5	0.5	0.5	**2**	**3**	**0.5**
C_6	0	0	0.5	0.5	0.5	0.5	**2**	**3**	**0.5**

Considering the data presented in the previous table, the journals were compared based on the identified and linearized criteria from table 3.

***Table 5**. Journals' importance factors*

		Journal of Economic Theory		European Economic Review		American Economic Review		American Economic Literature		American Economic Perspectives	
Criterion	**Weight**	**Values**	**Weight x Values**	**Values**	**Weight x Values**	**Values**	**Weight x Values**	**Values**	**Weight x Values**	**Values**	**Weight x Values**
C_1	5.0	0.19	0.95	0.14	0.70	1	5,00	0,18	0,90	0,21	1,05
C_2	5.0	0.16	0.80	0.2	1.00	0,43	2,15	1	5,00	0,62	3,10
C_3	0.5	0.42	0.19	0.27	0.12	0,93	0,42	1	0,45	0,6	0,27
C_4	0.5	0.46	0.21	0.3	0.14	1	0,45	0,08	0,04	0,18	0,08
C_5	0.5	0.26	0.12	0.12	0.05	1	0,45	0,17	0,08	0,28	0,13
C_6	0.5	0.25	0.11	0.18	0.08	0,58	0,26	1	0,45	0,69	0,31
Importance factors		**2.4**		**2.1**		**8.7**		**6.9**		**4.9**	

In the previous table the importance factors for each journal were obtained and these factors were then used to rank the relevance and importance of each article, depending on the journal's origin.

Next, after the sources of information were identified, we established the methods of information extraction and systematization. Thus, in this research we used the following variables:

***Table 6**. Variables used in the research*

V1. Journal	➢ Journal of Economic Theory ➢ European Economic Review ➢ American Economic Review ➢ Journal of Economic Literature ➢ Journal of Economic Perspectives
V2. Article title	
V3. Article's authors	
V4. Article publication date	➢ Month of article publication in the 2008-2011 period ➢ Corresponding month period was numbered successively from January 2008 (month 1) and until December 2011 (month 48)
V5. Authors' affiliated institution	
V6. Type of authors' affiliated institution	➢ University ➢ Research institute ➢ Private ➢ Public ➢ Central bank ➢ BIS ➢ IMF ➢ World Bank
V7. Institution's region	➢ United States; ➢ European Union – for institutions from the European Union, Austria, Belgium, Czech Republic, Denmark, Finland, France, Germany, Italy, Netherlands, Poland, Portugal, Spain, Sweden, United Kingdom; ➢ International - for international financial institutions: Bank for International Settlements, International Monetary Fund, World Bank; ➢ Rest of the world - Australia, Chile, Israel, Switzerland, Turkey, Canada, China, Japan, Singapore.
V8. Institution's country	United States, European Union – for the EU's institutions, Austria, Belgium, Czech Republic, Denmark, Finland, France, Germany, Italy, Netherlands, Poland, Portugal, Spain, Sweden, United Kingdom; Bank for International Settlements, the International Monetary Fund, World Bank, Australia, Chile, Israel, Switzerland, Turkey, Canada, China, Japan, Singapore.
V9. Reference theme	E0 - General E1 - General Aggregative Models E2 - Macroeconomics: Consumption, Saving, Production, Employment, and Investment E3 - Prices, Business Fluctuations, and Cycles E4 - Money and Interest Rates E5 - Monetary Policy, Central Banking, and the Supply of Money and Credit E6 - Macroeconomic Policy, Macroeconomic Aspects of Public Finance, and General Outlook

V10. Scientific importance and relevance of article based journals' importance factors	Each article is classified in relation to its theme and receives an importance factor according to the following values: ➢ 0 – not referring to that topic/theme ➢ 2,1 – article published in *European Economic Review* ➢ 2,4 – article published in *Journal of Economic Theory* ➢ 4,9 – article published in *American Economic Perspectives* ➢ 6,9 – article published in *American Economic Literature* ➢ 8,7 – article published in *American Economic Review*

After data extraction, for the following stage, we considered the contribution of each author as an individual research before a collective research. Thus, each individual research was regarded as an observation in the analysis process, i.e. in the informational input.

Further, the secondary data of the research was extracted manually by analyzing the volumes published by the five international journals in 2008-2011. The extracted data represented the input information that has been transferred to a database further processed with statistical analysis software SPSS and Microsoft Excel to accomplish the purpose of research and its derived objectives and hypotheses.
For attaining the objectives and related hypotheses we followed this research methodology:

(i) Obtaining descriptive statistics:
- frequencies analysis of the studies based on the journal in which the article was published,
- frequencies analysis of the studies based on the region of the institutions,
- frequencies analysis of the studies based on the country of the institutions,
- correspondence analysis of the research based on the region of the institutions and the institution's type,
- frequencies analysis of the studies based on the theme of the research,

(ii) Factor analysis on the topic of the studies carried out in 2008-2011.
(iii) Analysis of the resulted components from the factor analysis.

3. Empirical Analysis and Results

3.1. Obtaining descriptive statistics

This first phase of the empirical analysis consisted in setting up the descriptive statistics based on the articles published in the macroeconomic field within the 5 international journals chosen for this study: American Economic Review, European Economic Review, Journal of Economic Theory, The Journal of Economic Literature, and The Journal of Economic Perspectives.

Thus, the table below shows the frequencies of the article publications in each journal:

***Table** 7. Frequencies analysis of the article publication for each journal*

Journal	Article frequency	Percentage (%)	Cumulative percentage (%)
American Economic Review	157	45.91%	45.91%
European Economic Review	68	19.88%	65.79%
Journal of Economic Theory	66	19.30%	85.09%
The Journal of Economic Literature	23	6.73%	91.81%
The Journal of Economic Perspectives	28	8.19%	100.00%
Total	**342**	**100.00%**	-

Further, Table 7 shows these journals from the perspective of the research frequencies published between 2008 and 2011.

***Table 8**. Descriptive statistics regarding the journals used in the analysis of the theoretical context*

Journal	Research frequency	Percentage (%)	Cumulative percentage (%)
American Economic Review	314	47,2	47,2
European Economic Review	143	21,5	68,7

Journal of Economic Theory	120	18,0	86,8
The Journal of Economic Literature	35	5,3	92,0
The Journal of Economic Perspectives	53	8,0	100,0
Total	**665**	**100,0**	

It is noted that 47.2% of the researches published between 2008 and 2011 were published in the American Economic Review. The distribution of the research published in journals included in the analysis can be seen in the following figure.

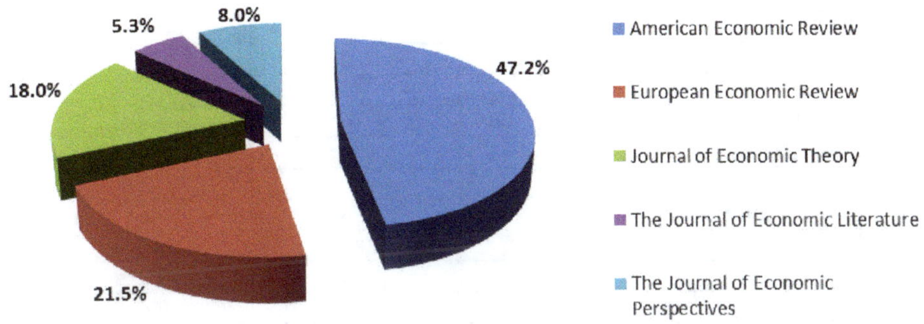

***Figure 1**. Research distribution according to the article's journal*

Table 9 and Figure 2 show to the regions of provenance of the 665 researches considered in the context of the analysis for the period 2008 - 2011. It is observed that 62.9% of these studies are from the United States of America, and 27.7% are from the European Union.

***Table 9**. Descriptive statistics for the institutions' regions of provenance*

Region	Research frequency	Percentage (%)	Cumulative percentage (%)
International	17	2.6	2.6
Rest of the world	45	6.8	9.3
European Union	185	27.8	37.1
United States	418	62.9	100.0
Total	**665**	**100.0**	

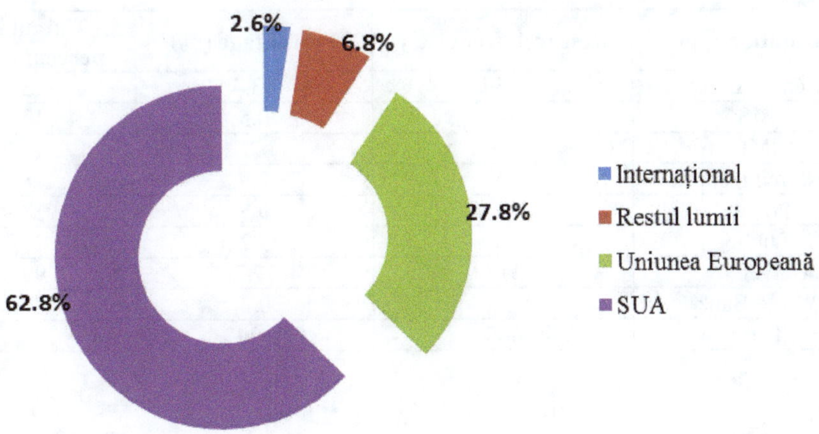

***Figure 2**. Distribution of research according to the region of provenance of the institutions*

Table 10 shows the distribution of research according to the institutions' countries of provenance where the scientific work included in this analysis was conducted.

Table 10*. Descriptive statistics on the countries of origin of the institutions used in the analysis of the theoretical context*

Country	Research frequency	Percentage (%)	Cumulative percentage (%)
Australia	3	0.5	0.5
Austria	3	0.5	0.9
Belgium	4	0.6	1.5
Canada	18	2.7	4.2
Czech Republic	2	0.3	4.5
Chile	1	0.2	4.7
China	1	0.2	4.8
Denmark	4	0.6	5.4
Switzerland	11	1.7	7.1
Finland	4	0.6	7.7
France	16	2.4	10.1
Germania	13	2	12
International	17	2.6	14.6
Israel	4	0.6	15.2
Italia	25	3.8	18.9
Japan	3	0.5	19.4
The Netherlands	7	1.1	20.5
Poland	1	0.2	20.6
Portugal	4	0.6	21.2
Singapore	1	0.2	21.4
Spain	23	3.5	24.8
Sweden	7	1.1	25.9
Turkey	3	0.5	26.3
European Union	18	2.7	29
United Kingdom	54	8.1	37.1
US	418	62.9	100
Total	**665**	**100**	

Table 11*. Descriptive statistics on the institution type of the researchers*

Institution type	Research frequency	Percentage (%)	Cumulative percentage (%)
Central Bank	89	13.4	13.4
BIS	3	0.5	13.8
IMF	13	2	15.8
Research institute	19	2.9	18.6
Private	2	0.3	18.9
Public	21	3.2	22.1
University	517	77.7	99.8
World Bank	1	0.2	100
Total	**665**	**100**	

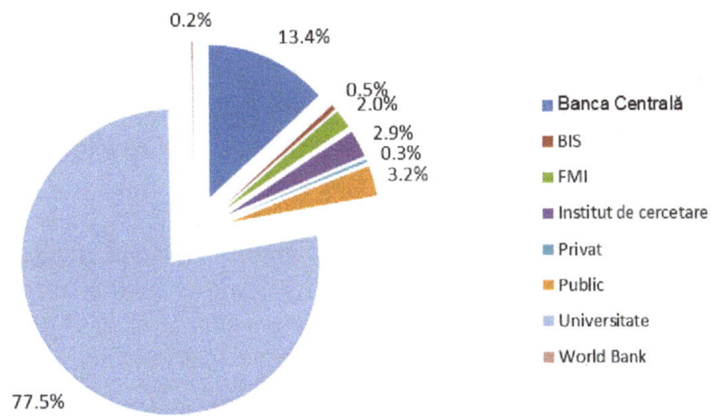

Figure 3. *Distribution of studies based on the researchers' affiliation*

Next we examined an analysis of the correspondence shown in Table 12 between the institution's region of origin and the institution's type. Correspondence analysis is a descriptive and exploratory technique used in this case to determine the correlation between the type of organization and its region, for the scientific research conducted during 2008-2011.

Table 12. *Correspondence analysis between the region and type of the institution*

Institution type	Region				
	US	EU	International	Rest of the world	Total
University	337	140	0	40	**517**
Research institute	9	9	0	1	**19**
Private	0	2	0	0	**2**
Public	17	4	0	0	**21**
Central Bank	55	30	0	4	**89**
BIS	0	0	3	0	**3**
IMF	0	0	13	0	**13**
World Bank	0	0	1	0	**1**
Total	**418**	**185**	**17**	**45**	**665**

From the previous table it is noted that 337 of the 665 studies (i.e. 50.68% of the total) were conducted by authors who come from United States academia. The second category, in terms of size, is represented by researchers from European Union academia, which totaled 140 scientific studies (i.e. 20.99% of the total), published as articles in the analyzed journals.

3.2. Factor Analysis on the Topic of the Studies Carried Out in 2008-2011

In this process, as a general linear model technique, factor analysis was used to reduce the number of variables of the research types conducted on the subject matter and the scientific importance of the studies, leading to obtain a limited number of main components, which represent the research directions that were addressed in the 2008-2011 framework.

Initially, a KMO test (Kaiser-Meyer-Olkin Measure of Sampling Adequacy) was conducted to indicate the data adequacy to achieve the factor analysis. For the variables introduced in this analysis we obtained a value of 0.535 of the KMO test therefore factor analysis is relevant, because this value is higher than the 0.5 acceptable threshold.

Table 13. *Communalities for each examined variable*

Variable	Initial	Extraction
E0	1.000	0.348
E1	1.000	0.429
E2	1.000	0.727
E3	1.000	0.533
E4	1.000	0.551
E5	1.000	0.588
E6	1.000	0.743

Table 13 shows the common variance of each variable analyzed (communalities) and presents the common level before and after the extraction of factors. Principal components analysis is based on the initial assumption that all variance is common, therefore, before extracting the factors, all variables have a variance factor equal to 1 (as seen in the column labeled Initial). All variance associated with a variable is accepted as common variance. The values in the Extraction column represent the extent to which a variable's variance is common to the variance of the extracted factor, more specifically of the newly created variable.

All values after factor extraction are high, indicating that all extracted components reflect the variables included in the factor analysis. Also, it is noted that variables E2 and E6 denote the highest variance (72.7% for E2 and 74.3% for E6) which are transposed onto the newly created factors that include these variables.

After establishing the variance transposed to the newly formed factors, factor analysis involves two stages: extraction of the factors (using principal components analysis method) and then rotation of the factors (using Varimax method) to assist in interpretation.

In Table 14, it is noted that the factor analysis developed three new variables or extracted factors, because this analysis was framed under the Kaiser criterion, which retains only factors with Eigenvalues greater than 1.

***Table 14**. Total variance explained for the 3 extracted factors*

	Initial Eigenvalues			**Extraction Sums of Squared Loadings**			**Rotation Sums of Squared Loadings**		
	Total	% of Variance	Cumulative %	Total	% of Variance	Cumulative %	Total	% of Variance	Cumulative %
1	1.608	22.969	22.969	1.608	22.969	22.969	1.390	19.857	19.857
2	1.194	17.057	40.026	1.194	17.057	40.026	1.346	19.232	39.089
3	1.118	15.965	55.991	1.118	15.965	55.991	1.183	16.903	55.991
4	0.978	13.977	69.969						
5	0.809	11.559	81.528						
6	0.679	9.695	91.223						
7	0.614	8.777	100.000						

Table 13 shows the number of selected factors (in this case, three factors) and the variance in each new variable, before and after rotation.

In the first section of the table entitled 'Initial eigenvalues', the 'Total' column indicates the amount of variance of the original variables explained by each component. Thus, further, only the first three factors will be considered because they display Eigenvalues greater than 1. The second column of the first section (% Variance) presents the Eigenvalues in terms of the percentage of explained variance of the total variance of all the variables included in the analysis. Column 'Cumulative %' shows the cumulative percentage for the first *n* components of the factor analysis.

The second section of the table ('Extraction Sums of Squared Loadings') presents the extracted components that exhibit three factors that explain 55.99% of the variability of the seven original variables.

The third section of the table ('Rotation Sums of Squared Loadings') involves applying the Varimax rotation method, whereby the cumulative percentage of variance explained by the extracted components is maintained (55.99%), but the variance is propagated more equally on other components. Before rotation, the first factor explains 22.969% of the total variance, but after rotation (the final part of the table labeled 'Rotation Sums of Squared Loadings') the first factor explains 19.857% of the total variance. Therefore, the rotation has the effect of optimizing the factor's structure and the immediate consequence of this is the equivalence of the relative importance of the factors.

Table 'Matrix of rotated components' helps to determine the representativeness of the components by showing which variables have the highest influence on each of the three newly formed factors.

***Table 15**. Matrix of rotated components*

	Components		
	F1	F2	F3
E0	**-0.562**	0.118	0.133
E1	**0.557**	0.342	0.050
E2	0.302	**-0.792**	0.096
E3	**0.718**	0.000	0.133
E4	0.127	0.319	**0.658**
E5	0.364	**0.661**	0.137
E6	0.096	0.222	**-0.827**

Following the factor analysis conducted in this study, we obtained three principal components, namely three directions of research carried out in the 2008-2011 period:

F1 - the first research direction relates to the studies that approached the interaction of general aggregated models with economic fluctuations and prices and dealt less with general aspects of macroeconomics

F2 - second direction is characterized by the research that approached monetary policy and money supply and did not address real variables (consumption, savings, production, employment, and investment)

F3 - the third direction encompasses studies regarding currency and interest rates which did not address macroeconomic policies and macroeconomic aspects of public finances.

3.3. Analysis of the Resulted Components from the Factor Analysis

The first factor (F1) is formed by the following subdomains E0 – 'General', E1 – 'General Aggregative Models'and E3 – 'Prices, Business Fluctuations, and Cycles'. E3 denotes the highest score of 0.718 which appears in the development of the first factor, accounting for articles that address:

- general aspects regarding prices, business fluctuations, and cycles (E30);
- price level, inflation, deflation (E31);
- business fluctuations and cycles (E32);
- forecasting and simulation: models and applications (E37);
- other articles in this macroeconomics sphere (E39).

Variable E1 – 'General Aggregative Models' presents a score of 0.557 influencing in a positive way the first factor which consists of articles that approach:

- general theoretical and empirical studies about issues related to aggregative models (E10);
- aggregative models that cover the Marxian, Sraffian, Institutional, and Evolutionary schools (E11);
- research surrounding Keynes's general theory, Keynesian and post- Keynesian macroeconomics (E12);
- neoclassical models (E13);
- forecasting and simulation of aggregative models (E17);
- other articles in this topic of general aggregative models (E19).

The second factor (F2) consists of two variables E2 and E5, but the scores of these two variables indicate that scientific research mainly focused on issues related to monetary policy, central banks and money supply (E5 = 0.661), and they were less related to the real macroeconomic variables (consumption, saving, production, employment and investment), due to it negative registered score (E2 = -0.792). Thus, research in the 2008-2011 period addresses:

- general aspects of monetary policy, central banking, and the supply of money and credit (E50);
- money supply, credit, and money multipliers (E51);
- monetary policy (E52);
- central banks and their policies (E58);
- other related themes to this area (E59).

It should also be noted that in these studies, there were not included themes from the area of variable E2 (real macroeconomic variables: consumption, saving, production, employment and investment), such as:

- general aspects(E20);
- consumption, saving, wealth (E21);
- capital, investment (including inventories and capital), capacity (E22);
- production (E23);
- employment, unemployment, wages, intergenerational income distribution, aggregate human capital (E24);
- aggregate factor income distribution (E25);
- informal economy and underground economy (E26);
- forecasting and simulations of models and applications of this real environment (E27);
- other research in this category (E29).

The last factor (F3) presents the research context dealing with themes of currency and interest rates (E4 = 0.658), but lacks in studies that fall under the E6 variable (macroeconomic policy, macroeconomic issues of public finance, and general outlook). This lack of theoretical context is highlighted by a negative score of -0.827 for variable E6. In this category are also included articles that did not approach topics such as:

- general aspects of macroeconomic policy and public finance (E60);
- policy objectives, designs and projections of policies and their consistency in time, policy coordination (E61);
- fiscal policy, public expenditures, investment, finance and taxation (E62);
- comparative or joint analysis of fiscal and monetary policy, economic stabilization, treasury (E63);
- incomes Policy, price policy (E64);
- studies of particular macro- policy episodes (E65);
- general macroeconomic outlook and conditions (E66);
- other aspects of this field of research (E67).

However, the examined studies have made numerous references to the E4 theme, namely 'Money and Interest Rates', with the following subcategories:

- general aspects related to money and interest rates (E40);
- demand for money (E41);
- monetary systems, standards, regimes, government and the monetary system, payment systems (E42);
- determination of interest rates, term structure of interest rates (E43);
- financial markets and the macroeconomy (E44);
- forecasting and simulation of money demand and/or interest rates (E47);
- other topics related to money and interest rates (E49).

Table 16 shows the weights to be used in obtaining the factor scores by multiplying the coefficients from this table with the standardized variables of the analysis.

***Table 16**. Coefficient matrix of factor scores*

	Components		
	F1	F2	F3
E0	-0.438	0.141	0.152
E1	0.374	0.202	-0.012
E2	0.294	-0.634	0.088
E3	0.521	-0.075	0.059
E4	0.012	0.206	0.542
E5	0.193	0.461	0.066
E6	0.112	0.189	-0.723

The factors represent linear combinations of the original variables that can be calculated as follows:

$$F_i = W_{i1}X_0 + W_{i2}X_1 + W_{i3}X_2 + \ldots + W_{ik}X_k$$
$$F_1 = -0.438E_0 + 0.374E_1 + 0.294E_2 + 0.521E_3 + 0.012E_4 + 0.193E_5 + 0.112E_6$$
$$F_2 = 0.141E_0 + 0.202E_1 - 0.634E_2 - 0.075E_3 + 0.206E_4 + 0.461E_5 + 0.189E_6$$
$$F_3 = 0.152E_0 - 0.012E_1 + 0.088E_2 + 0.059E_3 + 0.542E_4 + 0.066E_5 - 0.723E_6$$

The results obtained by calculating factors based on the data used, according to the region and type of the institute are shown in Table 17.

Table 17*. Factor values in relation to region and institution type*

		Region				
		US	EE	International	Rest of the world	
Institution type	University	0.178	-0.191	0.000	-0.188	F1
		-0.043	-0.043	0.000	-0.141	F2
		0.066	-0.191	0.000	0.095	F3
		24.92	24.06	0.00	23.67	Data
	Research institute	-0.111	-0.347	0.000	-0.748	F1
		-0.151	0.056	0.000	0.161	F2
		0.189	-0.091	0.000	0.274	F3
		30.56	24.22	0.00	40.00	Data
	Private	0.000	-0.340	0.000	0.000	F1
		0.000	-0.152	0.000	0.000	F2
		0.000	-0.897	0.000	0.000	F3
		0.00	32.00	0.00	0.00	Data
	Public	-1.399	-0.425	0.000	0.000	F1
		-0.058	0.120	0.000	0.000	F2
		-1.399	0.323	0.000	0.000	F3
		20.88	36.00	0.00	0.00	Data
	Central Bank	0.129	-0.135	0.000	0.067	F1
		0.148	0.591	0.000	0.433	F2
		0.215	-0.129	0.000	-0.724	F3
		25.80	16.00	0.00	19.00	Data
	BIS	0.000	0.000	0.313	0.000	F1
		0.000	0.000	-0.187	0.000	F2
		0.000	0.000	0.170	0.000	F3
		0.00	0.00	11.00	0.00	Data
	IMF	0.000	0.000	0.080	0.000	F1
		0.000	0.000	0.126	0.000	F2
		0.000	0.000	-0.824	0.000	F3
		0.00	0.00	29.54	0.00	Data
	World Bank	0.000	0.000	-0.018	0.000	F1
		0.000	0.000	-1.601	0.000	F2
		0.000	0.000	0.060	0.000	F3
		0.00	0.00	30.00	0.00	Data

Based on the table presented above, Figure 4 presents visually the evolution of the studies in relation to their topic, more specifically to the resulted components of the factor analysis:

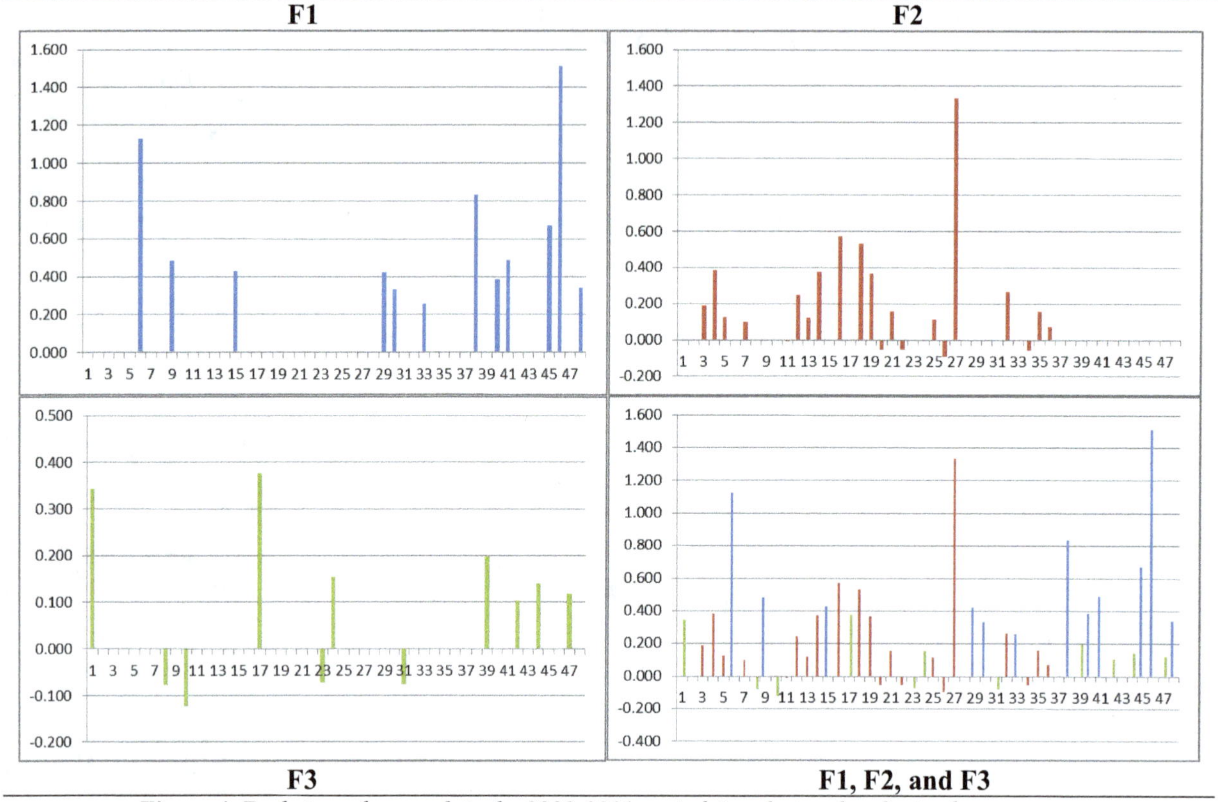

***Figure 4**. Evolution of research in the 2008-2011 period, in relation the obtained components*

As seen in the first part of the analyzed period (2008-2009, months 1-24 of the analysis period) the F2's studies prevailed (which addressed monetary policy), and second examined period (2010-2011, months 25-48 of the analysis period) the F1's studies were the most predominant (which addressed economic fluctuations and macroeconomic models). Regarding the F3 component, these researches were intertwined with the other two components in the all the analyzed periods.

4. Conclusion

Through this secondary research, the present study sought to group, on research directions, state of scientific research in macroeconomic theory, in the period that followed the outbreak of the 2008-2009 crisis considering the research published between 2008 and 2011, taking into account five international journals (American Economic Review, European Economic Review, Journal of Economic Theory, The Journal of Economic Literature, and The Journal of Economic Perspectives).

The results of the study consist of the existence of three main directions in scientific research in 2008-2011.

The first direction refers to studies that addressed general aggregative models with economic fluctuations and prices, but did not encompass general macroeconomic aspects: Barnett and Bhattacharya (2008), Termin (2008), Justiniano and Primiceri (2008), Barillas, Hansen and Sargent (2009), Chetty et al. (2011).

The second direction is characterized by the researches that approached monetary policy and money supply, however these studies did not address the real variables of macroeconomics (consumption, savings, production, employment, and investment): Blinder and Morgan (2008), Besley, Meads and Surico (2008), Gaspar, Pérez Quirós and Rodríguez Mendizábal (2008), Benoît (2008), Buffie et al (2008), Ravenna and Walsh (2008), Berger, Ehrmann and Fratzscher (2008), Blinder et al (2008), Badinger (2009), Shleifer and Vishny (2010), Rose (2010), Blinder (2010), Feldstein (2010), Sanches and Williamson (2010), James and Lawler (2011), Engel (2011).

The third direction is characterized by studies that examined money and interest rates, but did not address macroeconomic policies and macroeconomic aspects of public finance: Caballero, Farhi and Gourinchas (2008), Favero and Giavazzi (2008), Kikuchi (2008), Ferraris and Watanabe (2008), Stulz (2009),

Lagos, Rocheteau and Weill (2009), Reinhart and Rogoff (2012), Hoffmann and MacDonald (2009), Kannan (2009), Koeppl and MacGee (2009), Martin (2009), Gollier (2009), Wright (2010), Engel and West (2010), Fleming, Hrung and Keane (2010), Greenwood and Vayanos (2010), Piazzesi and Schneider (2010), Ferraris (2010), Jouini, Marin and Napp (2010), Arellano and Heathcote (2010), Gomis-Porqueras and Peralta-Alva (2010), Shy and Wang (2011), Reinhart and Rogoff (2011), Chudik and Fratzscher (2011), Korinek (2011), Schmeling and Schrimpf (2011), Tirole (2011), Sanches (2011), Ferraris and Watanabe (2011), Krusell, Mukoyama and Smith Jr. (2011), Kamiya and Shimizu (2011).

The analyses conducted to accomplish the main purpose of the secondary research are relevant in the presented context, but there are some limitations and criticisms related to secondary research. The most important criticism concerns to the subjectivity of the research, particularly the inclusion and investigation of a limited number of economic scientific journals.

Acknowledgements

This work was supported by the strategic grant POSDRU/159/1.5/S/133255, Project ID 133255 (2014), cofinanced by the European Social Fund within the Sectorial Operational Program Human Resources Development 2007-2013.

References

Arellano, C. and Heathcote, J., 2010. Dollarization and financial integration. *Journal of Economic Theory*, 145(3), pp.944-973

Badinger, H., 2009. Globalization, the output–inflation tradeoff and inflation. *European Economic Review*, 53(8), pp.888-907

Barillas F., Hansen, L.P. and Sargent, T.J., 2009. Doubts or variability? *Journal of Economic Theory*, 144(6), pp.2388-2418

Barnett, R.C. and Bhattacharya, J., 2008. Rejuveniles and growth. *European Economic Review*, 52(6), pp.1055-1071

Benoît, M., 2008. When did unsystematic monetary policy have an effect on inflation? *European Economic Review*, 52(3), pp.487-497

Berger H., Ehrmann, M., and Fratzscher, M., 2008. Forecasting ECB monetary policy: Accuracy is a matter of geography. *European Economic Review*, 53(8), pp.1028-1041

Besley T., Meads N., and Surico, P., 2008. Insiders versus Outsiders in Monetary Policy-making. *American Economic Review*, 98(2), pp.218-223

Blinder, A.S., 2010. How Central Should the Central Bank Be? *Journal of Economic Literature*, 48(1), pp.123-133

Blinder, A.S. et al., 2008. Central Bank Communication and Monetary Policy: A Survey of Theory and Evidence. *Journal of Economic Literature*, 46(4), pp.910-945

Blinder, A.S. and Morgan, J., 2008. Do Monetary Policy Committees Need Leaders? A Report on an Experiment. *American Economic Review*, 98(2), pp.224-229

Bloise, G., and Reichlin, P., 2008. Asset prices, debt constraints and inefficiency. *Journal of Economic Theory*, 146(4), pp.1520-1546

Buffie, E. et al., 2008. Riding the wave: Monetary responses to aid surges in low-income countries. *European Economic Review*, 52(8), pp.1378-1395

Caballero, R.J., Farhi, E. and Gourinchas, P.O., 2008. An Equilibrium Model of "Global Imbalances" and Low Interest Rates. *American Economic Review*, 98(1), pp.358-393

Chetty et al., 2011. Are Micro and Macro Labor Supply Elasticities Consistent? A Review of Evidence on the Intensive and Extensive Margins. *American Economic Review*, 98(3), pp.604-641

Chudik, A., and Fratzscher, M., 2011. Identifying the global transmission of the 2007–2009 financial crisis in a GVAR model. *European Economic Review*, 55(3), pp.325-339

Engel, C., 2011. Currency Misalignments and Optimal Monetary Policy: A Reexamination. *American Economic Review*, 101(6), pp.2796-2822

Engel, C., and West, K.D., 2010. Global Interest Rates, Currency Returns, and the Real Value of the Dollar. *American Economic Review*, 100(2), pp.562-567

Favero, C., and Giavazzi, F., 2008. Should the Euro Area Be Run as a Closed Economy? *American Economic Review*, 98(2), pp.138-145

Feldstein, M., 2010. What Powers for the Federal Reserve? *Journal of Economic Literature*, 48(1), pp.134-145

Ferraris, L., 2010. On the complementarity of money and credit. *European Economic Review*, 54(5), pp.733-741

Ferraris, L., and Watanabe, M., 2008. Collateral secured loans in a monetary economy. *Journal of Economic Theory*, 143(1), pp.405-424

Ferraris, L., and Watanabe, M., 2011. Collateral fluctuations in a monetary economy. *Journal of Economic Theory*, 146(5), pp.1915-1940

Fleming, M.J., Hrung W.B., and Keane, F.M., 2010. Repo Market Effects of the Term Securities Lending Facility. *American Economic Review*, 100(2), pp.591-596

Gaspar,V., Pérez Quirós, G., and Rodríguez Mendizábal, H., 2008. Interest rate dispersion and volatility in the market for daily funds. *European Economic Review*, 52(3), pp.413-440

Gollier, C., 2009. Ecological discounting. *Journal of Economic Theory*, 145(2), pp.812-829

Gomis-Porqueras, P., and Peralta-Alva, A., 2010. Optimal monetary and fiscal policies in a search theoretic model of monetary exchange. *European Economic Review*, 54(3), pp.331-344

Greenwood, R., and Vayanos, D., 2010. Price Pressure in the Government Bond Market. *American Economic Review*, 100(2), pp.585-590

Hoffmann, M., and MacDonald, R., 2009. Real exchange rates and real interest rate differentials: A present value interpretation. *European Economic Review*, 53(8), pp.952-970

James, J.G. and Lawler, P., 2011. Optimal Policy Intervention and the Social Value of Public Information. *American Economic Review*, 101(4), pp.1561-1574

Jouini, E., Marin, J.-M.and Napp, C., 2010. Discounting and divergence of opinion. *Journal of Economic Theory*, 145(2), pp.830-859

Justiniano, A., and Primiceri, G.E., 2008. The Time-Varying Volatility of Macroeconomic Fluctuations. *American Economic Review*, 98(3), pp. 604-641

Kamiya, K., and Shimizu, T., 2011. Stationary monetary equilibria with strictly increasing value functions and non-discrete money holdings distributions: An indeterminacy result. *Journal of Economic Theory*, 146(5), pp.2140-2150

Kannan, P., 2009. On the welfare benefits of an international currency. *European Economic Review*, 53(5), pp.588-606

Kikuchi, T., 2008. International asset market, nonconvergence, and endogenous fluctuations. *Journal of Economic Theory*, 139(1), pp.310-334

Koeppl, T.V., and MacGee, J.C., 2009. What broad banks do, and markets don't: Cross-subsidization. *European Economic Review*, 53(2), pp.222-236

Korinek, A., 2011. Foreign currency debt, risk premia and macroeconomic volatility. *European Economic Review*, 55(3), pp.371-385

Krugman, P., 2008. *The Return of Depression Economics and the Crisis of 2008*. London: Penguin BooksKrusell, P., Mukoyama T., and Smith Jr., A.A., 2011. Asset prices in a Huggett economy. *Journal of Economic Theory*, 146(3), pp.812-844

Lagos, R., Rocheteau, G., and Weill, P.-O., 2009. Crises and liquidity in over-the-counter markets. *Journal of Economic Theory*, 146(6), pp.2169-2205

Martin, A., 2009. A model of collateral, investment, and adverse selection. *Journal of Economic Theory*, 144(4), pp.1572-1588

Piazzesi, M., and Schneider, M., 2010. Interest Rate Risk in Credit Markets. *American Economic Review*, 100(2), pp.579-584

Ravenna, F., and Walsh, C., 2008. Vacancies, unemployment, and the Phillips curve. *European Economic Review*, 52(8), pp.1494-1521

Reinhart, C.M., and Rogoff, K.S., 2009. The Aftermath of Financial Crises. *American Economic Review*, 99(2), pp.466-472

Reinhart, C.M., and Rogoff, K.S., 2011. From Financial Crash to Debt Crisis. *American Economic Review*, 101(5), pp.1676-1706

Rose, A.K., 2010. Exchange Rate Regimes in the Modern Era: Fixed, Floating, and Flaky. *Journal of Economic Literature*, 49(3), pp.652-672

Sanches, D., 2011. A dynamic model of unsecured credit. *Journal of Economic Theory*, 146(5), pp.1941-1964

Sanches, D., and Williamson, S., 2010, Money and credit with limited commitment and theft. *Journal of Economic Theory*, 145(4), pp.1525-1549

Schmeling, M., and Schrimpf, A., 2011. Expected inflation, expected stock returns, and money illusion: What can we learn from survey expectations? *European Economic Review*, 55(5), pp.702-719

Shleifer, A., and Vishny, R.W., 2010. Asset Fire Sales and Credit Easing. *American Economic Review*, 100(2), pp.46-50

Shy, O., and Wang, Z., 2011. Why Do Payment Card Networks Charge Proportional Fees? *American Economic Review*, 101(4), pp.1575-1590

Stulz, R.M., 2009, Credit Default Swaps and the Credit Crisis. *Journal of Economic Perspectives*, 24(1), pp.73-92

Temin, P., 2008. Real Business Cycle Views of the Great Depression and Recent Events: A Review of Timothy J. Kehoe and Edward C. Prescott's Great Depressions of the Twentieth Century. *Journal of Economic Literature*, 46(3), pp.669-684

Tirole, J., 2011. Illiquidity and All Its Friends. *Journal of Economic Literature*, 49(2), pp.287-325

Wright, R., 2010. A uniqueness proof for monetary steady state. *Journal of Economic Theory*, 145(1), pp.382-391

18

Impact of Monetary Policy and Fiscal Policy on Indonesian Stock Market

Rossanto Dwi HANDOYO[1*], Mansor JUSOH[2], and Mohd. Azlan SHAH ZAIDI[2]

[1]Airlangga University, Surabaya, Indonesia
[2]National University of Malaysia, Bangi Selangor, Malaysia

This paper attempts to investigate the effect of fiscal and monetary policy on Indonesian Stock price as well as main sectors stock price such as agricultural, mining, manufacture, and financial sector indexes. We consider the world oil price as a foreign variable that will influence domestic economy as in regular small open economy model. In this paper, we employ the Monte Carlo algorithm to Near-SVAR models (if some of the VAR equations have regressors not included in the others). We find that there is a positive stock price response to monetary policy shock both aggregated and sectoral stock price. In term of interaction between fiscal policy shock and stock market, we find that all sectors respond negative relationship. From this empirical finding, fiscal policy crowd out private sector activity in market, thus, its effect will be impotent in economy. We also provide the evidence that not only both policies are able to influence the stock price individually, but also the interaction between monetary and fiscal policy is important in explaining stock market performance.

Keywords: *monetary policy, fiscal policy, stock price, Monte Carlo SVAR model, impulses response*

1. Introduction

Many empirical studies attempt to scrutinize both impact fiscal and monetary policies on output and inflation rather than stock price. The objective of our paper is to investigate the effect of fiscal and monetary policy on Indonesian Stock price. We use stock prices because they are the most responsive, while output and

[*] Corresponding Author:
Rossanto Dwi Handoyo, Department of Economics, Faculty of Economics and Business, Airlangga University Indonesia, 4th Airlangga Road, Surabaya, East Java, Indonesia, 60285

inflation are the sluggish ones due to many restrictions to various sort of adjustment costs in determining the quantities of most goods and services (Sims and Zha, 2006; Cheng and Jin, 2013). Several authors have discussed in detail the effect of monetary policy shock on stock market (e.g., Thorbecke, 1997; Bernanke and Kuttner, 2005; Cheng and Jin, 2013; Bouakez, et al., 2010; Laeven and Tong, 2012; Pirovano, 2012). Studies that attempt to test the impact of fiscal policy on stock market are also voluminous (e.g., Darrat, 1990; Laopodis, 2009; Afonso and Sousa, 2011 and 2012; Agnello and Sousa, 2012). On the other hand, the studies of incorporating the effect of fiscal and monetary policy on the stock market performance are not voluminous (e.g., Jansen, et. al., 2008; Chatziantoniou, 2013). Our study perhaps complements this literature gap.

The study of the effect of monetary and fiscal policy is important in case of Indonesia that implements the inflation targeting framework because of the potential conflicting objectives between fiscal and monetary policies will lead to a crucial strategic interaction between two policy instruments. The interaction arises as both monetary and fiscal policies have implication for the output gap and inflation. Fiscal authorities are more concern about output, otherwise the monetary authorities emphasize on controlling inflation. Under standard economic theory, the sign of the budget deficit is expected to be positive, which means that the larger the budget deficits will lead to larger the interest rate. Under these circumstances, the Central Bank needs to stabilize the economy from overheating and inflationary pressure. Meanwhile, many empirical studies that attempt to scrutinize the effect of impact fiscal and monetary policies focus more on output and inflation rather than stock price.

In the context of Indonesia, to our best knowledge, study relating to stock market response on both fiscal and monetary policy shocks is not well documented and sometimes only in individually rather than jointly (e.g., Praptiningsih, 2013). Meanwhile, studies relating to both the effect of monetary and fiscal policy analysis emphasized on those policies shocks on macroeconomic objective mainly on inflation and output not on stock market (e.g., Surjaningsih, et al., 2012; Hermawan and Munro, 2008). Our study perhaps fills this literature gap.

This paper also attempts to investigate the effect of monetary and fiscal policy on main sectors stock price index in Indonesian Stock market such as agricultural, mining, manufacture, and financial sectors indexes. We use only 4 main sectors in our analysis that represent three kinds of aggregated development sectors group namely primary, secondary and tertiary sectors. We use mining and agriculture sectors to represent the primary sector as well as the top stock price index. As a developing country, the contribution of these two sectors is still quite high to national output which are 12.7% and 7.67% in 2011, respectively (Indonesian Statistics Bureau, 2011). Meanwhile, the manufacture and financial sectors contribute 25.7% and 10.7% of total output, respectively. The last two sectors represent secondary and tertiary sectors as well as the medium and the low stock price sector index. This analysis is crucial in order to investigate the strength of such an association whether tend to varies extensively across sectors. Under these circumstances, sector stockholder will be affected by the change of the policies and then, in turn the firm's ability to finance the production level will vary across sectors due to different consumption (wealth effect) and investment pattern.

From the methodological perspective, we employ a near-SVAR model because some of the VAR equations have regressors not included in the others. This model provides an extension of the structural VAR approach, as it does not impose the same variables treated in all right-hand side of the equations of the reduced form model since we employ the world oil price as an exogenous variables and unaffected by any domestic variables. In the context of the present paper, the near-SVAR model is estimated using the method of seemingly unrelated regressions (SUR). SUR offers a robust statistical framework with the ability to give consistent and efficient estimates of the coefficients (Enders, 1995; Zaidi and Fisher, 2010; Piroli et al, 2012) particularly if the lag length is long because this erodes the degree of freedom. Numerous studies have attempted to improve the better SVAR methods by applying Bayesian analysis to obtain accurate infinite sample inferences from the posterior distribution (Sims and Zha, 1999; Wagonner and Zha, 2003). In this paper, we employ the Monte Carlo simulation method, particularly Gibbs Sampler, to our near SVAR model which has been proposed by Sims and Zha (1999), and developed extensively by Wagonner and Zha (2003).

This study is organized as follows. Section 2 explores the data used in the models. Section 3 mentions the methodological and model identification strategy. Section 4 reports the estimation results and discusses the empirical results. Section 5 concludes with the main findings and policy recommendations.

2. Data Description

As a small open economy, we employ the world oil price rather than output or commodity price as the foreign variables that affect Indonesian economy. The oil price data is crude oil or petroleum price in US$/barrel and taken from Dubai Fateh oil market. Our studies decompose variables into two blocks as a standard form model of SVAR for small open Economy. The first block consists of one foreign variable that is world oil price. The reason why we use the world oil price is that regarding the fact that since 2003, Indonesia becomes net importer oil country and suffer from any increase of such shock in which the deficit of trade balance on oil become larger as the world oil price tend to rise for over the last decade. Hence, rising oil prices are bad for stock market of oil importing country such as Indonesia. Kim and Roubini (2000) use oil prices rather than commodity prices as a proxy for future inflation and the world economic variable. On the other hand, Zaidi et. al., (2011) use the world commodity prices for Malaysia cases due to the fact that Malaysia is oil producing country and the oil price in the domestic market is heavily regulated.

The second block contains the domestic variables consisting of: industrial production index (LY), Debt to GDP ratio (DYR), the inflation rate (INF, the growth rate of consumer price index/CPI), money market interest rate (R, 3 month SBI rate), real exchange rate (LXR, nominal exchange rate times the ratio of US CPI/Indonesian CPI), and stock price both in composite index (LSP) and sector price index (LAGR for agriculture, LMINE for mining, LFINE for banking and finance). We use Industrial production index to represent national output (we also use this indicator due to the data availability in monthly basis instead of national income that employed in quarterly basis), Debt to GDP ratio for the fiscal policy variables and 3 months SBI rate for monetary policy variable. For this purpose, we decompose the shock of domestic and foreign shock on stock price both composite index and sectors index into 5 models; model 1 for the composite index, model 2 (mining), model 3 (agriculture), model 4 (finance), and model 5 (manufacture industry). We use industrial production index rather than GDP that has been used in stock market studies, such as Binswanger (2000, 2001, 2004), and Mackowiak (2006). All variables (except the inflation rate, Debt to GDP ratio and interest rate) are transformed by taking natural logarithms. All variables are in real term (constant price at certain base year depending the published report or if not available, we calculated them ourselves with base year 2003, similar to BPS or Indonesian Statistic Agency base year) and seasonally adjusted using X11 multiplicative provided by Eviews6 and RATS. Our SVAR model is specified in levels rather than in the first difference following Zaidi et. al., (2011) since there is no theoretically foundation to impose cointegration restriction on VAR model.

We use monthly data from 2001.1 until 2011.12. We start our data from January in year 2001 is to avoid the turbulence 1998 economic Crisis and of course data treatment using structural break are no longer needed. Data are collected from various sources such as the Monthly Indonesian Economics and Financial Statistics produced by Bank Indonesia (www.bi.go.id), Economic Indicators of Indonesian Statistics Agency or BPS/Badan Pusat Statistik (www.bps.go.id), Indonesian Stock Exchange market (www.idx.co.id), Directorate General of Debt Management of treasury department (www.djpu.kemenkeu.go.id), our world oil price data taken from the website www.indexmundi.com. Some variables that are not available in monthly data, such as GDP and Debt (data from 2000 until 2008 are not provided on monthly but quarterly) are interpolated using cubic match. The detailed formula of cubic match last is available at EVIEWS 6 user's guide.

3. Methodology and Identification

We investigate the dynamic relationship among fiscal and monetary policies and the stock market performance using near SVAR framework. In estimation, we emphasized on identifying only the monetary and fiscal policies shock and we do not aim to identify all structural shock. Our estimations follow the step by the step the methodology developed by Wagonner and Zha (2003). In order to choose the optimal lag length for our SVAR model, the residual of each equation are examined for evidence of serial correlation using Akaike's Information Criterion (AIC) and Schwarz Bayesian Criterion (SBC).

Following Wagonner and Zha (2003), the structural VAR models typically take the form of

$$y_t' A = \sum_{t=1}^{p} y_{t-l}' A_l + z_t' D + \varepsilon_t', \quad \text{for } t = 1, \ldots, T, \tag{1}$$

where A and A_l are 6×6 parameter matrices, D is an $h \times 6$ parameter matrix, y_t is an 6×1 column vector of endogenous variables at time t, z_t is an $h \times 1$ column vector of exogenous variables at time t, ε_t is an 7×1 column vector of structural disturbances at time t; p is the lag length, and T is the sample size. The parameters of individual equations in (1) correspond to the columns of A, A_l and D. The structural disturbances have a Gaussian distribution with

$$E(\varepsilon_t | y_1, \ldots, y_{t-1}, z_1, \ldots, z_T) = 0$$
$$E(\varepsilon_t \varepsilon_t' | y_1, \ldots, y_{t-1}, z_1, \ldots, z_T) = I. \tag{2}$$

The structural disturbances in (2) are normalized to have an identity covariance matrix. Right multiplying the structural form (1) by A^{-1}, the usual representation of a reduced-form VAR can be obtained with the reduced-form variance matrix being

$$\Omega = (AA')^{-1} \tag{3}$$

Equation (4) below indicates the set of restriction that are imposed on the contemporaneous parameters of the SVAR model of Indonesian Stock market. Our identification structures are more likely the upper triangular rather than the lower one. The coefficient β_{ij} indicates of how variable j contemporaneously influence on variable i. The coefficients on the diagonal are set to be unity, while the number of zero restriction on the coefficient is 23, hence the model is over-identified since exactly identified require 49-7=42/2=21 restrictions. If there are $(n^2 - n/2)$ additional restrictions, meaning that the the system is over-identified, hence χ^2 test of statistic need to be conducted. Following Zaidi and Karim (2012), χ^2 test of statistic is $\chi^2 = |\Sigma_e^R| - |\Sigma_e|$, where R (number of resctriction exceeding $(n^2 - n/2)$) degrees of freedom can be used to test the restricted system, $|\Sigma_e^R|$ is the restricted variance-covariance matrix, $|\Sigma_e|$ is the unrestricted variance-covariance matrix.

The short-run restrictions applied in this model are the following:

$$\begin{bmatrix} \varepsilon_{LSP} \\ \varepsilon_{LXR} \\ \varepsilon_{R} \\ \varepsilon_{INF} \\ \varepsilon_{DYR} \\ \varepsilon_{LY} \\ \varepsilon_{LOIL} \end{bmatrix} = \begin{bmatrix} 1 & A_{12} & A_{13} & A_{14} & A_{15} & A_{16} & A_{17} \\ A_{21} & 1 & A_{23} & A_{24} & 0 & A_{26} & A_{27} \\ 0 & A_{32} & 1 & A_{34} & 0 & 0 & A_{37} \\ 0 & 0 & 0 & 1 & 0 & A_{46} & A_{47} \\ 0 & 0 & 0 & 0 & 1 & A_{56} & A_{57} \\ 0 & 0 & 0 & 0 & 0 & 1 & A_{67} \\ 0 & 0 & 0 & 0 & 0 & 0 & 1 \end{bmatrix} x \begin{bmatrix} e_{LSP} \\ e_{LXR} \\ e_{R} \\ e_{INF} \\ e_{DYR} \\ e_{LY} \\ e_{LOIL} \end{bmatrix} \tag{4}$$

where, industrial production index (LY), Debt to GDP ratio (DYR), the inflation rate (INF), money market interest rate or 3 month SBI rate (R), real exchange rate (LXR), and stock price both in composite index (LSP) and World oil price (LOIL). We put the foreign variables at the last ordering to adjust the equation in the SUR model that place the oil equation at the last. Consequently, our restriction structure is more likely upper triangular rather than the lower one. In addition, Waggoner and Zha (2003) state that for the methodological purpose, the Gibbs sampler will produce independent draws of A matrix if the transformed form of A matrix is upper triangular after an appropriate reordering of equations and variables (for detailed discussion, see Waggoner and Zha, 2003).

We focus on examining the interaction between the macroeconomic policies and stock price. Our restrictions follow the previous studies that concern on macroeconomic modeling and stock market analysis. Below we provide the explanation of the model's restriction. Stock prices are contemporaneously influenced by all variables (Afonso and Sousa, 2011; Bouakez et al., 2010; Chatziantoniou et.al, 2013). Exchange rate is contemporaneously influenced by all variables except debt to GDP ratio (Kim and Roubini, 2000; Zaidi,et.al., 2011; Dungey and Fry, 2009). Monetary policy is also contemporaneously influenced by exchange rate. The interdependence between exchange rate and interest rate has been assumed because it helps to solve the exchange rate puzzle (Kim and Roubini, 2000; Zaidi et al., 2011). The foreign shock contemporaneously affects all domestic variables. Inflation reacts contemporaneously only to income shock and foreign shock (Bjornland and Leitemo, 2009; Kim and Roubini, 2000; Chatziantoniou et.al, 2013). Monetary policy tool is contemporaneously affected by inflation. However the national income cannot be contemporaneously influenced by any other domestic variables (Kim and Roubini, 2000). In contrast, it can contemporaneously influence all domestic variables.

We conduct inference from a Bayesian approach, as is common in the VAR literature (see Sims and Zha, 1998, 1999; Waggoner and Zha, 2003). We take draws from the posterior pdf of the parameters of the reduced-form VAR. This pdf is a product of an inverse-Wishart density for Ω and a Gaussian density for the equation's coefficients $B(s)$ for all $s > 0$, conditional on Ω. In the past, researchers have used an importance sampler to approximate the posterior density function of A.

4. Result Estimation

To begin with, we start our estimation with determining optimal lag length using Akaike Information Criteria (AIC) and Schwartz Bayesian Criterion (SBC). According to the two tests (Table 1), our five model both composite index and 4 sector index recommend to employ two lag orders. By using 2 lag orders, our models are expected to have consistent and efficient coefficient since they do not consume degrees of freedom.

***Table 1.** Optimal Lag Length*

Lags	AIC	SBC
1	-26.4542	-25.2818*
2	-26.8719*	-24.7688
3	-26.5634	-23.6441
4	-26.2624	-22.6743
5	-25.4871	-21.4222
6	-24.8955	-20.6076
7	-23.9693	-19.8012
8	-22.3896	-18.8150
9	-20.2409	-17.9369
10	-16.9447	-16.9192
11	-12.9457	-16.7851
12	-6.3145	-16.7159

*Note: * represents lag recommended by AIC or SBC*

Next, we develop our Seemingly Unrelated Regression (SUR) model to estimate our near-SVAR model. We treat world oil price as an exogenous variable against all equation and only be influenced by its own lag. Table 2 presents the estimates of the coefficients of A Matrix in equation (4). From the table, we find that all models produce the same sign on each coefficients, except coefficient (a_{17}) in model 5; (a_{23}) in model 4; (a_{26}) in model 2 and 3. The sign and the coefficient significancies across the models look similar. Unfortunately, many coefficients are insignificant. For the stock price variable, all coefficients are of expected sign except the real output which produce the negative sign (a_{16}). Stock price decreases contemporaneously with an increase in exchange rate, interest rate, real output, and oil price whereas the other variables such as inflation rate and fiscal policy rate move in the same direction. For the inflation variable, the estimation also indicates that inflation has significant contemporaneous relationship with monetary policy. Furthermore, the oil price has significant contemporaneous effect on interest rate and budget deficit. From this finding, the inflation and the oil price play an important role in determining the interest rate adjustment undertaken by the Central Bank. Meanwhile, these results imply that a change in oil price takes into account the fiscal policy.

***Table 2.** SVAR Result – Contemporaneous Coefficient*

Variables	Coefficient	Model 1 (composite)	Model 2 (mining sector)	Model 3 (agriculture sector)	Model 4 (finance sector)	Model 5 (manufacture industry sector)
LSP	a_{12}	-7.507	-9.897	-7.628*	-9.284	-9.005
	a_{13}	-30.892	-39.932	-27.796	-36.921	-32.679
	a_{14}	1.473	2.292	0.862	0.021	0.011
	a_{15}	0.489	0.656	0.597*	0.639	0.604
	a_{16}	-0.076	-0.581	-0.479	-0.732	-0.678
	a_{17}	-0.069	-0.430	-0.383	-0.026	0.133
LXR	a_{21}	0.801*	0.567*	0.363*	0.731*	0.907*
	a_{23}	1.053	0.923	1.843	-0.303	2.347*
	a_{24}	0.801*	1.233*	0.298	0.014	0.004
	a_{26}	-0.039	0.054	0.057	-0.047	-0.089
	a_{27}	-0.116*	-0.247*	-0.163*	-0.107*	-0.052
R	a_{32}	-0.048*	-0.047*	-0.046*	-0.043*	-0.046*
	a_{34}	-0.201*	-0.199*	-0.195*	-0.001*	-0.002*
	a_{37}	0.007*	0.008*	0.008*	0.007*	0.008*
INF	a_{46}	0.022	0.018	0.020	2.314	2.901
	a_{47}	-0.002	-0.007	-0.003	-0.178	-0.073

DYR	a_{56}	0.438	0.134	0.212	0.188	0.458
	a_{57}	1.056*	1.025*	1.164*	1.044*	1.253*
LY	a_{67}	0.047	0.038	0.051	0.058	0.069
Diagnostic Test:						
χ^2 statistic test		3.999	4.370	3.767	3.403	5.103
p-value		0.135	0.112	0.152	0.182	0.077
Convergence in (iteration)		71	74	52	72	67

*Note: Sign * Indicates that the coefficients are statistically significant at the 10% level. Model 1-5 represent model for composite stock price index, mining, agriculture, finance and manufacture industrial sectors index, respectively.*

To test the over identifying restrictions on the SVAR model, we employ a chi-squared with 2 degrees of freedom provided by RATS program output. We find the value of chi-square test for model 1of 3.999 with the χ^2 value of 0.135. It means that the overidentifying restrictions cannot be rejected. All models perform the same result (except model 5) and based on our calculation all models also perform well since they converge below 100 iterations. Our identification strategy is also valid since our model generates the significant of the contemporaneous coefficients outside the upper triangular of A matrix ($a_{21}$and a_{32}) as seen in equation (4).

Figure 1 and 4 plot the impulse response function of macroeconomic (stock price, exchange rate, inflation and output) response to one standard deviation shocks in monetary policy and fiscal policy for the aggregated stock price (model 1). Figure 2 and 5 display the sectors stock price response to one standard deviation shocks in monetary policy and fiscal policy respectively. The solid line corresponds to the median response and we provide 68% posterior confidence intervals from near-SVAR model. The confidence bands are constructed by using a Monte-Carlo Gibbs sampling algorithm as developed further for SVAR model by Waggoner and Zha (2003) and calculated by taking the estimated coefficient in structural model to form the data generating process on 2,000 burns and 10,000 draws.

4.1. The Effect of Monetary Policy Shocks

As shown, in a response to the positive innovation in the central bank policy rate (tightening monetary policy shock), Composite Stock price (figure 1) rise initially and then fall until reaches the peak in 16 months. This finding is in line with the work of Praptiningsih (2013) and Handoyo et al., (2014). These delayed responses of stock prices imply that stock prices adjust sluggishly to a monetary policy shock. The falling of stock price initially is to earn the higher discount factor which reduces the present value of expected future earnings of firms. Theoretically, a rise in interest rate is predicted to have a negative effect on the stock market. This sluggish response may be due to investing in the Indonesian stock market has grown significantly since the last two decades and become an interesting option for the investor to expand their business for both local and foreign investors regardless the policy undertaken by the central bank in the short horizon although in medium and long horizon stock price will fall.

From the perspective of the sectoral stock price, similar response patterns exist in all models (see figure 2) except model 4 (Finance and banking sector). The positive initial responses of both composite and sectoral stock prices are short-lived. The different response between the sectoral and the composite stock prices is in the period of initial response. Composite stock prices responds positively to the monetary policy shocks in month 5 and then negatively after that. Meanwhile, the mining, agriculture and manufacture industry responds positively in 3, 2, and 4 month, respectively. These findings reveal that the strength of the correlation between the monetary policy and the stock prices does not vary across sectors. The sector stockholder will be affected by the change in monetary policy. There are several reasons why initially they respond positively to monetary policy shock. First of all, this may be due to the probability of the asset price bubble increase for the last two decades regardless the policy actions conducted by monetary authority. In short run, Investors expect that as long as the future business prospect still profitable and the government perform the economy well, the demand for the asset still high. Secondly, this finding confirms that monetary policy is not effective for the Bank Indonesia (Indonesian Central bank) to intervene the Stock market. This is because the rapid development in financial market is not only affected by the monetary policy but also by the liberalization policy and reform in the financial sector that has been done so far.

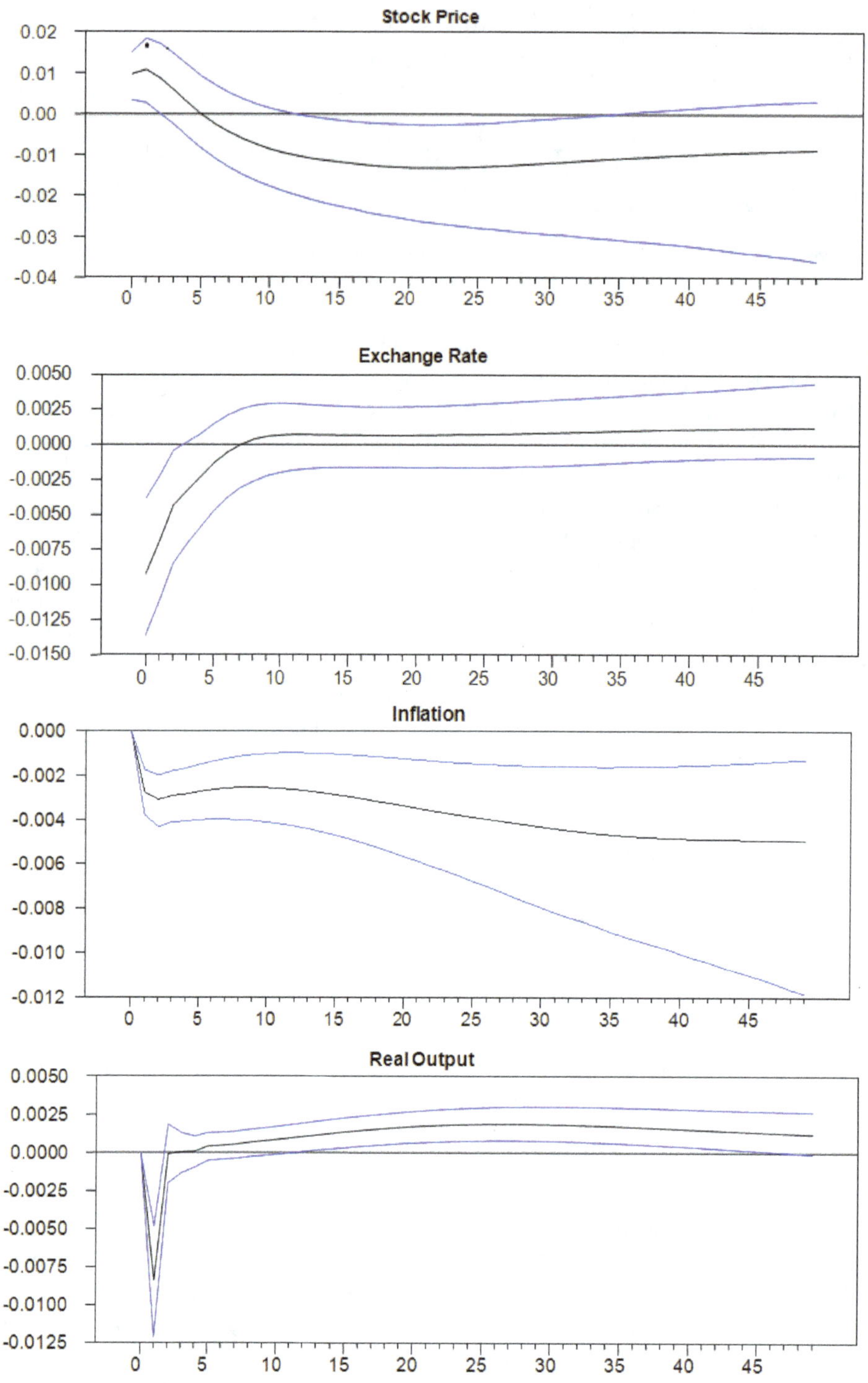

Figure 1. *Impulse Response to Monetary Policy Shock for Model 1 (Composite Stock Price Index)*

With so many studies on investigating in monetary policy shocks, the model has an appropriate behavior of the components of the model to domestic interest rate. The Impulse response functions for a domestic interest rate shock shown in Figure 1 reveals that many problems associated with identification of interest rate effects in a small open economy SVAR models are not present in the model. A rise in domestic interest rate generates a decline in domestic output and the real exchange rate (REER) appreciates. As the consequences of a decline in domestic output and the appreciation of the exchange rate, inflation rate falls. The inflation rate falls immediately after the increase in the domestic interest rate, the peak decline occurs 38 months after the shock. From this finding, the output puzzle, prize puzzle and the exchange rate puzzle do not exist in our model.

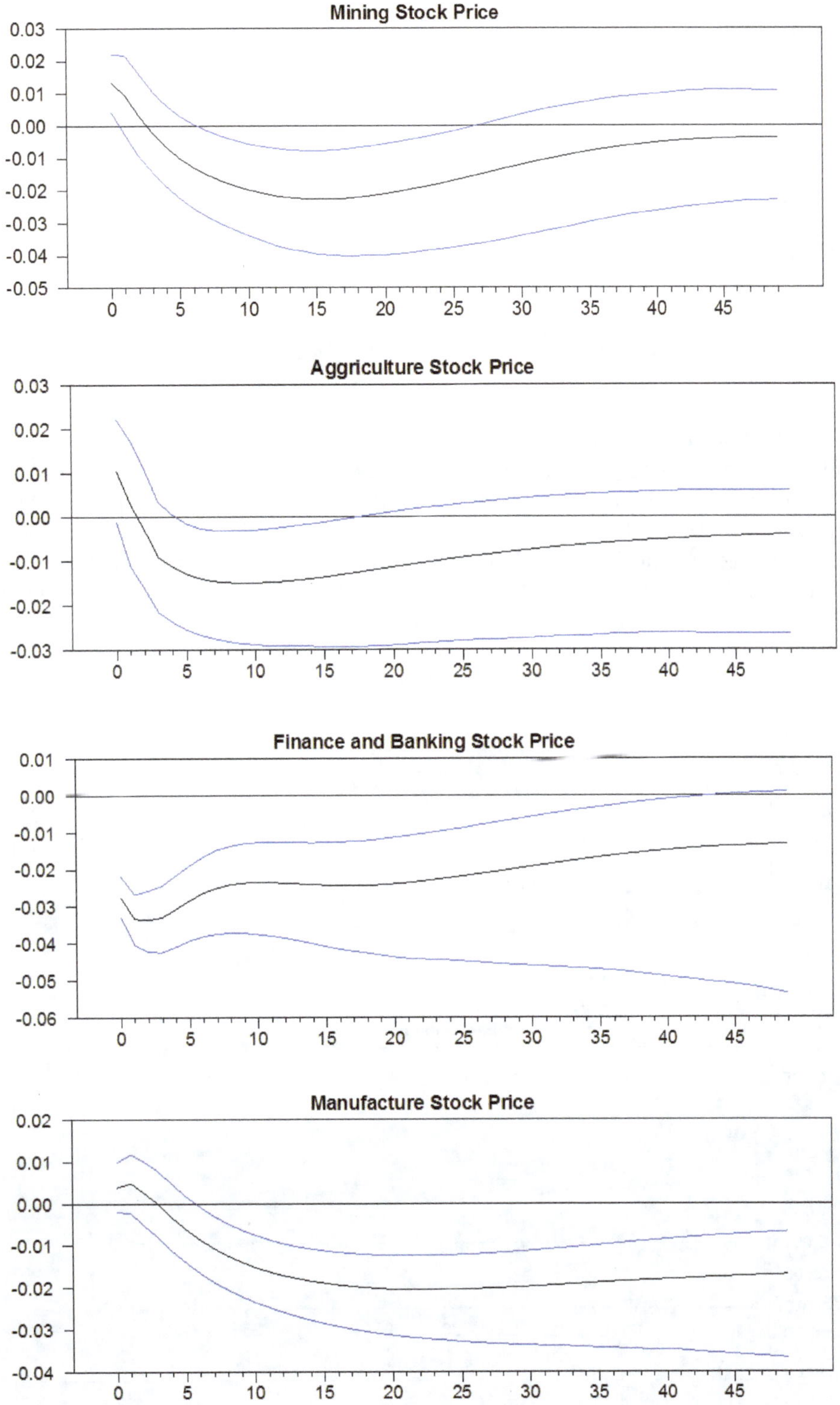

Figure 2. *Sector Stock Price Responses to Monetary Policy Shock*

In figure 3, our model also produces the responses the innovations of composite stock price. In response to a rise in stock price, the income increase immediately. This income response is consistent with a Tobin's q effect. The increase in income in turn will lead to create higher investment demand by firms and a wealth effect will lead to higher consumption demand by household.

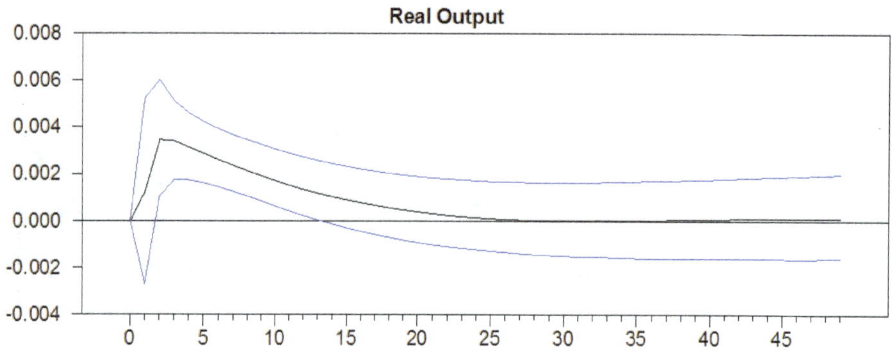

Figure 3. *Real Output Responses to Stock Price Shock*

4.2. The Effect of Fiscal Policy Shocks

In contrast to monetary policy shock, the stock market's response to one standard deviation increase in fiscal policy is similar since all models perform the similar pattern of initially response which all falls both composite stock price (see figure 4) and sectors stock price (figure 5). Looking at the reaction of stock price both composite and its sectors, the fiscal shock has a negative impact but it is less persistent. This finding is in line with the findings of Darrat (1990), Agnella and Sousa (2012), Afonso and Sousa (2011) which stated that there is a negative response of stock prices to fiscal policy shocks.

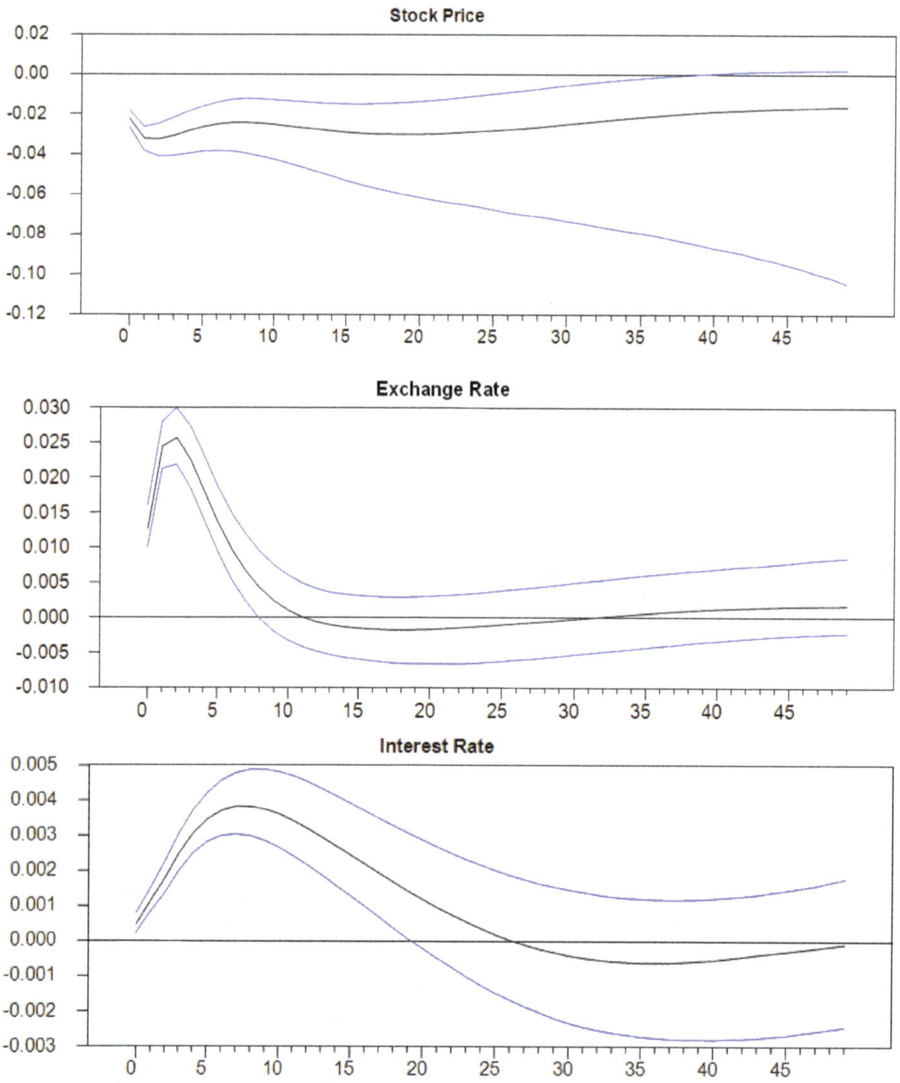

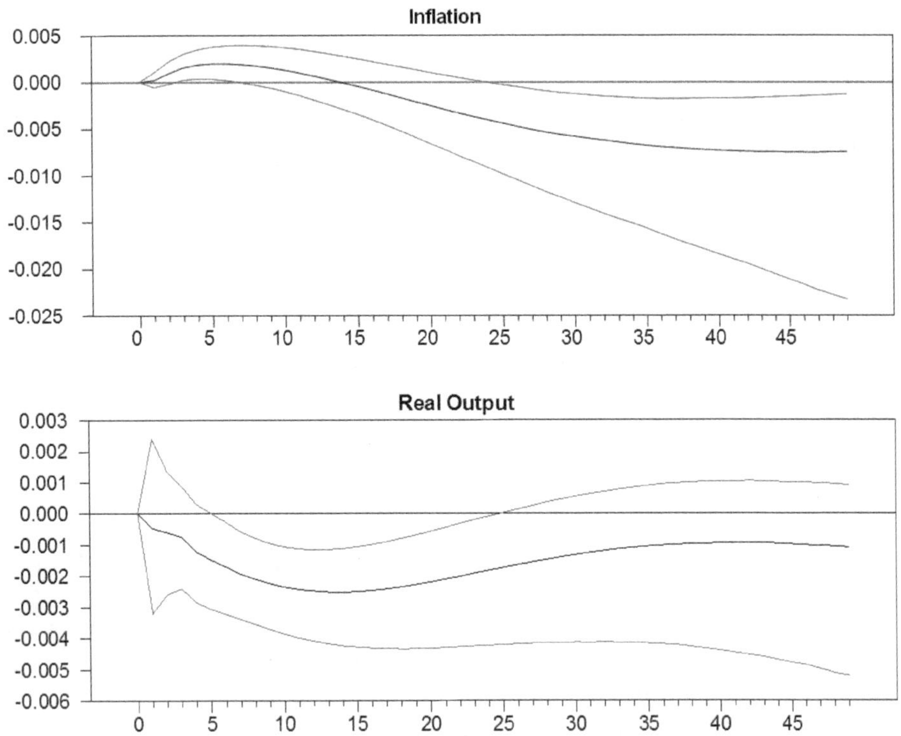

Figure 4. *Impulse Response to Fiscal Policy Shock for Model 1 (Composite Stock Price Index)*

In figure 4, the effect of fiscal policy shock on output is negative and this is in line with the study of Afonso and Sousa (2011), who also find a negative effect of government budget deficit on GDP. With reference to inflation, we have evidenced that they react positively to fiscal policy shock. This finding is also in line with the work of Perotti (2005).

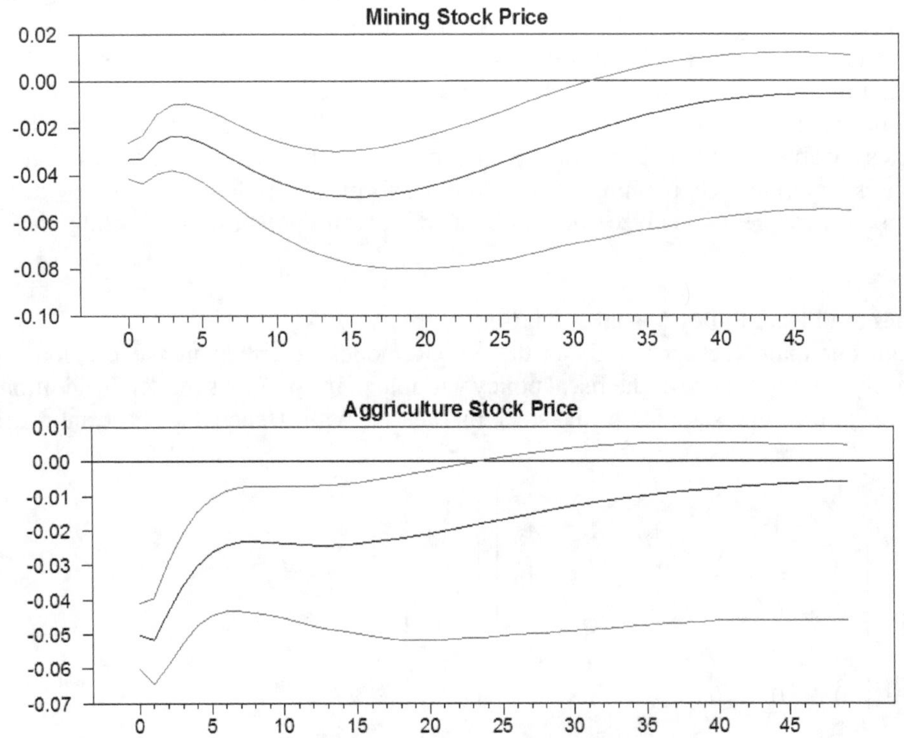

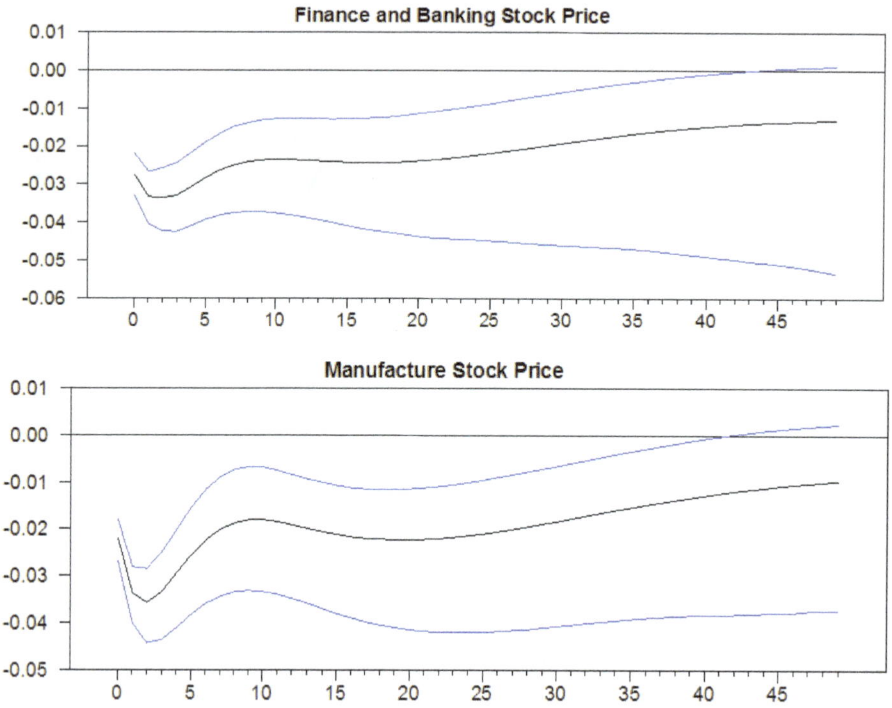

Figure 5. *Sectors Stock Price Response to Fiscal Policy Shock*

Response of interest rate seems to react positively to a fiscal shock. This reaction of the interest rate to fiscal policy is in the direction with the crowding out hypothesis. From this empirical finding, fiscal policy crowd out private sector activity in market, thus, its effect will be impotent in economy. This is in line with the work of Gale and Orszag (2003), Afonso and Sousa (2011) and Handoyo et al., (2014) who argue that there are two important reasons for why budget deficits may raise interest rates. Firstly, public deficits reduce aggregate savings when private savings do not increase by the same amount and there are no compensating foreign capital inflows. Secondly, deficits increase the stock of government debt. Furthermore, the effect of government budget deficits on long-term interest rates and emphasizes the "crowding-out" hypothesis, whereby fiscal policy can negatively influence investment expenditures. After the fiscal shock occurs, the rise in the interest rates makes the stock market a less attractive place for the allocation of savings. As a consequence, share prices immediately fall. However, as the shock erodes, stock prices start recovering in anticipation of the expansionary effects of fiscal policy on output. We provide this evidence to prove that not only both policies are able to influence the stock price individually, but also the interaction between monetary and fiscal policy is important in explaining stock market performance. Below we will provide the model that excludes the fiscal variable to analyze the importance of both policies in affecting the stock market performance.

4.3. Does the Fiscal Policy Variable Matter?

Although our main focus of study is the SVAR model described in the previous sections, it is interesting to verify the importance of the fiscal policy variable in the previous model. In addition, this can add a significant value to the understanding of the stock market behavior. Hence, the short run restrictions are as follows.

$$\begin{bmatrix} \varepsilon_{LSP} \\ \varepsilon_{LXR} \\ \varepsilon_{R} \\ \varepsilon_{INF} \\ \varepsilon_{LY} \\ \varepsilon_{LOIL} \end{bmatrix} = \begin{bmatrix} 1 & A_{12} & A_{13} & A_{14} & A_{15} & A_{16} \\ A_{21} & 1 & A_{23} & A_{24} & A_{25} & A_{26} \\ 0 & A_{32} & 1 & A_{34} & 0 & A_{36} \\ 0 & 0 & 0 & 1 & A_{45} & A_{46} \\ 0 & 0 & 0 & 0 & 1 & A_{56} \\ 0 & 0 & 0 & 0 & 0 & 1 \end{bmatrix} x \begin{bmatrix} e_{LSP} \\ e_{LXR} \\ e_{R} \\ e_{INF} \\ e_{LY} \\ e_{LOIL} \end{bmatrix} \quad (5)$$

Focusing on the responses of all variables to monetary policy shocks, we expect important findings compare to our original model's findings which take into account the fiscal policy instrument. In the absence of fiscal policy instrument (see fig. 6), interest rates do not seem to have the significant impact on stock market development and our study is in line with the study of Chatziantoniou, et al., (2013). Furthermore, contrary to the fiscal inclusion model, the fiscal exclusion model experiences the exchange rate puzzle. Comparing these results with the original model, we are able to suggest that the fiscal exclusion variables does not provide a better representation of the Indonesian stock market model. Hence, the incorporation of the fiscal policy variable has added to the insight value in determining the stock market behavior.

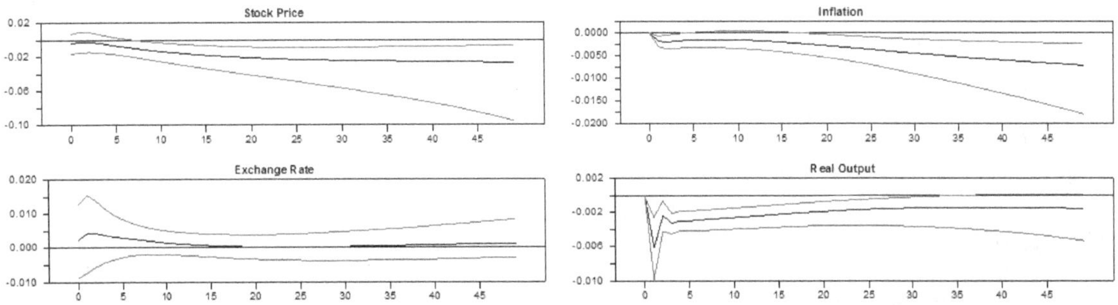

Figure 6. *Impulse Responses to Monetary policy Shocks for Fiscal Exclusion Model.*

5. Summary and Policy Recommendation

Our main conclusion is that the stock market responds positively to monetary policy shock on the short horizon although in medium and long horizon stock price will respond negatively. These delayed responses of stock prices suggest that stock prices adjust sluggishly to a monetary policy shock. From this empirical finding, it seems ineffective for the Bank Indonesia to intervene in the stock market on the short run. The monetary policy seems effective to influence the stock prices only on the Banking and finance sectors as suggested in the study. The change in stock market is not only affected by the monetary policy but also by the liberalization policy in the financial sector such as abolition of foreign exchange control, investment policies consistent with global economic development, free flow of foreign exchange, the development of technology in communications and trading systems, the introduction of innovative financial product, information availability, implementation of international accounting standard and the relaxation of foreign ownership. This generally supports the role of financial system in improving the economy. Continuing this liberalization policy in the future would seem beneficial for the economy as a whole.

In term of interaction between fiscal policy shock and stock market, we find that all sectors respond homogeneously in a negative relationship. From this empirical finding, fiscal policy crowd out private sector activity in market, thus, its effect will be impotent in economy. The ineffectiveness of fiscal policy on stimulating the economy can be due to the fact that most of the government spending (30%-40%) is used to pay the interest and the principal of debt rather than to finance the public investment which take less than 10% of government spending. Hence, it is important for the government to increase its expenditure for the public goods, in particular for the infrastructure sector. This policy perhaps will improve the macroeconomic performance and the investors' confidence and eventually will increase the stock price.

In this study, we also prove that not only both monetary and fiscal policy are able to influence the stock price individually, but also the interaction between two policies is important in explaining stock market performance. Due to different focused objectives between the fiscal and monetary authorities under the inflation targeting framework, the coordination between two authorities are needed. In the absence of coordination, the government may fail to attain the objective of stable and non-inflationary economic growth.

As in other time series modeling, this study also has some limitations. First of all, this study covers the sample period from January 2001 to avoid the effect of 1998 economic crisis. Nevertheless, the sample period still covers the period of global financial crisis of 2008. Then there exists a structural break and one should treat it carefully and we do not take into account the structural break. Secondly, in developing the model of Indonesian stock market, the oil price is the only variable that represents the foreign variable. Many studies have taken into account other foreign variables such as world commodity price, US monetary policy, US output, US inflation and world energy price in constructing the stock market model in particular.

References

Afonso, A., Sousa, R.M., 2011. What are the effects of fiscal policy on asset markets? *Economic Modelling, 28*(4), pp. 1871-1890. doi: http://dx.doi.org/10.1016/j.econmod.2011.03.018

Afonso, A., Sousa, R.M., 2012. The macroeconomic effects of fiscal policy. *Applied Economics, 44*(34), pp. 4439-4454.

Agnello, L., Sousa, R.M., 2012. Fiscal policy and asset prices. *Bulletin of Economic Research.*

Bank Indonesia, 2012. http://www.bi.go.id (Accessed on January 29th , 2013)

BAPEPAM-LK, 2011. *Statistical Database. Indonesian Capital Market and Other Financial Institution Supervisory Agency* (BAPEPAM-LK), Indonesian Stock Exchange, http://www.idx.co.id (Accessed on January 29th , 2013)

BPS, 2012. *Statistical Database. Indonesian Statistics Bureau or Badan Pusat Statistik* (BPS). http://www.bps.go.id (Accessed on January 5th , 2013)

Binswanger, M., 2000. Stock market booms and real economic activity: Is this time different? *International Review of Economics & Finance, 9*(4), pp. 387-415.

Binswanger, M., 2001. Does the stock market still lead real activity?—an investigation for the g-7 countries. *Financial Markets and Portfolio Management, 15*(1), pp. 15-29.

Binswanger, M., 2004. How important are fundamentals?—evidence from a structural var model for the stock markets in the US, Japan and Europe. *Journal of International Financial Markets, Institutions and Money, 14*(2), pp. 185-201.

Bernanke, B.S., Kuttner, K.N., 2005. What explains the stock market's reaction to federal reserve policy? *The Journal of Finance, 60*(3), pp. 1221-1257.

Bouakez, H., Essid, B.O., Normandin, M., 2010. Stock returns and monetary policy: Are there any ties? *Cahier de recherche/Working Paper, 10*, pp. 26.

Bjørnland, H.C., Leitemo, K., 2009. Identifying the interdependence between us monetary policy and the stock market. *Journal of Monetary Economics, 56*(2), pp. 275-282.

Chatziantoniou I., Duffy D., Filis G., 2013. Stock market response to monetary and fiscal policy shocks: Multi-country evidence. *Economic Modelling*, 30(0), pp. 754-769. doi: http://dx.doi.org/10.1016/j.econmod.2012.10.005

Cheng, L., Jin, Y., 2013. Asset prices, monetary policy, and aggregate fluctuations: An empirical investigation. *Economics Letters, 119*(1), pp. 24-27.

Ioannidis, C., Kontonikas, A., 2008. The impact of monetary policy on stock prices. *Journal of Policy Modeling, 30*(1), pp. 33-53.

Darrat, A.F., 1990. Stock returns, money, and fiscal deficits. *Journal of Financial and Quantitative Analysis, 25*(03), pp. 387-398.

DGDMTD, 2012. *Statistical Database. Directorate General of Debt Management of Treasury Department.* http://www.djpu.kemenkeu.go.id (Accessed on February 5th , 2013)

Doan TA, 1992. RATS User's manual version 4. Estima. USA

Dungey, M., Fry, R., 2009. The identification of fiscal and monetary policy in a structural var. *Economic Modelling, 26*(6), pp. 1147-1160.

Enders, W., 1995. *Applied Econometric time series: Wiley series in probability and mathematical statistics*, John Wiley & Sons.

Eviews User Guide, 2007. Quantitative Micro Software, CA.

Gale, W, Orszag P.R., 2003. Economic effects of sustained budget deficits. *National Tax Journal*, 56(3).

Handoyo, R.D., Jusoh, M., Zaidi, M.A.S., 2014. Oil Price, Monetary and Fiscal Policy: Indonesia Evidence. *Proceeding - Kuala Lampur International Business, Economics and Law Conference*, Vol. 3, November 29-30, 2014, Kuala Lampur, Malaysia

Hermawan, D., Munro, A., 2008. Monetary-fiscal interaction in indonesia. *Journal on Bank for International Settlements, 272.*

Ioannidis, C., Kontonikas, A., 2008. The impact of monetary policy on stock prices. *Journal of Policy Modeling, 30*(1), pp. 33-53.

Jansen, D.W., Li, Q., Wang, Z., Yang, J. 2008. Fiscal policy and asset markets: A semiparametric analysis. *Journal of Econometrics, 147*(1), pp. 141-150.

Kim, S., Roubini, N., 2000. Exchange rate anomalies in the industrial countries: A solution with a structural VAR approach. *Journal of Monetary Economics, 45*(3), pp. 561-586.

Laopodis, N.T., 2009. Fiscal policy and stock market efficiency: Evidence for the united states. *The quarterly Review of Economics and finance, 49*(2), pp. 633-650.

Laeven, L, Tong, H., 2012. US monetary shocks and global stock prices. *Journal of Financial Intermediation*, pp. 530-547

Maćkowiak, B., 2006. What does the Bank of Japan do to East Asia? *Journal of International Economics*, 70(1), pp. 253-270.

Perotti, R., 2005. Estimating the effects of fiscal policy in OECD countries. Bocconi University, *IGIER Working Paper*. No. 276.

Piroli, G., Ciaian, P., Kancs, d.A., 2012. Land use change impacts of biofuels: Near-var evidence from the us. *Ecological Economics, 84*(0), pp. 98-109. doi: http://dx.doi.org/10.1016/j.ecolecon.2012.09.007

Pirovano, M. (2012). Monetary policy and stock prices in small open economies: Empirical evidence for the new eu member states. *Economic System.*,36(3), pp. 372-390

Praptiningsih, M., 2013. The Effect of Monetary Policy On MacroEconomic Stability And Stock Market: Evidence From Indonesia. *AU Journal of Management*, 9(1), pp. 13-22.

Sims, C.A., Zha, T., 1998. Bayesian methods for dynamic multivariate models. *International Economic Review, 39*(4), pp. 949-968. doi: 10.2307/2527347

Sims, C.A., Zha, T., 1999. Error bands for impulse responses. *Econometrica, 67*(5), pp. 1113-1155.

Sims, C.A., Zha, T,. 2006. Does monetary policy generate recessions? *Macroeconomic Dynamics, 10*(02), pp. 231-272.

Surjaningsih, Utari, Trisnanto, 2012. The Impact of Fiscal Policy on the Output and Inflation. *Bulletin of Monetary Economics and Banking*, 14(4), pp. 367-396.

Thorbecke, W., 1997. On stock market returns and monetary policy. *The Journal of Finance*, 52(2), pp. 635-654.

Waggoner, D.F., Zha, T., 2003. A Gibbs sampler for structural vector autoregressions. *Journal of Economic Dynamics and Control*, 28(2), pp. 349-366.

World Bank, 2012. *Statistical Database*. http:// www.indexmundi.com (Accessed on March 5th, 2013)

Zaidi, M.A.S., Fisher, L.A., 2010. Monetary Policy and Foreign Shocks: A SVAR Analysis for Malaysia. *Korean and The World Economy*, 11(3), pp.527-550.

Zaidi, M.S.A., Kariem Z.A., Azman-Saini, 2011. Relative price effects of monetary policy shock in Malaysia. *MPRA Paper* No. 38768, posted 13. May 2012 / 06:58. Online at http://mpra.ub.uni-muenchen.de/38768/

Zaidi, M.S.A., Karim, Z.A., 2012. Relative Importance of Singapore, US and Japanese Shocks on Malaysian Economy: An SVAR with Sign Restriction Analysis. *Paper presented at the Persidangan Kebangsaan Ekonomi Malaysia VII (PERKEM VII)*, Malaysia.

19

Exchange Rate Volatility and Investment: A Panel Data Cointegration Approach

Ibrahima Amadou DIALLO*

University of Auvergne,
Centre d'Études et de Recherches sur le Développement International (CERDI), France

This paper examines the link between real exchange rate volatility and domestic investment by using panel data cointegration techniques. We study the empirical connection between real effective exchange rate volatility and investment for 51 developing countries (23 low-income and 28 middle-income countries). The theoretical relationship between investment and real exchange rate volatility predicts that the effects of exchange rate uncertainty on profits are ambiguous. The empirical results illustrate that real effective exchange rate volatility has a strong negative impact on investment. This outcome is robust in low income and middle income countries, and by using an alternative measurement of exchange rate volatility.

Keywords: *exchange rate volatility, investment, appreciation, depreciation, panel data cointegration, capacity principle*

1. Introduction

Multiples efforts have been deployed by governments and international organizations to maintain a stable macroeconomic environment in developing countries but, unfortunately,_instability still remains one of their greatest economic problems.

The theoretical link investment-exchange rate volatility has been the subject of many studies. (Campa and Goldberg, 1995) model predicts that the effects of exchange rate uncertainty on profits are ambiguous. Increases in exchange rate augment expected profit if the firm exports more than it imports and lower expected profit in the opposite case. (Goldberg, 1993), using a duality theory, and (Darby et al., 1999) an adapted model of (Dixit and Pindyck, 1994), found the same threshold effects of exchange rate uncertainty on investment.

Empirical investigations of the relation between exchange rate volatility and investment in developing countries use, in general, OLS, Two-Stage Least Squares, Fixed effects, GMM and system GMM. A significant

---

* Corresponding Author:
Ibrahima Amadou Diallo, University of Auvergne, Centre d'Études et de Recherches sur le Développement International (CERDI), 65, bd François Mitterrand, 63000 Clermont-Ferrand, France

negative impact of exchange rate volatility on investment is reported by the major part of the studies (Serven, 1998, Bleaney and Greenaway, 2001, and Serven, 2002). The impact of exchange rate instability on investment is nonlinear. (Serven, 2002) illustrates that the effect is large when, firstly, volatility is high and secondly, when there is large trade openness combined with low financial development. Contrary, in an environment with low openness and high financial development, exchange rate volatility tends to act positively on investment. Furthermore, (Guillaumont et al., 1999) find that "primary" instabilities (climatic, terms of trade and political instabilities) act on Africa growth through the negative effect that "intermediate" instabilities (instability of real exchange rate and instability of the rate of investment) exert on growth.

This paper fits in these researches of the link between investment and real exchange rate volatility. But it distinguishes itself in the following way. We apply panel data cointegration techniques to study the empirical relation between investment and exchange rate volatility for 51 developing countries (23 low-income and 28 middle-income countries presented in Appendix 1, note that countries and time period selection depend on the availability of data). There are some previous studies which employ microeconomic panel data methods (Fixed Effects, GMM, etc.) on annual data with a relatively long period. But given the existence of potential unit roots in variables, these estimations could be seriously affected by spurious regressions effects (See Kao, 1999 for further details on spurious regressions in panel data). This is why we think using panel data cointegration methods is more appropriate. For this study we use the original Program of Pedroni (1999) converted in RATS Procedure by Estima Corporation. Kao and Chiang (2000) have put together a set of GAUSS subroutines called NPT, for studying nonstationary panel data (Available online at: http://www.maxwell.syr.edu/maxpages/faculty/cdkao/working/npt.html). The latest version of Eviews (Eviews 8) also provides many tests on panel data cointegration. I have also introduced a new User-Written Stata command named **"xtdolshm"** which performs Dynamic Ordinary Least Squares for Cointegrated Panel Data with homogeneous covariance structure (Kao and Chiang, 2000).

The application of panel data cointegration techniques has several advantages. Initially, annual data enable us not to lose information contrary to the method of averages over sub-periods. Then, the addition of the cross sectional dimension makes that statistical tests are normally distributed, more powerful and do not depend on the number of regressors in the estimation as in individual time series. Among the panel data cointegration techniques, we utilize (Pedroni, 1999) *Fully Modified Ordinary Least Squares* (FMOLS) estimator which deals with possible autocorrelation and heteroskedasticity of the residuals, takes into account the presence of nuisance parameters, is asymptotically unbiased and, more importantly, deals with potential endogeneity of regressors. The results demonstrates firstly, that exchange rate volatility has a strong negative impact on investment, secondly, the effect of REER volatility is higher in countries which rely heavily on imports. Furthermore, robustness checks shows that this negative impact of REER volatility on investment is stable to the use of an alternative measurement of REER volatility and on subsamples of countries (low-income and middle-income developing countries).

The remaining of the paper is organized as follow: section 2 gives the estimation methods, section 3 presents the data and variables, section 4 provides the results of the study and the last part concludes.

2. Estimation Methods

Since our data base is composed of annually data going from 1975 to 2004, we run panel data unit root tests on all variables. Table 1 shows that among the five unit root tests, there exist at least one which tells us that each variable is non-stationary and I(1).

This outcome led us to apply recent panel data cointegration techniques to estimate a model of the form

$$\frac{I_{it}}{K_{it-1}} = \gamma EV_{it} + \beta' X_{it} + \alpha_i + \varepsilon_{it} \qquad (1)$$

Where $\frac{I_{it}}{K_{it-1}}$ is investment I_{it} over lagged capital stock K_{it-1}, EV_{it} the exchange rate volatility, X_{it} all other explanatory variables, α_i country individual specific effects, and ε_{it} the idiosyncratic error. i specifies countries and t the time. To estimate equation (1), we use the FMOLS *(Fully Modified Ordinary Least Squares)* estimator developed in panel data context by (Pedroni, 1996) and (Phillips and Moon, 1999).

This estimator was initially introduced in time series context by (Phillips and Hansen, 1990). The advantage of the FMOLS estimator over the OLS estimator (which is super-consistent but is asymptotically biased and is function of nuisance parameters; Kao and Chen, 1995, 2000; Pedroni, 1996). is that it deals with possible autocorrelation and heteroskedasticity of the residuals, potential endogeneity of the regressors, takes into account the presence of nuisance parameters and is asymptotically unbiased (A good survey on recent panel data cointegration is provided by Baltagi and Kao, 2000 and Hurlin and Mignon, 2006). Other estimators used for estimations and inferences in panel data cointegration are the DOLS *(Dynamic Ordinary Least Squares)*, (Kao and Chiang, 2000), (Mark and Sul, 1999), (Pedroni, 2001), PMGE *(Pooled Mean Group Estimator)*, (Pesaran et al. 1999), and the vector error-correction representation, (Breitung, 2005), (Mark and Sul, 2003). (Pedroni, 1996) and (Phillips and Moon, 1999) showed that the FMOLS estimator is normally distributed. Analogous results were also obtained by (Kao and Chiang, 2000) for the methods FMOLS and DOLS.

The use of panel data cointegration techniques in estimating equation (1) has several advantages. Initially, annual data enable us not to lose information contrary to the method of averages over sub-periods employed in some previous studies. Then, the additions of the cross sectional dimension makes that statistical tests are normally distributed, more powerful and do not depend on the number of regressors as in individual time series.

To test the presence of cointegration in equation (1), we utilize (Pedroni, 1999) tests. To explain the tests procedure, we rewrite equation (1) in the following manner

$$y_{it} = \alpha_i + \delta_i t + \beta_{1i} x_{1,it} + \beta_{2i} x_{2,it} + \ldots + \beta_{Mi} x_{M,it} + \varepsilon_{it} \quad (2)$$

Where δ_i are time specific effects, $i=1,\ldots,N$, $t=1,\ldots,T$ and $m=1,\ldots,$M. (Pedroni, 1999) compute four within tests and three between tests. If we write the residuals in equation (2) as an *AR(1)* process $\hat{\varepsilon}_{it} = \rho_i \hat{\varepsilon}_{it-1} + u_{it}$ the alternatives hypothesis for the tests are formulated in the following manner

- For within tests, the alternative hypothesis is $H_A : \rho_i = \rho < 1 \;\; \forall i$
- For between tests, the alternative hypothesis is $H_A : \rho_i < 1 \;\; \forall i$

We have seven (4 within and 3 between) tests in (Pedroni, 1999). See that paper for more details.

Table 1. *Panel unit root tests*

Variables	Levin, Lin and Chu t	Breitung t-stat	Im, Pesaran and Shin W-stat	Maddala Wu		Hadri Z-stat
				ADF - Fisher Chi-square	PP - Fisher Chi-square	
Investment, t / Capital stock, t-1	1.2975	0.3458	-1.9590	116.8340	139.6890	9.7625
	(0.9028)	(0.6352)	(0.0251)	(0.1496)	(0.0079	(0.0000)
GDP, t / Capital stock, t-1	3.3161	0.8132	0.4463	93.9174	104.5540	12.0348
	(0.9995)	(0.7919)	(0.6723)	(0.7035)	(0.4114)	(0.0000)
REER volatility 1, t	3.4882	-1.2381	-1.1465	122.8660	3021.0700	6.6479
	(0.9998)	(0.1078)	(0.1258)	(0.0781)	(0.0000)	(0.0000)
Real interest rate, t	-1.5507	-3.5656	-2.9037	94.2369	658.1490	13.4941
	(0.0605)	(0.0002)	(0.0018)	(0.3592)	(0.0000)	(0.0000)
Investment deflator, t / GDP deflator, t	-0.2080	-0.6727	-1.5745	108.5020	188.7280	6.5644
	(0.4176)	(0.2506)	(0.0577)	(0.3112)	(0.0000)	(0.0000)
Long term debt, t / GDP, t	1.6168	-3.0040	2.2875	69.1210	59.2335	9.8184
	(0.9470)	(0.0013)	(0.9889)	(0.9948)	(0.9998)	(0.0000)
ln(1+Inflation), t	1.8531	-2.9731	-2.4724	134.8430	782.8750	8.6758
	(0.9681)	(0.0015)	(0.0067)	(0.0163)	(0.0000)	(0.0000)
REER volatility 1, t × Imports of GS, t	-0.6414	-0.5348	-0.9650	103.9010	1136.6900	6.9685
	(0.2606)	(0.2964)	(0.1673)	(0.4290)	(0.0000)	(0.0000)
Terms of trade, t	2.02646	1.2532	-3.5582	188.3260	211.3420	7.5547
	(0.9786)	(0.8949)	(0.0002)	(0.0000)	(0.0000)	(0.0000)
REER Volatility 2, t	2.5109	-0.5354	-2.7373	133.3530	2501.2300	7.6559
	(0.9940)	(0.2962)	(0.0031)	(0.0202)	(0.0000)	(0.0000)
REER volatility 1, t × Exports of GS, t	0.3174	-1.0508	-0.1375	98.9928	931.1110	8.2079
	(0.6245)	(0.1467)	(0.4453)	(0.5659)	(0.0000)	(0.0000)

Note: The p-values are in parenthesis. All tests include intercepts (fixed effects) and individual trends. For the autocorrelation correction methods, the specified lags are 3 or 4 and Newey-West bandwidth selection using either Barlett, Parzen or Quadratic Spectral kernel depending on the variable and the test type

Source: Author's Calculations

3. Data and Variables

To study the effect of volatility on investment, we utilize annually data from 1975 to 2004 of 51 developing countries (23 low-income and 28 middle-income countries). The choice of the sample is based on the availability of data. The data are from World Development Indicators (WDI) 2006, International Financial Statistics (IFS), April, 2006 and CERDI 2006. The REER is calculated in foreign-currency terms meaning that an increase of the REER indicates an appreciation and, hence a potential loss of competitiveness. A decrease is considered as a depreciation.

After calculating the exchange rate, we compute as in (Serven, 1998; Serven, 2002) and (Bleaney and Greenaway, 2001) real exchange rate volatility using ARCH family methods. We proceed as such because many ARCH family methods can take account asymmetric chocks effects. We employ two ARCH-Family methods: GARCH (Generalized Autoregressive Conditional Heteroskedasticity), (Bollersev, 1986), and GARCH-M (GARCH-in-Mean), (Engle et al., 1987). The former specification implies symmetric effect of innovations while the second assumes asymmetric impact of good and bad news. The two estimated models, for each country of the sample, are

GARCH(1,1)

$$\begin{aligned} \ln(REER_t) - \ln(REER_{t-1}) &= \beta_0 + \varepsilon_t \\ \sigma_t^2 &= \gamma_0 + \gamma_1 \varepsilon_{t-1}^2 + \delta_1 \sigma_{t-1}^2 \end{aligned} \quad (3)$$

GARCH-M(1,1)

$$\begin{aligned} \ln(REER_t) - \ln(REER_{t-1}) &= \beta_0 + \psi\sigma_t^2 + \varepsilon_t \\ \sigma_t^2 &= \gamma_0 + \gamma_1 \varepsilon_{t-1}^2 + \delta_1 \sigma_{t-1}^2 \end{aligned} \quad (4)$$

Where $\varepsilon_t \sim N\left(0,\sigma_t^2\right)$, ε_t^2 is the squared residuals, σ_t^2 the variance of the regression model's disturbances, γ_0 and γ_1 the ARCH parameters, δ_1 the GARCH parameter and ψ the GARCH-M parameter. We compute the exchange rate volatility as the square root of the conditional variance of the regression. In the paper, the GARCH(1,1) measure of exchange rate volatility is referred to as *REER volatility 1, t* and the GARCH-M(1,1) measure as *REER volatility 2, t* (The weights used to generate the REER, from which these two measurements come, are respectively: general trade including oil countries, general trade without oil countries).

As dependent variable, we use the ratio of actual investment over lagged capital stock (computed by the perpetual-inventory method). Formulating investment this way is known as capacity principle, (Chenery, 1952). Other formulations close to this are the capital stock adjustment principle, (Goodwin, 1951) and the flexible accelerator, (Koyck, 1954). Traditional determinants of investment are considered as control variables: GDP over lagged capital stock, real interest rate, user cost of capital (investment deflator over GDP deflator), inflation, long term debt and the terms of trade. Table 2 gives summary statistics on all variables.

***Table 2.** Summary statistics on variables*

Variables	Observations	Mean	Std. Dev.	Min	Max
Investment, t / Capital stock, t-1	1472	0.0725	0.0296	-0.0050	0.1994
GDP, t / Capital stock, t-1	1475	0.3599	0.1928	0.0584	1.6920
Real interest rate, t	1087	0.0767	0.2799	-0.9781	7.8980
Investment deflator, t / GDP deflator, t	1523	1.0586	0.3474	0.1198	3.4958
REER volatility 1, t	1499	0.1323	0.2534	0.0000	6.8452
REER volatility 1, t × Imports of GS, t	1498	0.0437	0.1409	0.0000	4.4626
ln(1+Inflation), t	1530	0.1733	0.3717	-0.2763	4.7749
Long term debt, t / GDP, t	1517	0.6140	0.6023	0.0233	8.2349
Terms of trade, t	1518	1.0853	0.3759	0.3213	6.0800
REER volatility 2, t	1499	0.1213	0.1364	0.0000	2.2887

REER volatility 1, t × Exports of GS, t	1498	0.0338	0.0698	0.0000	2.2272

Source: Author's Calculations

4. Estimation Results

In this section, we describe first the panel data cointegration tests and second present the estimation results.

Table 3 illustrates that among the seven tests of (Pedroni, 1999), there is at least one that shows that we reject the null hypothesis of no cointegration in all 5 equations (See Table 4 for a list of these equations). This allows us to estimate the panel data cointegration relationships.

As mentioned earlier, panel data cointegration estimators, in particular the FMOLS, deal with possible autocorrelation and heteroskedasticity of the residuals, takes into account the presence of nuisance parameters, are asymptotically unbiased and, more importantly, deal with potential endogeneity of the regressors. Table 4 present the results of (Pedroni, 1999) panel data cointegration estimation results.

All five equations illustrates that the real exchange rate volatility is statistically significant and has the expected sign. Regression 1 represents the *capacity principle* model in which we add the real exchange rate volatility. In this model, the REER volatility is negative and marginally significant. The coefficient increases in magnitude and statistical significance when we control for traditional investment determinants, beginning from regression 2. These regressions show that the impact of REER volatility is high. Referring to regression 2, an increase in REER volatility by one standard deviation reduces the ratio of investment to lagged capital stock by an amount approximately equivalent to eight standard deviations. If we take regression 5, the impact become higher because an increase of REER volatility equal to the its interquartile range make the ratio of investment to lagged capital pass from the ninetieth percentile to approximately the tenth percentile, a drop higher than the interquartile range. The absolute value of REER volatility coefficient diminish by more than a half when we introduce long term debt in regression 4, suggesting that the effect of volatility on investment may pass through long term debt. The coefficient of actual GDP over lagged capital stock is positive and highly significant in all regressions. This is in line with (Chenery, 1952) capacity principle which state that an augmentation in capacity usage rise investment. The real interest rate and the user cost of capital have the expected signs and are, generally, statistically significant. Meaning that large costs of capital reduce investment. The other remaining variables have the expected signs and are, generally, statistically significant.

Table 5 presents the results of the interaction of the real exchange rate volatility with the variable imports, in the first place, and with the variable exports, in the second place.

In all four regressions, the REER volatility coefficient is negative and significant at 1 percent level. The interaction of REER volatility with imports of goods and services is negative, statistically significant with a high coefficient in absolute value in all first three equations. This suggests that the effect of REER volatility is higher in countries which rely heavily on imports. This outcome corroborates the theoretical predictions cited in the introduction. In regression 4, the interaction of REER volatility with exports of goods and services has the expected sign. This result implies that, the more an economy exports, the less exchange rate volatility has negative impact on investment. The export threshold for which the marginal impact of REER volatility on investment is nil is 2.54. This value is out of range of exports of goods and services in the sample (The minimum of export of goods and services over GDP is 0.0290 and the maximum 1.2441). Then in our sample, we could consider that the effect of REER volatility on investment is negative in regression 4.

Table 6 gives an estimation using an alternative measurement of REER volatility. It also provides regressions on subsamples of low-income and middle-income countries.

As mentioned, the alternative measurement of REER volatility, the GARCH-M(1,1), takes into account asymmetric effects of innovations. Regression 1 in Table 6 shows that the impact of the GARCH-M(1,1) measurement is significant and very high. This demonstrates that if we take account asymmetric effects, volatility can have a strong negative impact on investment. The coefficients of the REER volatility for regressions on the subsamples of countries are significant and have the expected signs. The absolute value of the coefficient of the REER volatility for low-income countries is larger than that of middle-income countries. Thus the effect of exchange rate volatility on investment is higher in low-income countries than in middle-income countries. This is the case because low income countries are more vulnerable to shocks.

Table 3. *Panel data cointegration tests*

Pedroni Panel Cointegration Tests		(1)	(2)	(3)	(4)	(5)
Panel Cointegration tests	panel v-stat	-0.2949	-2.6656	-2.9809	-3.1164	-3.6536
	panel rho-stat	0.4283	4.1791	4.9366	4.8765	6.5996
	panel pp-stat	-3.1529	-2.1764	-3.9206	-3.0677	-2.9631
	panel adf-stat	-2.4911	2.0490	5.6660	-0.4804	0.3043
Group mean cointegration tests	group rho-stat	2.5166	7.3718	8.1990	8.2804	9.6908
	group pp-stat	-1.9672	-1.6667	-4.2611	-2.9673	-4.6715
	group adf-stat	-1.4405	0.3701	1.9417	0.5910	2.8247

Note: All reported values are distributed N(0,1) under null of no cointegration

Source: Author's Calculations

Table 4. *Panel data cointegration estimation results. Dependent Variable: Investment, t / Capital stock, t-1*

Regressors	(1)	(2)	(3)	(4)	(5)
GDP, t / Capital stock, t-1	0.2361***	0.1391***	0.2217***	0.2194***	0.3585***
	(0.0000)	(0.0000)	(0.0000)	(0.0000)	(0.0000)
Real interest rate, t		-0.0121*	-0.1675	-0.0170***	-0.5345***
		(0.0778)	(0.1575)	(0.0006)	(0.0000)
Investment deflator, t / GDP deflator, t		-0.0506***	-0.0663***	-0.0257***	-0.0611***
		(0.0000)	(0.0000)	(0.0000)	(0.0000)
REER volatility 1, t	-0.0213*	-0.9431***	-0.7822***	-0.3318***	-1.0195***
	(0.0595)	(0.0000)	(0.0000)	(0.0000)	(0.0000)
ln(1+Inflation), t			-0.1615		-0.6314***
			(0.1989)		(0.0000)
Long term debt, t / GDP, t				-0.0987***	
				(0.0000)	
Terms of trade, t					0.0695***
					(0.0000)

Source: Author's Calculations

Note: ***, ** and * significant at 1%, 5% and 10% respectively. P-values in brackets

Table 5. *Exchange rate volatility pass-through. Dependent Variable: Investment, t / Capital stock, t-1*

Regressors	(1)	(2)	(3)	(4)
GDP, t / Capital stock, t-1	0.2459***	0.2929***	0.2933***	0.3043***
	(0.0000)	(0.0000)	(0.0000)	(0.0000)
REER volatility 1, t	-1.4319***	-0.9161***	-1.3506***	-0.5971***
	(0.0016)	(0.0042)	(0.0045)	(0.0049)
Imports of GS, t	0.3553	0.3565***	0.3242***	
	(0.1328)	(0.0013)	(0.0005)	
REER volatility 1, t × Imports of GS, t	-0.1067***	-0.4744***	-0.1905***	
	(0.0033)	(0.0044)	(0.0023)	
Terms of trade, t	0.0254***		0.0128***	
	(0.0000)		(0.0000)	
Investment deflator, t / GDP deflator, t		-0.0525***	-0.0498***	-0.0421***
		(0.0000)	(0.0000)	(0.0000)
ln(1+Inflation), t		0.0073	0.0066	0.0118
		(0.4298)	(0.3045)	(0.1891)
Exports of GS, t				0.0115**
				(0.0220)
REER volatility 1, t × Exports of GS, t				0.2349**
				(0.0117)

Source: Author's Calculations

Note: ***, ** and * significant at 1%, 5% and 10% respectively. P-values in brackets

Table 6. *Estimation results using an alternative measurement of real effective exchange rate volatility and on sub-samples of countries. Dependent Variable: Investment, t / Capital stock, t-1*

	Full sample	Middle-Income Countries	Low-Income Countries
Regressors	(2)	(2)	(5)
GDP, t / Capital stock, t-1	0.4308***	0.3096***	0.4067***
	(0.0000)	(0.0000)	(0.0000)
Real interest rate, t	-0.0119***	-0.0411***	-1.2375***
	(0.0000)	(0.0000)	(0.0000)
Investment deflator, t / GDP deflator, t	-0.0827***	-0.0463***	-0.1172***
	(0.0000)	(0.0000)	(0.0000)
REER volatility 1, t		-0.0489***	-1.8454***
		(0.0040)	(0.0000)
REER volatility 2, t	-7.7435***		
	(0.0000)		
ln(1+Inflation), t			-1.3942***
			(0.0000)
Terms of trade, t			0.0578***
			(0.0000)

Source: Author's Calculations

Note: ***, ** and * significant at 1%, 5% and 10% respectively. P-values in brackets

5. Conclusion

This paper examines the relationship between REER volatility and investment empirically. The theory indicates that exchange rate volatility have nonlinear effects on investment. Using new developments on panel data cointegration techniques, we find that real exchange rate volatility has a strong negative impact of investment. An increase in REER volatility by one standard deviation reduces the ratio of investment to lagged capital stock by an amount approximately equivalent to eight standard deviations. The robustness checks illustrates that this negative impact of REER volatility on investment is stable to the use of an alternative measurement of REER volatility and on subsamples of countries (low-income and high-income countries).

Though the results found were informative, some caveats remain. If data on both public and private investment are available, some regressions on these two variables would allow us to compare the effects of REER between these two variables and domestic investment. Some studies on structural change in the context of panel cointegration could also provide helpful information on the impact of REER volatility on investment.

From economic policy perspectives, the results illustrate that macroeconomic instability, in particular exchange rate volatility could have negative impacts on investment and that efforts made to reduce them might revive investment and productivity.

References

Baltagi, B. H. and Kao C., 2000. Nonstationary Panels, Cointegration in Panels and Dynamic Panels: A Survey, in *Advances in Econometrics 15*. Edited by Baltagi, B., and Kao C., pp.7-51, Elsevier Science.

Bleaney, M. and Greenaway D., 2001. The impact of terms of trade and real exchange rate volatility on investment and growth in Sub-Saharan Africa. *Journal of Development Economics 65*, pp. 491-500.

Bollersev, T., 1986. Generalized autoregressive conditional heteroskedasticity. *Journal of Econometrics 31*, pp. 307-327.

Breitung, J., 2005. A parametric approach to the estimation of cointegrating vectors in panel data. *Econometric Reviews 24*, pp. 151-173.

Campa, J. and Goldberg L. S., 1995. Investment in manufacturing, exchange rates and external exposure. *Journal of International Economics 38*, pp. 297-320.

Chenery, H. B., 1952. Overcapacity and the acceleration principle. *Econometrica* 20, pp. 1-28.

Darby, J., Hallett A. H., Ireland J. and Piscitelli L., 1999. The impact of exchange rate uncertainty on the level of investment. *The Economic Journal 109(454),* pp. C55-C67.

Dixit, A. and Pindyck R., 1994. *Investment under uncertainty*. Princeton University Press, Rinceton, N.J.

Engle, R. F., Lilien D. M. and Robins R. P., 1987. Estimating time varying risk premia in the term structure: the arch-m model. *Econometrica 55*, pp. 391-407.

Goldberg, S. L., 1993. Exchange rates and investment in United States industry. *The Review of Economics and Statistics 75(4),* pp.575-588.

Goodwin, R., 1951. The nonlinear accelerator and the persistence of business cycles. *Econometrica 19*, pp. 1-17.

Guillaumont, P., Guillaumont-Jeanneney S., and Brun J. F, 1999. How instability lowers African growth. *Journal of African Economies 8(1),* pp. 87-107.

Hurlin, C. and Mignon V., 2006. Une Synthèse des Tests de Cointégration sur Données de Panel. *Working Paper from LEO, Université d'Orléans.*

Kao, C. and Chen B., 1995. On the estimation and inference for cointegration in panel data when the cross section and time series dimensions are comparable. *Manuscript, Center for Policy Research, Syracuse University, New York.*

Kao, C. and Chiang M. H, 2000. On the estimation and inference of a cointegrated regression in panel data. *Advances in Econometrics 15.*

Kao, C., 1999. Spurious regression and residual-based tests for cointegration in panel data. *Journal of Econometrics 90*, pp. 1-44.

Koyck, L., 1954. *Distributed lags and Investment Analysis*. North Holland Publishing Company, Amsterdam.

Mark, N. and Sul D., 1999. A computationally simple cointegration vector estimator for panel data. *Manuscript, Ohio State University.*

Mark, N. and Sul D., 2003. Cointegration vector estimation by panel DOLS and long-run money demand. *Oxford Bulletin of Economics and Statistics 65*, pp. 655-680.

Pedroni, P., 1996. Fully modified OLS for heterogeneous panels and the case of purchasing power parity. *Working Paper in Economics Indiana University.*

Pedroni, P., 1999. Critical values for cointegration tests in heterogeneous panels with multiple regressors. *Oxford Bulletin of Economics and Statistics 61*, pp. 653-678.

Pedroni, P., 2001. Purchasing power parity tests in cointegrated panels. *Review of Economics and Statistics 83*, pp. 727-731.

Pesaran, H., Shin Y. and Smith R., 1999. Pooled mean group estimation of dynamic heterogeneous panels. *Journal of the American Statistical Association 94*, pp. 621-634.

Phillips, P. C. B. and Hansen B. E., 1990. Statistical inference in instrumental variables regression with I(1) processes. *Review of Economic Studies 57*, pp. 99-125.

Phillips, P. C. B. and Moon H., 1999. Linear regression limit theory for nonstationary panel data. *Econometrica 67*, pp. 1057-1111.

Serven, L., 1998. Macroeconomic uncertainty and private investment in LDCs: an empirical investigation. *World Bank Policy Research Working Paper 2035.*

Serven, L., 2002. Real exchange rate uncertainty and private investment in developing countries. *World Bank Policy Research Working Paper 2823.*

Appendix

Appendix 1. *List of 51 countries*

Low Income countries			Middle Income countries		
N°	**Word Bank Code**	**Countries**	**N°**	**Word Bank Code**	**Countries**
1	BDI	Burundi	**1**	ARG	Argentina
2	BEN	Benin	**2**	BOL	Bolivia
3	BFA	Burkina Faso	**3**	CHL	Chile
4	BGD	Bangladesh	**4**	CHN	China
5	CIV	Cote d'Ivoire	**5**	COL	Colombia
6	CMR	Cameroon	**6**	CRI	Costa Rica
7	COG	Congo, Rep.	**7**	DOM	Dominican Republic
8	GHA	Ghana	**8**	DZA	Algeria
9	GMB	Gambia, The	**9**	ECU	Ecuador
10	GNB	Guinea-Bissau	**10**	EGY	Egypt, Arab Rep.
11	IND	India	**11**	GAB	Gabon

12	KEN	Kenya	12	GTM	Guatemala
13	LSO	Lesotho	13	HND	Honduras
14	MDG	Madagascar	14	HUN	Hungary
15	MLI	Mali	15	IDN	Indonesia
16	MRT	Mauritania	16	LKA	Sri Lanka
17	MWI	Malawi	17	MAR	Morocco
18	NIC	Nicaragua	18	MEX	Mexico
19	RWA	Rwanda	19	MYS	Malaysia
20	SEN	Senegal	20	PER	Peru
21	TGO	Togo	21	PHL	Philippines
22	ZMB	Zambia	22	PRY	Paraguay
23	ZWE	Zimbabwe	23	SWZ	Swaziland
			24	THA	Thailand
			25	TTO	Trinidad and Tobago
			26	TUN	Tunisia
			27	URY	Uruguay
			28	VEN	Venezuela, RB

Note: This subdivision is from the Word Development Indicators 2006 classification based on countries 2004 GNI per capita: Low Income Countries (GNI/per capita ≤ US $825); Middle Income Countries (US $826 ≤ GNI per capita ≤ US $10065).

Source: Author's Calculations

20

The Structural Stability of a One-Day Risk Premium in View of the Recent Financial Crisis

Krzysztof DRACHAL*

Warsaw University of Technology

The aim of this research is to analyze a short-term risk premium in Poland between 2005 and 2015. In particular one-day periods are considered. It is studies whether the same GARCH type model can be applied for the whole period, or whether the estimated parameters differ significantly for selected sub-periods.

Keywords: *financial crisis, GARCH, risk premium, structural stability*

1. Introduction

The risk premium is quite an important measure in economic. Both in theory and practice. Not only can it be estimated on different theoretical basis (i.e., one usually considers term "risk premium" for many slightly different concepts like "required market risk premium", "historical market risk premium", "expected market risk premium", "implied market risk premium", etc.).

For example the expected risk premium is a measure of expectations on the future returns over some small risk investments (usually: treasuries). Required risk premium is connected with portfolio diversification. Finally, the implied risk premium is derived from pricing models under the assumption that the real market can be modeled by a certain description.

Here, the historical risk premium is considered. In particular – the difference between returns from stocks over treasury bonds. Measuring the risk premium is important due to various arguments, indeed. For example, it can be used as some kind of indicator of the risk aversion of investors. Moreover, its estimation is used in estimating the cost of capital and asset valuation (Damodaran, 2011).

In this article the risk premium volatility is studied. In particular, with a help of GARCH model. This model uses two equations: one describing the behavior of the risk premium itself, and the second – describing volatility. In other words, the second equation is responsible for the variation of the error term from the first equation. Choosing such a model is reasonable, because it is expected that the risk premium is characterized by volatility clustering, i.e., there are periods of high volatility, then periods of small volatility, and so on.

* Corresponding Author:
Krzysztof Drachal, Warsaw University of Technology, Faculty of Mathematics and Information Science, Poland

2. Literature Review

Quite comprehensive review of various kinds of risk premium is presented by Fernandez (2004). Estimations of various types of risk premium for many countries are presented by Damodaran (2015). Yet, these estimates are based on quite long time horizon. Yet, taking too long time horizon can make a significant bias, as too long investments seem practically useless. Indeed, various methodologies and restrictions lead to very different outcomes in the estimation of a risk premium.

The discussion from the theoretical point of view is still interesting for economists. Among plenty of literature, for example, works of Asness (2000), Duang and Zhang (2013), Mehra and Prescott (1985) and Sfiridis (2012) can be of a first interest.

Chen et al. (1990) discussed the time-variability of a risk premium. Recently, Heryan (2014) discussed the volatility of a risk premium in context of GARCH models. For the recent empirical estimations of a risk premium in Poland, the Reader should consult, for example, papers of Sekuła (2011) and Waszczuk (2013). For example, Sekuła (2011) estimated the risk premium for Poland in the period of 1995 – 2010 to be between 2.9% and 8.6%.

On the other hand, in 1986 Bollerslev proposed a GARCH model. In particular, the variable x_t is said to follow AR(m)-GARCH(p,q) process, if

$$x_t = a_0 + a_1 \cdot x_{t-1} + \ldots + a_m \cdot x_{t-m} + e_t ,$$

where $e_t = u_t \sqrt{h_t}$ and $u_t \sim N(0,1)$ and

$$h_t = c_0 + c_1 \cdot (e_{t-1})^2 + \ldots + c_p \cdot (e_{t-p})^2 + d_1 \cdot h_{t-1} + \ldots + d_q \cdot h_{t-q} .$$

Actually, the above equations describe a particular kind of GARCH-type model, i.e., AR-GARCH. Yet, this type was found were useful in applications. Especially, in the context of Polish capital market (see, for example: Fiszeder, 2009; Fiszeder and Kwiatkowski, 2005; Małecka, 2011).

More information about GARCH family of models can be found in the book of Xekalaki and Degiannakis (2010) and a chapter by Zivot (2009). Later, in this paper, also the methods described by Alexander (2001) and Andersen et al. (2009) will be used.

Yet, as the mentioned researches for Poland indicate AR-GARCH type model is especially useful. Usually, in practice there is no need to consider GARCH(p,q) with p or q higher than 1 (Hansen et al., 2005; Chou, 1988; Matei, 2009).

3. Methodology

The daily data for WIG (Warsaw Stock Exchange all-stocks index) and the yield of 10-year treasury Polish bonds were obtained from Stooq. If wig_t denotes the level of WIG index in points and ytm_t – a 10-year bond rate in percentages, and t stands for time index, then the daily risk premium, x_t, is computed by the following formula:

$$x_t = [(wig_t / wig_{t-1}) - 1] - [(1 + ytm_t)^{1/360} - 1] .$$

It should be noticed that usually a risk premium is considered for much longer time horizon than one day. However, the aim of this research is to analyze such a specific "high-frequency" estimate. (Yet, notice that this has nothing to do with high-frequency data which term is used to describe sec or min frequencies or market microstructure, etc.). It is just emphasized that more frequent than usual time series is considered.

The computations were done in R programme (R Core Team, 2015) in rugarch package (Ghalanos, 2014).

4. Analysis and Results

The graphical analysis suggests that the obtained time series is stationary and there exists the clustering of variance (see Fig. 1). Therefore, it seem reasonable to use the GARCH methodology further.

Yet, as mentioned, for example, by Heryan (2014), it seems interesting also to analyze the structural stability if some sub-periods are considered. The initial data consist of 2336 observations beginning on 28/11/2005 and ending on 27/03/2015. On 27/02/2007 Freddie Mac announced that they will no longer buy the most risky sub-prime mortgages and mortgage-related securities. On 15/09/2008 Lehman Brothers filed for bankruptcy protection. On 23/04/2010 Greece supplied for an initial loan from EU and IMF to cover its financial needs for the remaining part of the year, S&P rated Greece's sovereign debt as "junk" and Euro currency declined. Theses events divide the whole analyzed period into 4 sub-periods.

However, first some descriptive statistics are presented for the whole sample. The minimum daily risk premium for the considered period is -7.97% and the maximum one is 6.25%. The mean (arithmetic) is 0.015%, which corresponds to 5.46% annual rate. The geometric mean is 0.0059%, which corresponds to 2.15% annual rate.

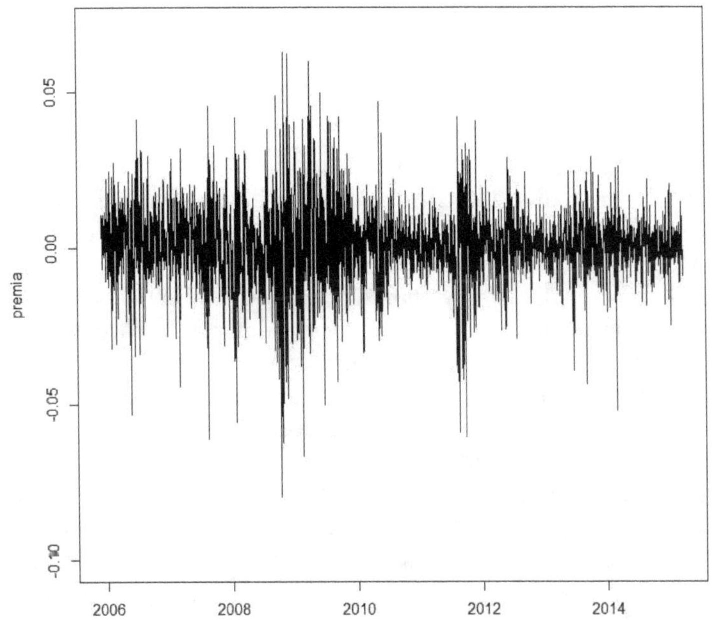

***Figure 1**. Risk premium (x_t)*
Source: Own calculations in R

As stated before, AR(1)-GARCH(1,1) was *a priori* taken as the most suitable type of model for the present research. In particular, it is assumed that

$$x_t = a_0 + a_1 \cdot x_{t-1} + e_t ,$$

where $e_t = u_t \sqrt{h_t}$ and $u_t \sim N(0,1)$ and

$$h_t = c_0 + c_1 \cdot (e_{t-1})^2 + d_1 \cdot h_{t-1} .$$

Table 1. Estimates of AR(1)-GARCH(1,1)

	2005-11-28/ 2015-03-27	**2005-11-28/ 2007-02-27**	**2007-02-27/ 2008-09-15**	**2008-09-15/ 2010-04-23**	**2010-04-23/ 2015-03-27**
Augmented Dickey-Fuller (p-value)	0.01	0.01	0.01	0.01	0.01
ARCH LM (p-value)	0.0000	0.1376	0.0000	0.0000	0.0000
a_0	0.000395 *	0.001668	-0.000723 *	0.000848 *	0.000299 *
a_1	0.067740	0.064227 *	0.038342 *	0.110164	0.058222 *
c_0	0.000001 *	0.000006	0.000015	0.000000 *	0.000002 *
c_1	0.078482	0.051288	0.100333	0.028394	0.078981
d_1	0.914829	0.919600	0.824101	0.966963	0.897321
$c_1 + d_1$	0.993311	0.970888	0.924434	0.995357	0.976302
Ljung-Box (p-value)	0.4689	0.8785	0.8913	0.68690	0.4667
ARCH LM on st. resid. (p-value)	0.6367	0.9175	0.03533	0.3375	0.6125

* not significant at $p = 0.05$

Source: Own calculations in R

The augmented Dickey-Fuller test allows to assume that all considered time series are stationary (see p-values reported in Tab. 1). If not stated otherwise, the significance level is assumed to be 0.05. For every period, except 28/11/2005 – 27/02/2007, the LM test suggest that there exists the ARCH effect (see p-values Tab. 1). Yet, it is reasonable to perform GARCH models, indeed.

Unfortunately, the parameter a_0 is not stable for all sub-periods. Moreover, it is statistically not significant for all periods, except 28/11/2005 – 27/02/2007. Similarly, the parameter a_1 varies significantly with time periods. Moreover, for there sub-periods it is statistically not significant. It suggests that the AR(1) specification should be somehow modified and is not the best one by itself.

On the other hand, the variance equations present better estimations. Although, the parameter c_0 is not significant for three models, it can be assumed to be equal to 0. The parameter c_1 takes (statistically significant) the smallest value for 15/09/2008 – 23/04/2010 sub-period and the highest for 27/02/2007 – 15/09/2008 sub-period. This can be interpreted as if shocks and innovations would have smaller impact on the present volatility than the past volatility. For the parameter d_1 the conclusions are just opposite. The variance equation seems to be quite stable, except the sub-period 27/02/2007 – 23/04/2010. This suggests that the root period of financial crisis is described by different parameters (see Tab. 1).

Yet, all evaluated models are free of autocorrelation of residuals. This is indicated by high p-values of the Ljung-Box test. Also, the LM test for standardized residuals suggests that after the GARCH type estimation there remained no further ARCH effects (see reported p-values in Tab. 1).

For all sub-periods, except 27/02/2007 – 15/09/2008 and 23/04/2010 – 27/03/2015, sign bias tests (Engle and Ng, 1993) do not indicate any problems (not reported here). In particular, positive and negative innovations affect the future volatility in the same way. The practical aspects of these tests in a more general context and other examples are explained, for example, by Kumar (2014) and Seddighi (2012).

From the news impact curve (see Fig. 2) it can be seen that the impact of shocks on volatility is different in certain periods (Pagan and Schwert, 1990; Jondeau et al., 2007). The highest impact is in the beginning of the financial crisis and the smallest – just afterwards.

Finally, it should be clearly emphasized that even the statistical significance of the AR model does not violate the efficient market hypothesis. This hypothesis requires no arbitrage, but some kind of predictability of returns can remain (Timmermann and Granger, 2004; Timmermann, 1993; Woooldridge, 2013). Moreover, the estimation of the parameters of models is done *ex-post*, i.e., basing on the already known observations. Therefore, it is not known if an information obtained in such a way could have been used in the past. Moreover, no transactional costs were incorporated into the estimated models, etc.

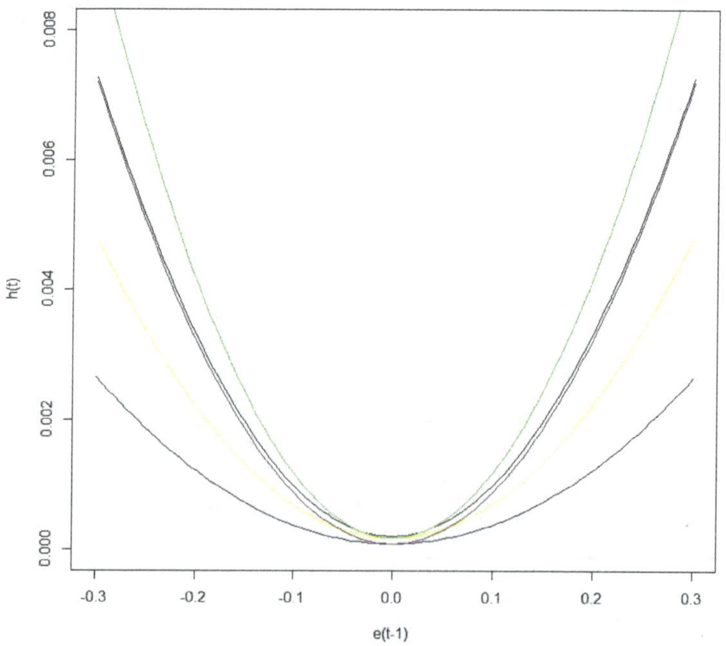

Figure 2*. News impact curves (28/11/2005 - 27/03/2015 black, 28/11/2005 - 27/02/2007 yellow, 27/02/2007 - 15/09/2008 green, 15/09/2008 - 23/04/2010 blue, 23/04/2010 - 27/03/2015 brown)*

Source: Own calculations in R

Of course, also the rolling estimation can be used to determine the discussed structural stability. The first estimation was done after the first 500 observations. Such a number of observations correspond to approximately two calendar years. Then, the re-fitting was done after every 25 new observations, which corresponds to approximately a period a bit longer than a one calendar month. As a result, 74 evaluations of GARCH type models were done. The results are presented on Fig. 3.

It can be observed that in 2009 and 2010 all estimated parameters were very volatile. The parameters a_0 and a_1 are more stable in the period after the occurrence of the recent global financial crisis. However, parameters connected with the variance equation, i.e., c_1 and d_1 are more volatile after the occurrence of the recent global financial crisis. Although, the numerical values seem to follow quite stable paths, the standard deviations of the estimations are very explosive in 2009 and 2010. Also, their confidence intervals significantly widened after the occurrence of the recent global financial crisis (see Fig. 3).

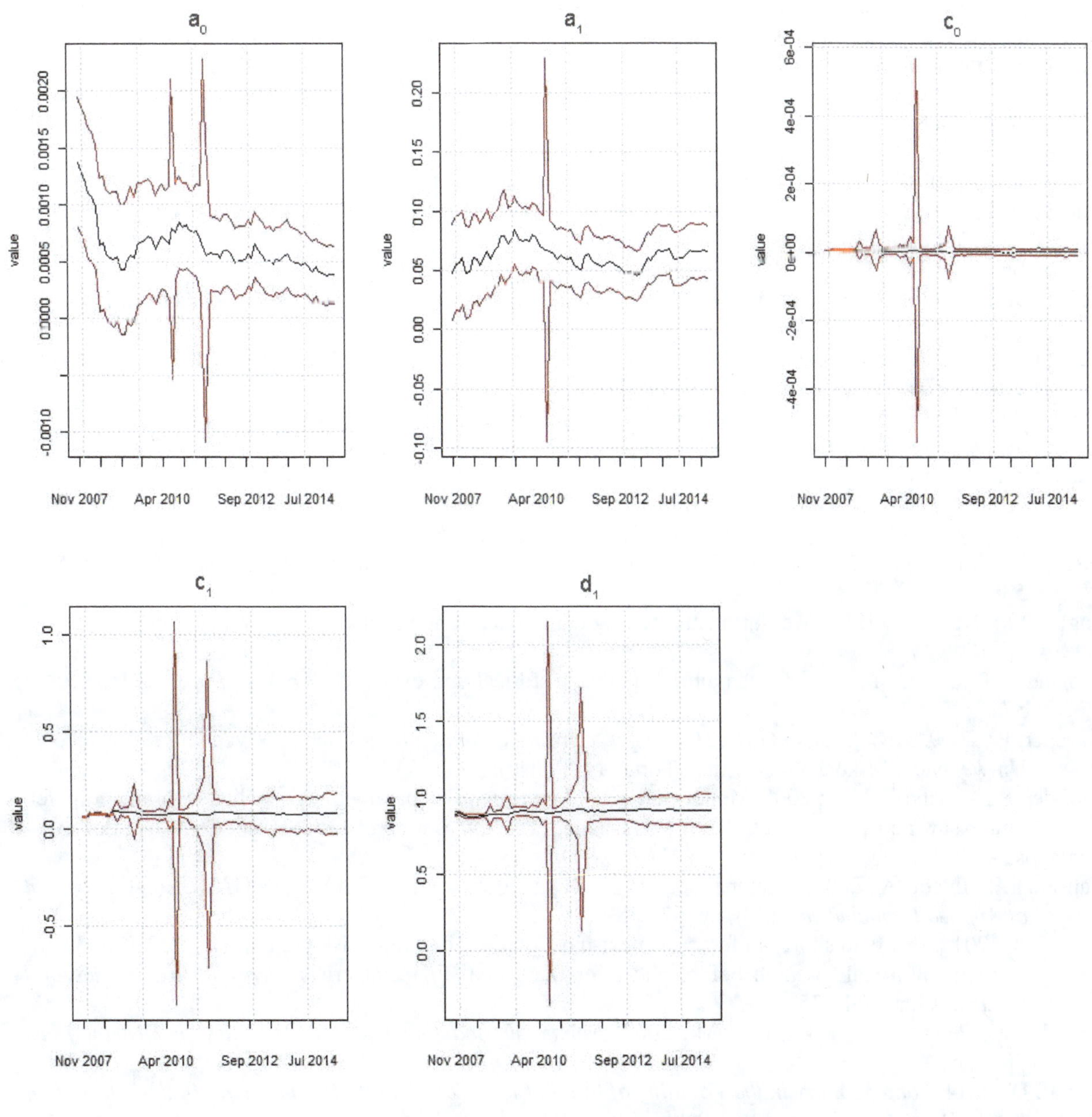

***Figure 3**. Rolling estimations (recursive)*
Source: Own calculations in R

5. Discussion and Conclusion

The daily risk premium was estimated to be between -7.97% and the maximum one is 6.25% in the period of 28/11/2005 – 27/03/2015. The arithmetic mean was estimated to 0.015% and the geometric mean to 0.0059% (daily). It corresponds to values between 2.15% and 5.46% *per annum*. Although, the base period for computing the premium was just one day, the outcomes are quite consistent with some other researches.

The AR(1)-GARCH(1,1) model estimation failed. However, the estimation of the variance equation was quite successful. This seems to be of the interest of some future researches with a help of the GARCH family of models. In case of the structural stability, a significant evidence was found to support the hypothesis that the parameters of the GARCH model vary significantly with time, depending on the sub-period of the recent global financial crisis. This is also with an agreement with some other researches reported in this paper.

In this sense, there is a clear evidence that investors have different attitude towards the risk in different periods of a business cycle. From the news impact curves, it could be observed that the impact of shocks on volatility has different size depending on the time period. On the other hand, the choice of the time horizon for computing the risk premium was quite specific in this paper. Therefore, it seems interesting to lead similar researches, but with different time horizons.

References

Alexander, C., 2001, *Market Models: A Guide to Financial Data Analysis*. Wiley.

Andersen, T.G., Davis, R.A., Kreiss, J.-P., Mikosch, T., 2009, *Handbook of Financial Time Series*, Springer.

Asness, C.S., 2000, Stocks versus bonds: explaining the equity risk premium, *Financial Analysts Journal* 56, pp. 96-113.

Bollerslev, T., 1986, Generalized autoregressive conditional heteroskedasticity, *Journal of Econometrics* 31, pp. 307-327.

Chen, N.-F., Grundy, B., Stambaugh, R.F., 1990, Changing risk, changing risk premiums, and dividend yield effects, *The Journal of Business* 63, pp. 51-70.

Chou, R.Y., 1988, Volatility persistence and stock valuations: Some empirical evidence using GARCH, *Journal of Applied Econometrics* 3, pp. 279-294.

Damodaran, A., 2011, *Risk premiums: Looking backwards and forwards...*, presentation.

Damodaran, A., 2015, Equity risk premiums (ERP): determinants, estimation and implications, *http://papers.ssrn.com/sol3/papers.cfm?abstract_id=2581517*.

Duan, J.-C., Zhang, W., 2013, Forward-looking market risk premium. *Management Science* 60(2), pp. 521-538.

Engle, R.F., Ng, V.K., 1993, Measuring and testing the impact of news on volatility, *Journal of Finance* 48, pp. 1749-1778.

Fernandez, P., 2004, Market risk premium: required, historical and expected, *Working Paper of IESE CIIF* 574.

Fiszeder, P., 2009, *Modele klasy GARCH w empirycznych badaniach finansowych,* Wydawnictwo Naukowe Uniwersytetu Mikołaja Kopernika: Toruń, (in Polish).

Fiszeder, P., Kwiatkowski, J., 2005, Model GARCH-M ze zmiennym parametrem - analiza wybranych spółek i indeksów notowanych na GPW w Warszawie, *Przegląd Statystyczny* 52(3), pp. 73-88, (in Polish).

Ghalanos, A., 2014, *rugarch: univariate GARCH models*.

Hansen, P.R., Lunde, A., 2005, A comparison of volatility models: does anything beat a GARCH(1,1)? *Journal of Applied Econometric* 20(7), pp. 873-889.

Heryan, T., 2014, Errors in short run forecasts next-day volatility of equity risk premium in the UK and U.S. market: Empirical research before and after the global financial crisis, *Procedia Economics and Finance* 14, pp. 243-252.

Jondeau, E., Poon, S.-H., Rockinger, M., 2007, *Financial Modeling Under Non-Gaussian Distributions,* Springer.

Kumar, D., 2014, *Long Memory in the Volatility of Indian Financial Market: An Empirical Analysis Based on Indian Data,* Anchor Academic Publishing.

Małecka, M., 2011, Prognozowanie zmienności indeksów giełdowych przy wykorzystaniu modelu klasy GARCH. *Ekonomista* 6, pp. 843-859, (in Polish).

Matei, M., 2009, Assessing volatility forecasting models: why GARCH models take the lead. *Romanian Journal of Economic Forecasting* 4, pp. 42-65.

Mehra, R., Prescott, E.C., 1985, The equity premium – a puzzle, *Journal of Monetary Economics* 15, pp. 145-

161.

Pagan, A.R., Schwert, G.W., 1990, Alternative models for conditional stock volatility, *Journal of Econometrics* 45, pp. 267-290.

R Core Team, 2015, *R: A Language and Environment for Statistical Computing*, R Foundation for Statistical Computing, Vienna, Austria, http://www.R-project.org

Seddighi, H., 2012, *Introductory Econometrics: A Practical Approach,* Routledge.

Sekuła, P., 2011, Szacunek premii za ryzyko dla Polski – próba empirycznej weryfikacji premii ex post i ex ante, *Acta Universitatis Lodziensis – Folia Oeconomica* 258, pp. 95-108, (in Polish).

Sfiridis, J.M., 2012, Revisiting the market risk premium. *Journal of Financial and Economic Practice* 12(2), pp. 10-22.

Stooq.pl, 2015, http://stooq.pl

Timmermann, A., 1993, How learning in financial markets generates excess volatility and predictability in stock prices, *The Quarterly Journal of Economics* 108, pp. 1135-1145.

Timmermann, A., C.W.J. Granger, 2004, Efficient market hypothesis and forecasting, *International Journal of Forecasting* 20(1), pp. 15-27.

Waszczuk, A., 2013, A risk-based explanation of return patterns – Evidence from the Polish stock market. *Emerging Markets Review* 15, pp. 186-210.

Wooldridge, J., 2013, *Introductory Econometrics: A Modern Approach*, Cengage Learning.

Xekalaki, E., Degiannakis, S. 2010, *ARCH Models for Financial Applications*, Wiley.

Zivot, E., 2009, Practical issues in the analysis of univariate GARCH models. In: (eds.) Andersen, T.G., Davis, R.A., Kreiss, J.-P., Mikosch, T., *Handbook of Financial Times Series*, Springer, pp. 113-155.

21

Human Trafficking and National Morality

William R. DI PIETRO*

Daemen College, Amherst, New York

The paper proposes that national morality is an important variable for explaining national anti-trafficking policy. It uses cross country regression analysis to see whether or not empirically national morality is a determinant of anti-trafficking policy. The findings of the paper are consistent with the notion that improved levels of national morality lead to better national anti-trafficking policy. National morality is found to be statistically relevant for national anti-trafficking policy when controlling for the extent of democracy, the share of the private sector in the economy, and the degree of globalization.

Keywords: *Human Trafficking, Human Trafficking Policy, National Morality*

1. Introduction

Human trafficking can be defined as the forced transportation of human beings against their will for the purpose of exploitation. While presumably, slavery was abolished long ago in most western countries, and, in the U.S.A. a horrendous civil war was fought to decide the issue of slavery, it is thoroughly reprehensible that, in our modern, technologically sophisticated, civilized world, human trafficking flourishes. Gaining some understanding of the causes of human trafficking and of the determinants of effective anti-trafficking policy is essential in order to begin to rationally address this inhumane problem.

This paper hypothesizes that higher levels of national morality can lead to better national anti-trafficking policy. If this proves to be the case, then improving national morality in countries around the world is one promising avenue for reducing human trafficking

Anticipating the results, upgrading national morality in order to better anti-trafficking policy can be undertaken by using two fundamental steps. The first is to make people more moral, and more sensitive to immoral behavior. Even from a strictly secular basis, a country can move in this direction by incorporating moral behavior as significant part of its national identity, and through its educational system. The second step is to make people more aware of the existence, the extent, and the horrific nature of human trafficking, that is to say, to bring it before their eyes, to the forefront of their consciousness. A hidden problem is a problem that is not likely to be addressed. Hiding the ugly consequences of immoral behavior is apt to increase immoral behavior by lowering its cost both in terms of personal guilt and with regard to social opprobrium.

The paper, aiming to see whether anti-trafficking policy depends on national morality, is divided into additional sections. The second section provides an overview of some of the recent literature with regard to anti-trafficking policy. The third section presents a model of anti-trafficking policy. The fourth section

* Corresponding Author:
William R. DiPietro, Daemen College, Amherst, New York, United States of America

discusses the variables that will be included in the empirical analysis. The fifth presents and discusses the results of cross country regressions of anti-trafficking policy on national morality and on other variables. Lastly, the sixth section summarily concludes.

2. Some Relevant Literature

In addition to creating their index of anti-trafficking policy, Cho, Dreher, and Neumayer employ spatial autoregression on a panel consisting of one hundred seventy seven countries for the years 2000 through 2009 with their anti-trafficking index as the dependent variable to see if policy choices in one country are spatially dependent on policy choices made by other countries (Cho, Dreher, and Neumayer 2011). They find that both a contiguity weighted spatial variable and a voting weighted spatial variable are statistically relevant for overall country anti-trafficking policy. What is more, among their control variables, the level of democracy, the control of corruption, and the extent of woman's rights also appear to be favorable forces for anti-trafficking policy, while U.S. aid, and the level of economic development do not appear to matter.

Rudolph and Schneider use a holistic multiple indicators multiple cause's structural equation model to obtain measures of the unobservable variable of interest, human trafficking inflows, for the years 2000 to 2010 (Rudolph and Schneider 2013). For getting their human trafficking inflows estimates and for providing insights into human trafficking, their basic model considers four causes of human trafficking intensity (log of GDP per capita, log of FDI stock, percentage of agriculture to GDP, and language fractionalization), and three indicators of human trafficking intensity (the crime rate, the Cho, Dreher, and Neumayer's policy index, and the number of identified victims).

Cho employs extreme bound analysis on an enormous number of regressions she runs on three different human trafficking data sets consisting of data on one hundred eighty countries for the years are 1995 through 2010 in order to identify robust determinants of outflows and of inflows of human trafficking (Cho 2012). Out of seventy eight push factors that she considers as potential sources of human trafficking outflows, her most robust negatively related push factors are log of per capita income, the percentage of Muslims in the population, the fertility rate, and the size of the food, beverage and tobacco industries. Her two most robust positively related push factors are the size of the information flow, and being a transition economy. From the sixty seven potential pull factors that she investigates as possible reasons for human trafficking inflow into countries, her single most robust negatively related pull factor is the size of the information flow, while her most robust positively related pull factors are the log of per capital income, the log of FDI to GDP, and language fractionalization.

Using averages over the period 2000 to 2010 for the Cho, Dreher, and Neumayer anti-trafficking policy index and its three components, Potrafke undertakes cross country regression analysis to investigate the effect of religion on anti-trafficking policy (Potrafke 2013). He finds that countries with greater Moslem majorities have more lax anti-human trafficking policies, and that the effect is more pronounced the more dictatorial (less democratic) the country. In addition, among the control variables the uses, he discovers that lower corruption and bigger population size are favorable for anti-trafficking policy, but that per capita GDP does not seem to be important.

Contrary to what one might expect on the basis of economic theory that greater scarcity of women relative to males would make women more valuable and thereby give women greater rights, Prakash proposes that, at least for India, given India's particular cultural characteristics, that higher sexual imbalance (more females to males in the population) leads to greater trafficking of women (Prakash 2014). Consistent with his contention, his regressions on a panel of Indian states for the years 1980 through 2011 show that a higher child sex ratio, measured in terms of males per thousand in the population, is associated with increased trafficking between Indian States.

In contrast to many who argue that internal factors, such as poverty, war, and cultural factors, are the major drivers of human trafficking in Africa, Njoh and Ayuk-Etang believe that external factors, such as the replacement of indigenous culture by foreign culture, are the real problem (Njoh and Ayuk-Etang 2012). Using data on forty seven African countries, they run regressions of Cho, Dreher, and Neumauyer's overall anti-trafficking policy index and its three sub-indexes of prevention, prosecution, and protection on the percentage of Christians, the percentage of Moslems, the percentage of African Religion, and literacy rates. Their results show that while greater literacy rates, which they interpret as a marker of greater western influence, has, in line with their beliefs, a statistically significant negative influence on anti-trafficking policy, the percentage of the population with African Religion, contrary to their expectations, also has a statistically significant negative influence.

Hernandez and Rudolph use a gravity style model to try to explain the number of human trafficking victims per year for each of one hundred and twenty source countries to thirteen European host countries for the years 1998 to 2009 (Hernandez and Rudolph 2011). Among their findings are, first, that income differentials between source and host country, the total population of source and destination countries, the amount of origin country migrants in the destination country, and the number of origin country refugees in the destination country are all significantly positively related to trafficking from a source country to a destination country; second, that both geographic distance between origin and source country, and the extent of law and order in the host country are significantly negatively related to human trafficking from a source country to a destination country; and, finally, third, that neither prostitution regulation in the host country, the extent of women's rights in the source country, the homicide rate in the host country, or the homicide rate in the source country are significant drivers of trafficking from a source country to a destination country.

3. Simple Anti-Human Trafficking Policy Model

The theoretical model of anti-human trafficking policy consists of a single equation with an accompanying partial derivative. The equation with its associated partial derivative is as follows.

$$A = f(M, \mathbf{C}) \quad \delta A/\delta M>0$$

In the model's equation, A stands for the extent of national anti-trafficking policy, M represents the level of national morality, and **C** is a set of control variables. The model's lone partial derivative between national anti-trafficking policy and the level of morality is positive. As a whole, the model suggests that national anti-trafficking policy depends on national morality and on a set of control variables, and that, after adjusting for other relevant variables, the relationship between anti-trafficking policy and national morality is positive.

If morality means anything, then at a minimum it provides some constraint on individual undertaking of undesirable behavior. The whole notion of morality is to get people to behave in an ethically appropriate manner, and to avoid behaving in an ethically inappropriate manner. Morality develops and molds individual conscience, which becomes a force in individual decision making. It makes it more costly for an individual to engage in abhorrent behavior because of guilt, and because of perceived or actual negative views of others, and because of potential consequences from the judgment of others.

Besides national morality, three control variables are also considered as possible determinants of anti-trafficking policy.

The first is the extent of democratic government. Greater democracy is expected to have a positive effect on anti-trafficking policy. The reason is that, because democracy gives some political power to the common man, democracy has more concern for the common man, and it allows all groups, even highly marginalized groups, to have some impact on the government and on government policy. That is to say, as a general rule, a more democratic government is more sensitive and more responsive to the people.

The second control variable is the share of the private sector in the economy. It is anticipated that a bigger private sector share in the economy leads to better anti-trafficking policy. Culturally, societies can range all the way from an individualistic orientation, with individuals as individuals being important in and of themselves, to a more collective orientation, in which it is the nation that matters, and individuals are seen solely from the perspective of the nation as a whole. To say it a little differently, at the one extreme, there is no real society and society is simply a collection of individual human beings, and, at the other extreme, only the collective such as the nation matters, with individual identify completely subsumed in the collective identity. Thus, the more privatized an economy, the more capitalistic the economy, the more people define themselves as individuals , and as a consequence, the greater will be the tendency of the society to place emphasis on the individual and on individual rights.

Given the continuing integration of the world economy, the final control variable included is the extent of globalization. The expected sign on this variable is ambiguous. On the one hand, greater integration of a country with the world economy is likely to make a country more sensitive to world pressure, including world pressure in terms of improved human rights. This suggests a positive relationship between anti-trafficking policy and globalization. On the other hand, globalization increases the channels for movement of goods and services, including the trafficking of human beings, between nations. This latter suggests a negative relationship between anti-trafficking policy and globalization

4. Data Sources for Variables

The measure of the strength of anti-trafficking policy is the anti-trafficking policy index developed by Cho, Breher, and Neumayer (Cho, Dreher, and Neumayer 2011). The data is downloaded from the Human Trafficking website (human Trafficking 2014).The index ranges from a low value of three to a high value of fifteen with higher values representing better anti-trafficking policy. It is constructed by rating three component of anti-trafficking policy the prosecution of traffickers, the prevention of trafficking, and the protection of victims, from one to five, and adding the results.

National morality is quantified by using Crabtree's measure of national morality for the first, and, at present, the only year for which it is available, 2013 (Crabtree 2013). Crabtree's national morality measure is fairly comprehensive as it considers a wide variety of factors in its construction. For 2013, the Crabtree index ranges from 27.4 to 90.7. Higher values of the Crabtree index indicate greater national morality.

The measure of democracy is the 2010 democracy index of the economist intelligence unit of economist magazine (The Economist 2010). The democracy index can range from one to ten with higher values signifying greater levels of democracy.

The share of the private sector in the economy in 2010 is computed simply by subtracting the percentage of government spending to GDP for the year 2010 from one hundred percent. The numbers for the percentage of government spending to GDP for 2010 come from the World Bank (World Bank 2014).

Globalization is captured by utilizing the percentage of trade to GDP for the year 2010 with trade defined as exports plus imports. The data for the percentage of trade to GDP also comes from the World Bank.

5. Empirical Results

Table I shows the results of cross country regressions of the Human anti-trafficking policy index on national morality and on other variables.

***Table 1.** Cross Country Regressions of Anti-Trafficking Policy Index on National Morality and Other Variables*

	(1)	(2)	(3)	(4)
CONSTANT	3.612 (4.46) *	4.500 (6.02) *	-.0888 (-.047)	.0745 (.034)
MORALITY	.1071 (8.04) *	.0425 (2.27) **	.0431 (2.41) **	.0572 (3.06) *
DEMOCRACY		.5817 (4.75) *	.5878 (4.74) *	.5319 (4.26) *
PERPRIVATETOGDP			.0566 (2.91) *	.0556 (2.95) *
PERTRADETOGDP				-.0075 (-2.35) **
RSQ	.275	.411	.435	.459
N	173	159	144	143

The table consists of four different regression equations. The first is a simple regression using national morality as the sole explanatory variable. The next three equations cumulatively add a control variable as an additional explanatory variable, first starting with democracy in the second equation, followed by the percentage of the private sector to GDP in equation three, and, finally adding the percentage of trade to GDP in fourth equation.

The construction of the table is as follows. The first row numbers the regressions, the second to last row provides the r-squared values for the regressions, and the last row shows the number of countries (sample observations) for the regressions. The first column provides the potential explanatory variables. Each of the remaining columns shows the results of a single regression. For any variable that enters an equation the estimated coefficient is provided with its individual t-statistic underneath in parenthesis. Variables significant at the one percent level of significance or better in an equation are marked with a single asterisk under their individual t-statistic, while those significant at the five percent level or better are given two asterisks.

The results lend real support to paper's central hypothesis that higher levels of national morality positively influence anti-trafficking policy. National morality, as measured by Crabtree's morality index, is positive in all of the four regressions equations in table I. It is significant at the one percent level of significance or better in two of the four equations, equations one and four, and significant at the five percent level in the other two equations, equations two and three. When used on its own in the first equation, national morality explains over twenty seven percent of the cross country variation in the anti-trafficking index in a sample consisting of one hundred and seventy three countries.

The three control variables, democracy, the percentage share of the private sector in the GDP, and the percentage share of trade to GDP also appear to be relevant for anti-trafficking policy.

In line with theoretical expectations and the findings of past studies, the estimated coefficient on democracy is positive in the three equations that it enters, equations, two, three, and four. In every one of these equations democracy is significant at the one percent level of significance or better.

The percentage share of the private sector in the total economy is positive and significant at the one percent level of significance or better in both equations in which it appears, equations three and four, suggesting, as anticipated, that a more privatized economy with its greater focus on the importance of the individual is more conducive to better anti-trafficking policy.

Finally, in the single equation, equation four, that the measure of globalization, the percentage of trade to GDP, is employed, it is negative and significant at the five percent level of significance or better. This suggests that the negative channel enlargement effect on anti-trafficking policy due to globalization overwhelms any potential positive effect on anti-trafficking policy such as a country becoming more globally sensitive or globally influenced. Thus, while, perhaps, globalization may be favorable for economic development and economic growth, there appears to be a potential negative externality from globalization due to its negative effect on anti-trafficking policy that needs to be taken into consideration when a country considers greater globalization.

6. Conclusion

The cross country analysis of the paper provides support for the notion that greater country morality leads to better national anti-trafficking policy. Whether national morality is used alone in regressions to explain anti-trafficking policy or adjusting for various control variables, national morality proves to be a statistically significant positive determinant of anti-trafficking policy. In addition, the findings of the paper suggest that greater democracy and increased privatization of the economy are favorable for anti-trafficking policy, while greater globalization appears to be detrimental for anti-trafficking policy. Thus, in order to improve national anti-human trafficking policy it would be advisable for a country to work to improve national morality, to try to extend the scope of democracy and democratic institutions, and, culturally, to steer the country away from collective identity and more towards individual identity.

References

Cho, S.Y., 2012. *Modeling for Determinants of Human Trafficking*. Ibero America Institute for Economic research, Working Paper. No 216, [online] Available at: http://www.econstor.eu/bitstream/10419/57315/1/685774678.pdf_ [Accessed on December 18, 2014]

Cho, S. Y., Dreher,A., Neumayer., E., 2011. *The Spread of Anti-trafficking Policies-Evidence from a New Index*. Cege Discussion Paper Series. No. 119, Georg-August-University of Goettingen, Germany. (also IZA discussion paper No. 5559 and CESifo working Paper 3376), [online] Available at: http://ftp.iza.org/dp5559.pdf_[Accessed on December 24, 2014]

Crabtree, V., 2013. *What is the Best Country in the World? An index of Morality, Conscience, and Good Life*. [online] Available at: http://www.vexen.co.uk/countries/best.html [Accessed on July 25, 2014]

Hernandez, D., Rudolp, A., 2011. *Modern Day slavery: what Drives Human trafficking in Europe? Courant Research Centre 'Poverty, Equity and Growth'*, Discussion Paper. No. 97, Georg-August-University of Goettingen, Germany. [online] Available at: http://www2.vwl.wiso.uni-goettingen.de/courant-papers/CRC-PEG_DP_97.pdf_ [Accessed on December 24, 2014]

Human Trafficking - Research and Measurement, 2014. *Human Trafficking, Alfred Weber Institute, University of Heidelberg*. [online] Available at: http://www.human-trafficking-research.org [Accessed December 2014]

Njoh, A. J., Ayuk-Etang, E., 2012. Combating Forced Labour and Human Trafficking in Africa: The Role of Endogenous and Exogenous Forces. *African Review of Economics and Finance*, 4(1), pp. 30-52.

[online] Available at: http://www.google.com/url?sa=t&rct=j&q=&esrc=s&source=web&cd=1&ved=0CCAQFjAA&url=http%3A%2F%2Fwww.ajol.info%2Findex.php%2Faref%2Farticle%2Fdownload%2F87231%2F76963&ei=rbiiVPOpK8qANtSbgrAO&usg=AFQjCNEg_31inXbJVgDi3xJz3-ZTHHtqrQ&bvm=bv.82001339,d.eXY [Accessed on December 20, 2014]

Portrafke, N., 2013. *Policies against Human Trafficking: The Role of Religion and Political Institutions*, CESifo working Paper series, No. 4278. [online] Available at: http://econpapers.repec.org/paper/cesceswps/_5f4278.htm [Accessed on December 24, 2014]

Prakash, N., Vadlamannati, K.C., 2014. *Girls for Sale? Child Sex Ratio and Girls trafficking in India.* [online] Available at: http://www.uni-heidelberg.de/md/awi/humantrafficking/prakash__vadlamannati_2014__girls_for_sale-child_sex_ratio_and_girls_trafficking_in_india.pdf [Accessed on December 24, 2014]

Rudolph, A., Schneider, F., 2013. *International Human Trafficking: Measuring Clandestinity by the Structural Equation Approach.* IZA discussion paper. No 7867. [online] Available at: http://ftp.iza.org/dp7867.pdf [Accessed on December 24, 2014]

The Economist, 2010. *Economist Intelligence Unit, Democracy Index 2010*, [online] Available at: http://graphics.eiu.com/PDF/Democracy_Index_2010_web.pdf [Accessed on August 21, 2014]

World Bank, 2014. *World Development Indicators*, [online] Available at: http://databank.worldbank.org/data/views/variableSelection/selectvariables.aspx?source=world-development-indicators [Accessed on May 20, 2014]

22

Is the Development of WIG Index Determined by Certain Macroeconomic and Financial Factors?

Krzysztof DRACHAL*

University of Warsaw, Poland

The aim of this paper is to present an analysis whether certain financial ratios can have a significant impact on the development of a stock exchange index. In particular the benchmark stock exchange index is considered, as well as, the selected ratios are considered as the average ones for the whole economy. Quarterly data between 2005 and 2015 were analyzed for the Warsaw Stock Exchange (Poland).

Keywords: *efficient market hypothesis, financial ratios, ratio analysis, stock exchange*

1. Introduction

The ratio analysis is an important tool for a potential investor on the market. It helps to determine the evaluation of a company based on objective criteria. Moreover, it allows to compare a selected company with other ones from the similar market sector. As a result, a company can be valued in comparison to its competitors. Actually, it can happen that the data from financial reports of various companies cannot be compared with each other, but in general there are certain commonly accepted rules and guides to assess a business organization. For example, Micherda (2005) stated that a company has to obtain a relatively high profitability in order to survive on the market. This is however not a sufficient condition. Moreover, Mayo (2008) stated that investors on any stock market usually make choices based on technical analysis and (or) fundamental analysis.

Indeed, according to Bauman (1996) and Penman (1992) the most important task for an analysts is to derive the information on the potential future earnings of a company from the already available financial statements. In other words, the aim of the fundamental analysis is to use the core accounting data available into a reliable prediction on the company's value.

Herein, it will be checked whether the development of WIG index (a benchmark index on the Warsaw Stock Exchange) can be determined by certain macroeconomic and financial factors within a linear regression framework.

* Corresponding Author:
Krzysztof Drachal, Faculty of Economic Sciences, University of Warsaw, Poland

2. Literature Review

Within the above presented context, it can be expected that investors make their decision based on the profitability of companies. Narrowing the considerations to the companies listed on a stock exchange, companies with good financial ratios should be more attractive to investors. And, vice versa, if a company has poor financial ratios, it should be not interesting for the majority of investors. This conclusion assumes that investors are risk averse. In other words, there can always be an investor who would rather buy poorly performing stocks, because they are currently cheap, but he or she expects that if in the future the financial performance will be better, then the price of the stocks will go higher. This is connected with extraordinary risk, because if a company has already poor financial situation it is already connected with higher probability of bankruptcy than in the case of a well financially performing company.

As a result, one can expect that if a company announces good financial information, then its stock prices are going higher, and vice versa. If a company announces bad financial information, then its stock prices are going down. Such a behavior can be also extrapolated on the whole market. In other words, it can be expected that if financial ratios are on average good for the whole market, than a certain benchmark measure of this market indicates this situation. If the financial situation reflected by poor financial ratios on average is bad, than it should also be reflected by decrease of a benchmark index.

The above hypothesis is however connected with certain very important assumptions. First of all, it is assumed that the market reaction through stock prices happens after the announcement of financial statements. In other words, the financial ratios cannot be know before the publication of a financial statement. Secondly, that the financial fundamental information plays a role significant enough to impact stock prices. The first assumption is quite important and significant. If one could somehow forecast future stock prices, based on previous data, then the semi-strong market efficiency hypothesis would not be true (Fama, 1970). Although such a hypothesis is a classical topic already, it is still highly disputable whether markets are efficient or not (Dimson and Mussavian, 1998; Constantinides et al., 2003). In other words, if the market is efficient, then the prices always reflect all the available information.

It has to be emphasized the efficient market hypothesis is based on certain assumptions about the underlying market structure. For example, Fama (1970) assumed that there are no transaction costs and the method of valuing the impact of a new information available on the prices are the same for every market player. These assumptions are hardly met in practice. Therefore, sometimes it is also assumed that there are a lot of market players, the products are homogeneous (i.e., roughly the same), the market is organized (for example, there is a supervised stock exchange, regulated by law, supervised by a certain commission, etc.), and the information arrives on the market in a random way (Dimson and Mussavian, 1998; Constantinides et al., 2003).

Usually, the market efficiency is discussed in a three stage classification. In particular, it is said that the market is weakly efficient in no market player can gain abnormal returns from the market by a strategy based on historical data. This should be due to the fact that such historical information is already reflected in the current prices. The semi strong efficiency is understood as the fact that no market player can obtain abnormal gains by using all publicly available sources of information. This is assumed because of the fact that such information are already reflected in the current prices. The third – strong efficiency – assumes that no market player can gain extraordinary returns, even if he or she would use all the information, both publicly available and hidden. This is assumed due to the fact that such information should be already reflected in the current prices (Dimson and Mussavian, 1998; Constantinides et al., 2003).

Testing the strong version of market efficiency is very hard. It is questionable how the hidden information can be measured. However, in case of semi strong efficiency hypothesis usually most important financial ratios are included in the analyzed model. Bulski and Gorski (2012) have, for example, indicated the following ratios: market capitalization, price to earnings ratio, price to book value, dividend yield, and beta risk factor.

The problem of the relevance of financial information has been discussed in literature. Usually, such considerations have been done within the context of a simple linear regression model. The independent variables have been taken as several financial ratios and the dependent variable is then the stock price. Often, instead of stock prices and financial ratios for several stocks a benchmark reflecting various stocks is taken and certain average of financial ratios.

It should also be mentioned that financial and non-financial organizations prepare in Poland financial statements ruled by different law regulations. In particular, banks are financial institutions, whose balance sheets and income statements differ slightly from those of non-financial institutions. As a result, their ratio analysis looks a bit different.

The most exploited by researchers are of course the developed markets. Among them a lot of studies have been taken on the U.S. market. For example, Baruch and Thiagarajan (1993) considered in their model several fundamental factors like: the change of inventories, the change of accounts receivables, the change of sales, the change of industry capital expenditures on research and development, the change of gross margin, the change of sales and administrative expenses, the change of gross receivables, the change of doubtful receivables, the effective tax rate, the change in order backlog, the change of labor efficiency, LIFO earnings and audit qualification. Currently, their research can seem to be a bit old. Indeed, they have examined selected financial reports from the period beginning on 1974 and ending on 1990.

Baruch and Thiagarajan (1993) constructed year by year cross sectional regressions. For each year they have taken between 140 and 180 sample consisting of companies' financial reports and their stock prices. They have not found a one significant behavior patterns. Certain variables impacted stock prices in some years positively, whereas in some year the impact was opposite. Also, the predictive power of the constructed models have been quite marginal. It was between 4% and 21% measured by R squared. Nevertheless, they have found that certain variables included in their models are statistically significant.

If the developed markets can be more efficient, the emerging ones can be less efficient in the context of accounting information. This can be the result of the fact that beginning investors are not used to developed analysis. If this statement is just a hypothesis, it is commonly accepted among researchers that emerging markets needs a careful attention and findings from the developed markets cannot be moved without any consideration on emerging markets. Indeed, they can be even more likely than developed countries to be influenced by local information (Harvey, 1995).

More recent analysis has been provided by Jung et al. (2015). They have examined a sample beginning on 2002 and ending on 2009. They have found that the analysis interest (i.e., the onset of analysts not covered in a company, but just participating in its earnings conference call) is positively correlated with future stock prices. Abarbanell and Bushee (1998) examined a sample of data beginning on 1974 and ending on 1993. For each year they have examined a sample of a size between 469 and 785 observations. As a result, they have found that the fundamental analysis can lead to abnormal returns from the market. In other words, the market efficiency was indicated no to be fulfilled. The significant determinants of stock returns were found to be inventories levels, accounts receivables, gross margin, selling expenses, capital expenditures, effective tax rate, inventory methods, audit qualifications, labor sales productivity. With these information they have claimed that the abnormal return of 13.2% yearly can be generated.

Bartram and Grinblatt (2015) have claimed that fundamental analysis can lead to abnormal returns of 9% per year. They have examined a sample beginning on 1977 and ending on 2012. They have not constructed simple linear models with independent variables as financial ratios, but rather estimated more developed financial models. Moreover, they focused on estimation of a fair value and mispricing of stocks.

Piotroski (2002) has constructed a specific factor score for a company. This score is based on return on assets, cash flow from operations, net income before extraordinary items depreciated by cash flow from operations, gross margin ratio, asset turnover ratio, leverage ratio, current ratio, and the binary variable indication issuing common equity. He has analyzed the period beginning on 1976 and ending on 1996. The finally selected sample consisted of over 14 000 observations (companies) from the American market. Piotroski (2002) has shown that by using certain strategies based on these financial information an investor can generate between 7.5% and 23% annual return.

Omran (2004) have examined a quite exotic emerging market, i.e., Egyptian one. For such a market it is important to notice that except common risks, a political risk is extremely high. Such effect can significantly influence its stock market. Omran (2004) have studies 46 Egyptian companies beginning the sample on 1996 and ending on 2000. Initially the sample consisted of more companies, but due to through check certain companies were excluded from the sample. The reliability of data is quite high as they were obtained from the Egyptian Capital Market Authority. Omran (2004) initially included as potential independent variables return on sales, return on assets, return on equity, earnings per share, assets turnover, inventory turnover, current ratio, quick ratio, debt ratio and inverse time interest earnings. By the stepwise backward regression variables were excluded from the model until all included variables become statistically significant at 5% significance level. As a result, only return on equity remained in the model as the independent variable. Omran (2004) considered two models: buy and hold strategy and cumulative one. However, this has not impacted the number of significant independent variables. The first model had quite poor predictive power – R-squared was only 14% for the buy and hold model and 6% for the cumulative strategy.

Lopes and Galdi (2007) have examined selected stock from Sao Paulo Stock Exchange (Brasil) between 1994 and 2004. They have found that returns between 6% and 27% can be generated if an investor would stick to fundamental analysis. As a potential stock returns determinants they have selected book value of equity, market value of equity, return on assets, current year change in cash and cash equivalents, net income, changes on non cash current assets decreased by current liabilities (except short term debt) and depreciation, changes in current ratio, changes in gross debt, changes in sales and changes in gross margin.

Martani et al. (2009) have analyzed the Indonesian Stock Exchange between 2003 and 2006. They have constructed simple linear regression models with independent variables as net profit margin, return on equity, current ratio, debt to equity ratio, total assets turnover, price to book value, total assets and cash flow from operations dividend by sales. For each year they have analyzed 195 companies. The obtained R squared for models were around 40%. It have been found that net profit margin, return on equity, sales divided by total assets, price to book value and total assets are statistically significant determinants of returns from stocks. Finding that total assets is significant determinant is an interesting result. It means that the returns from stocks depends on whether the firm is small or big (i.e., the size effect exists). Such an effect has been first observed by Banz (1981).

In case of the Polish stock market, there have also been some researches in the considered direction. For example, Czekaj et al. (2001) have examined the period beginning on 1994 and ending on 2000. In this time, Poland was not a member of the European Union and the country was during the economy transition. Indeed, the Warsaw Stock Exchange has been set up in 1991, and initially only five share were quoted. It is therefore not surprising that Czekaj et al. (2001) have found that although the market was usually efficient in this period, there used to be significant periods of notable market inefficiency. Indeed, Papla (2003) have examined also the very beginning period, dating back to 1991. He has found that the big stocks with high turnover and high market share behaved in an efficient way. On the other hand, small companies could have been assumed as inefficient ones. Drachal (2011) considered a small sample of biggest companies listed on the Warsaw Stock Exchange (from the WIG 20 list), and found no significant linear correlations between changes in total assets, net profit, sales, ROS, ROE and ROA with the change in a share price for the quarterly data from 2001 – 2010.

3. Methodology and Data

Basing on the above literature review and data availability, five financial information indicators have been selected for the purpose of this research. Additionally, five macroeconomic indicators have also been included. The following notation has been used herein:

- WIG – level in points of the benchmark index WIG,
- GM – average gross margin of firms (in percentages),
- ROS – average return on sales for firms (in percentages),
- CR – average current ratio for firms,
- PN – (in percentages) the number of firms generating positive net income divided by the number of all registered firms,
- SALES – total revenues of all firms (in mln PLNs),
- R – average interest rate for short term deposits (in percentages),
- INF – inflation (in percentages),
- GDP – gross domestic product in current prices (in mln PLNs),
- U – unemployment rate (in percentages),
- CA – current accounts divided by gross domestic product (in percentages).

The selection of the variables has been based on data availability and reliability. Indeed, all time series (except WIG) have been obtained from the Central Statistical Office of Poland (CSO, 2015). The WIG time series has been taken from Stooq (2015). Quarterly data have been used. The analysis has covered the period beginning on the first quarter of 2005 and ending on the second quarter of 2015.

The computation has been done in a free econometric software package (Gretl). A standard statistical and econometric methods have been applied (Brooks, 2008).

From Figure 1 it can be seen that when stock price are high, gross margin is also high, and vice versa. It can also be seen (although it seems less clear) that higher deposit rate occurs when stock prices are high and vice versa. It seems like deposit rate follows stock prices (the reaction is delayed in time). However, the selected time series presented on Figure 1 are not stationary. In other words, they do not look like scattered randomly around some flat axis, but indicate some trend patterns.

In order to fulfill the assumptions of the linear regression models the analyzed time series have been transformed. The subscript t denotes time indexing. For example, WIG_t represents the value of the variable WIG in time t.

In particular, the following linear equation has been at first estimated and analyzed:

$$\Delta WIG = \alpha_0 + \alpha_1 * \Delta GM + \alpha_2 * \Delta ROS + \alpha_3 * \Delta CR + \alpha_4 * \Delta PN + \alpha_5 * \Delta SALES + \alpha_6 * \Delta R + \alpha_7 * \Delta INF + \alpha_8 * \Delta GDP + \alpha_9 * \Delta U + \alpha_{10} * \Delta CA, \quad (1)$$

where

$\Delta WIG = \ln (WIG_t / WIG_{t-1})$,
$\Delta GM = GM_t - GM_{t-1}$,
$\Delta ROS = ROS_t - ROS_{t-1}$,
$\Delta CR = CR_t - CR_{t-1}$,
$\Delta PN = PN_t - PN_{t-1}$,
$\Delta SALES = \ln (SALES_t / SALES_{t-1})$,
$\Delta R = R_t - R_{t-1}$,
$\Delta INF = INF_t - INF_{t-1}$,
$\Delta GDP = \ln (GDP_t / GDP_{t-1})$,
$\Delta U = U_t - U_{t-1}$,
$\Delta CA = CA_t - CA_{t-1}$.

***Figure 1**. Selected time series*
Source: Own elaboration in Gretl

***Table 1**. ADF test*

variable	statistics	p-value
ΔWIG	-4.0980	0.0001
ΔGM	-6.2625	0.0000
ΔROS	-6.4058	0.0000
ΔCR	-2.5992	0.0091
ΔPN	-2.5992	0.0091
ΔSALES	-1.4194	0.1454
ΔR	-3.9728	0.0001
ΔINF	-4.7755	0.0000
ΔGDP	-0.8946	0.3288
ΔU	-2.1721	0.0287
ΔCA	-7.4697	0.0000

Source: Own elaboration in Gretl

Such transformations helped to obtain stationary data. The stationarity has been checked at 5% significance level by the ADF test. Lag order for the ADF test has been taken as 9, testing down from maximum lag order has been done with respect to the AIC criterion. The test without constant has been performed. The results have been presented in Table 1. After transformations all-time series (except SALES and GDP) are stationary. However, the KPSS test (p-value = 0.05) has indicated that SALES are stationary at 1% significance level. Also, for GDP (p-value = 0.01) KPSS test indicated that this variable is stationary at 1% significance level. In order to maintain the simplicity of the model no further transformations were made.

The above considerations allow to perform the linear regression for the Equation (1).

4. Results

Unfortunately, the first model estimated is not good. Assuming the 5% significance level, none of the included variables are statistically significant. On the other hand, the obtained model has moderate R squared (58%). Very high R squared would indicate very good predictive power, which could contradict the efficient market hypothesis. Therefore, moderate values seem to be more reasonable. The results of the first estimation are presented in Table 2.

In order to continue the analysis the backward regression has been performed. This method assumes that first all potential independent variables are included in the model. Then, such a model is estimated and it is checked whether all variables (except the constant term) are statistically significant at the given significance level. If yes, the model is further diagnosed. If not – the variable with highest p-value is dropped and such a modified model is estimated. The dropping of variables is performed until a model with all variables statistically significant is found.

Table 2. *First regression estimation*

OLS, using observations 2005:2-2015:2 (T = 41) Dependent variable: ΔWIG

	Coefficient	Std. Error	t-ratio	p-value
α_0	0.0170713	0.0197987	0.8622	0.3954
α_1	0.228099	0.195052	1.1694	0.2514
α_2	−0.0971563	0.212301	−0.4576	0.6505
α_3	1.02741	0.629921	1.6310	0.1133
α_4	0.00665947	0.0123705	0.5383	0.5943
α_5	−0.0622827	0.0970669	−0.6416	0.5260
α_6	−0.0972201	0.109548	−0.8875	0.3819
α_7	−0.0130641	0.0244371	−0.5346	0.5969
α_8	0.198215	0.58456	0.3391	0.7369
α_9	0.0400666	0.0278675	1.4378	0.1609
α_{10}	−0.0149587	0.0111237	−1.3448	0.1888

Mean dependent var	0.016360	**S.D. dependent var**	0.114511
Sum squared resid	0.221464	**S.E. of regression**	0.085919
R-squared	0.577770	**Adjusted R-squared**	0.437026
F(10, 30)	4.105128	**P-value(F)**	0.001261
Log-likelihood	48.85536	**Akaike criterion**	−75.71071
Schwarz criterion	−56.86142	**Hannan-Quinn**	−68.84684
rho	0.327765	**Durbin-Watson**	1.332021

Source: Own elaboration in Gretl

By the stepwise backward regression the model presented in Table 3 has been found. Finally, from ten initial variables only three remained in the model. Only one accounting information has remained in the model, i.e., the gross margin. However, two macroeconomic variables have remained: unemployment rate and current accounts. Herein, 10% significance level has been assumed. But, even at a 5% significance level GM and U are still statistically significant.

The model has moderate R squared, i.e., 51%. It means that only 51% of the variability of ΔWIG can be explained by the variability of the changes of gross margin, unemployment rate and current accounts. Therefore, it cannot be said that this research managed to beat the efficient market hypothesis in case of Poland.

Also, the diagnostic of the final model has been performed. The White's test has slightly indicated the heteroskedasticity of the residuals. However, from the Breusch-Pagan test there is no evidence at 5% significance level of heteroskedasticity. In other words, the variance of the error term of the model is constant with time, as the assumptions of the linear regression model require.

By the Jarque-Bery test there is also no evidence (a very high p-value) that errors are not normally distributed at 5% significance level. Therefore, another assumption of a linear regression is met.

By the Lagrange Multipliers test there is also no evidence of autocorrelation of residuals (p-value higher than 5%) at the 5% significance level. This is in agreement with the linear regression model assumptions.

Finally, the RESET specification test has indicated that the model specification is adequate at the 5% significance level.

The above considerations allow to state that the constructed model is good from the theoretical point of view. In other words, the estimated model has not violated the underlying theoretical assumptions. (Notice also that all the variables are stationary according to the ADF test at 5% significance level.)

Table 3. *Final regression estimation*

OLS, using observations 2005:2-2015:2 (T = 41) Dependent variable: ΔWIG

	Coefficient	Std. Error	t-ratio	p-value	
α_0	0.0305104	0.0136376	2.2372	0.0314	**
α_1	0.162412	0.0290544	5.5899	<0.0001	***
α_9	0.0614518	0.0178973	3.4336	0.0015	***
α_{10}	−0.0181726	0.00939557	−1.9342	0.0608	*

* stands for 10% significance level, ** for 5% and *** for 1%

Mean dependent var	0.016360	**S.D. dependent var**	0.114511
Sum squared resid	0.257773	**S.E. of regression**	0.083468
R-squared	0.508546	**Adjusted R-squared**	0.468698
F(3, 37)	12.76224	**P-value(F)**	7.09e-06
Log-likelihood	45.74308	**Akaike criterion**	−83.48616
Schwarz criterion	−76.63187	**Hannan-Quinn**	−80.99020
rho	0.357111	**Durbin-Watson**	1.263461

White's test for heteroskedasticity - Null hypothesis: heteroskedasticity not present Test statistic: LM = 16.9929 with p-value = P(Chi-square(9) > 16.9929) = 0.0488278	**Test for normality of residual -** Null hypothesis: error is normally distributed Test statistic: Chi-square(2) = 0.83169 with p-value = 0.659783
Breusch-Pagan test for heteroskedasticity - Null hypothesis: heteroskedasticity not present Test statistic: LM = 5.52053 with p-value = P(Chi-square(3) > 5.52053) = 0.137416	**LM test for autocorrelation up to order 4 -** Null hypothesis: no autocorrelation Test statistic: LMF = 2.30751 with p-value = P(F(4,33) > 2.30751) = 0.0787195
RESET test for specification - Null hypothesis: specification is adequate Test statistic: F(2, 35) = 1.46498 with p-value = P(F(2, 35) > 1.46498) = 0.244906	

Source: Own elaboration in Gretl

As a result, the Equation (1) has been modified and estimated to have finally the following form:
ΔWIG = 0.03 + 0.16 * ΔGM + 0.06 * ΔU − 0.02 * ΔCA.

(Scatter plot and correlation matrix are presented in the Appendix.) The obtained estimates are interesting. First of all, the positive constant term indicate that there is a steady trend of increase of stock prices. Secondly, it seems natural that increase in gross margin results in an increase in stock prices, and vice versa. Third, it can be seen that increase in current accounts results in decrease of stock prices. This can be understood, if much of the demand on Polish stocks would be generated by foreign investors. Indeed, the negative current accounts indicate net borrowing by Poland from the rest of the world. The net inflow of foreign capital results then in increase of stock prices. But the forth conclusion seems to be a bit strange and shocking. The increase of unemployment rate results in higher stock prices. This result seems quite unnatural. High unemployment is not a positive sign in economy, therefore in such an economy investors should rather avoid investing their money. However, one can remind that there is a negative relationship between unemployment rate and inflation. Actually, the inflation variable and other interest rates has been dropped from the model. But one can follow the reasoning that if unemployment goes up, it is connected with smaller inflation. This can be connected with general decline in interest rates. This leads to "cheaper" capital, which can be invested on the market. So the demand on stocks can increase, and therefore, their prices.

5. Conclusions

The present research is robust to many factors. For example, it can be questioned whether the chosen ratios as the representatives of the information from the financial statements are proper. Indeed, it has been shown that although in literature there are certain sets of commonly used ratios, different researchers usually consider different ratios. Moreover, because of different habits, laws, policies, etc. the accounting information can slightly differ between various countries. As a result, the relevance of certain financial ratios can vary between countries and stock exchanges. Secondly, the financial ratios were considered for the whole economy - not restricted to stock exchange listed companies (this was done due to data availability).

Also, the behavioral aspect is an important one. In certain countries, investors can be more risk accepting, whereas in others the opposite may be true. On certain stock exchanges the role of investors using fundamental analysis can be higher and on others – smaller. This question can be widened on a following general problem: do the investors behave in a rational way? And finally, what is the quality of the used financial statement data (i.e., the audit quality).

Happily, in case of Poland most of the potential problems are the same as for the developed markets. Indeed, the Warsaw Stock Exchange is the biggest one in the Central and Eastern Europe. The audit standards are high and worldwide accepted. Poland is a member of European Union and perceived as a country with good "economic health". Nevertheless, it must be remembered that the problem of rationality of investors has been questioned and nowadays, it is not a dogma any more. Indeed, the behavioral finance are a dynamically expanding branch of finance in contrast with "homo oeconomicus" assumptions.

Herein, it has been shown that an increase in unemployment rate and/or gross margin leads to higher stock prices, whereas an increase in current account results in stock prices decrease. But the obtained model is characterized by relatively small R squared (indicator of a predictive power). The presented research, therefore, rather failed to show that the development of WIG index is really determined by certain macroeconomic and financial factors. However, such a result can still serve as another argument in favor of the efficiency of the Polish Stock Exchange.

6. References

Abarbanell, J.S. and Bushee, B.J., 1998. Abnormal returns to a fundamental analysis strategy. *The Accounting Review,* 73(1), pp. 19-45.

Banz, R.W., 1981. The relationship between return and market value of common stocks. *Journal of Financial Economics,* 9, pp. 3–18.

Baruch, L. and Thiagarajan, S.R., 1993. Fundamental information analysis. *Journal of Accounting Research,* 31(2), pp. 190-215.

Bartram, S.M. and Grinblatt, M., 2015. Fundamental analysis works. *Social Science Research Network.* [online] Available from: http://papers.ssrn.com/sol3/papers.cfm?abstract_id=2479817. [Accessed: 5th November 2015].

Bauman, M.P., 1996. A review of fundamental analysis research in accounting. *Journal of Accounting Literature,* 15, pp. 1-33.

Bolski, D. and Gorski, M., 2012. Wyniki testow hipotezy polsilnej efektywnosci informacyjnej Gieldy Papierow Wartosciowych w Warszawie w latach 2005-2011. *Problemy Zarzadzania,* 4(39), pp. 141-168. [in Polish]

Brooks, C., 2008. *Introductory Econometric for Finance.* Cambridge: Cambridge University Press.

Constantinides, G. et al. (eds.), 2003. *Handbook of the Economics of Finance: Financial Markets and Asset Pricing*. Amsterdam: Elsevier.

CSO, 2015. Poland macroeconomic indicators. *Central Statistical Office of Poland.* [online] Available from: http://stat.gov.pl/en/poland-macroeconomic-indicators. [Accessed: 5th November 2015].

Czekaj, J., Wos, M. and Zarnowski, J., 2001. *Efektywnosc gieldowego rynku akcji w Polsce z perspektywy dziesieciolecia.* Warszawa: PWN. [in Polish]

Dimson, E. and Mussavian, M., 1998. A brief history of market efficiency. *European Financial Management,* 4(1), pp. 91-103.

Drachal, K., 2011. Analiza korelacji liniowej zyskownosci wybranych spolek gieldowych i cen ich akcji na rynku polskim. *Gospodarka w Praktyce i Teorii*, 21(1), pp. 4-8. [in Polish]

Fama, E., 1970. Efficient capital markets: A review of theory and empirical work. *Journal of Finance,* 25(2), pp. 383-417.

Jung, M.J., Wong, M.H.F. and Zhang, X.F., 2015. Analyst interest as an early indicator of firm fundamental changes and stock returns. *The Accounting Review,* 90(3), pp. 1049-1078.

Harvey, C.R., 1995. Predictable risk and returns in emerging markets. *Review of Financial Studies,* 8(3), pp. 773-816.

Lopes, A.B. and Galdi, F.C., 2007. Financial statement analysis generate abnormal returns under adverse conditions? *Proceedings of Annual Meeting of the American Accounting,* pp. 988-1027.

Martani, D., Mulyono, and Kharirurizka, R., 2009. The effect of financial ratios, firm size, and cash flow from operating activities in the interim report to the stock return. *Chinese Business Review,* 8(6), pp. 44-55.

Mayo, H.B., 2008. *Investments: An Introduction*. Mason OH: Cengage Learning.

Micherda, B., 2005. *Podstawy rachunkowosci.* Warszawa: PWN. [in Polish]

Omran, M., 2004. Linear versus non-linear relationships between financial ratios and stock returns: Empirical evidence from Egyptian firms. *Review of Accounting and Finance,* 3(2), pp. 84-102.

Papla, D., 2003. *Teoria rynku efektywnego i jej zastosowanie na rynku polskim.* Wroclaw: University of Wroclaw. [in Polish]

Penman, S.H., 1992. Return to fundamentals. *Journal of Accounting, Auditing and Finance,* 7, pp. 465-483.

Piotroski, J.D., 2002. Value investing: The use of historical financial statement information to separate winners from losers. *Selected Papers of The University of Chicago Graduate School of Business,* 84, Chicago: The University of Chicago.

Stooq, 2015. WIG historical data. *Stooq.* [online] Available from: http://stooq.pl/q/d/?s=wig. [Accessed: 5th November 2015].

Appendices

Table 4. *Correlation matrix*

Correlation coefficients, using the observations 2005:2 - 2015:2
5% critical value (two-tailed) = 0.3081 for n = 41

ΔWIG	*ΔGM*	*ΔU*	*ΔCA*	
1.0000	0.5665	-0.0042	-0.2990	*ΔWIG*
	1.0000	-0.5535	-0.2247	*ΔGM*
		1.0000	0.2227	*ΔU*
			1.0000	*ΔCA*

Source: Own elaboration in Gretl

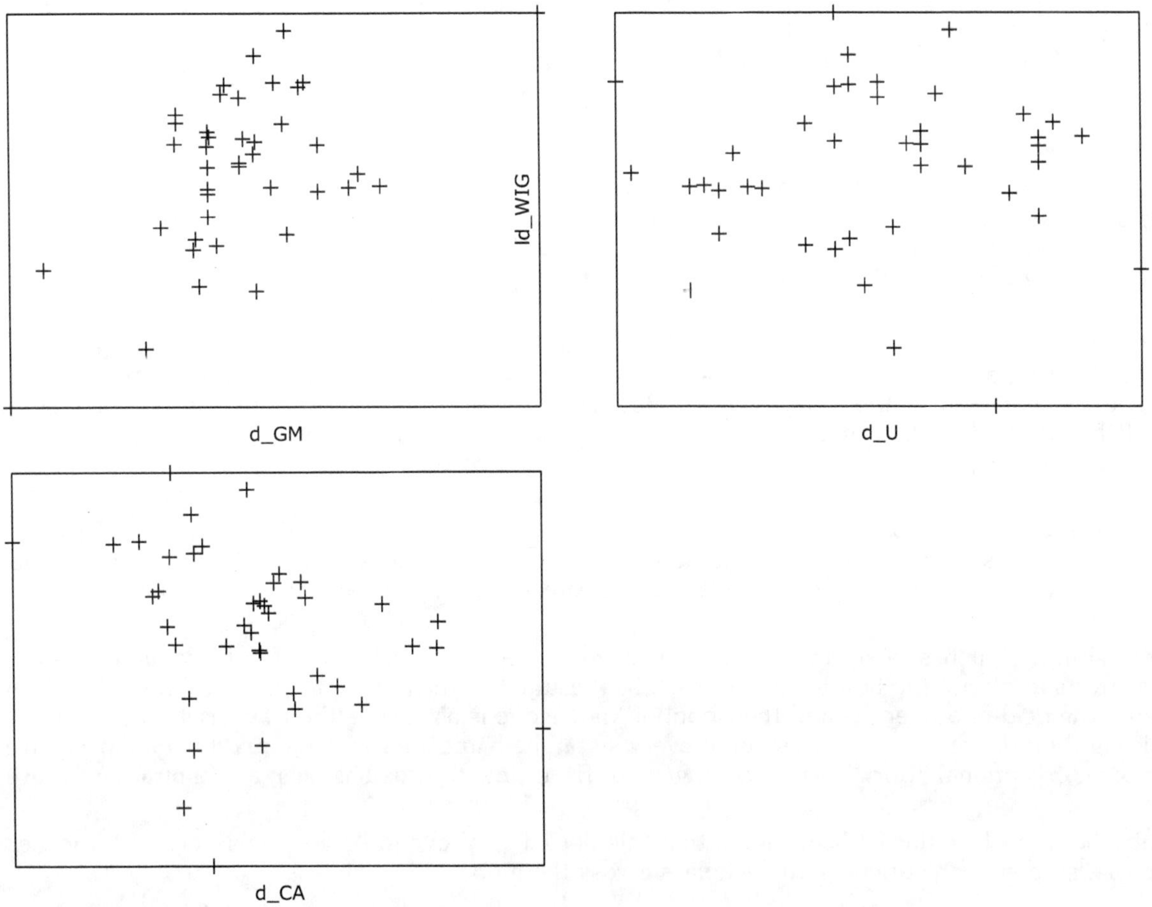

Figure 2*. Scatter plot of ΔWIG and ΔGM, ΔU and ΔCA*
Source: Own elaboration in Gretl

Permissions

All chapters in this book were first published in EJE, by Sprint Investify; hereby published with permission under the Creative Commons Attribution License or equivalent. Every chapter published in this book has been scrutinized by our experts. Their significance has been extensively debated. The topics covered herein carry significant findings which will fuel the growth of the discipline. They may even be implemented as practical applications or may be referred to as a beginning point for another development.

The contributors of this book come from diverse backgrounds, making this book a truly international effort. This book will bring forth new frontiers with its revolutionizing research information and detailed analysis of the nascent developments around the world.

We would like to thank all the contributing authors for lending their expertise to make the book truly unique. They have played a crucial role in the development of this book. Without their invaluable contributions this book wouldn't have been possible. They have made vital efforts to compile up to date information on the varied aspects of this subject to make this book a valuable addition to the collection of many professionals and students.

This book was conceptualized with the vision of imparting up-to-date information and advanced data in this field. To ensure the same, a matchless editorial board was set up. Every individual on the board went through rigorous rounds of assessment to prove their worth. After which they invested a large part of their time researching and compiling the most relevant data for our readers.

The editorial board has been involved in producing this book since its inception. They have spent rigorous hours researching and exploring the diverse topics which have resulted in the successful publishing of this book. They have passed on their knowledge of decades through this book. To expedite this challenging task, the publisher supported the team at every step. A small team of assistant editors was also appointed to further simplify the editing procedure and attain best results for the readers.

Apart from the editorial board, the designing team has also invested a significant amount of their time in understanding the subject and creating the most relevant covers. They scrutinized every image to scout for the most suitable representation of the subject and create an appropriate cover for the book.

The publishing team has been an ardent support to the editorial, designing and production team. Their endless efforts to recruit the best for this project, has resulted in the accomplishment of this book. They are a veteran in the field of academics and their pool of knowledge is as vast as their experience in printing. Their expertise and guidance has proved useful at every step. Their uncompromising quality standards have made this book an exceptional effort. Their encouragement from time to time has been an inspiration for everyone.

The publisher and the editorial board hope that this book will prove to be a valuable piece of knowledge for researchers, students, practitioners and scholars across the globe.

List of Contributors

Alin Opreana
Lucian Blaga University of Sibiu

Andrejs Jaunzems
Ventspils Augstskola, Latvia

Onur Tutulmaz and Burcu Doğan
Hitit University, Turkey

David Revilla
Instituto Nacional de Estadística y Geografía, Oaxaca, México

Adelaido García-Ándres
Universidad Autónoma de Nuevo León, Monterrey, México

Isaac Sánchez-Juárez
Universidad Autónoma de Ciudad Juárez, Chihuahua, México

Gioacchino De Candia
Studio de Candia, Italy

Sebastian-Ilie Dragoe
Lucian Blaga University of Sibiu, Romania

Arthelo P. Palma
University of Southeastern Philippines, Philippines
Davao Central College, Philippines

Diana Mihaiu
Lucian Blaga University of Sibiu, Romania

Elchin Suleymanov and Sabuhi Yusifov
Qafqaz University, Azerbaijan

Mehdi Monadjemi and John Lodewijks
Australian School of Business, University of New South Wales, Sydney, Australia

Abdullahi Olabode Abdulkadri
The University of the West Indies, Mona Campus, Jamaica

Wei-Bin Zhang
Ritsumeikan Asia Pacific University, Japan

Simona Vinerean
The Bucharest University of Economic Studies

Abel Ouko
The East African University, Kenya

Cheruiyot W. Kipkoech
Maasai Mara University, Kenya

Emily Kirimi
Technical University of Kenya

Ramzi Farhani, Ghrissi Mhamdi, Abdelkader Aguir and Mounir Smida
University of Sousse, Tunisia MO2FID Research Unit

Simona Vinerean
The Bucharest University of Economic Studies

Rossanto Dwi Handoyo
Airlangga University, Surabaya, Indonesia

Mansor Jusoh and Mohd. Azlan Shah Zaidi
National University of Malaysia, Bangi Selangor, Malaysia

Ibrahima Amadou Diallo
University of Auvergne, Centre d'Études et de Recherches sur le Développement International (CERDI), France

William R. DI Pietro
Daemen College, Amherst, New York

Krzysztof Drachal
University of Warsaw, Poland
Warsaw University of Technology

Index